Distributed Computing

PRINCIPLES and APPLICATIONS

Distributed Computing

PRINCIPLES and APPLICATIONS

M.L. Liu

California Polytechnic State University,
San Luis Obispo

PEARSON

Addison
Wesley

Boston San Francisco New York
London Toronto Sydney Tokyo Singapore Madrid
Mexico City Munich Paris Cape Town Hong Kong Montreal

Senior Acquisitions Editor: *Maite Suarez-Rivas*
Marketing Manager: *Nathan Schultz*
Marketing Coordinator: *Lesly Hershman*
Text Design, Composition and Art: *Gillian Hall, The Aardvark Group*
Cover Design: *Gina Hagen Kolenda*
Cover Image: *Dorling Kindersley, Ltd.*
Prepress and Manufacturing: *Caroline Fell/Hugh Crawford*

Access the latest information about Addison-Wesley titles from our World Wide Web site:
http://www.aw.com/cs

Many of the designations used by manufacturers and sellers to distinguish their products are claimed as trademarks. Where those designations appear in this book, and Addison-Wesley was aware of a trademark claim, the designations have been printed in initial caps or all caps.

Java, JDK, J2EE, J2SE, Java Naming and Directory Interface (JNDI), Jini, JavaSpaces are trademarks of Sun Microsystems, Inc. The following products developed by Sun Microsystems, Inc. are referred to in this book: Java, Java Socket API, Java Secure Socket Extension (JSSE), NIOS, Java Multicast API, Remote Method Invocation (RMI), Java Message Service (JMS), Jini, JavaSpaces, Java Shared Data Toolkit (JSDT), JSWDK.

CORBA, Unified Modeling Language (UML), Object Request Broker (ORB), Object Management Group Interface Definition Language (OMG IDL) are trademarks of the Object Management Group (OMG).

Apache is the trademark of the Apache Software Foundation.

The programs and applications presented in this book have been included for their instructional value. They have been tested with care, but are not guaranteed for any particular purpose. The publisher does not offer any warranties or representations, not does it accept any liabilities with respect to the programs or applications.

Library of Congress Cataloging-in-Publication Data

Liu, Mei-Ling L.
    Distributed computing : principles & applications / Mei-Ling L. Liu.
      p. cm.
    Includes bibliographical references and index.
    ISBN 0-201-79644-9
      1. Electronic data processing--Distributed processing. I. Title.

 QA76.9.D5L58 2003
 004'.36--dc21

                                                                              2002034187

ISBN 0-201-79644-9
1 2 3 4 5 6 7 8 9 10-DOC-06050403

Preface

In the *Year 2001 Model Curricula for Computing (Computing Curricula 2001)* *(http://www.computer.org/education/cc2001/report/index.html)* developed by the Joint IEEE Computer Society/ACM Task Force, net-centric computing is included as a key area in the Computer Science body of knowledge:

> *Recent advances in computer and telecommunications networking, particularly those based on TCP/IP, have increased the importance of networking technologies in the computing discipline. Net-centric computing covers a range of subspecialties, including computer communication network concepts and protocols, multimedia systems, Web standards and technologies, network security, wireless and mobile computing, and distributed systems.*
>
> *Mastery of this subject area involves both theory and practice. Learning experiences that involve hands-on experimentation and analysis are strongly recommended as they reinforce student understanding of concepts and their application to real-world problems. Laboratory experiments should involve data collection and synthesis, empirical modeling, protocol analysis at the source code level, network packet monitoring, software construction, and evaluation of alternative design models. All of these are important concepts that can be best understood by laboratory experimentation.*

The ACM model curricula lists a number of topics in this area, specifying a minimum of 15 hours of core topics and additional elective topics. Many of these topics are covered in a series of courses in distributed computing that I initiated and have taught at California Polytechnic State University (Cal Poly), San Luis Obispo, since 1996. For these courses I employed excerpts from various publications, as well as materials I developed, including overhead slides, code samples, and laboratory/problem/research assignments, which I provided as a course package to my students.

This textbook is a synthesis of the course materials I accumulated over a span of six years, designed for a sequence of technical elective courses for upper-division undergraduates.

Reasons for the Book

Traditionally, distributed computing courses are offered at the graduate level. With the growth of Internet and intranet applications, more and more under-graduate students are engaged in net-centric computing, either at the workplace or on their own initiative. Distributed computing is distinct from (1) communications and networks and (2) distributed operating systems. It operates at a higher level of abstraction than the network layer and the operating systems layer and deals with programming paradigms, application program interfaces (APIs) or toolkits, and protocols and standards in the context of net-centric computing. Although there are numerous books available on network programming and technologies, there is a lack of books written in a textbook style, combining the theory and practice of distributed computing.

This book has the following distinctive features:

- It is designed to introduce **undergraduate students** to the principles of distributed computing, topics formerly reserved for graduate students.

- It focuses on the upper layers of the architecture for net-centric computing, specifically on **computing abstractions** and **paradigms**.

- It incorporates both conceptual topics and practical topics, using program samples and hands-on exercises to illustrate and reinforce the concepts presented.

- It is designed as a textbook, with a narrative style suitable for academic settings, diagrams to illustrate the topics, exercises at the end of each chapter, and a list of references for student research.

- It is designed for **learn-by-doing teaching**: programming samples are used to reinforce the topics presented, and **laboratory** activities are incorporated in the exercises at the end of each chapter.

- **Supplementary teaching materials**, including presentation slides, program samples, a Web site, and an instructor's manual, will be provided by the author.

- In addition to printed books and articles, this book cites reliable references that are accessible via the World Wide Web. For example, the references include a link to the archival sites where Internet Requests for Comments (RFCs) can be looked up online. It is the author's belief that undergraduate students are more inclined to look up references that are readily available on the Web. (*Note*: Although I have chosen to include as references Web links that are reliable and stable, it is possible that some of the links may become obsolete over time. I would appreciate receiving reports of inactive links.)

What This Book Is Not About

- **This book is not about networking.** In a general sense, networking encompasses distributed computing in as much as distributed computing involves networked computers. But in academia, courses in networking typically focus on the lower layers of the network architecture and address topics such as signal transmission, error corrections, data link layer protocols, transport layer protocols, and the Internet layer protocol. By comparison, this book deals with the uppermost layers of the network architecture, namely the application, presentation, and session layers, and more from the viewpoint of computing paradigms and abstractions than from the viewpoint of system architecture.

- **This book is not about distributed systems.** Our focus is not on system architecture or system resources.

- **This book is not about Web application development.** Although the Internet is the most popular network, programming for the Internet is a specialized form of distributed computing. This book addresses distributed computing for networks in general, including the Internet, intranet, and local area networks.

- **This book is not about application program interfaces (APIs) or technologies.** Although a number of APIs are introduced in the book, they are presented as representative toolkits that support particular paradigms; the introduction of these APIs is meant to allow students to write programs for hands-on laboratory exercises that reinforce the concepts and principles.

A Word to Fellow Instructors

The book is designed for use in a technical elective course during an academic term. The entire twelve chapters of the book can be covered in a quarter at a fast pace or in a semester at a more leisurely pace. The material requires no advanced knowledge of networks, operating systems, or software engineering. A course taught using the book can be taken by an upper-division undergraduate student.

With a field as wide as distributed computing, it is impossible for one book to cover every corner of the discipline. In particular, there is no intention here to cover the latest technologies. The book is meant to convey fundamental concepts in interprocess communication.

A common thread that runs through this book is the idea of abstraction, in the sense of detail encapsulation—how that idea applies in the various paradigms of distributed computing and the trade-offs between tools that provide different levels of abstraction. It is my firm belief that these concepts and ideas are important to each student in computer science and computer engineering, regardless of the student's chosen area of specialization. With an understanding of these fundamental concepts, students should be well equipped to explore new tools and technologies on their own, as they will be expected to do throughout their career.

The first three chapters of the book contain introductory background material that can be covered in the first one or two weeks of an academic term, during which students are gently introduced to a multitude of issues to which they may or may not have been exposed already. Subsequent chapters are more technical and detailed and can be covered at roughly a chapter each week.

Broad as the subject of distributed computing is, you will likely feel compelled to supplement this text with additional material that you deem important. For example, you may be inclined to add an introduction to distributed algorithms, or to go into more depth in the area of security. To allow time for such additions, you may consider omitting selected chapters from this book.

It is not assumed that readers of this book have had prior expertise in distributed computing. At Cal Poly, I have used the material to teach students with diverse backgrounds, ranging from some students who had no experience with multiprocess programming, to those who were already sophisticated network software developers. While the material worked best with the former, those with advanced backgrounds would find the topics of interest nevertheless.

Readers, Please Note

A word on the use of typefaces in the narrative of this book:

- Key terms and phrases are emphasized through the use of boldface; for example: This book addresses **distributed computing**.
- A special word, such as one used as a program identifier, nonstandard protocol name, or operation name, is expressed in italic to distinguish it from the rest of the text in a sentence; for example: What do you expect the outcome to be when *RunThread3* is executed? Compile and run it.
- Reserved words and identifiers, such as those stipulated by the Java Language or by a well-known protocol, appear in italic; for example: To support threading in a program, Java provides a class named *Thread* as well as an interface named *Runnable* interface.

A word on the article inserts and Web links:

Throughout the text of this book, excerpts from articles previously published in various media are inserted. These articles were chosen for their relevance to the topics, and for the interest that they may bring to the readers.

Many of the references listed at the end of each chapter are Web links. This is a deliberate choice, because the author believes that the accessibility of Web-available contents will enhance a student's initiative to pursue research in a topic. The Web links chosen are those that the author deemed to be reliable and stable. But obsolescence of some links is inevitable, in which case the author offers an apology and welcomes your notification of such an occurrence.

Contacting the Author

The compilation of a textbook is a painstaking and consuming task. To the best of my ability, I have attempted to maximize the accuracy of the materials presented within the pages of this book. If you discover any errors or inaccuracy, or if you have suggestions for improvements, I shall be grateful to hear from you. Please email to *mliu@csc.calpoly.edu.*

Supplementary Materials

Supplementary materials, including the source files for programming samples and overhead slides, are available at URL www.aw.com.

Additional supplementary materials for instructors only are available by contacting your local Addison Wesley sales representative.

Acknowledgments

I thank the generosity of the various authors and publishers who granted reprint permission to allow the inclusion of previously published work in the text of this book.

I am forever indebted to my doctoral program advisors, Dr. Divyakant Agrawal and Dr. Amr El Abbadi, Computer Science Department, University of California at Santa Barbara, who introduced me to the field of distributed computing.

Gratitude is due to Cal Poly students Jared Smith, Domingo Colon, Vinh Pham, Hafeez Jaffer, Erik Buchholz, and Lori Sawdey for the gift of their time and efforts in reviewing the book. Thanks are also due to the students who enrolled in these courses at Cal Poly in school year 2001–2003: Computer Engineering 369, Computer Engineering 469, and Computer Science 569, for their patience with the numerous errors in the initial drafts of the manuscript for this book.

I thank my colleagues in the Computer Science Department and the College of Engineering at Cal Poly, who provided the opportunities for me to teach the courses that inspired this book, and without whose encouragement the book would not have been possible.

I thank the staff of Addison Wesley for their invaluable guidance and assistance that allows the book to come to fruition, and the following reviewers for the generosity of sharing their time and wisdom:

Anup Talukdar
Motorola Labs, Schaumburg

Dr. Ray Toal
Loyola Marymount University

Mr. David Russo
Computer Science and Engineering
Senior Lecturer, University of Texas at Dallas

Dr. Alvin Lim
Computer Science and Software Engineering Department
Auburn University

Isaac Ghansah, Professor
Computer Science and Computer Engineering
California State University, Sacramento

Bruce Char
Department of Computer Science
Drexel University

Finally, I thank my family and in particular my son, Marlin, for providing a reason for me to strive.

M. L. Liu
Cal Poly, San Luis Obispo
January, 2003

Contents

CHAPTER **2**

Interprocess Communications   47

CHAPTER **10**

CHAPTER **12**

Advanced Distributed Computing Paradigms   **387**

## CHAPTER 1

Distributed Computing, An Introduction

This book addresses **distributed computing**. In this chapter, we will begin by clarifying what is meant by distributed computing in the context of this book. We will do so by looking at the history of distributed computing and by comparing this type of computing with other forms of computing. We will then present some basic concepts in the disciplines of **operating systems**, **networks**, and **software engineering**, concepts that you will need to be familiar with in order to understand the material presented in later chapters.

1.1 Definitions

A source of confusion in the field of distributed computing is the lack of a universal vocabulary, perhaps because of the breathtaking pace with which new ideas evolve in the field. Following are the definitions of some of the key terms used in the context of this book. When you read the book, please keep these definitions in mind, and be aware that some of these terms may not have the same definition in other contexts.

Early computing was performed on a single processor. A **uni-processor**, or **monolithic computing**, makes use of a single central processing unit (CPU) to execute one or more programs for each application.

A **distributed system** is a collection of independent computers, interconnected via a network, that are capable of collaborating on a task. Computers are considered independent if they do not share memory or program execution space.

Such computers are called **loosely coupled** computers, as opposed to **tightly coupled** computers; the latter can share data using common memory space.

Distributed computing is computing performed in a distributed system. In this book, we explore the ways that computer programs, running on independent computers, collaborate with each other to perform computing such as network services and Web-based applications.

▤ A **network service** is a service provided by a special kind of program known as a server on a network. The World Wide Web is such a service, as is electronic mail (email) and file transfer (FTP). A server program is just half of the story in the so-called client-server model of distributed computing. Client-server will be studied extensively in later chapters of this book.

▤ A **network application** is an application that runs on networked computers for end users. Network applications range from enterprise applications such as online shopping carts and electronic auction sites to noncommercial applications such as chatrooms and network games.

The distinction between network services and network applications is not always clear-cut, and the terms are often used interchangeably.

1.2 The History of Distributed Computing

In the beginning there were stand-alone computers, each of which was capable of executing stored programs. Connecting stand-alone computers so that data could be exchanged among them was a natural progression. Rudimentary connection of computers using cables for file sharing was practiced as early as the 1960s. However, such an undertaking requires manual intervention and cannot be called a computer application when one or more computer programs execute autonomously to carry out a task. Such a computer application requires data communication, whereby two computers spontaneously exchange data using software and hardware in order to carry out the tasks inherent in the application.

Request for Comments are specifications proposed by Internet engineers to invite public comments. Over the years, thousands of such specifications have arisen, and they are archived and accessible in a number of Web sites, including The Internet RFC/STD/FYI/BCP Archives [faqs.org, 5].

The **ARPANET**, initiated in 1970, was the predecessor of the Internet.

The first Internet Request for Comments (RFC), RFC 1, is a proposal that specifies how participating hosts can exchange information with each other through **messages**. Whereas there may have been individual attempts to create network applications on a small scale (perhaps involving two or more computers connected via cables), the earliest network application was electronic mail, or email, by which the first message was reportedly sent in 1972 on a four-node ARPANET. (A **node** on a network is a computer, or host, that participates in the network.) Automated file transfer mechanisms, which allowed data files to be exchanged between hosts, were another natural progression, and as early as 1971 there was a proposal for such a mechanism (see RFC 114 and RFC 141). To this day, email and file transfer remain two of the most popular network services. The best-known network service, however, is undoubtedly the **World Wide Web** (**WWW**). The Web was originally conceived in the late 1980s by scientists at the Swiss research institute CERN in Geneva as an application that could support the access of hypertext over a network. The WWW has since become a platform for network applications and services, including email, search engines, and electronic commerce (e-commerce).

The WWW was responsible for an explosion in the scale of the Internet. Until 1990, ARPANET, the predecessor of the Internet as we know it, was primarily a data network used by scientists, researchers, and academicians. Spurred by the popularity of the WWW, the network grew spectacularly in the 1990s, as illustrated in Figures 1.1 and 1.2.

If you are interested in the history of network computing, some Web sites that are well worth visiting are [vlmp.museophile.com, 1], [zakon.org, 2], and [isoc.org, 38]. In addition, [Hafner and Lyon, 4] is a fascinating account of the early development of the Internet, including the people and the organizations involved in it.

Hypertext, a term coined by visionary Ted Nelson, refers to textual documents in which associative paths may be followed to access additional documents. The best-known example of hypertext is a Web page that contains Web links.

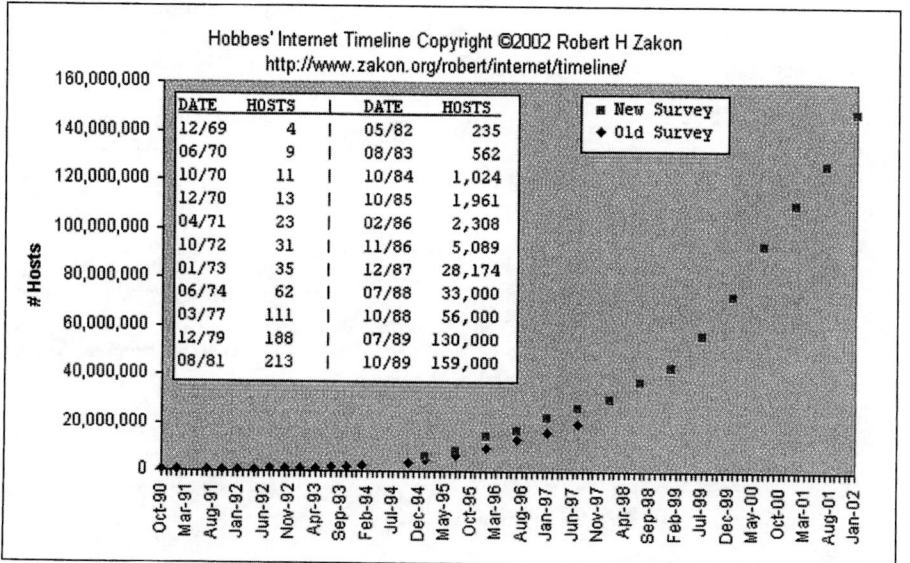

Figure 1.1 The growth of Internet hosts [zakon.org, 2] (reprinted by permission).

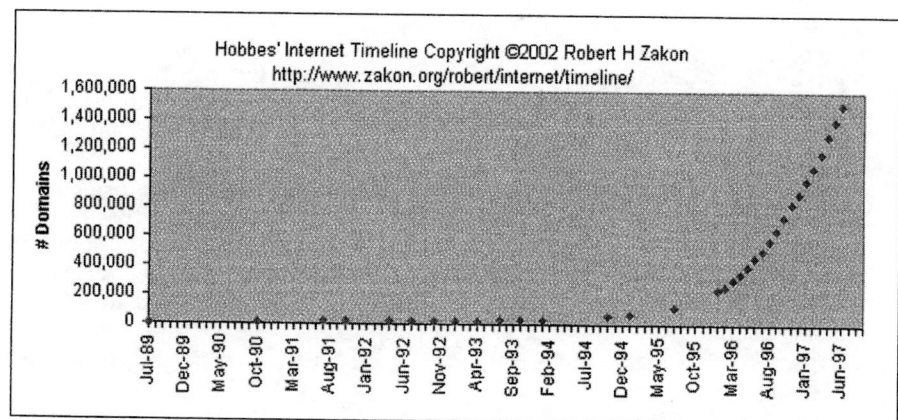

An Internet domain is part of the naming scheme of resources on the Internet.

Figure 1.2 Internet domains [zakon.org, 2] (reprinted by permission).

HISTORICAL TRENDS

by Richard Gabriel and Jim Waldo, Sun MicroSystems
(Excerpted from *http://www.sun.com/jini/overview/* [7])
Reprinted by permission of Jim Waldo.

How have we arrived at a place where connected services and devices are the driving forces for the next wave of computing?

The most significant reason is our better understanding of physics, chemistry, the physical bases for computation, and chip manufacturing process. Today, a significantly powerful computer can be built from one or two small chips and an entire computer system can be built on one small board.

There were three dimensions of improvement: size, cost, and computational power. Since the 1960s, size and cost of computers have decreased dramatically while computational power has gone through the roof.

The mainframe of the 1960s was a collection of boxes in a large room—it cost millions of dollars and set the bar for computational power. Only a company could afford one.

The minicomputer became possible when the functionality of a mainframe could be put in a few boxes. It had the computational power of the previous mainframe generation and could be bought by a single department. Most minicomputers were connected to interactive terminals—the beginnings of computer-based culture, a community.

When a computer with the power of a mini shrank to a box that fit beside a desk, we got the workstation. A department could afford to buy one for a couple of professionals. A workstation had enough computational power to support sophisticated design, engineering, and scientific applications, and to provide the graphical support for them.

The personal computer was small enough to fit on a desk and powerful enough to support intuitive graphical user interfaces, individuals could afford them, and companies bought them for every employee.

Eventually processors became small enough and cheap enough to put one in a car in place of an ignition system, or in a TV instead of discrete electronics. Today's cars can have fifty or more processors, the home over a hundred.

The computational power dimension has another fallout. The overall trend toward smaller, faster, cheaper processors meant that fewer people had to share a CPU, but it also meant that people in the organization could become isolated. When a tool is shared, it creates a community; as the tool shrinks, fewer people use it together, and the community disperses. But a community is hard to give up. Fortunately, computational power kept pace with the shrinking processor, and as the community served by a single computer system shrank, there was enough power to support communication between systems. Thus, for example, workstations became successful once they could communicate and exchange data.

The final stretch of the computational power dimension is that now processors are powerful enough to support a high-level, object-oriented programming language in such a way to support moving objects between them. And such a processor is small enough and cheap enough to sit in the simplest devices.

Once there is sufficient computational power, the ability to connect and communicate is the dominant factor determining value. Today for most people, a computer runs only a few applications and mainly facilitates communication: email, the Web. Recall how fast Internet popularity soared first with email and, more recently, once the Web and browsers became prevalent.

1.3 Different Forms of Computing

To understand what is meant by distributed computing in the context of this book, it is instructive to look at various forms of computing using computers.

Monolithic Computing

In the simplest form of computing, a single computer, such as a personal computer (PC), is used for computing. The computer is not connected to any network, and thus it may use only those resources within its immediate access. This form of computing may be called **monolithic computing**. In the most basic monolithic computing, the computer is used by a single user at a time. The user runs applications on the system with no access to resources beyond those available with the system. When you use applications such as a word processing program or a spreadsheet on a PC, you are practicing this form of computing, which may be called *single-user monolithic computing*.

Multiple users can engage in monolithic computing. This form of computing (see Figure 1.3a), where the resources of a single computer can be shared by concurrent users using a technique known as **timesharing**, was popular in the 1970s and 1980s. The computer that provides the centralized resource is usually called a *mainframe* to differentiate it from smaller computers such as minicomputers and microcomputers. Through devices known as *terminals*, users (who may be geographically dispersed) can be connected to the mainframe computer and interact with it during a terminal session. Some widely used mainframe computers include the IBM 360 series and the Univac 1100 series. Applications using this form of computing are typically separate programs designed to perform a single function, such as payroll or billing for a firm or a university.

Distributed Computing

In contrast, **distributed computing** involves computing performed among multiple network-connected computers, each of which has its own processor(s) and other resources (see Figure 1.3b). A user, using a workstation, has full use of the resources on the local computer to which its workstation is connected. In addition, through the interaction of the local computer and the remote computers, the user may access resources on the remote computers. The World Wide Web is an excellent example of this type of computing. When you use a browser to visit a Web site, a program such as Netscape or Internet Explorer runs on your local system and interacts with a program (known as a Web server) running on a remote system to fetch a file that may reside on yet another remote system.

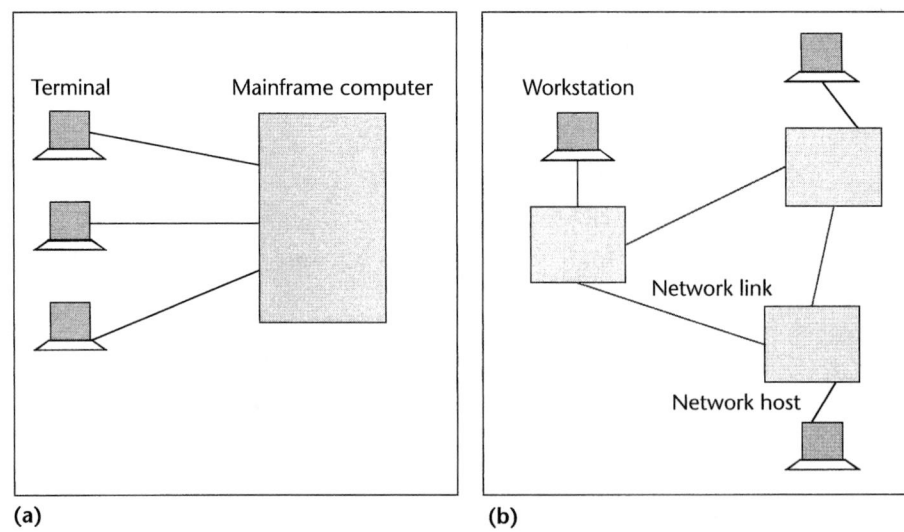

(a)   **(b)**

Figure 1.3 Centralized computing (a) versus distributed computing (b).

Parallel Computing

Similar to but distinct from distributed computing is a form of computing known as **parallel computing** or **parallel processing**, which uses more than one processor simultaneously to execute a single program. "Ideally, parallel processing makes a program run faster because there are more engines (CPUs) running it. In practice, it is often difficult to divide a program in such a way that separate CPUs can execute different portions without interfering with each other" [Koniges, 9]. Parallel computing is typically performed on a single computer that has multiple CPUs, but, according to Koniges, it is also possible to "perform parallel processing by connecting the computers in a network. However, this type of parallel processing requires very sophisticated software called distributed processing software" [Koniges, 9].

Using parallel computing, one can solve problems that are otherwise impossible to solve on one computer or solve computing-intensive problems that are otherwise economically untenable. Today, parallel computing is primarily used in large-scale scientific computing in areas such as biology, aerospace, weather forecasting, and semiconductor design. Although a fascinating subject, parallel computing is not within the scope of this book.

WHERE IT GOES

by Joseph Menn
(From *Los Angeles Times*, Los Angeles, Calif., Dec. 2, 1999, Joseph Menn.
Copyright © 1999, *Los Angeles Times*.)
Reprinted with permission.

EBay users rarely think about the bidding process—until the site crashes. Behind the scenes, the online auctioneer has a number of safeguards that rely increasingly on duplicated, or mirrored, technologies in case one piece of machinery or software fails. Buth the information must still pass through many different companies and types of equipment for everything to work properly.

1 Bidder at home registers and submits an electronic bid from a personal computer.

2 The bid travels from the consumer's Internet service provider, through switches and routers, to the ISP company's servers.

3 The bid is sent through the Internet backbone.

4 The bid travels to one of EBay's ISPs, most likely Sprint or UUNet, and through pipes to EBay.

5 The bid passes through EBay's Cisco switches and routers.

6 The Information reaches one of about 200 front-line Compaq servers running on Windows NT. The servers are mirrored, so that if any one fails, the others pick up the slack.

7 The bid is passed along to one of Sun Microsystems' Starfire servers, named Bull and Bear, that mirror each other.

8 The bid is added to two information-storage databases running Oracle software, where it is matched with the seller's information.

9 The information flow is reversed back out of EBay, into e-mails sent to both the seller and potential buyers who are outbid. Confirmation is also sent to the bidder.

10 From Bull, the bid amount and other details are sent to another Starfire server, called Anaconda, and recorded on mirrored storage disks.

Sources: Times staff, EBay

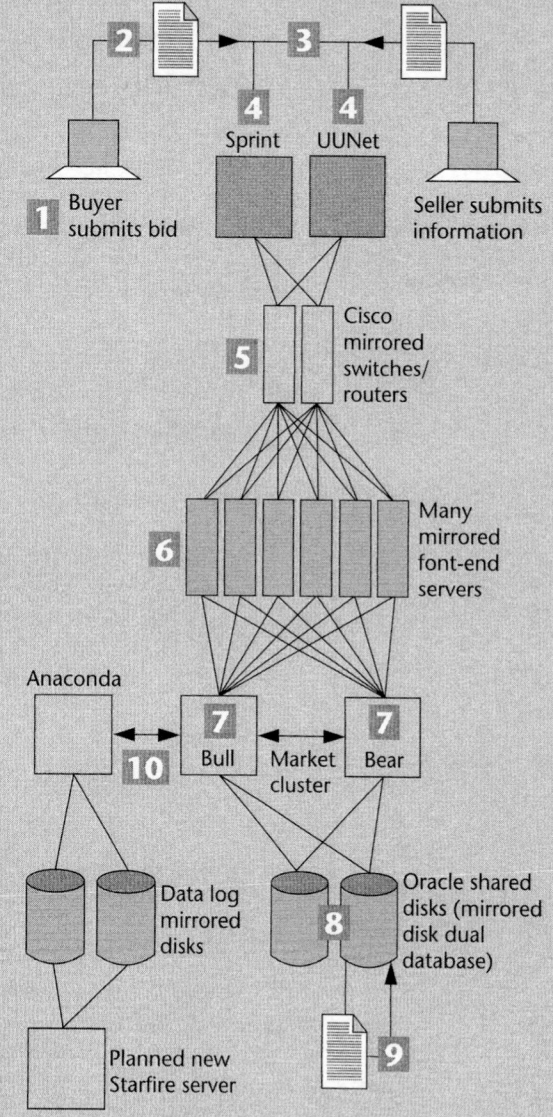

EBay is planning to add another Starfire attached to the final data disks, mirroring Anaconda.

An interested computer owner will download a free piece of software (for example, a screen saver) from SETI@home. Then, when his or her computer is idle while online, the software downloads a data file from an Internet site for analysis on his or her computer. The results of the analysis are sent back to the Internet site where they are combined with those contributed by other SETI@home participants and used to help in the search for extraterrestrial signals.

Cooperative Computing

Recently, the term *distributed computing* has also been applied to cooperative computing projects such as the Search for Extraterrestrial Intelligence (SETI) [setiathome.ssl.berkeley.edu, 10] and distributed.net [distributed.net, 33]. These are projects that parcel out large-scale computing to workstations on Internet hosts, making use of surplus CPU cycles, as described in the sidebar. (*Note:* Further discussion of this type of computing is not within the scope of this book.)

1.4 The Strengths and Weaknesses of Distributed Computing

Prior to the appearance of the World Wide Web, monolithic computing, such as business applications running on a mainframe computer, or a single user using a personal computer to perform word processing or spreadsheet functions, was the dominant form of computing. Thomas Watson, the founder of IBM, was said to have made the following statement in 1943: "I think there is a world market for maybe five computers." Since the 1980s, however, distributed computing has become as important as—if not more important than—monolithic computing.

There are a number of reasons for the popularity of distributed computing:

* **The affordability of computers and availability of network access.** Today's personal computer has computing power superior to that of the mainframe computers of the early days, at a fraction of the size and the cost. Coupled with the fact that connectivity to the Internet has become universally available and generally affordable, the large number of interconnected computers makes for an ideal community for distributed computing.

* **Resource sharing.** The architecture of distributed computing mirrors the computing architecture of modern organizations. Each organization independently maintains computers and resources that are local to the organization while sharing resources over the network. Using distributed computing, organizations can pool their resources very effectively. The Web, for example, is a powerful platform for sharing documents and other resources within and among organizations.

* **Scalability.** With monolithic computing, the available resources are limited to the capacity of one computer. By contrast, distributed computing provides scalability in that increasing demand for resources can be addressed effectively with additional resources. For example, more computers providing a service such as email can be added to the network to satisfy an increase in the demand for that service.

* **Fault tolerance.** Compared to monolithic computing, distributed computing provides the opportunity for fault tolerance in that a resource can be repli-

cated (or mirrored) to sustain its availability in the presence of failures. For example, backup copies of a database can be maintained on different systems on the network, so that when one system fails, other copies can be accessed without disrupting the service. Although it is not possible to build a distributed system that is completely reliable in the presence of failures [Fischer, Lynch, and Paterson, 30], it is the responsibility of a developer, when designing and implementing such a system, to maximize its fault tolerance. Fault tolerance in distributed computing is a complex topic that has received extensive attention in the research community. Interested readers may want to refer to sources such as the work of Pankaj Jalote [Jalote, 31].

In any form of computing, there is always a trade-off between advantages and disadvantages. The advantages already mentioned are offset by disadvantages. Some of the most significant ones are:

- **Multiple points of failure.** There are more points of failure in distributed computing. Since multiple computers are involved, all of which depend on the network for communication, the failure of one or more computers, or one or more network links, can spell trouble for a distributed computing system. There is a popular quote, attributed to noted computer scientist Leslie Lamport, which says that "a distributed system is one in which the failure of a computer you didn't even know existed can render your own computer unusable."

- **Security concerns.** In a distributed system, there are more opportunities for unauthorized attack. Whereas in a centralized system all the computers and resources are typically under the control of a single administration, in a distributed system management is decentralized, often involving a large number of independent organizations. The decentralization makes it difficult to implement and enforce security policies; hence distributed computing is vulnerable to security breaches and unauthorized access, which unfortunately can affect all participants on the system. This problem is clearly illustrated by well-known attacks on the Internet, such as worms and viruses [Eichen and Rochlis, 21; Zetter, 22].

  Because of its importance, computer security is a widely researched and studied topic, and successful techniques have been developed for writing and deploying secure applications. Such techniques include encryption, keys, certificates, digital signatures, sandboxes, authentication, and authorization. Security is a broad topic that is beyond the scope of this book. Readers are encouraged to pursue the topic in references such as [Oaks, 32].

Now that we have clarified the objective of this book, let's next look at some of the basic concepts in three related disciplines in computer science: operating systems, networks, and software engineering. Although no in-depth knowledge of these disciplines is required as a prerequisite for this course, this book does refer to some concepts and terminologies associated with these disciplines. In the rest of this chapter we will introduce these concepts and terminologies.

WEB ATTACKS MIGHT HAVE MANY SOURCES

by Matt Richtel and Sara Robinson (NYT), Feb. 11, 2000
(reprinted with permission of the *New York Times*)

SAN FRANCISCO, Feb. 10—Computer security experts said today that evidence now suggests that the three days of attacks on leading Web sites may have been the work of more than one person or group.

The analysis that more than one group was at work called into question the conclusion of some security experts who were initially skeptical that following Monday's attack on Yahoo, multiple vandals would have been able to muster large "copy cat" assaults on other sites.

And while the Internet community searched aggressively for leads, computer experts said that it would be difficult even to determine which computers initiated the attacks, let alone find the responsible parties.

CERT, a federally financed computer security organization formerly known as the Computer Emergency Response Team, said today that it was no longer seeing an unusual number of reports of attacks. From Monday through Wednesday, service on several leading Web sites, including those of the Yahoo portal, the E*Trade Group brokerage firm, the eBay auction company and Time Warner's CNN.com news site, were disrupted and in some cases halted by assaults involving dozens or more computers flooding them with data feeds.

But security experts said that Web sites and the Internet in general would remain vulnerable for the near future because so many organizations were failing to take steps to prevent their computers from being used by vandals to initiate the attacks.

One government official said today that tougher laws might be necessary to combat such attacks. "We don't consider this a prank," Deputy Attorney General Eric Holder said. "These are very serious matters."

Also today, it was disclosed that more major Web sites than had been previously known were hit on Wednesday, the last day of the assaults. Those included Excite@Home, a provider of high-speed access over cable modems, which was attacked early Wednesday evening despite having taken precautions to defend its network.

At least two other major e-commerce companies were hit with attacks on Wednesday, according to IFsec, a computer security firm in New York, though it declined to name the companies, saying that one of them was a client.

"We're seeing more of these than have appeared in the popular media," said David M. Remnitz, the chief executive of IFsec.

In addition, users of Internet Relay Chat, or I.R.C., said that the forum had been under intense fire in the last two weeks by attacks similar to those levied at the e-commerce companies.

Meanwhile, network service providers and investigators continued analyzing evidence, including the packets of data that had been used to overwhelm and paralyze the victim sites.

Computer security experts at Stanford University in Palo Alto, Calif., said that the preliminary evidence suggested the attacks might have been the work of more than one person or group.

David J. Brumley, assistant computer security officer for Stanford, said the type of data included in the packets used to attack Yahoo on Monday differed from the data in the Tuesday assault on eBay.

"The attacks were just completely different between those two days," Mr. Brumley said. "The people who did Yahoo are different than the people who did eBay and CNN."

Network service providers said that the recent assaults included two types of attacks, further suggesting that more than one party may have been involved. Both are what are known as denial of service attacks because they prevent the targeted site from serving its customers.

In the first, known as a SYN flood, attackers hack into—and install software on—a large number of computers, then use those machines to bombard the victim site with requests to start an e-commerce session. The large number of requests overwhelms the victim's servers, preventing customers from gaining access to the site.

To prevent any tracing of these requests, the vandals employ a practice called spoofing, which alters the initiating address.

The second type, known as a smurf attack, again involves the use of compromised machines, but it also employs a large third-party network of computers to "amplify" the data used in the attack and greatly increases the effectiveness of the assault. It is believed that Stanford's network of computers may have been used in this way in the attack on Yahoo.

Security experts say it is simple to configure networks so they cannot be used in a smurf attack, yet many sites do not know to take these steps.

Computer security experts noted that the large numbers of computers used to initiate the attacks this week made tracing those attacks very difficult.

"At this point, there's been so much traffic thrown at these people that it's pretty hard to do a trace," said Joel de la Garza of the Kroll-O'Gara Information Security Group, a risk mitigation company.

Moreover, companies whose computers are hijacked and then used as platforms for an assault often have no idea of the problem, even as the assault is going on, computer security experts said. Vandals can activate the assault from a remote location, and to a company or an individual whose computer is being used; the only impact may appear to be a slowdown in the activity of the network.

Victim companies and security experts said today that in some cases the attacks seemed more complicated than originally thought—reinforcing how difficult they are to prevent.

Excite@Home, for example, said it sought to take precautionary measures in light of the earlier attacks but was still unable to keep its Web site from being crippled for at least half an hour.

"To the best of our knowledge, a site cannot take preventative measures against the attacks without the help of others," said Kelly Distefano, an Excite@Home spokeswoman. She said the company would have needed more cooperation from the companies that provide Excite network services.

Peter Neumann, principal scientist at SRI International in Menlo Park, Calif., reiterated that the success of the attacks had shown that Internet sites were not taking adequate precautions to prevent themselves from being used for attacks.

"It's time people woke up," Mr. Neumann said. "People are racing to do electronic commerce on the Net without any understanding of the risks—and there are much greater risks than we've seen here."

1.5 Basics of Operating Systems

Distributed computing involves programs running on multiple computers. Let's look at some of the concepts involved with the execution of programs in modern-day computers.

Computer Programs and Processes

A software program is an artifact constructed by a software developer using some form of programming language. Typically, the language is a high-level one that requires a compiler or an interpreter to translate it into machine language. When a program is "run," or executed, on a computer, it is represented as a **process**. On modern computers, a process consists of an executing program, its current values, state information, and the resources used by the operating system to manage the execution of the program. In other words, a process is a dynamic entity that exists only when a program is run.

Figure 1.4 illustrates the state transitions during the lifetime of a process. A process enters a ready state when a program is at the start of its execution, when it is placed in a queue by the operating system, along with other programs that are to be executed. When system resources (such as the CPU) are available for its actual execution, the process is dispatched, at which point it enters the running state. It continues to execute until the process must wait for the occurrence of an event (such as the completion of some input/output operation), at which time it enters a blocked state. Once the anticipated event occurs, the process will be placed on the execution queue and await its turn to execute once again. The process repeats the ready-running-blocked cycle for as many times as necessary until the execution of the process is completed, at which time the process is said to be terminated.

In this book, we will use Java programs, or fragments of them, as code examples. There are three types of Java programs: **applications** (Figure 1.5), **applets** (Figure 1.6), and **servlets** (Figure 1.7). Regardless of which type of program you are writing, each one is written as a **Java class**. A Java application program has a main

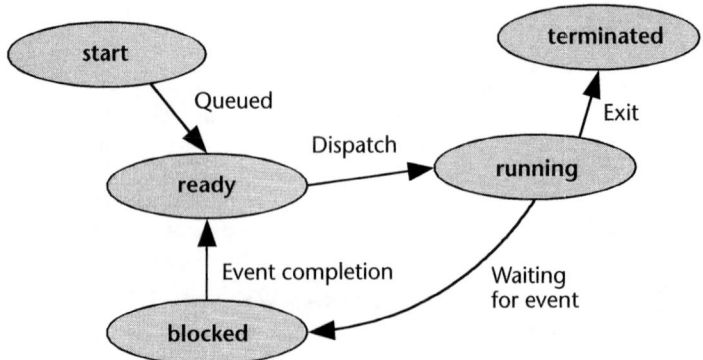

Figure 1.4 A simplified state transition diagram of a process.

method, and it is run as an independent (stand-alone) process. On the other hand, an applet does not have a main method, and it is run using a browser or the appletviewer. A servlet is similar to an applet in that it does not have a main method, and it is run in the context of a Web server. We will have occasion to see examples of all three types of programs and program fragments in this book, with applications being the form of programs most frequently employed.

A Java program is compiled into **bytecode**, a universal object code. When run, bytecode is translated by the Java Virtual Machine (JVM) to the machine code native to the computer, following the state transitions that we have studied ear-

A stand-alone Java application is run on a local machine.

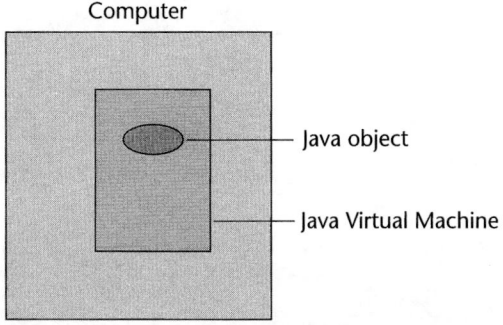

```
/*********************************************************
 * A sample of a simple Java application.
 * M. Liu 1/8/02
 *********************************************************/

import java.io.*;

class MyProgram{

  public static void main(String[ ] args)
    throws IOException{

    BufferedReader keyboard = new
      BufferedReader(new InputStreamReader(System.in));
    String theName;
    System.out.println("What is your name?");
    theName = keyboard.readLine( );
    System.out.print("Hello " + theName);
    System.out.println(" - welcome to CSC369.\n");

  } // end main

} //end class
```

Figure 1.5 A stand-alone Java application (top) and the code that activates it (bottom).

An applet is an object downloaded (transferred) from a remote machine and then run on a local machine.

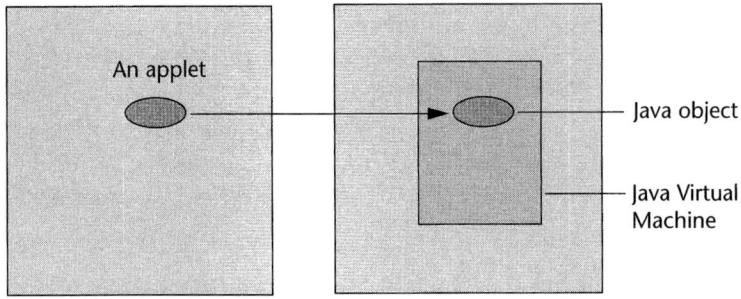

```
/****************************************************
 * A sample of a simple applet.
 * M. Liu 1/8/02
 ****************************************************/

import java.applet.Applet;
import java.awt.*;

public class MyApplet extends Applet{

  public void paint(Graphics g){
    setBackground(Color.blue);

    Font Claude = new Font("Arial", Font.BOLD, 40);
    g.setFont(Claude);
    g.setColor(Color.yellow);
    g.drawString("Hello World!", 100, 100);
  } // end paint

} //end class
```

```
<!-- A web page which, when browsed, will run>
<!-- the MyApplet applet>
<!-- M. Liu 1/8/02>

<title>SampleApplet</title>
<hr>

<applet code="MyApplet.class" width=500 height=500>
</applet>

<hr>
<a href=" Hello.java">The source.</a>
```

Figure 1.6 An applet (top) and the Web page (bottom) that activates it.

A servlet is an object that runs on a remote machine and interacts with a local process using a request-response protocol.

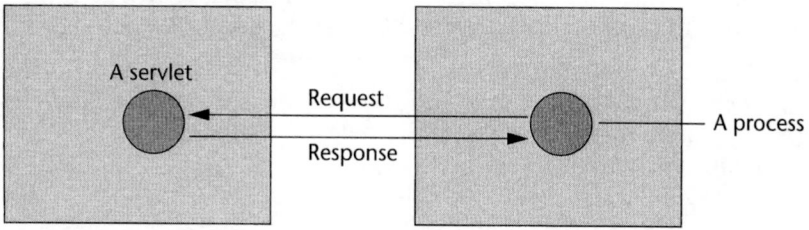

```
/*********************************************************
 * A sample of a simple Java servlet.
 * M. Liu 1/8/02
 *********************************************************/

import java.io.*;
import java.text.*;
import java.util.*;
import javax.servlet.*;
import javax.servlet.http.*;

public class MyServlet extends HttpServlet {

   public void doGet (HttpServletRequest request,
                       HttpServletResponse response)
      throws ServletException, IOException {

      PrintWriter out;
      String title = "MyServlet Output";
      //set content type and other response header
      //fields first
      response.setContentType("text/html");
      //then write the data of the response
      out = response.getWriter();
      out.println("<HTML><HEAD><TITLE>");
      out.println(title);
      out.println("</TITLE></HEAD><BODY>");
      out.println("<H1>" + title + "</H1>");
      out.println("<P>Hello World!");
      out.println("</BODY></HTML>");
      out.close();
   } //end doGet
} //end class
```

Figure 1.7 A servlet (top) and the code that activates it (bottom).

lier. Because the bytecode is an intermediate code that is the same regardless of machine types and is translated to the specific machine code at run time, Java programs are therefore said to be **platform-independent**, meaning that the same program can be run on any machine type that supports the JVM.

In this book, it is assumed that you have knowledge of basic Java programming, to the extent that you can compile and execute a **stand-alone** application or applet. A stand-alone program is one that executes on its own, without exchanging messages with another program.

Concurrent Programming

Distributed computing involves concurrent programming, which is programming that involves the simultaneous execution of processes. In the following paragraphs we look at three kinds of concurrent programming.

- **Concurrent processes executed on multiple computers.** Much of the material in this book deals with separate processes running concurrently on separate, independent computers interconnected via a network. The processes interact with each other by exchanging data over the network, but their execution is otherwise completely independent. When you access a Web page using a browser, a process of the browser program, running on your machine, interacts with a process running on the Web server machine.

    Concurrent programming involving multiple machines requires programming support; that is, the software for the participating program must be written to contain logic to support the interaction between processes. How this logic can be expressed in the programs is a main theme of this book.

- **Concurrent processes executed on a single computer.** Modern computers are supported by multitasking operating systems, which allow multiple tasks, or processes, to be executed concurrently. The concurrency may be real or virtual. True concurrent multitasking on a single computer is feasible only if the computer has multiple CPUs, so that each CPU can execute a separate process. On a computer that has only one CPU, timesharing (see Figure 1.8), or time-slicing, is used to allow processes to take turns being executed, creating the illusion that they are being executed in parallel.

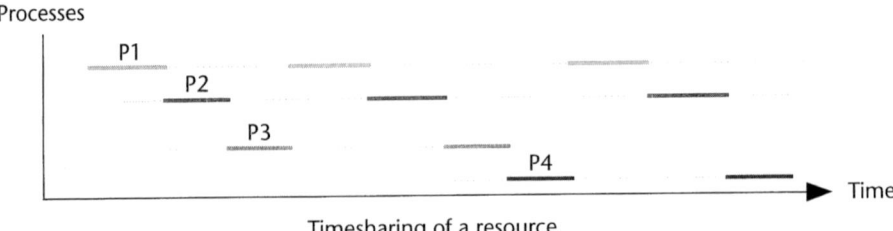

Timesharing of a resource

Figure 1.8 Timesharing on a computer.

Since multitasking is a functionality of the operating system, no programming is needed for this type of concurrent programming. No special software logic needs to be contained in a program to initiate multitasking.

■ **Concurrent programming in a process.** In addition to concurrent programming in separate processes, it is often necessary for a single program to initiate tasks that are to be executed concurrently. For example, it may be necessary for a program to perform other tasks while waiting indefinitely for user input in one user interface window. It may also be desirable for a program to execute tasks in parallel, for performance reasons. Concurrent programming within a process is performed using two types of facilities provided by the operating system.

Parent and Child Processes

At run time, a process may spawn subordinate processes, or **child processes**. Through real or virtual multitasking, the original process, called the **parent process**, continues to run simultaneously with the child processes (see Figure 1.9). A child process is a complete process, consisting of an executing program, its own current values, and state information, some of which is inherited from the parent process. A parent process can be notified when a child process has terminated.

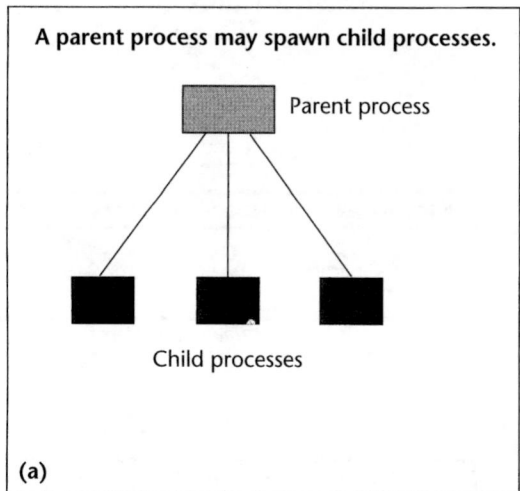
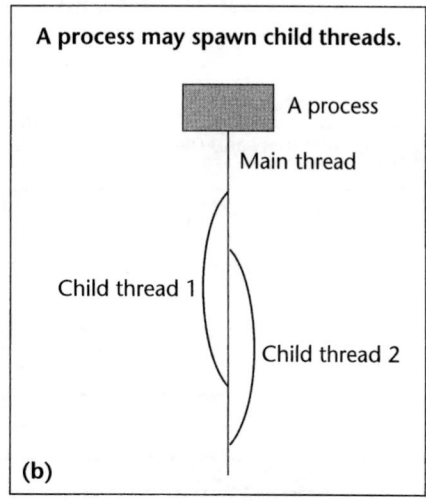

Figure 1.9 Concurrent processing within a process.

Threads

In lieu of child processes, a process may spawn **threads**, also known as **lightweight processes**. Threads carry a minimum of state information, but otherwise behave the same as processes. Since they incur less overhead, threads are preferred over child processes.

The spawning and coordination of child threads requires programming support. The software for the program must be written to contain logic to support the spawning of the threads and to coordinate, or synchronize, the execution of the family of threads spawned by the parent thread.

The concurrent execution of threads may result in a **race condition**. A race condition occurs when a series of commands in a program are executed in parallel, in an arbitrarily interleaved fashion, yielding nondeterministic execution outcome. Figure 1.10 illustrates such a situation. Suppose *counter* is a variable shared among two concurrent threads. Execution sequence 1, in which the instructions of the two processes are executed serially, will result in the counter value being incremented to 2. On the other hand, in execution sequence 2, in which the two sets of instructions are interleaved, the counter will only be incremented to 1.

Race conditions can be avoided if **mutual exclusion** is provided to a code segment to ensure that the commands in the segment can only be executed by one thread at a time. Such a code segment is called a **critical region**. For our example, the critical region comprises the code where the *counter* variable is accessed and incremented.

Programming using threads is called **multi-threaded programming**, or **threaded programming** for short. A multi-threaded program that is written to guard against race conditions is said to be **thread-safe**. The development of a complex thread-safe program requires advanced programming skills.

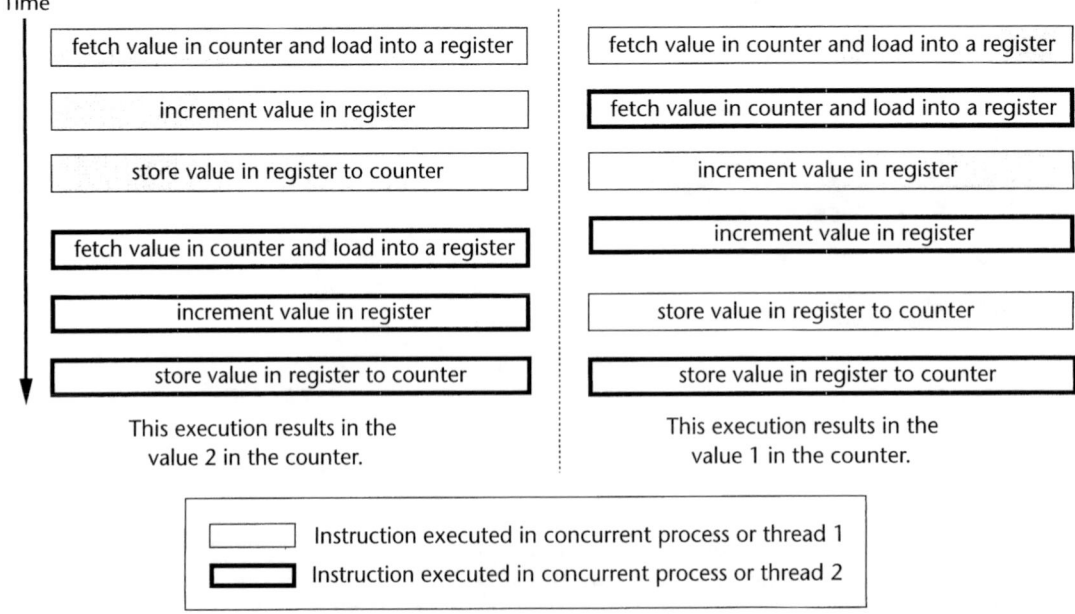

Time

fetch value in counter and load into a register	fetch value in counter and load into a register
increment value in register	fetch value in counter and load into a register
store value in register to counter	increment value in register
fetch value in counter and load into a register	increment value in register
increment value in register	store value in register to counter
store value in register to counter	store value in register to counter

This execution results in the value 2 in the counter.   This execution results in the value 1 in the counter.

☐ Instruction executed in concurrent process or thread 1
▭ Instruction executed in concurrent process or thread 2

Figure 1.10 A race condition resulting from unsynchronized concurrent processes or threads.

Fortunately, in this book we will seldom have to use threads explicitly, as threaded programming is often provided behind the scenes by the toolkits that support network applications.

Java Threads

The Java Virtual Machine enables an application to have multiple threads of execution running concurrently. When a Java Virtual Machine starts up, there is usually a single thread (although in some systems a program may start with more than one thread) that typically calls the method named *main* of some designated class, such as the class of an application that you wrote. Additional threads can be spawned from an active thread, and each thread will run independently and in parallel with other threads until it terminates.

To support threading in a program, Java provides a class named *Thread* as well as an interface named `Runnable` interface.

From within a Java program, there are two ways to create a new thread of execution:

1. Declare a class to be a subclass of *Thread*. This subclass should override the run method of class *Thread*. When an instance of the subclass is allocated and started, the code in the run method is executed concurrently with the main thread.

2. Declare a class that implements the *Runnable* interface. That class implements the *run* method of the interface. When an instance of the class is allocated and started, the code in the *run* method is executed concurrently with the main thread.

Figure 1.11 illustrates the use of the first means of creating a new thread of execution, while Figure 1.12 illustrates the use of the second way.

```
public class RunThreads
{
  public static void main (String[] args)
   {
     SomeThread p1 = new SomeThread(1);
     p1.start();

     SomeThread p2 = new SomeThread(2);
     p2.start();

     SomeThread p3 = new SomeThread(3);
     p3.start();
   }
}// end class RunThreads
```

```
public class SomeThread extends Thread {
  int myID;

  SomeThread(int id) {
    this.myID = id;
  }

  public void run() {
    int i;
    for (i = 1; i < 11; i++)
      System.out.println
        ("Thread"+ myID + ": " + i);
  }
} //end class SomeThread
```

Figure 1.11 Sample application that spawns three threads using a subclass of the *Thread* class.

```
public class RunThreads2
{
  public static void main (String[] args)
  {
    Thread p1 = new Thread(new
              SomeThread2(1));
    p1.start();

    Thread p2 = new Thread(new
              SomeThread2(2));
    p2.start();

    Thread p3 = new Thread(new
              SomeThread2(3));
    p3.start();
  }
} //end class RunThread2
```

```
class SomeThread2 implements Runnable {
  int myID;

  SomeThread2(int id) {
    this.myID = id;
  }

  public void run() {
    int i;
    for (i = 1; i < 11; i++)
      System.out.println ("Thread"+myID
                  + ": " + i);
  }
} //end class SomeThread2
```

Figure 1.12 Sample application that spawns three threads using an implementation of the *Runnable* interface.

In Java, the most straightforward way to guard against race conditions is by using **synchronized static methods**. A static method with the reserved word *synchronized* appearing in its signature can be executed by only one thread at a time. Hence the code in a synchronized static method is guaranteed to be mutually exclusive. For the example shown in Figure 1.10, the code for incrementing the *counter* variable should be enclosed in a synchronized **static** method so that the increments to the counter can only be made by one thread at a time. A Java code sample illustrating the use of threads and a synchronized static method can be found in Exercise 2(d.) at the end of this chapter.

In subsequent chapters, we will use the terms **process** and **thread** frequently. If you are not familiar with threading, there are some exercises at the end of this chapter that allow you to practice threading using Java programming.

1.6 Network Basics

Having looked at some key concepts in operating systems that are relevant to distributed computing, next we will do the same with network basics.

Protocols

In the context of communications, a protocol is a set of rules that must be observed by participants. In a face-to-face meeting, human beings instinctively follow an unspoken protocol based on eye contact, body language, and gestures. This protocol stipulates that only one person speaks at a time while the others listen. In a phone conversation, one party initiates the call, and then, after the call is answered, the parties at the two ends take turns speaking, using pauses or questions to signify when it is the other party's turn to talk.

In communications involving computers, protocols must be formally defined and precisely implemented. For each protocol, there must be rules that specify the following:

- How is the data exchange encoded?
- How are events (sending, receiving) synchronized (ordered) so that the participants can send and receive in a coordinated manner?

The concept of protocols will become more concrete when we study a number of protocols in the rest of this book.

It should be emphasized that a protocol is a set of rules. The specification of a protocol does not dictate how the rules are to be implemented. For example, Hypertext Transfer Protocol (HTTP) specifies the rules that must be observed between a Web browser process and a Web server process. Any Web server program written in conformance to these rules satisfies the protocol, regardless of what programming language or syntax is employed. Therefore, you should understand that a protocol (such as HTTP) is distinct from its implementations (such as the varieties of Web browsers, including Netscape and Internet Explorer).

> The **syntax** of a programming language is the set of language rules, including spelling and grammar, of the language.

As an analogy, the rules for a sport, say basketball, are specified by some authority, say the National Basketball Association (NBA), but it is up to each individual team and then each player to execute or implement the game while observing those rules.

Network Architecture

In the textbooks for data networks, the functionalities of a network are frequently presented using a network architecture (Figure 1.13). The classic network architecture, called the Open System Interconnect (OSI) architecture, divides the complex functionalities of a network into seven layers. All or part of these functionalities must be present on a computer that participates in data communication and hence also in distributed computing. If you are interested in the specifics of the OSI model, you should be able to find them in textbooks on networks such as [Tanenbaum, 35]. For the purposes of this book, a simplified architecture that is appropriate for the Internet will be presented.

> OSI stands for Open System Interconnect, the name given to a model of network architecture promoted by an organization called the International Organization for Standardization (ISO).

The network architecture for the Internet is illustrated in Figure 1.14, where there are four layers: physical, Internet, transport, and application. The **physical layer** provides the functionalities for the transmission of signals, representing a stream of data, from one computer to another. The **Internet layer** allows a packet of data to be addressed to a remote computer and delivered to that computer. The **transport layer** provides the functionalities for data packets to be delivered to a specific process running on a remote computer. Finally, the **application layer** allows messages to be exchanged between programs in support of an application such as the World Wide Web.

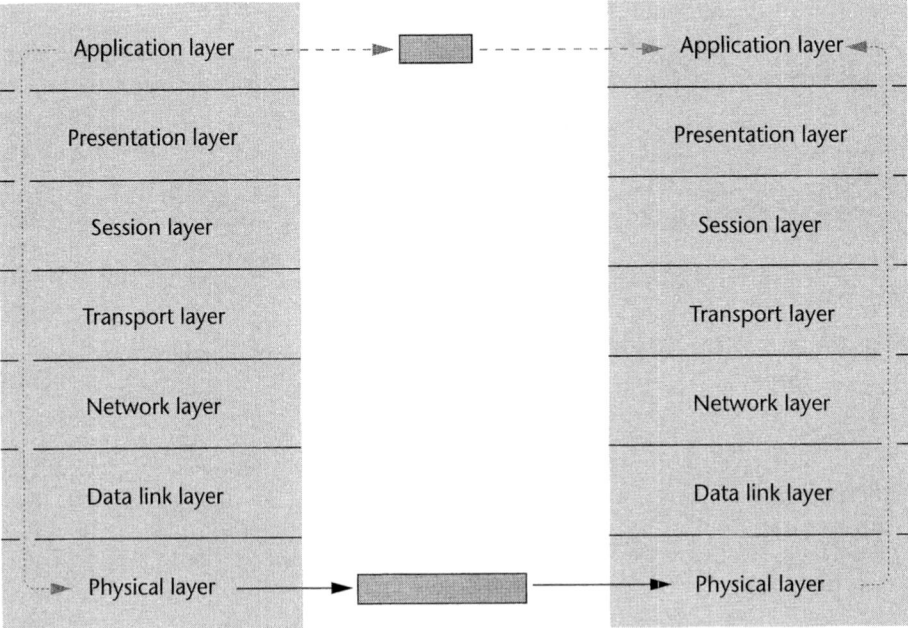

Figure 1.13 The OSI seven-layer network architecture.

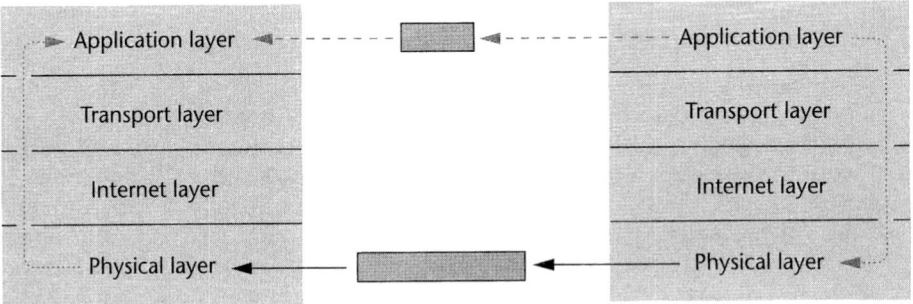

Figure 1.14 The Internet network architecture.

The division of the layers is conceptual: the implementation of these functionalities need not be clearly divided as such in the hardware and software that implement the architecture. The conceptual division of the architecture into layers serves at least two useful purposes. First, it enables protocols to be specified systematically; that is, using a network architecture, these protocols can be specified layer by layer, addressing the functionalities required at each layer.

Secondly, the layered architecture allows the details of the network's functionalities to be abstracted, or hidden. When writing an application, it is helpful when one does not have to be concerned with the details of data communication but can instead concentrate on the application protocol at hand. A layered architecture allows a program to be written as if data can be exchanged directly (see the dashed lines in Figures 1.13 and 1.14). In actuality and behind the scenes, a message sent from one application must be processed by all the functionalities in the lower layers of the network architecture (see the dotted lines). Eventually, the stream of data signals representing the message is transmitted over the physical link interconnecting the computers (see the solid lines). Upon arriving at the receiving computer, the data signals are then processed by the functionalities of the network architecture in the reverse order, until eventually the data is reassembled into a message and delivered to the appropriate process.

Network Architecture Protocols

Let's now look at some of the specific protocols for the Internet architecture. The protocol for the Internet layer is named, aptly enough, the Internet Protocol. This protocol uses a particular naming scheme, which we will soon study, for identifying computers on the network and for routing the data. At the transport layer, there are two widely used protocols: The Transmission Control Protocol (TCP) provides **connection-oriented** communication, while the User Datagram Protocol (UDP) supports **connectionless** communication. (A discussion of connection-oriented versus connectionless communication will be introduced in the next section and then discussed further in Chapter 2.) Finally, at the application layer, protocols such as File Transfer Protocol (FTP), Simple Network Mail Protocol (SNMP), and Hypertext Transmission Protocol (HTTP) are specified for network applications. The well-known Transmission Control Protocol/Internet Protocol (TCP/IP) is a set of protocols encompassing the Internet and transport layers of this architecture; these protocols are universally employed for data communication over the Internet. An Internet application therefore must be run on a computer that implements this portion of the Internet architecture, colloquially termed the **TCP/IP stack**.

Readers who are interested in the protocols at the lower layers may want to consult textbooks such as [Stallings, 12; Tanenbaum, 13]. This book is devoted to the study of protocols at the application layer. We will start by looking at some of the popular application protocols, such as those just mentioned in the previous paragraph. We will then go on to study how such applications are supported using distributed computing.

Connection-Oriented versus Connectionless Communication

Although connection-oriented and connectionless communication are more properly a topic for data networks discussion, we will have occasion to make a distinction between the two in our discussions.

In connection-oriented communication, a connection—which may be physical (i.e., tangible, provided using hardware such as cables, modems, and receivers) or **logical** (i.e., *abstract* or *virtual*, using software that emulates a connection)— is established between two parties, the caller and the callee. Such is the case when you (the caller) dial a number to make a phone call to a friend (the callee). Once a connection is established, data (voice, in the case of a phone call) can be sent repeatedly over the connection continuously until the session is over, such as when you hang up the phone at the end of a conversation, at which point the connection is severed. Note that in this mode of communication there is no need to address an individual data packet explicitly while a connection is in use.

As the name implies, connectionless communication involves no connection. Instead, data is sent a packet at a time. Each packet must be explicitly addressed by the sender to the receiver. An example of connectionless communication is when you correspond with a friend using rounds of email messages or letters. Each email or letter you send, containing a message, must be addressed to your friend. In reply, your friend sends an email or letter addressed to you. The exchange continues until the correspondence, or session, is over.

A data network transmits data; a voice network transmits voice. Modern networks transmit both data and voice.

On a data network, connectionless communication is simpler to provide, since there is no need to maintain separate connections. Yet the lack of a connection can result in data packets being lost during delivery or being delivered out of order. For example, if you send multiple emails or letters to your friend in succession, each one containing part of a message, it is entirely possible for your friend to receive the emails or letters in a scrambled order, since each email/letter is delivered independently.

On the other hand, connection-oriented communication can ensure that data packets are delivered safely and in order along an established connection, at the cost of additional processing overhead. This is another example of trade-offs.

Figure 1.15 graphically illustrates the difference between these two forms of communication. In exercise 3 at the end of this chapter, you will be guided through a simplified analysis of the trade-offs between the two forms.

At any layer of a network architecture, communication can be carried out using a connection-oriented facility or a connectionless facility. At the transport layer of the TCP/IP suite, the User Datagram Protocol (UDP) is a connectionless protocol, while the Transmission Control Protocol (TCP) is a connection-oriented protocol. A facility or protocol that uses UDP to transmit data is said to be connectionless at the transport layer, while one that uses TCP is said to be connection-oriented at the same layer. Note that it is possible for a communication facility to be connection-oriented at one layer but connectionless at another. For example, a Web application uses HTTP, a connection-oriented protocol, at the application layer, but actual data transmitted to and from the application may use UDP at the transport layer.

Table 1.1 compares the two modes of communication.

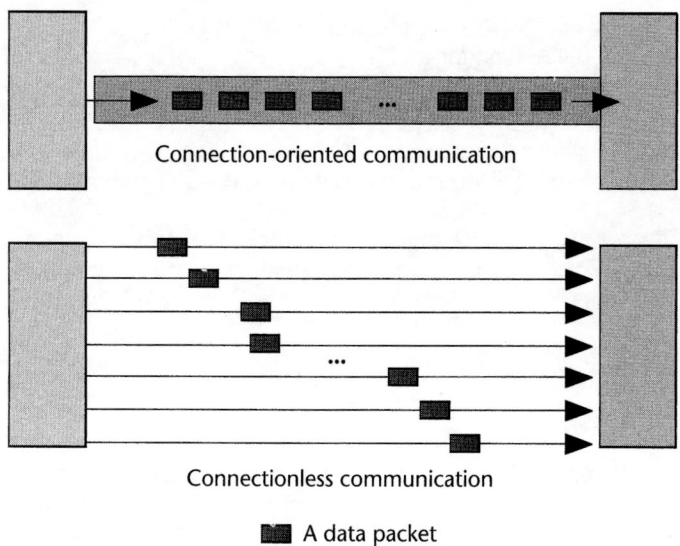

Connection-oriented communication

Connectionless communication

A data packet

Figure 1.15 Connection-oriented versus connectionless communication.

Table 1.1 Comparisons of Connection-Oriented and Connectionless Interprocess Communication (IPC).

	Connection-Oriented	**Connectionless**
Addressing	Specified at connection time; there is no need to re-specify with each subsequent operation (send or receive).	Addressing is specified with each operation.
Connection overhead	There is overhead for establishing a connection.	Not applicable.
Addressing overhead	There is no addressing overhead with each individual operation.	Overhead is incurred with each operation.
Data delivery order	The connection abstraction allows the IPC mechanism to maintain the order of delivering data packets.	The lack of a connection makes it difficult for the IPC facility to maintain delivery order.

(continued on next page)

Table 1.1 Comparisons of Connection-Oriented and Connectionless Interprocess Communication (IPC). (*continued*)

	Connection-Oriented	**Connectionless**
Protocols	This mode of communication is appropriate for protocols that require exchange of a large stream of data and/or a large number of rounds of exchange.	This mode of communication is appropriate for protocols that exchange a small amount of data in a limited number of rounds of exchange.

Network Resources

An **Internet host** is a computer that implements the Internet protocol architecture and hence is capable of participating in Internet communications.

A **router** is a computer that specializes in forwarding data between networks. On the Internet, a router implements the functionalities of the Internet layer.

Throughout this book you will often encounter the term **network resources**. By network resources we are referring to resources that are available to the participants of a distributed computing community. For example, on the Internet the network resources include hardware such as computers (including **Internet hosts** and **routers**) and equipment (printers, facsimile machines, cameras, etc.), and software such as processes, email mailboxes, files, and Web documents. An important class of network resources is **network services**, such as the World Wide Web (WWW) and file transfer service, which are provided by specific processes running on computers.

Although the idea may seem simple, one of the key challenges in distributed computing is the unique identification of resources that are available on the network. In the next section, we will look at how resource identification is accomplished on the Internet.

Host Identification and Internet Protocol Addresses

Physically, the Internet is a gigantic mesh of network links and computers. Conceptually (see Figure 1.16), the main arteries of the Internet are a set of high-bandwidth network links that constitute the "backbone" of the network. Connected to the backbone are individual networks, each of which has a unique identifier. Computers with TCP/IP support, called Internet **hosts**, are linked to individual **networks**. Through this system of "information highways," data can be transmitted from a host H_1 on network N_1 to another host H_2 on network N_2. To transfer data from within a program, it must be possible to uniquely identify the process that is to receive the data, similar to addressing the recipient of a letter delivered by the postal service.

As you recall, a process is a run-time representation of a program when the program is executed on a computer. Further, recall that on the Internet a computer, or a host, is linked to a network. In order to identify a process, it is therefore necessary to name the network, the host linked to that network, and then the particular process running on the host.

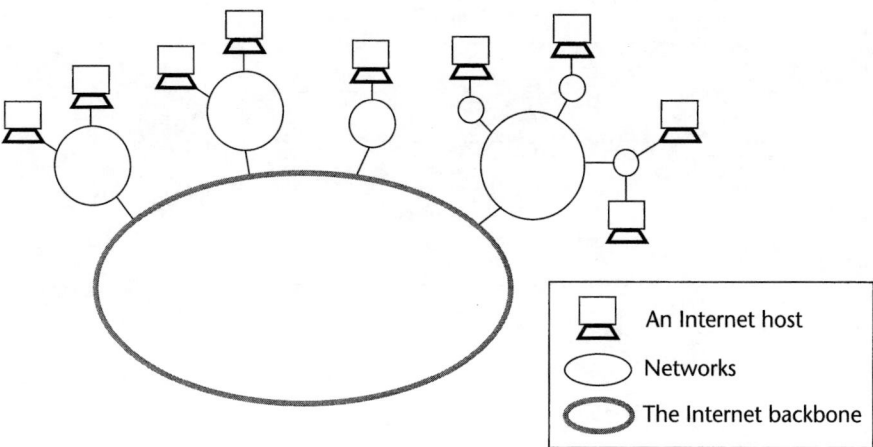

Figure 1.16 The Internet topology.

In the Internet architecture, host identification is part of the Internet protocol (IP), which, as you recall, is the protocol at the Internet layer of the TCP/IP suite. The discussion that follows refers to the host identification scheme specified in version 4 of IP, or IPv4. Although the scheme has been modified in IP version 6 (IPv6) to accommodate more Internet addresses, the principles of the scheme are unchanged in the two versions, and IPv4 is chosen here for its relative simplicity. In the context of this book, the distinctions between the two versions are not significant.

In IPv4, each host on the Internet is identified by a unique 32-bit string. Given a length of 32 bits, the total number of addresses allowable is 2^{32}. Put another way, the address space of IPv4 accommodates 2^{32} (4,294,967,296 or over 4 billion) addresses in total.

Each IP address must identify both the network on which a host resides and then the particular host on that network. The IPv4 addressing scheme does so as follows:

The address space is divided into five classes, A through E. As illustrated in Figure 1.17, each class has a unique prefix. Class A starts with a bit 0, Class B starts with a bit sequence of 10, Class C with 110, and so forth. The remaining bits in each address are used for identifying the network and the host on a particular network. Thus a Class A address has 31 bits for network-host identification, a Class B address 30 bits, and so forth. This means that a total of 2^{31} (about 2 billion) Class A addresses are available, while a maximum of 2^{30} (about 1 billion) Class B addresses are available. The maximum number of addresses in Class C, D, or E can be calculated similarly. It should be noted that within each class a small number of addresses (such as all 0s and all 1s) are reserved for special purposes.

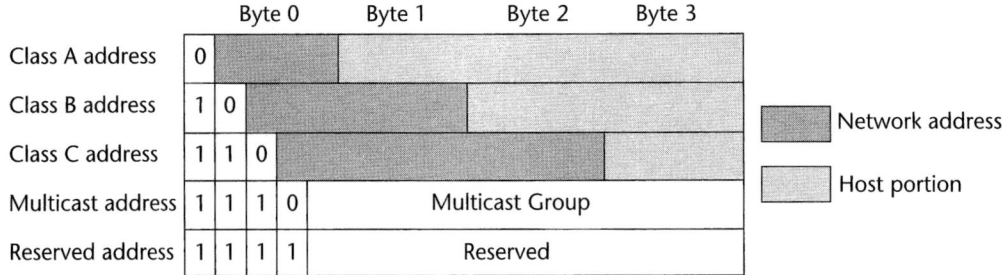

Figure 1.17 The IPv4 address scheme.

You may wonder why it is necessary to have different classes of addresses. This has to do with the number of computers that each individual network can accommodate. Consider a Class A address (see Figure 1.17): the 7 bits immediately following the prefix 0 are allotted for network identification, with the rest of the 32–8 = 24 bits devoted to the identification of hosts within a network. Therefore, each class A network can support 2^{24} (roughly 16 million) hosts, although there can be no more than 2^7, or 128, such networks. Using the same analysis, you can see that each of the 2^{14} (16,384) class B network addresses can accommodate up to 2^{16} (65,536) hosts. Likewise, there are far more Class C networks than there are Class B networks, but each Class C network can support far fewer hosts.

As has already been mentioned, we will seldom have occasion to identify IP hosts using the 32-bit address string. On the rare occasions when we do use a numerical network address, we most likely will use the so-called dotted decimal notation instead. The dotted decimal notation of an IP address uses a decimal value for each of the 4 bytes in the IP address.

For example, suppose the dotted-decimal notation for a particular Internet address is 129.65.24.50. The 32-bit binary expansion of the notation is as follows:

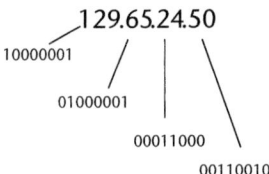

Since the leading bit sequence is 10, the address is a Class B address. Within the class, the network portion is identified by the remaining bits in the first 2 bytes, that is, 00000101000001, and the host portion consists of the values in the last 2 bytes, or 0001100000110010. For convenience, the binary prefix for class identification is often included as part of the network portion of the address, so we would say that this particular address is at network 129.65 and at host address 24.50 on that network.

Here is another example. Given the address 224.0.0.1, one can expand it as follows:

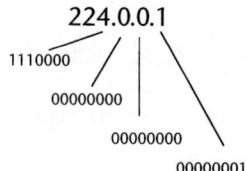

The binary prefix 1110 signifies that this is a class D, or multicast, address. Data packets sent to this address should therefore be delivered to the multicast group 00000000000000000000000000001.

An IP network address is assigned by an authority, known as the **Internet Assigned Numbers Authority** (**IANA**) [community-ml.org, 25] to an organization such as a university or an Internet Service Provider (ISP). (*Note:* The assignment of the authority is dynamic. See http://www.wia.org/pub/iana.html for a history of the evolution of this authority.) Within each network, the assignment of the host portion is internal to the organization. Typically, an organization makes use of this portion of the address to subdivide its network into a hierarchy of subnets, with a unique host number assigned to each computer attached to a subnet. For instance, the administrator of class B network 129.65 may choose to designate byte 2 (that is, the leftmost 8 bits of the host portion) in the address as a subnet identifier. Under this subnet scheme, the IP address 129.65.32.3 identifies a host of ID 3 on a subnet of ID 32 on this particular network.

Since the 1990s, the demand for IP addresses has skyrocketed, to the point that the address space has been exhausted. The static addressing scheme we have just described has since been augmented with numerous changes in response to ever-increasing demand for addresses, including the **dynamic addressing** scheme that is popular with Internet Service Providers (ISPs) such as America Online (AOL). Using dynamic addressing, an ISP or large organization can extend the address space for a given IP network by pooling the addresses. For example, a static class B network address may accommodate up to 2^{16} or 65,536 static hosts. By pooling the approximately 65 thousand addresses and allocating each to an active session on an as-needed basis, it is possible to support millions of IP hosts, assuming that no more than 65 thousand are active at the same time. For this reason, when you access the Internet through an ISP, the IP address of your computer may vary from one logon session to the next.

Most of us have problems memorizing a 32-bit string, even with the aid of the dotted decimal notation. Hence, a symbolic name for identifying a host is preferable. That is why the **Domain Name System** (**DNS**) was adopted by the Internet community. The acronym DNS also expands to Domain Name Service, which refers to the service provided by a Domain Name System. Every time you use email or browse a Web page, you identify an Internet host using a domain name based on the DNS protocol.

Every domain name contains two or more components separated by dots. In an address such as acme.com, the last component, com in this case, is called the **top-level domain**. To the left of the dot in that name, acme in this case, is what is called the **second-level domain**. It is also possible to have subdomains, such as marketing.acme.com. Domain names are not case-sensitive; that is, there is no distinction between the uppercase and the lowercase of the same character when a name is spelled.

Currently, the top-level domains are classified as shown in Table 1.2 [Brain, 15].

Table 1.2 Top-level Domain Names

.com	For commercial entities, which anyone, anywhere in the world, can register.
.net	Originally designated for organizations directly involved in Internet operations. This domain is increasingly being used by businesses when the desired name under .com is already registered by another organization. Today anyone can register a name in the .net domain.
.org	For miscellaneous organizations, including nonprofits.
.edu	For four-year accredited institutions of higher learning.
.gov	For U.S. federal government entities.
.mil	For the U.S. military.
Country codes	For individual countries based on the International Standards Organization; for example, .ca for Canada, and .jp for Japan. See [Connolly, 18] if you are interested in a list of the country codes.

The second-level domain combined with the first-level domain (e.g., calpoly.edu) typically, but not necessarily, maps to the network portion of an IP address while the rest of the domain name (e.g., www.csc) serves to identify the subnet, if any, and the host name. See Figure 1.18 for a pictorial depiction.

Each domain name is mapped to a corresponding IP address, although the mapping may not be permanent. For example, the domain name ebay.com currently maps to the IP address 216.32.120.133. The mapping of a domain name to its current corresponding IP address, and vice versa, can be performed using a network service known as **DNS naming resolution**. Exercise 4 shows you a way to experiment with this service.

Finally, the domain name *localhost* can be used to refer to the computer on which the process is run. The name is always mapped to the IP address 127.0.0.1 and simply addresses "this computer."

Once a host is located using either an IP address or domain name, we can then identify individual resources on that host. In the following paragraphs we will

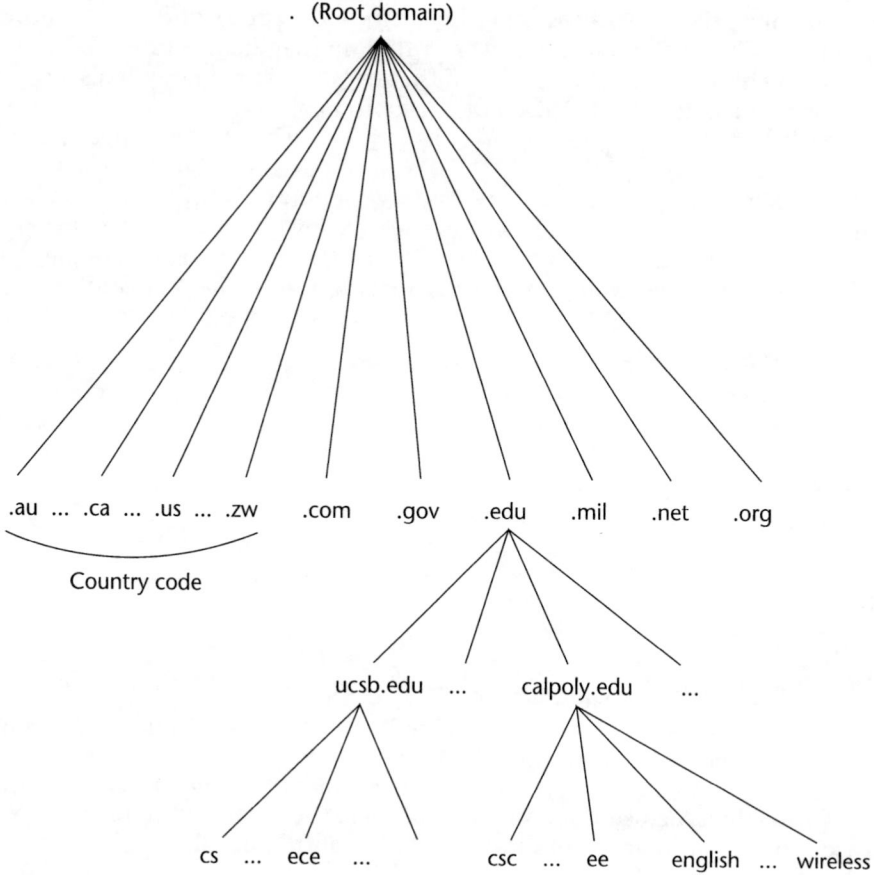

Figure 1.18 Domain name hierarchy.

look at three examples of such schemes for identifying a process, an email recipient, and Web documents, respectively.

Identifying Processes with Protocol Ports

Specifying the correct domain name or its corresponding IP address allows us to locate a computer or host on the Internet. But in network applications, data needs to be delivered to a specific process running on a computer. Thus we need a naming scheme to allow us to uniquely identify such a process. There are any number of possible schemes to do so. For example, one possibility is to make use of a unique **process identifier** (**PID**) assigned to the process by the operating system (see exercise 4). On the Internet, the protocol for process identification involves the use of a logical entity known as a **protocol port**, or a **port** for short. Recall that the transport layer in the Internet architecture is responsible for dispatching data to processes, and that two well-known protocols are in use at this layer: TCP and UDP. Each of these protocols uses a separate set of ports on each host for this purpose. A process that wishes to exchange data with another process using either TCP or UDP must be assigned one of the ports. To send data to a process currently associated with port p on host H, an application must address the data to (H, p) in the code. In Ipv4, there are 2^{16} ports (port 0 to port 65,535) on each host, under either TCP or UDP. For example, when browsing a Web site, you are typically making use of the service of a process running on TCP port 80 on the host (such as www.calpoly.edu) you specified.

In the TCP and UDP protocols, protocol numbers 0 through 1023 (2^{10}) are reserved for well-known services. Known as **well-known ports**, these numbers are assigned by the Internet Assigned Numbers Authority (IANA) [isoc.org, 38], and on some systems these numbers can only be used by system processes or by programs executed by privileged users. Each popular network service, such as telnet, FTP, HTTP, or SMTP, is assigned one of these port numbers (23, 21, 80, 25, respectively) where the process providing the service can be expected to be reached. We will have many occasions to specify port numbers in our coding examples.

Email Addresses

An email address takes the form of username@DomainName. For example, mliu@csc.calpoly.edu identifies the author of this book. When you send an email identifying that email address as the recipient, a mailer program on the IP host with the specified domain name delivers the email to the mailbox of the specified user on that system, in this case the author of this book.

URLs

Users of Web browsers are familiar with **Uniform Resource Locators** (**URLs**). When you enter a name string such as http://www.csc.calpoly.edu in the browser to visit a particular Web site, you are specifying a URL.

A URL is a naming scheme under the more general scheme known as **Uniform Resource Identifiers** (**URIs**). URIs are short strings that identify resources on the Web, including documents, images, downloadable files, services, and electronic mailboxes. The URI scheme provides a uniform way of addressing these resources under a variety of naming schemes used in individual application protocols such as HTTP, FTP, and Internet mail. By design, the URI scheme is an extensible scheme so that it can support more protocol naming schemes over time.

URL is an informal term associated with popular URI schemes for protocols such as HTTP, FTP, and mailto.

The **Uniform Resource Name** (**URN**) is a scheme specified by RFC2141 and related documents, intended to serve as persistent, location-independent, resource identifiers. A URN provides persistent names within a namespace, thus allowing a permanent object to be mirrored over several known sites; if a site is unavailable, the object could be found/resolved at another site. Several proposals for URNs exist, but none of them has been widely adopted yet [aboutdomains.com, 16].

Although informal, the URL is by far the best known of these terms. A URL provides a nonpersistent (that is, not necessarily permanent) means to uniquely identify an object within a **namespace**. A namespace, in the context of a naming system, refers to the set of names that the system provides. In its most general form, the format of a URL is

<protocol>//<user>:<password>@<host-ID>:<port-number>/<directory path>

where

<protocol> is the exact but case-insensitive name of the application-layer protocol you wish to use to access the resource; for example, HTTP if you are attempting to access a Web browser;

<user>:<password> is for access authorization, if required by the protocol;

<host-ID> is the domain name or dotted-decimal IP address of the host that provides the service allowing you to access the protocol; for example, www.calpoly.edu;

<port-number> is the transport-layer protocol port for the process that provides the service on the remote host; for example, 80 (by default) for HTTP or Web servers;

<directory path> specifies where in the file system of the remote host the resource can be located; for example, ~mliu/csc102/index.html.

When you are entering a URL in a browser, you may skip the specifications of the protocol (in which case HTTP is assumed), the user:password (not used in HTTP), the port-number (80 by default), and the directory path (the root of the document directory hierarchy is assumed). For example, the URL www.csc.calpoly.edu entered to Netscape specifies the home page of the California Polytechnic State University at San Luis Obispo, to be fetched from the host with the domain name www.csc.calpoly.edu, running on port 80.

A shortened form of a URL, termed a **relative URL**, can be used at times. During a session when a document (say http://www.csc.calpoly.edu/index.html) is accessed, you can use a *relative* URL to name another file in the same directory, to be fetched via the same Web server. For example, if another file exists in that same directory called courses.html, then the URL courses.html can be named in that document in lieu of the full URL, http://www.csc.calpoly.edu/courses.html.

Extensible Name Service

Extensible Name Service (XNS) is an Internet naming service managed by the XNS Public Trust Organization (XNSORG), an independent, open-forum organization. The service supports a naming scheme that allows a single, universal address to be used by a user to perform "communications of all types—email, phone, fax, Web pages, instant messaging, even postal mail. . . . As a naming and addressing service, XNS operates at a higher level than DNS. DNS is designed to resolve a name into the address of an Internet host computer. XNS is designed to resolve a universal address into any type of address on any type of communications network. You could say that XNS is to DNS what DNS is to a phone number (and, in fact, XNS uses DNS to resolve the Internet address of an XNS agency)" [omg.org, 27]. An XNS is a character string. There are three types of XNS names: personal names, business names, and general names, each of which starts with a unique leading character (=, @, and +, respectively) and each of which can contain up to 64 Unicode characters.

> **Unicode** is a standard for representing characters. According to the Unicode Home Page, "Unicode provides a unique [numerical representation] for every character, no matter what the platform, no matter what the program, no matter what the language" [unicode.org, 29].

Name Resolution

Whenever a symbolic name is used to identify a resource, the name must be translated to the corresponding physical address in order to locate the resource. We have already seen that a domain name such as

someComputer.someDivision.someCompany.com

for an Internet host must be translated to the numerical address, say 129.65.123.7, of that particular computer. The process of the translation is called **name resolution**, or more simply, **name lookup**.

To perform name resolution, a database (also called a directory or a registry) must exist containing the mappings between symbolic names and physical names. If the namespace of a naming scheme is of a limited size, then it is possible to perform name resolution manually. In the case of the DNS or XNS, a manual process is out of the question; instead, a network service has to be provided to support online name resolution.

For the DNS, the name lookup service is provided by machines that are called **DNS servers**. A central authority maintains the name database and sees to it that the database is distributed throughout the Internet to the DNS servers. When a domain name is specified—whether entered into a browser or coded in a program being executed—the name is submitted to the nearest DNS server for resolution. If the nearest server does not have the mapping, that server forwards the request to another DNS server. The propagation of the request continues until the name is resolved, at which time the mapping is sent back to the process that originated the request.

In later chapters of this book we will have many occasions to work with naming schemes and their supporting facilities.

1.7 Software Engineering Basics

Software engineering is a discipline in computer science that covers the process of developing applications. Although this book provides the technical background for building network applications, it is not intended to cover the process of developing such applications. At the same time, some of the basic concepts from the discipline of software engineering will be relevant to our discussions. These concepts are introduced in this section.

Procedural versus Object-Oriented Programming

In building network applications, there are two main classes of programming languages: procedural language and object-oriented language. (Although there are other classes of languages, such as functional language, they are not widely used in network applications.)

Procedural languages—the C language being the primary example—use procedures to break down the complexity of the tasks of an application. For example, an application may be coded using a **procedure** (also called a function, although in some contexts the term *procedure* is used for a void function) to perform the input, another procedure to perform the computation, and a third procedure for generating the output.

Object-oriented languages, exemplified by Java, the language chosen for this book, use objects to encapsulate the details. Each object simulates an object in real life, carrying state data as well as behaviors. State data is represented as instance data (in Java) or data members (in C++). Behaviors are represented as methods.

The Unified Modeling Language

An important step in software engineering is the production of **artifacts**, or documents, to record the conceptual design of the application being developed. For readability, these documents should be written using a universal set of notations and languages. The **Unified Modeling Language** (UML), developed by the Object Management Group [omg.org, 27], is such a facility. UML provides a common set of language and notations "for specifying, visualizing, constructing, and documenting the artifacts of software systems" [omg.org, 27].

OMG-UML provides a rich set of tools for all aspects of software engineering, the coverage of which belongs in software engineering courses. In this book we will occasionally make use of one of the notations: UML class diagrams (and only a subset of them), for documenting the relationships of some of the Java classes that appear in our presentation. Figure 1.19 presents the subset of class diagrams you will see in this book.

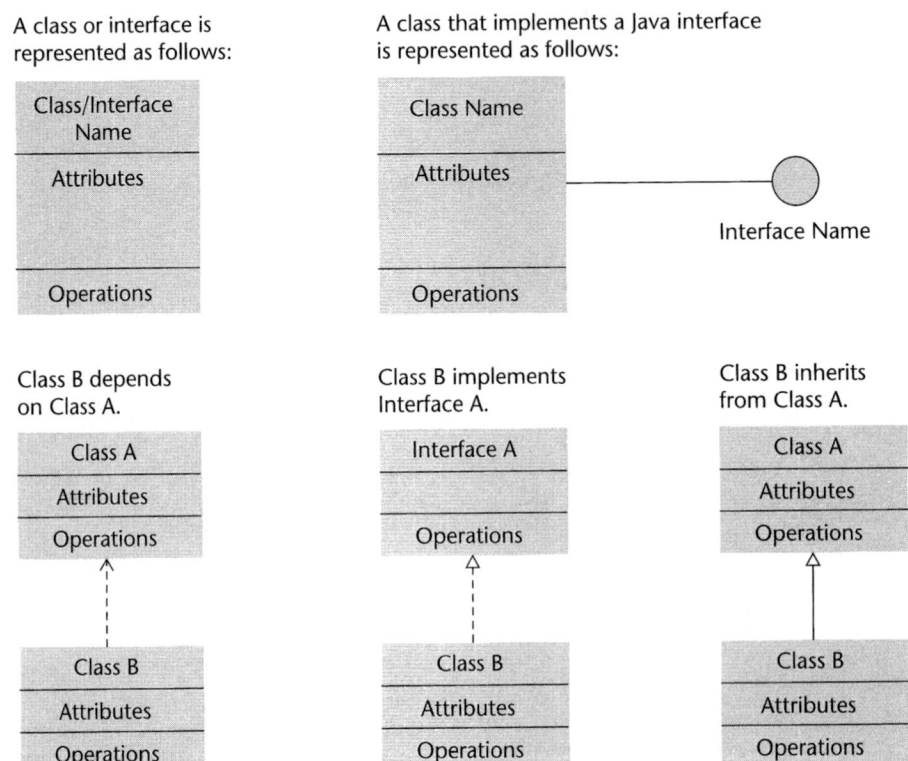

Note: The style of the lines and the shape of arrowheads are significant.

Figure 1.19 A subset of UML class diagrams.

The Architecture of Distributed Applications

The idea of using a multilayer architecture to organize the functionalities of a data network can be applied to distributed applications. Figure 1.20 presents an example of such an architecture.

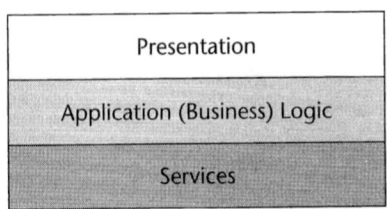

Figure 1.20 The architecture of distributed applications.

Using this architecture, the functionalities of a distributed application can be classified in three layers:

- The **presentation layer** provides the user interface. For example, if the application is a shopping cart, this layer generates the set of Web pages that are viewable by a shopper using a browser.

- The **application logic layer** provides the computation for the application. This layer is also called the **business logic layer** for enterprise applications. In a shopping cart application, this layer is responsible for such tasks as credit verification and computing the dollar amounts of the orders, sales tax, and delivery cost.

- The **service layer** provides the underlying services needed to support the functionalities of the top two layers. Services may include data access facilities (such as a database management system), directory services for name lookups (such as the Domain Name Service), and interprocess communication (which allows data to be exchanged among processes).

Of these layers, the service layer will be the focus of this book. The other two layers belong in the realm of software engineering.

Toolkits, Frameworks, and Components

Toolkits, frameworks, and components are terms associated with software engineering for enterprise systems (that is, large-scale commercial applications).

In the context of software development, a **toolkit** or **framework** is a collection of classes, tools, and programming samples. As examples, the Java Development Tookit (JDK) is such a collection for developing Java programs, while Microsoft's .NET framework is meant for building Web-based applications. It is assumed that you are proficient with the JDK for developing Java programs; other toolkits for distributed computing (for example, the Java Socket Toolkit) will be covered later in this book.

Component-based software development is an approach to building enterprise software systems. Using this approach, software is developed and evolved by assembling selected pre-engineered, pretested, and reusable software components. This approach promotes software reuse and has the potential to significantly reduce the cost and errors of development [Pour, 37]. The Enterprise Java Bean (EJB) and Microsoft's Component Object Model (COM) are platforms that support component-based applications. Although these platforms are important to enterprise distributed computing, their coverage is beyond the scope of this book.

Summary

In this introductory chapter, we have discussed the following topics:

- What is meant by distributed computing and how it is related to or different from terms such as distributed system and parallel computing.
- The basic concepts of operating systems that are important to our study. Such concepts include processes and threads.
- Basic concepts in data communication that are relevant to this book. Such topics include
  - Network architectures: the OSI model and the Internet model
  - Connection-oriented communication versus connectionless communication
  - Naming schemes for network resources, including
    - The Domain Name System (DNS)
    - The Extensible Name System (XNS)
    - Protocol port numbers
    - Uniform Resource Identifier (URI) and Uniform Resource Locator (URL)
    - Email addresses
- Basic concepts in software engineering that are important to our study. Such concepts include
  - Procedural programming compared to object-oriented programming
  - Class diagrams using the notations of the Unified Modeling Language (UML)
  - The three-layered architecture of distributed applications consisting of (i) the presentation layer, (ii) the application or business logic layer, and (iii) the service layer
  - The terms toolkit, framework, and component in the context of software engineering

Exercises

1. Distributed Computing

   a. Consider distributed computing as defined in this chapter. For each of the following activities, determine and explain whether it is an example of distributed computing:

      i.   Using Excel on a stand-alone personal computer

      ii. Web surfing

      iii. Instant messaging

      iv. Compiling and testing a Cobol program on a department machine that has no network connection

      v.   Using the electronic mail on your department's computer to send a message to yourself

      vi. Using Napster.com to download music

   b. In this exercise we will use a simplified mathematical model to analyze failures in a distributed system. Explain your answers.

      Suppose each computer in this question has a probability p of failing at any time, $p < 1$.

      i.   If n computers are interconnected and the availability of each computer is needed to maintain a service provided using distributed computing involving these computers,

           a. What is the probability p that the service will not be available at any time, assuming that no other components in the distributed system will fail? Express p as a mathematical function of n and p.

           b. Based on your answer for part a, what is the probability p when the computing is not distributed at all, that is, for the case of $n = 1$?

           c. Based on your answer for part a, use $p = 0.2$ and $n = 3$ to compute the probability p. How does that probability compare with the failure probability if the same computing is performed using monolithic computing, that is, on one computer only?

      ii. Now suppose the service provided using distributed computing requires only one of the three computers, with the other two computers serving as backups (that is, each of the three computers, on its own, is capable of providing the service). What is the probability that the service will not be available at any time, assuming that no other components in the distributed system will fail? How does the failure probability of this system compare with the failure probability if the same computing is performed using monolithic computing, that is, on one computer only?

Napster.com is a digital music service. AudioGalaxy and KaZaA offer similar services.

c. Do research on either the Internet worm [Eichin and Rochlis, 21] or a virus attack such as the I-Love-You virus [Zetter, 22] and summarize what each one is and how it happened. Why are such occurrences significant in distributed computing? Can you think of some measures to avoid these problems?

d. Do research on "distributed computing" (or, more accurately, collaborative computing) projects such as seti@home [setiathome.ssl.berkeley.edu, 10] and genome@home [genomeathome.stanford.edu, 23]. Choose one of them. Write a report to (i) explain the objective of the project, (ii) explain how the computing is performed in a distributed system, and (iii) explain what you have to do to participate in the project.

e. Do research on the early days of the Internet (see sources [vlmp.museophile.com, 1], [zakon.org, 2], [silkroad.com, 3], or [Hafner and Lyon, 4], for example) and write a short report on one of the key organizations and one of the prominent figures in the history of the Internet.

2. Concurrent Programming

a. Look up the online API specification for Java [java.sun.com, 20].

Choose the link for the *Runnable* interface and then the *Thread* class. Browse each carefully, reading the specifications for the methods of each.

i. According to the specifications, which of the two, *Runnable* interface or *Thread* class, is preferred if you only intend to implement the *run* method? Why?

ii. What does the *Thread* class method *sleep* do? Write the Java statement(s) that appears in the code for a thread to suspend the execution of the thread for 5 seconds.

iii. What does the *Thread* class method *activeCount* do? What should the method return in a program where three threads are spawned?

iv. The *Thread* class method stop is said to be *deprecated*. What is meant by a deprecated method?

v. How many methods are there in the *Runnable* interface? Name each.

vi. How do you use the *Runnable* interface to create a thread? Explain.

b. Compile and run the Java class files shown in Figure 1.11 and provided in the program sample folder. What is the outcome? Capture the output of the run and write a paragraph to explain the output, paying special attention to the order of the lines of output.

c. Compile and run the Java class files shown in Figure 1.12. What is the outcome? Capture the output of the run and write a paragraph to explain the output, paying special attention to the order of the lines of output. Also, how does the output compare with the output from part b (the second part)?

d. Consider the following Java classes:

i. What do you expect the outcome to be when *RunThread3* is executed? Compile and run it.

ii. Comment out the word *synchronized* in the heading of the method *update*. Compile and run *RunThread3* again. What is the outcome? Explain.

```java
public class RunThreads3
{
   public static void main (String[] args)
   {
     int originalThreadCount = Thread.activeCount( );
     for (int i=0; i<10; i++) {
       Thread p = new Thread(new SomeThread3());
       p.start( );
     System.out.println("thread count=" + Thread.activeCount( ));
     }
     while (Thread.activeCount( ) > originalThreadCount ){
       // loop until all child threads have exited.
     }
     System.out.println("finally, Count = " + SomeThread3.count);
   }
}//end class RunThreads3
```

```java
class SomeThread3 implements Runnable {
   static int count=0;

   SomeThread3() {
     super( );
   }

   public void run() {
     update( );
   }

   static public synchronized void update( ){
     int myCount = count;

     int second = (int)(Math.random( ) * 500.0);
     try {
       Thread.sleep(second);
     }
     catch (InterruptedException e) {
     }

     myCount++;
     count = myCount;
     System.out.println("count="+count+
     "; thread count=" + Thread.activeCount( ));
   }
} //end class SomeThread3
```

3. Connection-Oriented versus Connectionless Communication

In this exercise we will use a simplified mathematical model to analyze the trade-off between connection-oriented communication and connectionless communication. Explain your answer.

On a certain network both forms of communication are provided:

- Using connection-oriented communication, it takes 50 seconds to establish a connection, after which a packet of up to 10 characters can be sent in 1.0 seconds over the connection, in either direction.

- Using connectionless communication, a packet of up to 10 characters can be sent in 1.2 seconds (the sending of each packet takes slightly longer than in the connection-oriented case, since each packet must find its way to the receiver).

Suppose processes A and B exchange messages on this network. A initiates the communication and sends to B a message of 100 characters, which are partitioned into 10 packets. In reply, B sends a message of 50 characters, which are partitioned into 5 packets.

Assuming that there is no delay other than the time it takes for establishing a connection (in the connection-oriented case) and for packet transmission:

a. How long does the session between A and B last, using connection-oriented communication? Explain.

b. How long does the session between A and B last, using connectionless communication? Explain.

c. How much data (in number of characters) must be exchanged between A and B in order for the connection-oriented communication to yield a shorter session than the connectionless communication? Explain.

4. Naming

a. What is the size of the address space (that is, the total number of addresses allowable) in each of the five classes of the IPv4 addresses? Show your computation.

b. Find out the IP network address assigned to your organization. What class (A thorugh E) is it?

c. Find out the domain name of the Web server host of your organization. What is its IP address?

d. A network program, *nslookup*, can be used to obtain DNS name-lookup service. You can invoke this program in at least three ways:

- On a UNIX system, enter *nslookup* at the system prompt.

- On a Windows system, enter *nslookup* at the prompt in a command prompt window.

- Browse to the site http://cc-www.uia.ac.be/ds/nslookup.html.

Use the service to complete the following table:

IP Address	Domain Name
127.0.0.1	
	ifi.uio.no
	ie.technion.ac.il
204.198.135.62	
224.0.1.24	
	cse.cuhk.edu.hk
129.65.2.119	
	www.mit.edu

e. Complete the following table:

IP Address	Domain Name	Class of Address (A–E)	Net ID (in dotted decimal notation)	Host ID (in dotted decimal notation)
18.181.0.31				
129.65.2.119				
204.198.135.62				
224.0.1.24				

f. Using the country code top-level domains listed by the Internet Assigned Numbers Authority [iana.org, 19] to help, find out the domain name country code for the following nations:

> Armenia, Brazil, Canada, Cuba, Germany, Spain, France, Guatemala, India, Mexico, Qatar, Singapore, Sweden, El Salvador, Turkey.

Identify the nation for each of the following country codes:

> Td, tv, zw, nz, ph, pk, eg, bt, ao.

g. Consider this URI: http://www.someSite.org:8081/foo/index.htm.

i. What is the protocol specified?

ii. What is the host name of the service?

iii. What is the port number of the process that provides the service?

iv. Where is the document located?

h. Look up the well-known port number assignments by browsing the page http://www.iana.org/assignments/port-numbers.

i. Which port number is assigned to each of these services: (i) FTP, (ii) telnet, (iii) SMTP, and (iv) World Wide Web HTTP? Are these services available using TCP, UDP, or both?

 ii. What services are assigned to ports 13 and 17, respectively?

 iii. On a UNIX system, or from the command-prompt window of a Windows system, one way that you can access a network service is by issuing a command such as the following:

> telnet<space><domain name or IP address of a system that you know><space><port number assigned to the service>

For example, the command telnet foo.com 13 will access the service provided by the process running on port 13 on the Internet host telnet.foo.

Try using this method to access the services offered on port 13 on a machine you know. Describe the outcome.

 i. Instead of using the Internet scheme of using a protocol port number as part of an address to deliver data to a process on a given host, consider an alternative scheme where the process is located using a unique process ID (PID), such as that assigned to each active process by the Unix operating system. Note that a PID is assigned dynamically to a process when the process is started, so that it is not possible to know ahead of a program's execution what the ID will be at run time. The range of values for PIDs also varies from system to system. What, if any, is the problem with such an addressing scheme?

 j. A naming scheme is said to allow **location transparency** [community-ml.org, 25] if the scheme allows objects to be addressed without explicit knowledge of their physical location. For example, the U.S. phone number system is location transparent, since a caller does not need to know the whereabouts of the callee when dialing up. The U.S. Postal Service address system, on the other hand, does not allow location transparency, since you must address the recipient with his/her physical address (excluding post office box numbers, that is).

Consider each of the following naming schemes. For each, determine whether it is location transparent. Justify your answer.

 i. The Domain Name System (DNS).

 ii. Uniform Resource Locator (URL)

 iii. Uniform Resource Name (URN)

 iv. Extensible Name Service (XNS)

5. UML Class Diagrams

 a. Using the notations shown in Figure 1.19, draw the class diagram for the classes shown in Figure 1.11.

 b. Using the notations shown in Figure 1.19, draw the class diagram for the classes shown in Figure 1.12.

References

1. The Virtual Museum of Computing, *http://vlmp.museophile.com/computing.html*

2. Hobbes' Internet Timeline—the definitive ARPAnet & Internet history, *http://www.zakon.org/robert/internet/timeline/*

3. The Silk Road Group, Ltd, *A Brief History of Networking*, *http://www.silkroad.com/net-history.html*

4. Katie Hafner and Matthew Lyon. *Where Wizards Stay Up Late: The Origins of the Internet.* New York, NY: Simon & Schuster, 1996.

5. Internet RFC/STD/FYI/BCP, Archives, *http://www.faqs.org/rfcs/*

6. Todd Campbell, "The first email message," *PRETEXT Magazine*, 1998. *http://www.pretext.com/mar98/features/story2.htm*

7. *http://www.sun.com/jini/overview/*, September 2000.

8. webopedia, *http://webopedia.internet.com*

9. Alice E. Koniges. *Industrial Strength Parallel Computing.* San Francisco, CA: Morgan Kaufman Publishers, 2001.

10. SETI@home, the Search for Extraterrestrial Intelligence, *http://setiathome.ssl.berkeley.edu/*

11. Java Resources, *http://www.csc.calpoly.edu/~mliu/javaResources.html*

12. William Stallings. *Data and Computer Communications.* Upper Saddle River, NJ: Prentice Hall, 1999.

13. Andrew S. Tanenbaum. *Computer Networks.* Upper Saddle River, NJ: Prentice Hall, 1996.

14. Chuck Semeria, 3Com Corporation, *Understanding IP Addressing: Everything You Ever Wanted To Know*, 1996, *http://www.3com.com/other/pdfs/infra/corpinfo/en_US/501302.pdf*

15. Marshall Brain, Question of the Day, *http://www.howstuffworks.com/question549.htm*, *HowStuffWorks*

16. About Domains, *about domains, http://www.aboutdomains.com/News/basics.htm*

17. The National Center for Supercomputing Applications (NCSA). A Beginner's Guide to URLs, *http://archive.ncsa.uiuc.edu/SDG/Experimental/demoweb/url-primer.html*

18. Dan Connolly. *Naming and Addressing: URIs, URLs, ..., http://www.w3.org/Addressing/*

19. Internet Assigned Numbers Authority. Country Code Top-Level Domains, *http://www.iana.org/cctld/cctld.htm*

20. Java 2 Platform v1.4 API Specification, *http://java.sun.com/j2se/1.4/docs/api/index.html*

21. Mark W. Eichin and Jon A. Rochlis, Massachusetts Institute of Technology. *With Microscopes and Tweezers: An Analysis of the Internet Virus of 1988*, *http://www.mit.edu/people/eichin/virus/main.html*

22. Kim Zetter. PCWorld.com, "When Love Came To Town: A Virus Investigation," Monday, November 13, 2000.

23. The genome@home project homepage, *http://genomeathome.stanford.edu/*

24. Internet Assigned Numbers Authority, *http://www.iana.org/*

25. Reference Model for Open Distributed Processing (RM-ODP), ISO/IEC IS 10746|ITU-T X.900, *http://community-ml.org/RM-ODP/*

26. XNS—frequently asked questions, *http://www.xns.org/*, XNSORG.

27. What Is OMG UML? *http://www.omg.org/gettingstarted/what_is_uml.htm*

28. UML Notation Guide–Version 1.1, *http://www.informatik.fh-luebeck.de/~st/UML/ UML1.1/*

29. Unicode Home Page, *http://www.unicode.org/*

30. Michael Fischer, Nancy Lynch, and Michael S. Paterson. "Impossibility of distributed consensus with one faulty process." *Proceedings of the 2nd ACM Symposium on Principles of Database Systems*, pages 1–7, 1983.

31. Pankaj Jalote. *Fault Tolerance in Distributed Systems*. Upper Saddle River, NJ: Prentice Hall, 1994.

32. Scott Oaks. *Java Security*. Sebastopol, CA: O'Reilly Press, 2001.

33. distributed.net: Node Zero, *http://www.distributed.net/*

34. Internet Security Alliance, *http://www.isalliance.org/*

35. Andrew Tanenbaum. *Computer Networks*. Upper Saddle River, NJ: Prentice Hall, 1996.

36. *http://www.iana.org/assignments/port-numbers*

37. Gilda Pour. "Web-Based Architecture for Component-Based Application Generators." *The International Multiconference in Computer Science*, Las Vegas, Nevada, 2002.

38. Internet Society (ISOC), All About the Internet: History of the Internet, *http://www.isoc.org/internet/history/*

CHAPTER **2**

Interprocess Communications

The backbone of distributed computing is **interprocess communications** (IPC):
the ability for separate, independent processes (as you will recall, *processes* are run-
time representations of a program) to communicate among themselves to collaborate on a task. In this chapter, we will look at the fundamentals, the issues, the
paradigms, and the implementations of IPC.

A **paradigm** is an
abstract model of how a
certain task can be car-
ried out.

Figure 2.1 illustrates basic IPC: Two independent processes, possibly running on
separate machines, exchange data over the interconnecting network. In this case,
process 1 acts as the **sender**, which transmits data to process 2, the **receiver**.

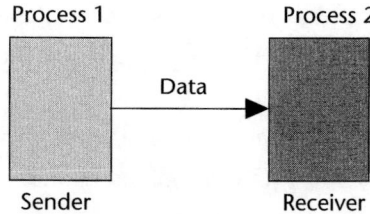

Figure 2.1 Interprocess communication.

In distributed computing, two or more processes engage in IPC in a protocol—
a set of rules that must be observed by the participants in data communication—
agreed upon by the processes. A process may be a sender at some points during a

protocol, a receiver at other points. When communication is from one process to a single other process, the IPC is said to be a **unicast**. When communication is from one process to a group of processes, the IPC is said to be a **multicast**, a topic that we will explore in Chapter 6. Figure 2.2 illustrates the concept of the two types of interprocess communications.

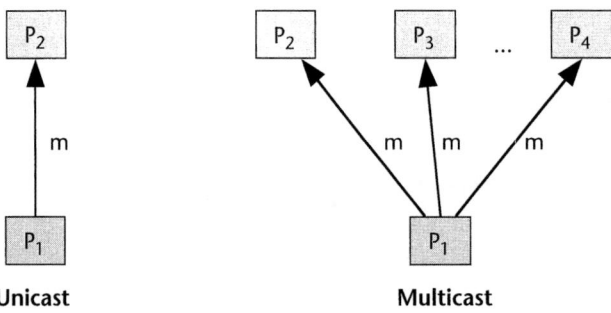

Figure 2.2 Unicast versus multicast.

Modern-day operating systems such as UNIX and Windows provide facilities for interprocess communications. We will call these facilities operating system-level IPC facilities, to distinguish them from higher-level IPCs. System-level IPC facilities include message queues, semaphores, and shared memory. (If you have not taken a course in operating systems, do not be concerned if you are not familiar with these terms; they are not subjects that we will study in this course.) It is possible to develop network software using these system-level facilities directly. Examples of such programs are network device drivers and system evaluation programs. Rudimentary distributed applications can also be developed using these facilities, although that is not normally done, since typically the complexities of the application require the use of some form of **abstraction** to spare the programmer of system-level details. You will find details on operating system-level IPC in books on operating systems. In this book, we will confine our attention to IPC at a higher level of abstraction.

An IPC **application program interface** (API), also commonly expanded to **application programming interface**, provides an abstraction of the details and intricacies of the system-level facilities, thereby allowing the programmer to concentrate on the application logic; we will spend the rest of this chapter investigating IPC program interfaces.

In software engineering, **abstraction** refers to hiding of the underlying complexities of a task at hand. For example, a higher-level language such as Java provides an abstraction that allows a program to be written without the programmer having to understand the details at the operating system level.

2.1 An Archetypal IPC Program Interface

Consider a basic API that provides the minimum level of abstraction to facilitate IPC. Four primitive operations are needed. The details of these operations (such as arguments and return values) will be given with specific tools or facilities presented in subsequent chapters. These operations are:

- **Send.** This operation is issued by a sending process for the purpose of transmitting data to a receiving process. The operation must allow the sending process to identify the receiving process and specify the data to be transmitted.

- **Receive.** This operation is issued by a receiving process for the purpose of accepting data from a sending process. The operation must allow the receiving process to identify the sending process and specify a memory space that allows the data to be stored, to be subsequently accessed by the receiver.

- **Connect.** For connection-oriented IPC, there must be operations that allow a logical connection to be established between the issuing process and a specified process: one process issues a **request-to-connect** (**connect** for short) operation while the other process issues an **accept-connection** operation.

- **Disconnect.** For connection-oriented IPC, this operation allows a previously established logical connection to be deallocated at both sides of the communication.

A process involved in IPC issues these operations in some predetermined order. The issuance of each operation causes the occurrence of an **event**. For example, a send operation issued by a sending process results in the event wherein data is transmitted to the receiving process, while a receive operation issued by a receiving process results in data being delivered to the process. Note that the participating processes issue operations independently, as each has no way of knowing the status of the other process.

IPC operations are provided, implicitly or explicitly, in every distributed computing paradigm that we will study in subsequent chapters. The next chapter (Chapter 3) will provide an introduction to the hierarchy of distributed computing paradigms. In subsequent chapters, we will see examples of how these paradigms are used in protocols, tools, and facilities.

Network service protocols can be implemented using primitive IPC operations. For example, in basic HTTP (Hypertext Transfer Protocol, used extensively on the World Wide Web, which will be studied in later chapters) one process, a Web browser, issues a *connect* operation to establish a logical connection to another process, a Web server, followed by a *send* operation to the Web server, which transmits data representing a request. The Web server process in turn issues a *send* operation that transmits data requested by the Web browser process. At the end of the communication, each process issues a *disconnect* operation to terminate the connection. Figure 2.3 illustrates the sequence of operations. We will study network service protocols such as HTTP further in this chapter and in other chapters.

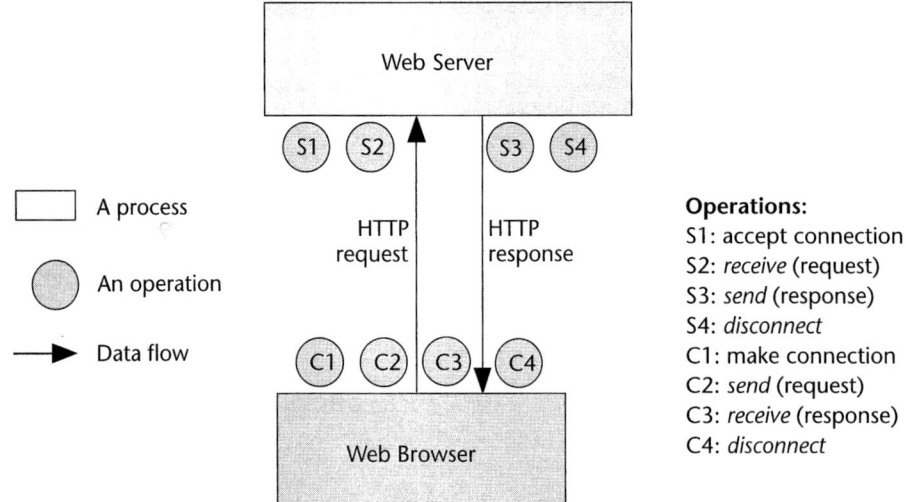

Figure 2.3 Interprocess communication in basic HTTP.

In the rest of this chapter we will look at some of the key issues associated with IPC operations.

2.2 Event Synchronization

A main difficulty with IPC is that the processes involved execute independently, with neither process knowing what takes place in the process at the other end.

Consider basic HTTP, as described above. As you can see, the two sides involved in the protocol must issue the IPC operations in a specific order. For example, the browser process must not issue the *send* operation until the *connect* operation has completed. It is also important that the Web server does not begin to transmit the requested data until the browser process is ready to receive it. Furthermore, the browser process needs to be notified when the requested data has been received so that it may subsequently process the data, including formatting and displaying the data to the browser user.

The simplest way for an IPC facility to provide for event synchronization is by using **blocking**, which is the suspension of the execution of a process until an operation issued by the process has been completed.

To illustrate the use of blocking for event synchronization, consider again the basic HTTP. A browser process issues a blocking *connect* operation, which blocks further execution of the process until the connection has been acknowledged by the server side. Subsequently, the browser process issues a blocking *receive* operation, which suspends execution of the process until the operation has completed (whether successfully or not). The blocking or unblocking is performed by the operating system and is initiated by the IPC facilities, not by the programmer. The programs for the two processes are shown in Figure 2.4.

During execution, the process is suspended after each blocking operation is issued. The blocking is initiated by the IPC facility and the underlying operating systems when a blocking operation issued in a process is executed. The blocking will terminate subsequently when and if the operation is fulfilled, at which time the process is said to be *unblocked*. An unblocked process transits to the ready state and will resume execution in time. In the event that the operation cannot be fulfilled, a blocked process will experience **indefinite blocking**, during which the process will remain in the blocked state indefinitely, unless intervening measures are taken.

Blocking operations are also referred to as **synchronous operations**. Alternatively, IPC operations may be **asynchronous** or **nonblocking operations**. An asynchronous operation issued by a process will not cause blocking, and therefore the process is free to continue with its execution once the asynchronous operation is issued to the IPC facility. The process will subsequently be notified by the IPC facility when and if the operation is fulfilled.

A nonblocking operation can be issued by a process when that process may proceed without waiting for the completion of the event that the operation initiates. For example, the *receive* operation issued by the Web browser must be blocking, because the browser process must wait for the response from the Web server in order to proceed with further processing. On the other hand, the *send* operation issued by the Web server can be nonblocking, because the Web server

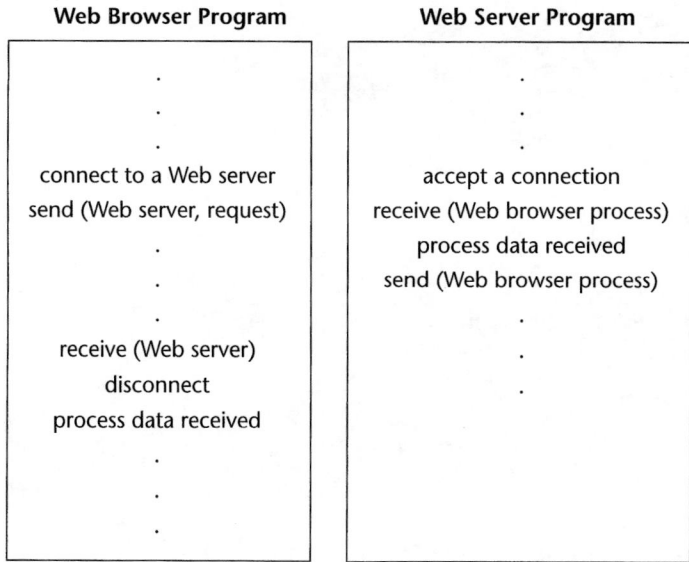

Figure 2.4 Program flow in two programs involved in IPC.

need not wait for the completion of the *send* operation before proceeding with the next operation (the *disconnect*), so that it may proceed to service other Web browser processes.

It is the programmer's responsibility to recognize the need for synchronization and to be cognizant of whether an operation is blocking. For example, if a non-blocking *receive* operation is used in coding the HTTP by an unwary programmer, and the data is assumed to have been received immediately after the issuance of the *receive* operation in the program, the subsequent processing may display invalid data or, worse yet, generate errors.

As the use of *send* and *receive* operations is fundamental to distributed computing, let's look at the different scenarios in which a combination of these operations can be used in different modes.

Synchronous *Send* and Synchronous *Receive*

Figure 2.5 is a diagram, which will be called an **event diagram** in this book, that illustrates the event synchronization for a protocol session implemented using synchronous *send* and *receive* operations. In this scenario, a *receive* operation

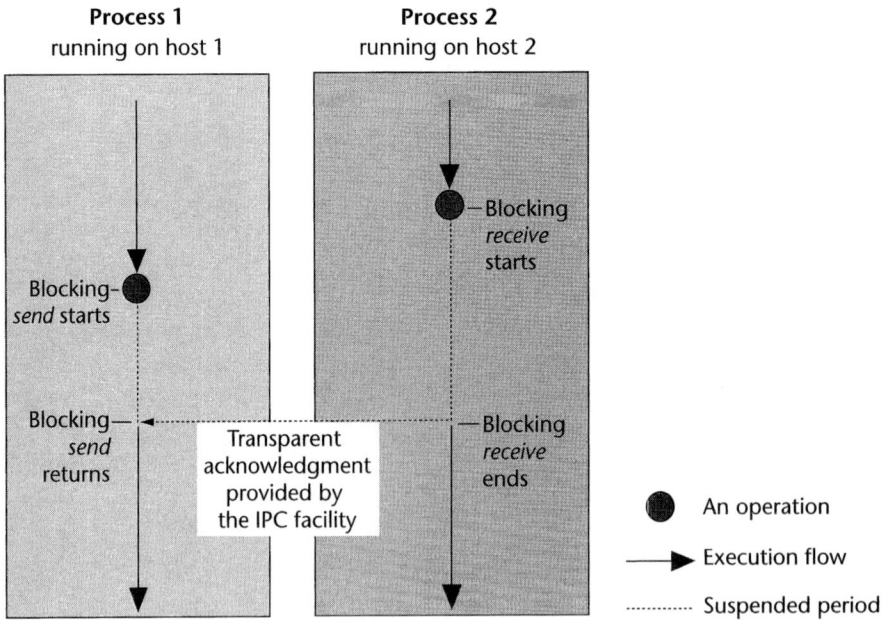

Figure 2.5 Synchronous *send* and *receive*.

issued causes the suspension of the issuing process (process 2) until data is received to fulfill the operation. Likewise, a *send* operation issued causes the sending process (process 1) to suspend. When the data sent has been received by process 2, the IPC facility on host 2 sends an acknowledgment to the IPC facility on host 1, and process 1 may subsequently be unblocked. Note that the acknowledgment is handled by the IPC facilities on both hosts and is transparent to the processes.

The use of synchronous *send* and synchronous *receive* is warranted if the application logic of both processes requires that the data sent must be received before further processing can proceed.

Depending on the implementation of the IPC facility, the synchronous *receive* operation may not be fulfilled until the amount of data the receiver expects to receive has arrived. For example, if process 2 issues a *receive* for 300 bytes of data, and the *send* operation brings only 200 bytes, it is possible for the blocking of process 2 to continue even after the first 200 bytes have been delivered; in such a case, process 2 will not be unblocked until process 1 subsequently sends the remaining 100 bytes of data.

Asynchronous *Send* and Synchronous *Receive*

Figure 2.6 illustrates an event diagram for a protocol session implemented using asynchronous *send* and synchronous *receive* operations. As before, a *receive* oper-

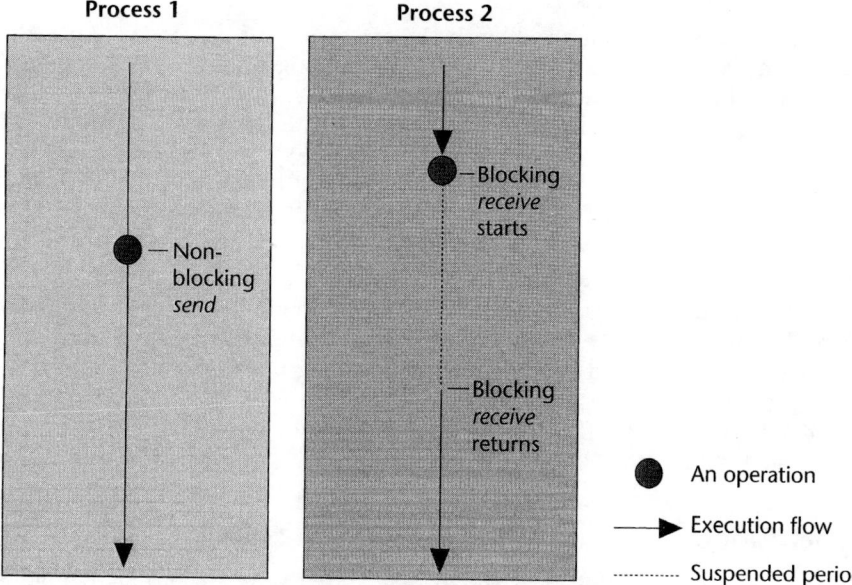

Figure 2.6 Asynchronous *send* and synchronous *receive*.

ation issued will cause the suspension of the issuing process until data is received to fulfill the operation. However, a *send* operation issued will not cause the sending process to suspend. In this case the sending process is never blocked, so no acknowledgment is necessary from the IPC facility on the host of process 2. This use of asynchronous *send* and synchronous *receive* is appropriate if the sender's application logic does not depend on the receiving of the data at the other end. However, depending on the implementation of the IPC facility, there is no guarantee that the data sent will actually be delivered to the receiver. For example, if the *send* operation is executed before the corresponding *receive* operation is issued on the other side, it is possible that the data will not be delivered to the receiving process unless the IPC facility makes provisions to retain the prematurely sent data.

Synchronous *Send* and Asynchronous *Receive*

Figure 2.7 illustrates different scenarios for a protocol session that employs synchronous *send* and asynchronous *receive* operations.

An asynchronous *receive* operation causes no blocking of the process that issues the operation, and the outcome will depend on the implementation of the IPC facility. The *receive* operation will, in all cases, return immediately, and there are three scenarios for what happens subsequently:

Scenario 1. The data requested by the receive operation has already arrived at the time when the *receive* operation is issued. In this case, the data is delivered to process 2 immediately, and an acknowledgment from host 2's IPC facility will unblock process 1.

Scenario 2. The data requested by the *receive* operation has not yet arrived; no data is delivered to the process. It is the receiving process's responsibility to ascertain that it has indeed received the data and, if necessary, repeat the *receive* operation until the data has arrived. (Note that it is common for the program to use a loop to issue the *receive* operation repeatedly until the awaited data has been received. The technique of such repeated attempts is called **polling**.) Process 1 is blocked indefinitely until process 2 reissues a *receive* request and an acknowledgment eventually arrives from host 2's IPC facility.

Scenario 3. The data requested by the *receive* operation has not yet arrived. The IPC facility of host 2 will notify process 2 when the data it requested has arrived, at which point process 2 may proceed to process the data. This scenario requires that process 2 provide a listener or event handler that can be invoked by the IPC facility to notify the process of the arrival of the requested data.

Asynchronous *Send* and Asynchronous *Receive*

Without blocking on either side, the only way that the data can be delivered to the receiver is if the IPC facility retains the data received. The receiving process

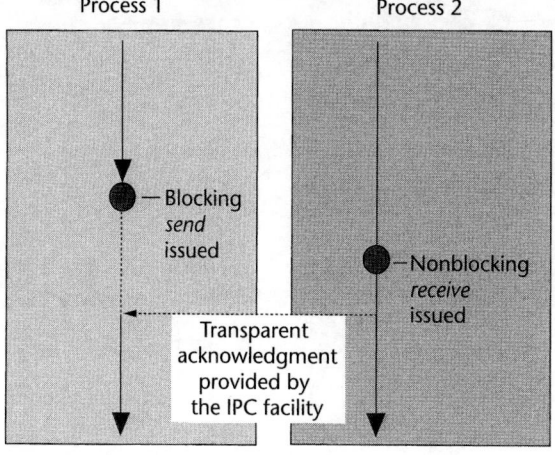

Scenario 1:
Synchronous *Send* and Asynchronous *Receive*

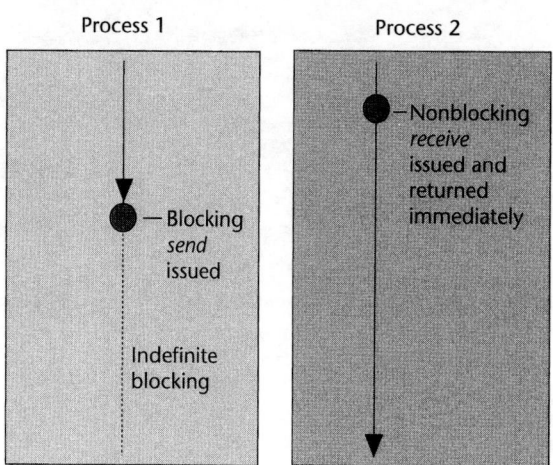

Scenario 2:
Synchronous *Send* and Asynchronous *Receive*

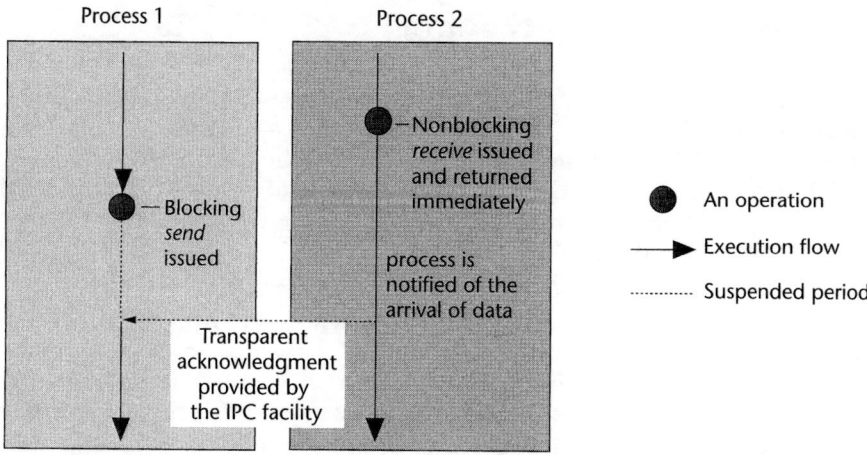

Scenario 3:
Synchronous *Send* and Asynchronous *Receive*

Figure 2.7 Synchronous *send* and asynchronous *receive*.

can then be notified of the data's arrival (see Figure 2.8). Alternatively, the receiving process may poll for the arrival of the data and process it when the awaited data has arrived.

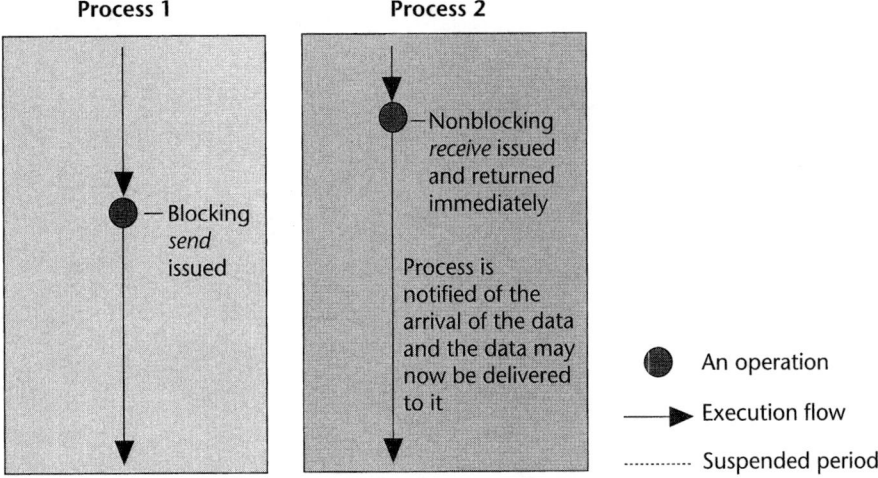

Figure 2.8 Asynchronous *send* and asynchronous *receive*.

2.3 **Timeouts and Threading**

Although blocking provides the necessary synchronization for IPC, it is generally unacceptable to allow a process to be suspended indefinitely. There are two measures to address this issue. First, **timeouts** may be used to set a maximum time period for blocking. Timeouts are provided by the IPC facility and may be specified in a program with an operation. Second, a program may spawn a **child process** or a **thread** to issue a blocking operation, allowing the main thread or parent process of the program to proceed with other processing while the child process or child thread is suspended. Figure 2.9 illustrates this use of a thread.

Timeouts are important if the execution of a synchronous operation has the potential of resulting in **indefinite blocking**. For example, a blocking *connect* request can result in the requesting process being suspended indefinitely if the connection is unfulfilled or cannot be fulfilled as a result of a breakdown in the network connecting the two processes. In such a situation, it is typically unacceptable for the requesting process to "hang" indefinitely. Indefinite blocking can be avoided by using a timeout. For example, a timeout period of 30 seconds may be specified with the *connect* request. If the request is not completed within approximately 30 seconds, it will be aborted by the IPC facility, at which time the requesting process will be unblocked, allowing it to resume processing.

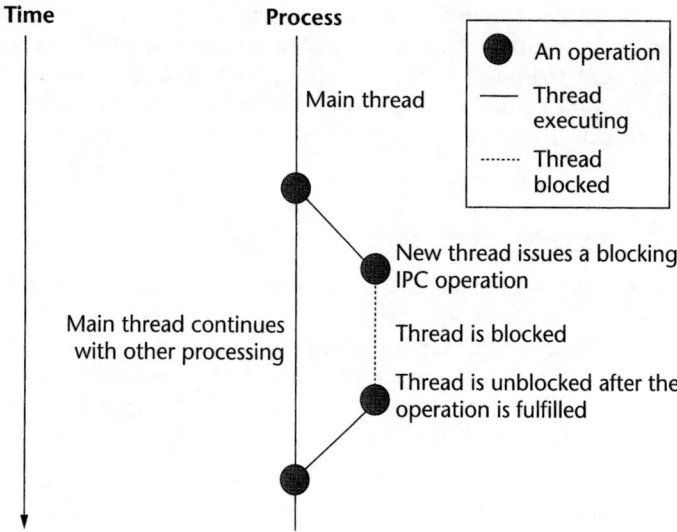

Figure 2.9 Using a thread for a blocking operation.

2.4 **Deadlocks and Timeouts**

Indefinite blocking may also be caused by a **deadlock**. In IPC, a deadlock can result from operations that were issued improperly, perhaps owing to a misunderstanding of a protocol, or owing to programming errors. Figure 2.10 illustrates such a case. In process 1, a blocking *receive* operation is issued to receive

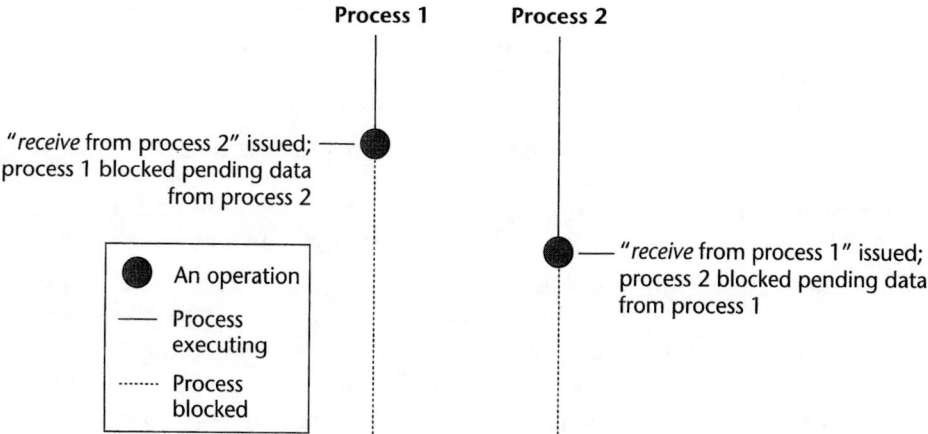

Figure 2.10 A deadlock caused by blocking operations.

data from process 2. Concurrently, process 2 issues a blocking *receive* operation where a *send* operation was intended. As a result, both processes are blocked awaiting data sent from the other, which can never occur (since each process is now blocked). As a result, each process will be suspended indefinitely until a timeout occurs, or until the operating systems abort the processes.

2.5 Data Representation

At the physical layer (that is, the lowest layer, as opposed to the application layer, which is the highest) of the network architecture, data is transmitted as **analog** signals, which represent a **binary stream**. At the application layer, a more complex representation of transmitted data is needed in order to support data types and data structures provided in programming languages, such as character strings, integers, floating point values, arrays, records, and objects.

> **Analog** is the opposite of digital: it refers to something mechanical, as opposed to something represented using data. Analog signal processing is a topic in networking.

Consider the simple case of two processes, process 1 on Host A and process 2 on Host B, engaged in a protocol that calls for the exchange of an integer value determined at run time. Process 1 computes the value and issues a *send* operation to transmit it to process 2, which issues a *receive* operation to accept the value, based on which process 2 performs further processing of the protocol.

> A **binary stream** is a stream of bits (0 and 1), such as 00101...1010111.

Consider the integer value that needs to be sent by process 1. This value is represented in the integer representation of Host A, which is a 32-bit machine that uses the "big-endian" representation for multi-byte data types. (The terms *big endian* and *little endian* refer to which bytes are most significant in multi-byte data types. In big-endian architectures, the leftmost bytes [those with a lower address] are most significant. In little-endian architectures, the rightmost bytes are most significant.)

Host B, on the other hand, is a 16-bit machine that uses the "little-endian" representation. Suppose the value is sent as a 32-bit stream directly from process 1's memory storage and placed into process 2's memory location. Then (1) 16 bits of the value sent will need to be truncated, since an integer value only occupies 16 bits on host B, and (2) the byte order of the integer representation must be swapped in order for the value to be interpreted correctly by process 2.

> **Heterogeneous hosts** are computers that have different hardware and hence different representations of data.

As can be seen from the example, when **heterogeneous hosts** are involved in IPC, it is not enough to transmit data values or structures using raw bit streams unless the participating processes take measures to package and interpret the data appropriately. For our example, there are three schemes for doing so:

1. Prior to issuing the *send* operation, process 1 converts the value of the integer to the 16-bit, little-endian data representation of process 2.

2. Process 1 sends the data in 32-bit, big-endian representation. Upon receiving the data, process 2 converts it to its 16-bit, little-endian representation.

3. A third scheme is for the processes to exchange the data in an **external representation**: data will be sent using this representation, and the data received will be interpreted using the external representation and converted to the native representation.

As another example, suppose process 1, running on host A, wishes to send a single character *a* to process 2, running on host B. The program for process 1 uses ASCII representation for characters, while the program for process 2 uses Unicode representation. Scheme 1 will call for process 1 to convert the *a* to Unicode before sending. Scheme 2 will call for process 2 to receive the data, then convert it from ASCII representation to the corresponding Unicode representation. Scheme 3 will call for the two sides to agree on an external representation, say ASN.1 (Abstract Syntax Notation Number 1), so that process 1 will convert the *a* to its ASN.1 representation before sending, while process 2 will convert the data received from the ASN.1 representation to the Unicode representation for *a*. (The ASN.1 data representation will be explained in section 2.6.)

Consider another case where the transmission of a data structure, such as a list of values, is called for. In addition to the need for an external representation of data values, there is now a need to "flatten" or serialize the data structure at the sender's end and to unpack the data at the other end to reconstruct the data structure.

The term **data marshaling** is used in the context of IPC to refer to the processing necessary to transmit data values and data structures. Data marshaling is needed for all IPC and includes necessary steps for conditioning the data to be transmitted: (1) serializing the data structures, and (2) converting the data values to an external representation. Figure 2.11 illustrates the data marshaling concept.

For network applications written in object-oriented programming languages such as Java, an important data structure that requires special attention for data marshaling is an object. Unlike static data structures such as arrays or records of data, an object encapsulates both data (representing the state of an object) and methods (representing the behavior of an object). If an object is to be transmitted using IPC, it is necessary for the data marshaling (again, flattening and encoding) to cover both the data and the representation of the methods—including the execution state—so that an object, once un-marshalled by the receiving process, can function as an object in the execution space of the receiving process. Because of the complexity involved, data marshaling of objects poses a bigger challenge than data marshaling of other data structures, and has been given a special term: **object serialization** [java.sun.com, 11]. In Java, "(O)bject serialization supports the encoding of objects, and the objects reachable from them, into a stream of bytes; and it supports the complementary reconstruction of the object ... from the stream" [Harold, 12].

ASCII stands for American Standard Code for Information Interchange, an encoding scheme for mapping a character used in the English language to a numeric value in the range of 0 to 127.

Unicode is a complex encoding scheme for mapping a character, not limited to those used in the English language, to a numeric value in the range of 0 to 65,535. For a precise definition of the scheme, see http://www.unicode.org

2.6 Data Encoding

Although customized programs can be written to perform IPC using any mutually agreed upon scheme of data marshaling, general-purpose distributed applications require a universal, platform-independent scheme for encoding the exchanged data. Hence there exist network data encoding standards.

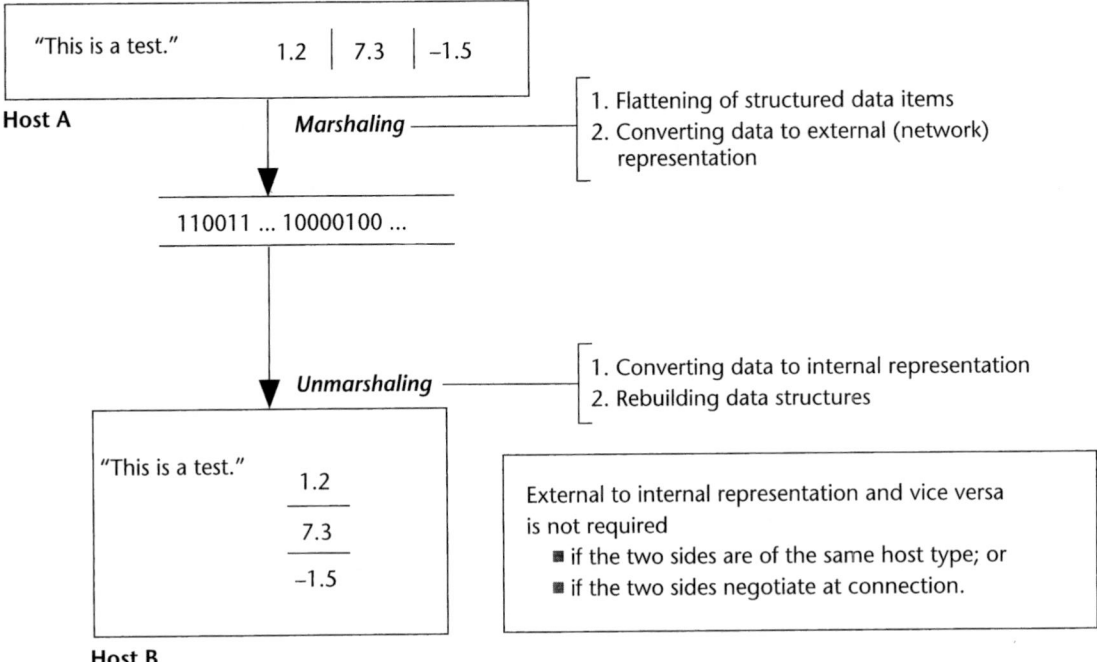

Figure 2.11 Data marshaling.

As illustrated in Figure 2.12, data encoding standards are available at varying levels of abstraction.

At the simplest level, an encoding scheme such as **External Data Representation (XDR)** [ietf.org, 1] allows a selected set of programming data types and data structures to be specified with IPC operations. The data marshaling and unmarshaling are performed automatically by the IPC facilities on the two ends, transparent to the programmer.

At a higher level of abstraction (that is, detail hiding; more on this concept in the next chapter), standards such as **ASN.1 (Abstract Syntax Notation Number 1)** [oss.com, 2] exist. ASN.1 is an Open Systems Interconnection (OSI) standard that specifies a transfer syntax for representing network data. The standard covers a wide range of data structures (such as sets and sequences) and data types (such as integer, Boolean, and characters) and supports the concept of data tagging. Each data item transmitted is encoded using syntax that specifies its type, its length, its value, and optionally a tag to identify a specific way of interpreting the syntax.

At an even higher level of abstraction, the **Extensible Markup Language (XML)** [w3.org, 9] has emerged as a data description language for data sharing

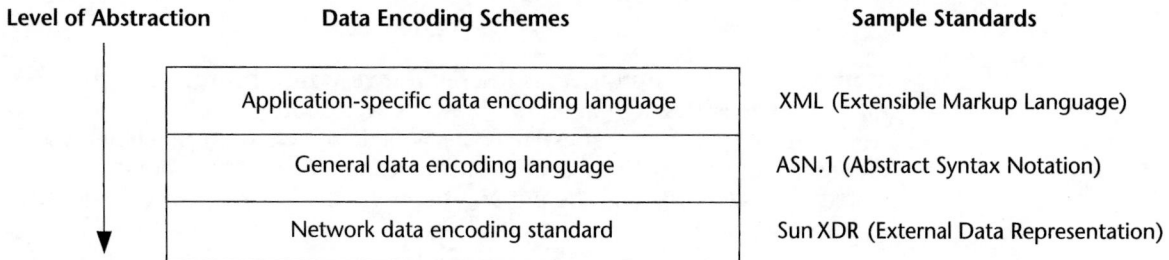

Level of Abstraction   **Data Encoding Schemes**   **Sample Standards**

Application-specific data encoding language	XML (Extensible Markup Language)
General data encoding language	ASN.1 (Abstract Syntax Notation)
Network data encoding standard	Sun XDR (External Data Representation)

Figure 2.12 Network data representation standards.

among applications, primarily Internet applications, using syntax similar to the Hypertext Markup Language (HTML), which is the language used for composing Web pages. XML goes one step beyond ASN.1 in that it allows a user to use customized tags (such as the tags *<message>*, *<to>*, and *<from>* in the example in Figure 2.13) to specify a unit of data content. XML can be used to facilitate data interchange among heterogeneous systems, to segregate the data content of a Web page (written in XML) from the display syntax (written in HTML), and to allow the data to be shared among applications. Since its introduction in 1998, XML has gained considerable attention and is now widely employed in computer applications.

```
<message>
  <to>MaryJ@BigU.edu</to>
  <from>JohnL@OpenU.edu</from>
  <subject>Interprocess Communications</subject>
  <text> IPC is the backbone of distributed computing ... </text>
</message>
```

Figure 2.13 A sample XML file.

2.7 Text-Based Protocols

Data marshaling is at its simplest when the data exchanged is a stream of characters or text encoded using a representation such as ASCII. Exchanging data in text has the additional advantage that the data can be easily parsed in a program and displayed for human perusal. Hence it is a popular practice for protocols to exchange requests and responses in the form of character strings. Such protocols are said to be **text-based**. Many popular network protocols, including FTP (File Transfer Protocol), HTTP, and SMTP (Simple Mail Transfer Protocol), are text-based. You will have a chance to investigate and experiment with these protocols in the exercises at the end of this chapter, and we will study some of these protocols in detail in subsequent chapters.

2.8 **Request-Response Protocols**

An important type of protocol is the **request-response protocol**. In this protocol, one side issues a request and awaits a response from the other side. Subsequently, another request may be issued, which in turn elicits another response. The protocol proceeds in an iteration of request-response, until the desired task is completed. The popular network protocols FTP, HTTP, and SMTP are all request-response protocols.

2.9 **Event Diagram and Sequence Diagram**

An event diagram, introduced in Section 2.2, is a diagram that can be used to document the detailed sequence of events and blocking during the execution of a protocol. Figure 2.14 is an event diagram for a request-response protocol involving two concurrent processes, A and B. The execution of each process with respect to time is represented using a vertical line, with time increasing downward. A solid line interval along the execution line represents a time period during which the process is active. A broken line interval represents when the process is blocked. In the example, both processes are initially active. Process B issues a blocked *receive* operation in anticipation of request 1 from

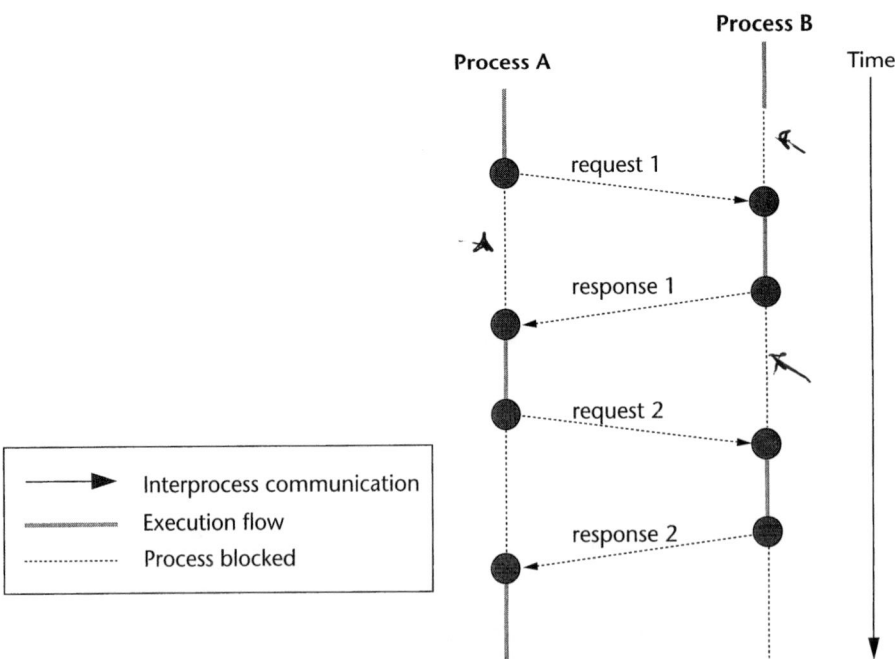

Figure 2.14 An event diagram.

process A. Process A meanwhile issues the awaited request 1 using a nonblocking *send* operation, then subsequently a blocking *receive* operation in anticipation of process B's response. The arrival of request 1 reactivates process B, which processes the request before issuing a *send* operation to transmit response 1 to process A. Process B then issues a blocking *receive* for request 2 from process A. The arrival of response 1 unblocks process A, which resumes execution to work on the response and to issue request 2, which unblocks Process B. A similar sequence of events follows.

Note that each round of request-response entails two pairs of *send* and *receive* operations to exchange two messages. The protocol can extend to any number of rounds of exchange using this pattern.

Note also that it is essential that the programs implementing the protocol must be written to issue the *send* and *receive* operations in the order prescribed, otherwise one or both of the participating processes may wait for a request or a response that never arrives, and the processes may become blocked indefinitely.

Figure 2.15 uses an event diagram to describe basic HTTP. In its basic form, HTTP is a text-based, request-response protocol that calls for only one round of exchange of messages. A Web server process is a process that constantly listens for incoming requests from Web browser processes. A Web browser process makes a connection to the server, then issues a request in a format dictated by the protocol. The server processes the request and dispatches a response composed of a status line, header information, and the document requested by the browser process. Upon receiving the response, the browser process parses the response and displays the document. (We will study the client-server model and HTTP in further detail in Chapter 5.)

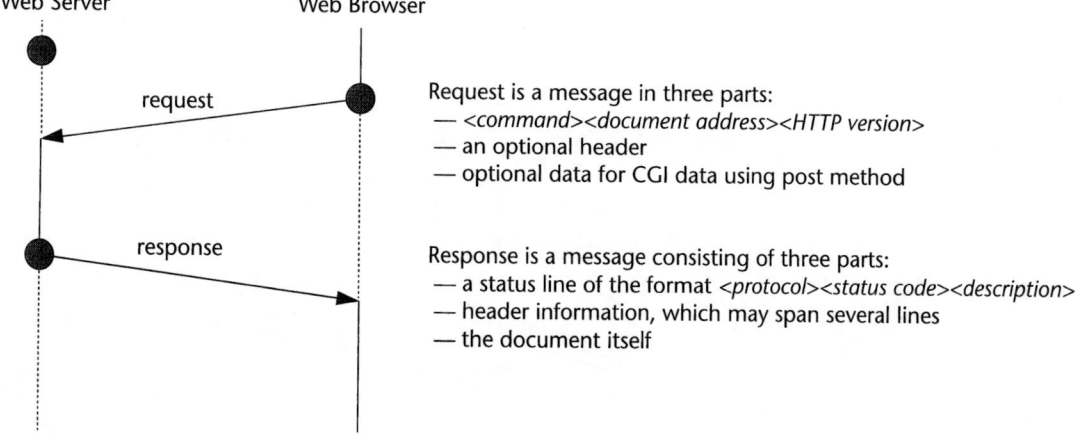

Figure 2.15 Event diagram for an HTTP session.

An event diagram is a useful device for illustrating the synchronization of events. It is, however, too detailed for documenting complex protocols. A simplified form of diagram, known as a **sequence diagram** and part of the UML notations, is more commonly used to document interprocess communications.

In a sequence diagram, the execution flow of each participant of a protocol is represented as a dashed line and does not differentiate between the states of blocked and executing. Each message exchanged between the two sides is shown using a directed line between the two dashed lines, with a descriptive label above the directed line, as illustrated in Figure 2.16.

The sequence diagram for the basic HTTP is shown in Figure 2.17.

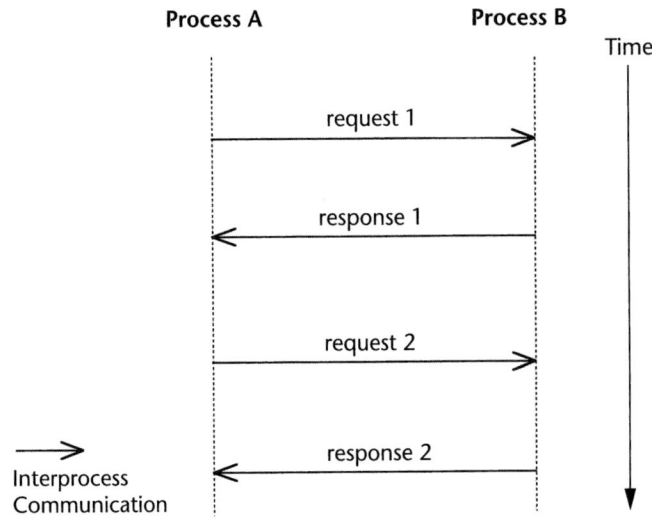

Figure 2.16 A sequence diagram.

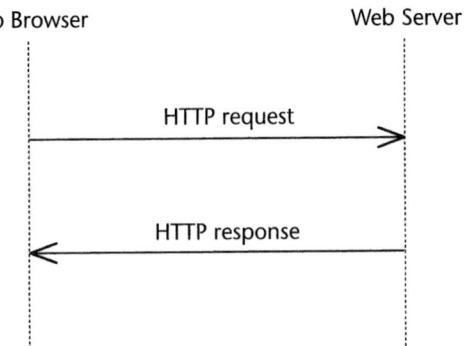

Figure 2.17 The sequence diagram for HTTP.

Figure 2.18 captures the text of the messages exchanged during a sample HTTP session. Using a **telnet** client (telnet is a protocol normally used for a terminal session to a remote machine), it is possible to make a connection to a Web server process and enter the text of an HTTP request by hand. (Using telnet to communicate with a process in the way described here allows you to experiment with IPC without having to write a program; be aware that it is *not* the normal way to interact with such a process. In subsequent chapters we will learn about how to use programming to do the same thing.) In this case, the Web server process runs on port 80 of the host named www.csc.calpoly.edu. The request GET /~mliu/ HTTP/1.0 is keyed in. The response from the Web server process then follows. In Chapter 9 we will study the meanings of the requests and the responses when we explore HTTP in detail.

```
Script started on Tue Oct 10 21:49:28 2000
9:49pm telnet www.csc.calpoly.edu 80
Trying 129.65.241.20...
Connected to tiedye2-srv.csc.calpoly.edu.
Escape character is '^]'.
GET /~mliu/ HTTP/1.0  ◄───────────────────────  HTTP request

HTTP/1.1 200 OK
Date: Wed, 11 Oct 2000 04:51:18 GMT  ◄──────────  HTTP response status line
Server: Apache/1.3.9 (Unix) ApacheJServ/1.0 ◄───  HTTP response header
Last-Modified: Tue, 10 Oct 2000 16:51:54 GMT
ETag: "1dd1e-e27-39e3492a"
Accept-Ranges: bytes
Content-Length: 3623
Connection: close
Content-Type: text/html

<HTML>
<HEAD>
<TITLE> Mei-Ling L. Liu's Home Page
</TITLE>                                        ─── Document content
</HEAD>
<BODY bgcolor=#ffffff>
...
```

Figure 2.18 The dialog during an HTTP session.

2.10 Connection-Oriented versus Connectionless IPC

In Chapter 1 we introduced the distinction between connection-oriented and connectionless communication. We can now apply that distinction to IPC.

Using a connection-oriented IPC facility, two processes establish a connection (which, as a reminder, may be logical—that is, implemented in software—rather than physical), then exchange data by inserting data to and extracting data from the connection. Once a connection is established, there is no need to identify the sender or the receiver.

Using a connectionless IPC facility, data is exchanged in independent packets, each of which needs to be addressed specifically to the receiver.

When we study the socket API in Chapter 4, we will look at how connection-oriented and connectionless IPCs are provided at the application layer.

2.11 The Evolution of Paradigms for Interprocess Communications

Now that we have explored the concept of IPC, we will next look at the different models, or paradigms, through which IPC can be provided to a programmer who wishes to make use of IPC in a program. Earlier in this chapter we have seen that data encoding schemes exist at different levels of abstraction. The same can be said of paradigms for IPC, as illustrated in Figure 2.19.

Serial data transfer refers to transmitting data one *bit* at a time. The opposite of **serial data transfer** is **parallel data transfer**, in which several bits are transmitted concurrently.

At the least abstract, IPC involves the transmission of a binary stream over a connection, using low-level serial or parallel data transfer. This IPC paradigm may be appropriate for network driver software, for instance. IPC of this form falls in the realm of network or operating system programming and will not be covered in this book.

At the next level is a well-known paradigm called the **socket application program** interface (the **socket API**). Using the socket paradigm, two processes exchange data using a logical construct called a **socket**, one of which is established at either end. Data to be sent is written to the socket. At the other end, a receiving process reads or extracts data from its socket. We will study the socket API in the Java language in the next chapter.

Socket is a term borrowed from the early days of telephone communications, when an operator had to manually establish a connection for two parties by inserting the two ends of a cable into the correct sockets.

The **remote procedure call** or **remote method invocation** paradigm provides further abstraction by allowing a process to make procedure calls or method invocations to a remote process, with data transferred between the two processes as arguments and return values. We will study one implementation of this paradigm, the Java remote method invocation, in Chapter 8.

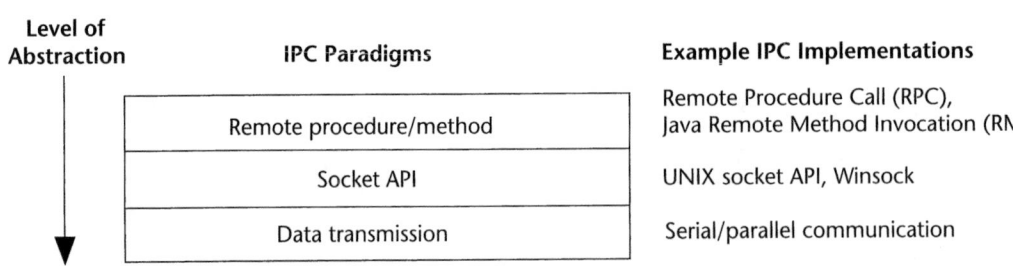

Figure 2.19 IPC paradigms.

Summary

Interprocess communications (IPC) form the backbone of distributed computing. In this chapter we have looked at the principles of IPC, including the following:

- Interprocess communications (IPC): the ability for separate, independent processes to communicate among themselves to collaborate on a task. When communication is from one process to a single other process, the IPC is said to be a unicast. When communication is from one process to a group of processes, the IPC is said to be a multicast.

- A basic API that facilitates IPC must provide the following:

  - Primitive operations: send, receive, connect, and disconnect.

  - Event synchronization, which allows the processes involved to execute independently, with no knowledge of what takes place at the other end. The simplest way for an IPC facility to provide for event synchronization is by using blocking. Operations that are blocking are also called synchronous operations, while operations that are nonblocking are also called asynchronous operations. Deadlocks can result from blocking operations. Threading or process forking can be used by a program to perform separate tasks while awaiting the fulfillment of a blocked operation.

  - Data marshaling, which includes these steps needed to condition the data to be transmitted: (i) serializing the data structures, and (ii) converting the data values to an external or network data representation.

- Different network data representation schemes exist at different levels of abstraction. Some well-known schemes are the Sun XDR (External Data Representation), ASN.1 (Abstract Syntax Notation Number 1), and the XML (Extensible Markup Language).

- Data marshaling is at its simplest when the data exchanged is a stream of characters or text encoded using a representation such as ASCII. Protocols that use text encoding are called text-based protocols.

- Request-response protocols are protocols that proceed in an iteration of request-response until the desired tasks are completed.

- An event diagram can be used to document the detailed sequence of events and blocking in a protocol. A solid interval along the execution line represents a time period during which the process is active. A broken line interval represents when the process is blocked.

- A sequence diagram is part of the UML notations and is used to document complex interprocess communications. In a sequence diagram, the execution flow of each participant of a protocol is represented as a dashed line and does not differentiate between the states of blocking and executing.

- IPC facilities can be connection-oriented or connectionless:
  - Using a connection-oriented IPC facility, two processes establish a logical connection, then exchange data by inserting data to and extracting data from the connection. Once a connection is established, there is no need to identify the sender or the receiver.
  - Using a connectionless IPC facility, data is exchanged in independent packets, each of which needs to be addressed specifically to the receiver.
- IPC facilities can be classified according to their levels of abstraction, ranging from serial or parallel data transfer at the lowest level, to socket API at the next level, to remote procedure or method call at the highest level.

Exercises

1. Consider interhuman communications.

   a. Classify each of the following scenarios in terms of **unicast** or **multicast**:

      i.   A student speaking to a friend on a wireless phone

      ii. An executive speaking on a conference phone with managers in different cities

      iii. A teacher lecturing in a classroom

      iv. A child playing with another child using a "walkie-talkie"

      v.   The president addressing the nation on television

   b. How are event synchronization and data representation handled during a session of face-to-face conversation, such as when you speak to someone seated next to you?

   c. How are event synchronization and data representation handled during a session of remote conversation, such as when you speak to someone over the phone?

   d. How are event synchronization and data representation handled during a meeting of two heads of nations who speak different languages?

2. Process A sends a single message to process B using connectionless IPC. To do so, A issues a *send* operation (specifying the message as an argument) sometime during its execution, and B issues a *receive* operation. Suppose the *send* operation is asynchronous (nonblocking) and the *receive* operation is synchronous (blocking). Draw an event diagram (*not* a sequence diagram) for each of the following scenarios:

   a. Process A issues its *send* operation prior to process B issuing its *receive* operation.

   b. Process B issues its *receive* operation prior to process A issuing its *send* operation.

3. Repeat the last question. This time both operations (*send, receive*) are blocking.

4. Consider the following interprocess communication API:

   Using this API, messages are sent to and received from mailboxes. A process can communicate with another process using a mailbox shared by the two processes. For example, if process A wishes to communicate with processes B and C, it has to share mailbox 1 with B, and another mailbox, mailbox 2, with C. Messages between A and B are deposited into and retrieved from mailbox 1, while messages between B and C are deposited into and retrieved from mailbox 2. See Figure 2.20.

   The *send* and *receive* operations are defined as follows:

   ▪ send (n, message): send a message to mailbox n, blocking (that is, the sender will be suspended indefinitely until a response arrives in the shared mailbox)

■ receive (n, message): examines mailbox n in anticipation of receiving a message; this is a blocking operation, meaning that the receiving process will be suspended until the message arrives in the named mailbox

A process blocked waiting for a message coming to one mailbox will not be able to receive any message arriving at any other mailbox.

a. Suppose a process P expects to receive two messages, one from mailbox 1 and one from mailbox 2. It is not known ahead of time which message will arrive first. What sequence of *send* and *receive*, if any, can it execute to make sure that process P does not block forever?

b. What sequence of *send* and *receive*, if any, should process P execute if it wants to wait for a message either from mailbox 1 or from mailbox 2 (or from both)? Again, it is not known ahead of time which message will arrive first. Also, your sequence should not cause indefinite blocking.

(*Note:* Your answer should use the given operations only; you should not use threading or other operating system support.)

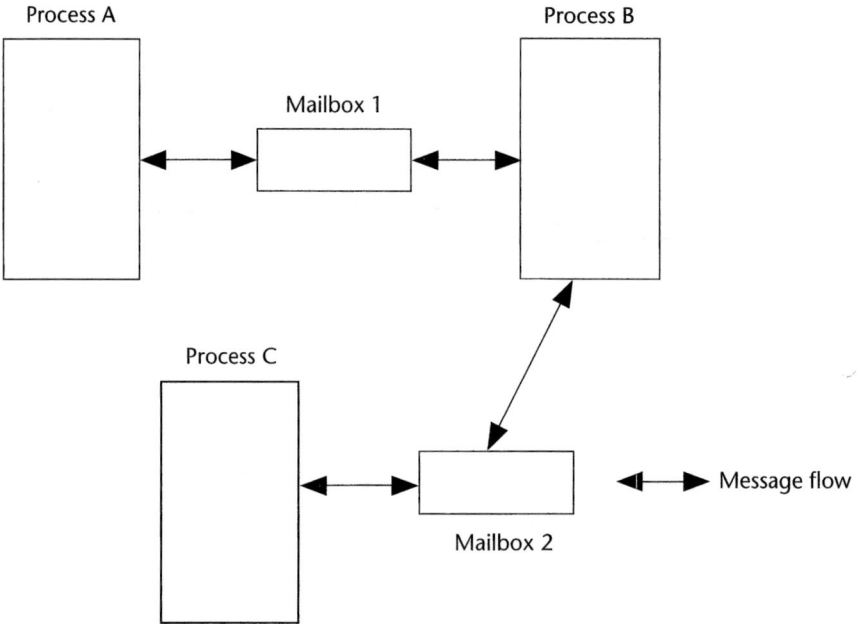

Figure 2.20 An IPC application program interface for Exercise 4.

5. Is it possible for a deadlock to occur during interprocess communications (involving *send/receive* operations)

a. on a communications system that provides a blocking *send* operation and a blocking *receive* operation?

b. on a communications system that provides a nonblocking *send* operation and a blocking *receive* operation?

Justify your answers. If the answer is yes, give an example. If the answer is no, give a brief argument.

6. Consider the provision of an API for multicasting built on an existing unicast API. The unicast API provides *send* and *receive* operations between two processes. The multicast API provides operations for (1) sending to a group of processes, and (2) receiving from a multicasting process. Describe how you would provide the multicast operations using the unicast operations only. (*Note:* Your answer should use the given operations only; you should not use threading or other operating system support.)

7. In a distributed system, three processes P1, P2, and P3 are engaged in interprocess communication. Suppose the following sequence of events occurred:

    At time 1, P3 issues a *receive* from P2.

    At time 2, P1 *sends* m1 to P2.

    At time 3, P2 issues a *receive* from P1.

    At time 4, P2 *receives* m1.

    At time 5, P2 *sends* message m1 to P3.

    At time 6, P3 *receives* m1; P1 issues a *receive* from P2.

    At time 7, P2 issues a *receive* from P3.

    At time 8, P3 *sends* m2 to P2.

    At time 9, P2 *receives* m2.

    At time 10, P2 *sends* m2 to P1.

    At time 11, P1 *receives* m2.

    a. For each of the following scenarios, draw an event diagram to show the sequence of events and the blocking and unblocking of each process:

       i. on a communication system that provides blocking for the *send* operations and blocking *receive* operations,

       ii. on a communication system that provides nonblocking *send* operations and blocking *receive* operations.

    b. Draw a sequence diagram to document the interprocess communication between P1, P2, and P3.

8. This is an exercise on data marshaling.

    a. In the context of IPC:

       i.   What is meant by data marshaling? There are two components to data marshaling; name and describe each. Why is data marshaling necessary?

       ii. What is meant by object serialization?

       iii. How do the two components of data marshaling apply to (i) an array of integers, and (ii) an object? Describe in general terms what needs to be done with the data.

    b. Process A sends to process B a single data item, a date. Process A uses the American date format: *<month>/<day>/<year>* (for example, 01/31/2001). Process B uses the European date format: *<day>/<month>/<year>* (for example, 31/01/2001).

i. Suppose no external data representation has been agreed upon.

    a. How can A send the date to B so that A does not have to do any conversion?

    b. How can A send the date to B so that B does not have to do any conversion?

ii. Suppose the same date has to be communicated to process C, which uses a date format of *<year>-<month>-<date>* (for example, 2001-01-31).

    How can A send the date to both B and C so that A does not have to do any conversion?

iii. Describe an external representation of the date so that any sending process may convert a date of its local representation to the external representation prior to sending, and any receiving process may convert the date received from this representation to its native representation.

It may be of interest for you to read reference [saqqara.demon.co.uk, 10].

9. Use telnet to interact with a *Daytime* [RFC 867, 4] server process on a machine that you have access to. *Daytime* server processes reside on port 13 of an IP host. From a console screen on a command prompt screen, enter

    `telnet<space> <domain name or IP address of the machine><space>13`

    Example: `telnet somehost.someU.edu 13`

Provide a script of the session and describe your observations.

10. Draw a sequence diagram for the *Daytime* protocol.

11. Is it possible for a *Daytime* client to be blocked indefinitely? Explain.

12. Use telnet to interact with an *echo* [RFC 862, 6] server process on a machine to which you have access. By default, *Echo* server processes reside on port 7 of an IP host.

    a. Draw a time event diagram for the *echo* protocol.

    b. Is it possible for an *echo* client to be blocked indefinitely? Explain.

13. Consider the FTP (File Transfer Protocol) [RFC 959, 5].
Note that this protocol uses two connections: one for transmitting requests and responses, the other for transmitting data of the files being sent/received.

    a. Use telnet to connect to an FTP server that you have access to. Then issue a command to list the contents of the root directory on the server.

    b. Use an event diagram to describe the interactions among the participating processes.

    c. What is the format of each request?

    d. What is the format of each response?

    e. Consider the MODE command of the protocol: it allows a client to specify what type of file (text or binary) is to be transferred. What is the data representation for different modes of files?

14. Consider the Simple Mail Transfer Protocol (SMTP) [RFC 821, 3]. An excerpt from the RFC for this protocol provides the following sample session:

```
R: 220 USC-ISI.ARPA Simple Mail Transfer Service Ready
S: HELO LBL-UNIX.ARPA
R: 250 USC-ISI.ARPA
S: MAIL FROM:<mo@LBL-UNIX.ARPA>
R: 250 OK
S: RCPT TO:<Jones@USC-ISI.ARPA>
R: OK
S: DATA
R: 354 Start mail input; end with <CRLF>.<CRLF>
S: Blah blah blah...
S: ...etc. etc. etc.
S: .
R: 250 OK
S: QUIT
R: 221 USC-ISI.ARPA Service closing transmission channel
```

a. Use a sequence diagram to describe the interactions among the participating processes.

b. What is the format of each request?

c. What is the format of each response?

d. Use telnet to connect to a system on which you have an SMTP email account, and then send yourself an email. Log onto the system and check that the email indeed arrived.
    Provide a script of the session and describe your observations.

References

(*Note:* All Requests for Comments [RFCs] can be browsed online at this archival site: IETF RFC Page, http://www.ietf.org/rfc.html)

1. RFC 1014, External Data Representation.

2. "ASN.1 Overview," *http://www.oss.com/asn1/overview.html*

3. RFC 821, SMTP.

4. RFC 867, Daytime Protocol.

5. RFC 959, FTP Protocol.

6. RFC 862, Echo Protocol.

7. John Shapley Gray. *Interprocess Communications in UNIX.* Upper Saddle River, NJ: Prentice Hall, 1997.

8. RFC 742, Finger protocol.

9. Extensible Markup Language (XML), *http://www.w3.org/XML/*

10. International Date Format Campaign, *http://www.saqqara.demon.co.uk/datefmt.htm*

11. Java Object Serialization, *http://java.sun.com/j2se/1.3/docs/guide/serialization/*

12. Elliotte Rusty Harold. *Java I/O*, Sebastopol, CA: O'Reilly Press, 1999.

## CHAPTER 3

Distributed Computing Paradigms

Distributed computing is one of the most vibrant areas in computer science. There is an ongoing evolution of new technologies for supporting network applications, bringing with them new conceptual models and terminologies. Seemingly a new buzzword, another acronym, or yet one more groundbreaking technology surfaces everyday. To a casual observer or a beginning student, sorting out the terminologies and technologies proves a daunting task.

This chapter presents a classification of the various paradigms for distributed applications, as well as an introduction to some of the existing well-known tools and protocols based on these paradigms. In subsequent chapters we will explore some of the paradigms, tools, and protocols in detail.

3.1 Paradigms and Abstraction

The terms **paradigms** and **abstraction** have already been used in previous chapters. Here we will examine them closely.

Abstraction

Arguably the most fundamental concept in computer science, *abstraction* is the idea of **encapsulation**, or **detail hiding**. To quote David J. Barnes [Barnes, 1]:

We often use abstraction when it is not necessary to know the exact details of how something works or is represented, because we can still make use of it in its simplified form. Getting involved with the detail often tends to obscure what we are trying to understand, rather than illuminate it. . . . Abstraction plays a very important role in programming because we often want to model, in software, simplified versions of things that exist in the real world . . . without having to build the real things.

In software engineering, abstraction is realized with the provision of tools or facilities that allow software to be built without the developer having to be cognizant of some of the underlying complexities. It is not an overstatement to say that the tools for abstraction are the force behind modern-day software, and they exist in every aspect of application development. As examples, we make use of compilers to abstract the detail of the machine languages, and Java programmers use the *Abstract Window Toolkit (AWT)* to rapidly develop graphic displays.

In the area of distributed applications, there has been an explosion of tools and facilities based on a wide variety of paradigms that offer varying degrees of abstraction.

Paradigms

Webster's Dictionary defines the word *paradigm* as "a pattern, example, or model." In the study of any subject of great complexity, it is useful to identify the basic patterns or models and classify the details according to these models. This chapter aims to present a classification of the paradigms for distributed applications. The paradigms will be presented in the order of their level of abstraction, as shown in Figure 3.1. At the lowest level of abstraction is **message passing**, which encapsulates the least amount of detail. **Object space** occupies the other extreme of the spectrum, as it is the most abstract of all the paradigms.

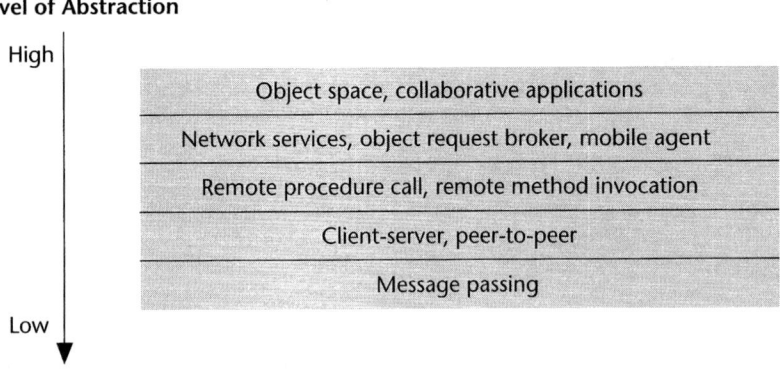

Figure 3.1 Distributed computing paradigms and their level of abstraction.

3.2 An Example Application

Throughout the discussion that follows, a common application will be used to illustrate how each paradigm may be applied.

The example application is an online auctioning system. (Note that the implementations described in this chapter intentionally skip the details [such as user interface and data storage] for an actual application. The example implementations are meant to serve as a common thread in this chapter. Using these implementations, you may compare and contrast the differences and the effects of the abstractions provided by the different paradigms.) We will simplify the system to one that handles only one auctioned item per session. During each auctioning session, an item is open for bids placed by the auction participants. At the end of a session, the auctioneer announces the outcome. In the description of the various implementations, we will confine our attention to the distributed computing aspects of the service layer (that is, within a three-layered architecture of distributed applications, the layer that provides the underlying services in support of the upper layers) of the application's architecture.

3.3 Paradigms for Distributed Applications

Message Passing

The basic approach to interprocess communications is **message passing**. In this paradigm, data representing messages are exchanged between two processes, a **sender** and a **receiver**.

Message passing is the most fundamental paradigm for distributed applications. A process sends a message representing a request. The message is delivered to a receiver, which processes the request and sends a message in response. In turn, the reply may trigger a further request, which leads to a subsequent reply, and so forth. Figure 3.2 illustrates the message-passing paradigm.

The basic operations required to support the message-passing paradigm are *send* and *receive*. For connection-oriented communication, the operations *connect* and *disconnect* are also required. (The details of operations, such as arguments and return values, will be given with specific tools or facilities in later chapters.) With the abstraction provided by this model, the interconnected processes perform input and output to each other, in a manner similar to file input and output (I/O). As with file I/O, the operations serve to encapsulate the detail of network communication at the operating system level, so that a programmer may make use of the operations to send and receive message without having to deal with the underlying detail.

The **socket** application program interface (which will be studied in Chapter 4) is based on this paradigm. Using a socket, a logical construct, two processes may exchange data as follows: A sender writes or inserts a message into the socket; at the other end, a receiver reads or extracts a message from the socket.

The implementation of our auction system using message passing and the client-server paradigm will be described in the next section.

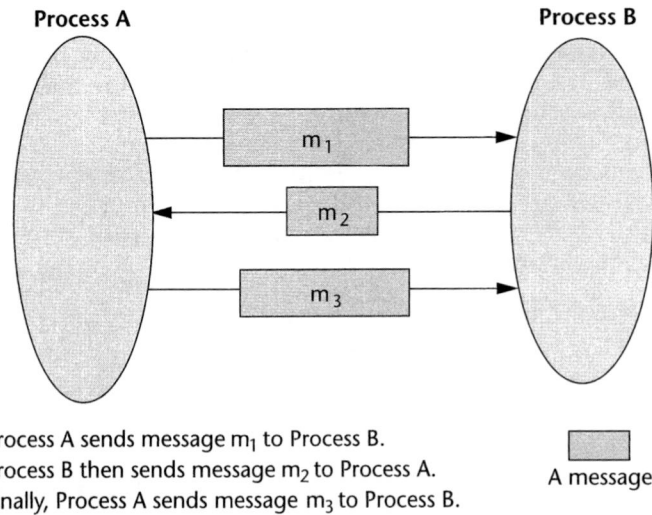

Process A sends message m_1 to Process B.
Process B then sends message m_2 to Process A.
Finally, Process A sends message m_3 to Process B.

A message

Figure 3.2 The message-passing paradigm.

The Client-Server Paradigm

Perhaps the best known paradigm for network applications, the **client-server model** [Comer and Stevens, 2] assigns asymmetric roles to two collaborating processes. One process, the *server*, plays the role of a service provider, waiting passively for the arrival of requests. The other, the *client*, issues specific requests to the server and awaits the server's response. Figure 3.3 illustrates the paradigm.

Simple in concept, the client-server model provides an efficient abstraction for the delivery of network services. Operations required include those for a server process to listen and to accept requests, and for a client process to issue requests and accept responses. By assigning asymmetric roles to the two sides, event synchronization is simplified: The server process waits for requests, and the client in turn waits for responses.

Many Internet services support client-server applications. These services are often known by the protocol that the application implements. Well-known Internet services include HTTP, FTP, DNS, finger, gopher, and so forth, some of which you have already been introduced to in Chapter 2.

The two basic models that we have looked at so far, *client-server* and *message passing*, are sufficient as a basis for the implementation of our auctioning system. Each participant, as well as the auctioneer program, assumes the role of both *client* and *server*, as follows:

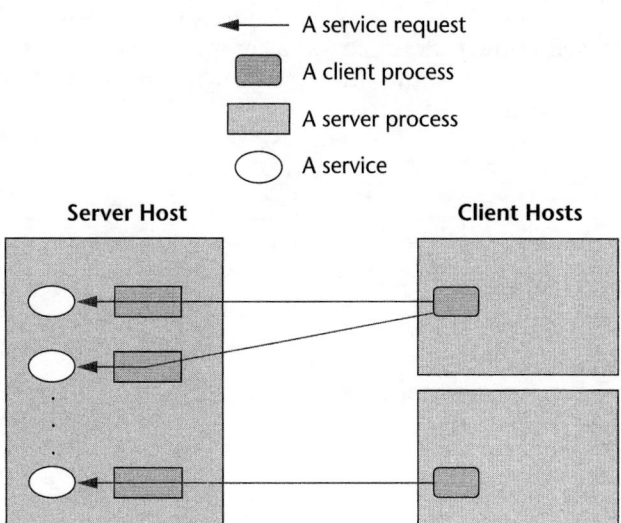

Figure 3.3 The client-server paradigm.

For session control:

- As a server, a participant waits to hear an announcement from the auctioneer (1) when the session starts, (2) whenever there is an update on the current highest bid, and (3) when the session ends.
- As a client, the auctioneer sends a request that announces the three types of events outlined in the previous item.

For accepting bids:

- As a client, a participant sends a new bid to a server.
- As a server, an auctioneer accepts new bids and updates the current highest bid.

The client-server paradigm is inherent in most of the programming facilities for distributed applications. The connection-oriented socket API provides operations designed specifically for servers and clients, respectively, and **Remote Procedure Call APIs** and **Java Remote Method Invocation API** (more on the latter will be presented later in this chapter) also refer to the participating processes as clients and servers.

The Peer-to-Peer Paradigm

In the client-server paradigm, the participating processes play different roles: Client processes issue requests while the server processes listen passively for service requests and provide the requested service in response. In particular, the paradigm makes no provision to allow a server process to initiate communication.

In the **peer-to-peer** paradigm (Figure 3.4), the participating processes play equal roles, with equivalent capabilities and responsibilities (hence the term *peer*).

Each participant may issue a request to another participant and receive a response. A well-known example of a peer-to-peer file transfer service is *Napster.com*; similar sites allow files (primarily audio files) to be transmitted among computers on the Internet.

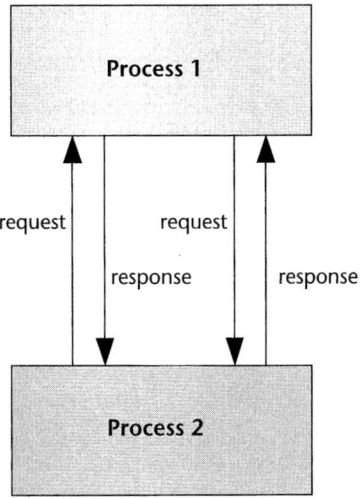

Figure 3.4 Peer-to-peer paradigm.

Whereas the client-server paradigm is an ideal model for a centralized network service (where a server process provides the service and client processes access the service through the server), the peer-to-peer paradigm is more appropriate for applications such as instant messaging, peer-to-peer file transfers, video conferencing, and collaborative work. It is also possible for an application to be based on both the client-server model and the peer-to-peer model. Napster.com makes use of a server for the directory in addition to the peer-to-peer computing.

The peer-to-peer paradigm can be implemented with facilities using any tool that provides message passing. For complex applications such as instant messaging and resource sharing, there is ongoing work to develop high-level protocols and tools for their development. Examples of such protocols and their accompanying tools include the **JXTA** project [jxta.org, 29] and **Jabber** [jabber.org, 30], an XML-based, open protocol for instant messaging and presence.

In the context of instant messaging, **presence** refers to the state of a participant, such as whether the participant is currently online or offline, and other status indicators.

The implementation of our auctioning system can be simplified significantly with the availability of a tool that supports the peer-to-peer paradigm. A participant can now contact the auctioneer directly to register for the auction. The auctioneer subsequently contacts each participant to initiate the auction session, during which individual participants may obtain the latest status and submit a bid. At the conclusion of the auction, the winning bidder can be notified by the auctioneer, and other participants may learn about the outcome by contacting the auctioneer.

THE FUTURE OF PEER-TO-PEER

by Matthew Fordahl, *Associated Press* writer
(http://www.hollandsentinel.com/stories/021801/bus_Napster.shtml,
Web posted Sunday, February 18, 2001)
Reprinted by permission of the Associated Press.

The future of peer-to-peer

The file-swapping technology popularized by Napster, known as peer-to-peer networking, is about to change how people and corporations use the Internet. Instead of relying on central servers to process and relay information, new applications being developed will allow users to turn any computing device into a server.

A virtual meeting room

Users logon to the Internet using a program that looks like an online chat room.

A file is placed into a "shared space" within the virtual meeting room, which allows users to work on data files at the same time.

Users work in real time and can instant message each other. In the future, this might be done through devices such as handhelds and cell phones.

What is on the screen

Names of online users ———

File that is being ——— worked on

Instant ——— messaging

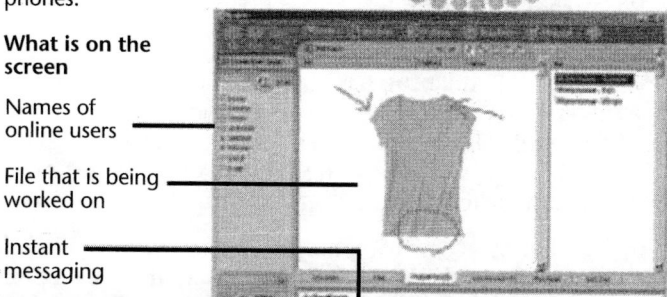

SOURCES: Groove Networks; compiled from AP wire reports

The Message System Paradigm

Middleware refers to software that serves as an intermediary between independent processes. Message systems are one type of middleware and request broker is another.

The use of an intermediary is a common technique in distributed computing.

The **Message System** or **Message-Oriented Middleware (MOM)** paradigm (see Figure 3.5) is an elaboration of the basic message-passing paradigm.

In this paradigm, a message system serves as an **intermediary** among separate, independent processes. The message system acts as a switch for messages, through which processes exchange messages asynchronously, in a decoupled manner. (Asynchronous, as you'll recall from Chapter 2, refers to nonblocking communication.) A sender deposits a message with the message system, which forwards it to a message queue associated with each receiver. Once a message is sent, the sender is free to move on to other tasks.

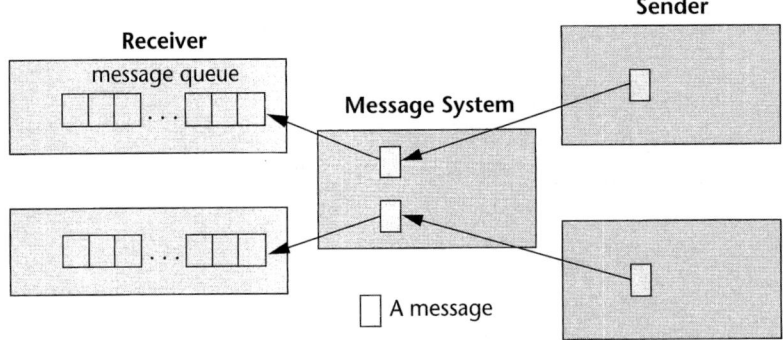

Figure 3.5 The message system paradigm.

There are two subtypes of message system models: the point-to-point message model and the publish/subscribe message model.

The Point-to-Point Message Model

In this model, a message system forwards a message from the sender to the receiver's message queue. Unlike the basic message-passing model, the middleware provides a message depository and allows the sending and the receiving to be decoupled. Via the middleware, a sender deposits a message in the message queue of the receiving process. A receiving process extracts the messages from its message queue and handles each message accordingly.

Compared to the basic message-passing model, the point-to-point message paradigm provides an additional abstraction for asynchronous operations. To achieve the same effect with basic message passing, a developer would have to make use of threads or child processes.

The implementation of our auctioning system using the point-to-point message model is the same as with the basic message-passing model. The only difference is that messages are channeled through the middleware, and the sending and receiving are thereby decoupled.

The Publish/Subscribe Message Model

In this model, each message is associated with a specific topic or event. Applications interested in the occurrence of a specific event may subscribe to messages for that event. When the awaited event occurs, the process publishes a message announcing the event or topic. The middleware message system distributes the message to all its subscribers.

The publish/subscribe message model offers a powerful abstraction for multicasting or group communication. The *publish* operation allows a process to multicast to a group of processes, and the *subscribe* operation allows a process to listen for such a multicast.

Using the publish/subscribe message model, the implementation of our auctioning system may proceed as follows:

- Each participant subscribes to a *begin-auction* event message.
- The auctioneer signifies the beginning of the auctioning session by sending a *begin-auction* event message.
- Upon receiving the *begin-auction* event, a participant subscribes to an *end-auction* event message.
- The auctioneer subscribes to messages for *new-bid* events.
- A participant wishing to place a new bid issues a *new-bid* event message, which will be forwarded to the auctioneer.
- At the end of the session, the auctioneer issues an *end-auction* event message to inform all participants of the outcome. If desired, additional message events can be added to allow the participants to monitor the status of the auction.

The MOM paradigm has had a long history in distributed applications. Message Queue Services (MQS) have been in use since the 1980s. The IBM MQ*Series [ibm.com, 6] is an example of such a facility. Other existing supports for this paradigm are Microsoft's Message Queue (MSMQ) [Dickman, 5; lotus.com, 21] and Java's Message Service [Wetherill, 7].

Remote Procedure Call Model

The message-passing model works well for basic network protocols and for basic network applications. But, as applications grew increasingly complex, it became necessary for further abstractions to be provided for network programming. In particular, it was desirable to have a paradigm that allows distributed software to be programmed in a manner similar to conventional applications that run on a single processor.

The Remote Procedure Call (RPC) model provides such an abstraction. Using this model, communication between two processes is carried out using a concept similar to that for a local procedure call, which is familiar to application programmers.

In procedural languages such as C, a **procedure call** is a call to a procedure (a void function) or a function (a value-returning function).

In a program that involves only one process, a call to a procedure such as *someFunc(arg1, arg2)* results in a detour of the execution flow to the code in the procedure. (See Figure 3.6.) Arguments can be carried into the procedure as parameters for its execution.

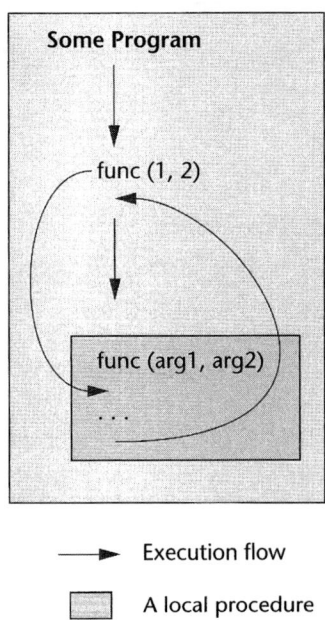

> ← Execution flow
>
> ▢ A local procedure

Figure 3.6 Local procedure call.

A remote procedure call involves two independent processes, which may reside on separate machines. A process, *A*, wishing to make a request to another process, *B*, issues a procedure call to *B*, passing with the call a list of argument values. As in the case of local procedure calls, a Remote Procedure Call triggers a predefined action in a procedure provided by process *B*. At the completion of the procedure, process *B* returns a value to process *A*.

Figure 3.7 illustrates the RPC paradigm. A procedure call is made by one process to another, with data passed as arguments. Upon receiving a call, the actions encoded in the procedure are executed as a result.

As a comparison, the message-passing model is *data-oriented*, with the actions triggered by the message exchanged, while the RPC model is *action-oriented*, with the data passed as arguments.

RPC allows programmers to build network applications using a programming construct similar to the local procedure call, providing a convenient abstraction for both interprocess communications and event synchronization.

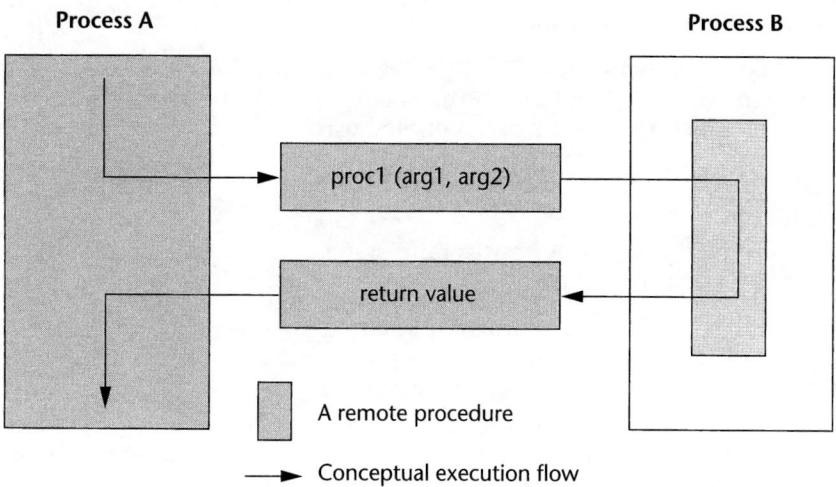

Figure 3.7 The Remote Procedure Call paradigm.

Since its introduction in the early 1980s, the Remote Procedure Call model has been widely used in network applications. There are two prevalent APIs for Remote Procedure Calls: One, the Open Network Computing Remote Procedure Call, evolved from the RPC API originated from Sun Microsystems in the early 1980s. Details of this API can be found in [ietf.org, 8]. The other well-known API is the Open Group Distributed Computing Environment (DCE) RPC [opennc.org, 9]. In addition, there is the Simple Object Access Protocol (SOAP), which will be studied in Chapter 11, and its implementations support Web-based Remote Procedure Calls.

Using RPC to implement our auctioning system will proceed as follows:

■ The auctioning program provides a remote procedure for each participant to register itself and another procedure for a participant to make a bid.

■ Each participant program provides the following remote procedures: (1) to allow the auctioneer to call a participant to announce the onset of the session, (2) to allow the auctioneer to inform a participant of a new highest bid, and (3) to allow the auctioneer to announce the end of the session.

The Distributed Objects Paradigms

The idea of applying object orientation to distributed applications is a natural extension of object-oriented software development. Applications access objects distributed over a network. Objects provide methods, through the invocation of which an application obtains access to services. A number of paradigms, described in the paragraphs that follow, are based on the idea of distributed objects.

Remote Method Invocation

Remote Method Invocation (RMI) (Figure 3.8) is the object-oriented equivalent of the Remote Procedure Call. In this model, a process invokes the methods in an object, which may reside on a remote host.

As with RPC, arguments may be passed with the invocation, and a value may be returned when the method call is completed.

The implementation of our auctioning system is essentially the same as with RPC, except that object methods replace procedures:

- The auctioning program provides a remote method for each participant to register itself and another method for a participant to make a bid.
- Each participant program provides the following remote methods: (1) to allow the auctioneer to call it to announce the onset of the session, (2) to allow the auctioneer to inform the program of a new highest bid, and (3) to allow the auctioneer to announce the end of the session.

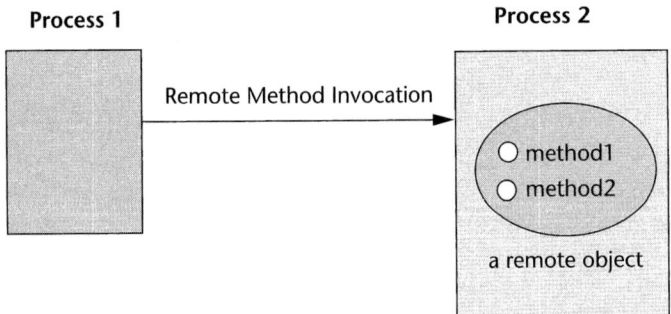

Figure 3.8 The Remote Method Invocation paradigm.

The Object Request Broker Paradigm

In the object broker paradigm (Figure 3.9), a process issues requests to an **object request broker (ORB)**, which directs the request to an appropriate object that provides the desired service. The paradigm closely resembles the Remote Method Invocation model in its support for remote object access. The difference is that the object request broker in this paradigm functions as middleware, allowing an application, as an object requestor, to potentially access multiple remote (or local) objects. The request broker may also function as a mediator for heterogeneous objects, allowing interactions among objects implemented using different APIs and /or running on different platforms.

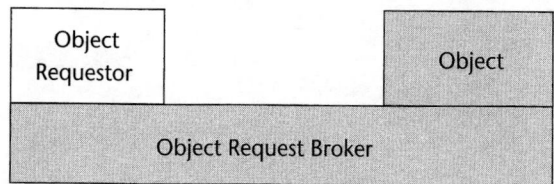

Figure 3.9 The object request broker paradigm.

Implementation of the auctioning system using ORBs is similar to using RMI, with the exception that each object (auctioneer or participant) must be registered with the ORB and requested from the ORB. Each participant issues requests to the auctioneer object to register for the session and to make bids. Through the ORB, the auctioneer invokes the methods of each participant to announce the start of the session, to update the bidding status, and to announce the end of the session.

This paradigm is the basis of the Object Management Group's **CORBA (Common Object Request Broker Architecture)** which is covered in Chapter 10. Toolkits based on the architecture include Inprise's Visibroker, Java Interface Definition Language (Java IDL), IONA's Orbix, and TAO from Object Computing, Inc.

Component-based technologies, such as Microsoft COM, Microsoft DCOM, Java Bean, and Enterprise Java Bean, are also based on distributed-object paradigms, since the components are essentially specialized, packaged objects designed to interact with each other through standardized interfaces. In addition, **application servers**, popular for enterprise applications, are middleware facilities that provide access to objects or components.

The Object Space

Perhaps the most abstract of the object-oriented paradigms, the object space paradigm assumes the existence of logical entities known as **object spaces**. The participants of an application converge in a common object space. A provider places objects as entries into an object space, and requestors who subscribe to the space may access the entries. Figure 3.10 illustrates the paradigm.

In addition to the abstractions provided by other paradigms, the object space paradigm provides a virtual space or meeting room among providers and requestors of network resources, as objects. This abstraction hides the details involved in resource or object lookup that are needed in paradigms such as Remote Method Invocation, object request broker, or network services. In addition, mutual exclusion is inherent in the paradigm, as an object in a space can be retrieved by only one participant at a time.

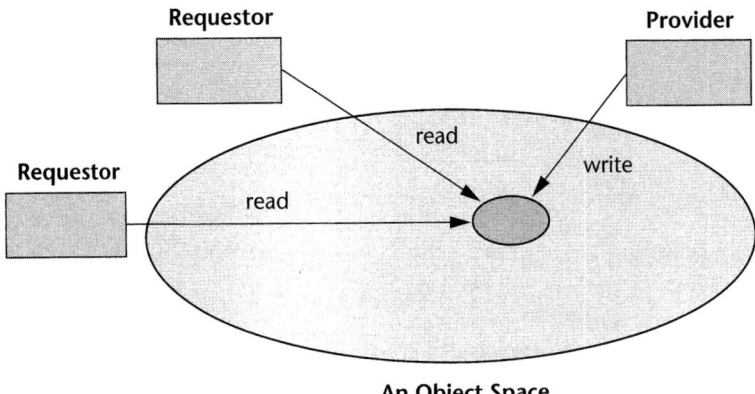

Figure 3.10 The object space paradigm.

For the auctioning system, all participants as well as the service provider subscribe to a common object space. Each participant deposits an object into the object space to register for the session and to be notified when the auctioning session starts. At the onset of the session, the auctioneer deposits an object into the object space. The object contains the item information and the bid history. A participant wishing to place a bid retrieves the object from the space and, if he/she so chooses, places a new bid in the object before returning the object to the space. At the end of the session, the auctioneer retrieves the object from the space and contacts the highest bidder.

An existing toolkit based on this paradigm is JavaSpaces [java.sun.com, 15].

The Mobile Agent Paradigm

A **mobile agent** is a transportable program or object. In this paradigm, an agent is launched from an originating host. The agent then travels autonomously from host to host according to an itinerary that it carries. At each stop, the agent accesses the necessary resources or services and performs the necessary tasks to accomplish its mission. The paradigm is illustrated in Figure 3.11.

The paradigm offers the abstraction for a **transportable program** or object. In lieu of message exchanges, data is carried by the program/object as the program is itself transported among the participants.

The mobile agent paradigm provides a novel way of implementing our auctioning system. At the onset, each participant launches a mobile agent to the auctioneer. The mobile agent carries with it the identity, including the network address, of the participant that it represents. Once the session starts, the auctioneer launches a mobile agent that carries with it an itinerary of the participants, as well as the current highest bid. The mobile agent circulates among

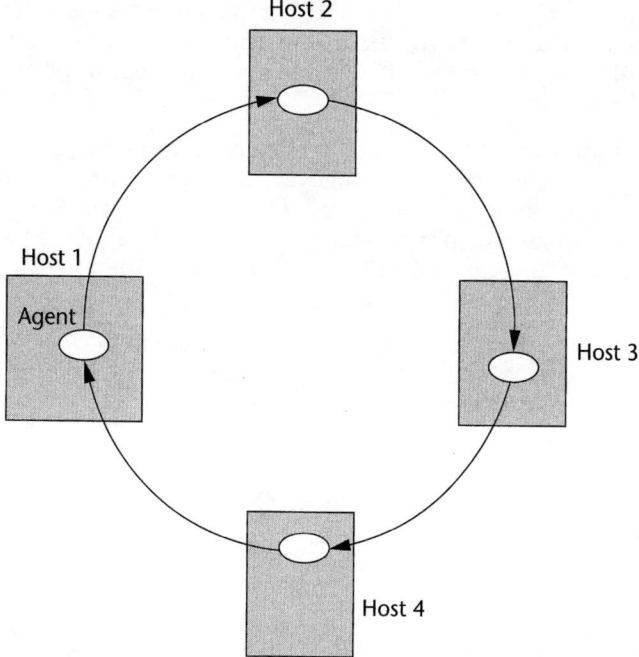

Figure 3.11 The mobile agent paradigm.

the participants and the auctioneer until the session ends, at which time the auctioneer launches the agent to make one more round among the participants to announce the outcome.

Commercial packages that support the mobile agent paradigm include the Concordia system [meitca.com, 16], and the Aglet system [trl.ibm.co.jp, 17]. There are also numerous research systems based on this paradigm, including the D'agent [agent.cs.dartmouth.edu, 13] and the Tacoma Project [tacoma.cs.uit.no, 14].

The Network Services Paradigm

In the paradigm shown in Figure 3.12, service providers register themselves with directory servers on a network. A process desiring a particular service contacts the directory server at run time, and, if the service is available, the process will be provided a reference to the service. Using the reference, the process interacts with the service.

This paradigm is essentially an extension of the Remote Method Invocation paradigm. The difference is that service objects are registered with a global directory service, allowing them to be looked up and accessed by service requestors on a federated network. Ideally, services may be registered and located using a

A **callback method** is a method provided by a service requestor so that the service provider may initiate a call to a particular requestor. Callback methods can also be employed in other paradigms, such as the distributed object paradigm. Chapter 8 covers callbacks in the Java RMI toolkit.

globally unique identifier, in which case, the paradigm offers an extra abstraction: **location transparency**. Location transparency allows a software developer to access an object or a service without having to be cognizant of the location of the object or service.

The implementation of our auctioning system is the same as under the RMI paradigm except that the auctioneer registers itself with the directory service, allowing the participants to locate it and, once the session has commenced, to make bids. The participants provide callback methods to allow the auctioneer to announce the start and the end of the session, and to update the status of the session.

Java's Jini [jini.org, 4] technology is based on this paradigm. The protocol SOAP (Simple Object Access Protocol), which we will study in Chapter 11, applies this paradigm to services that are accessible on the Web.

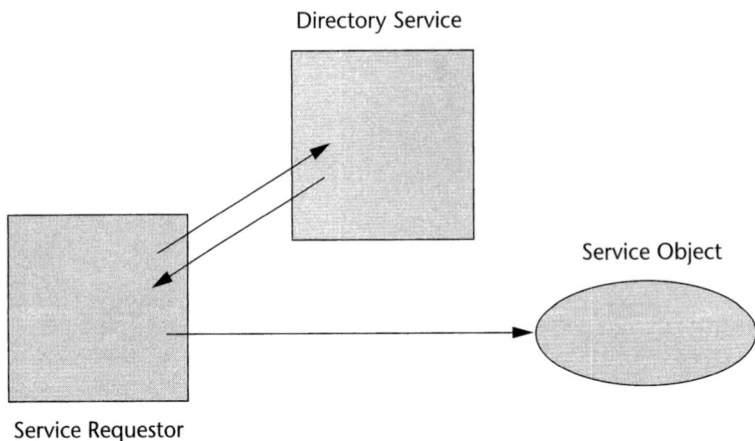

Figure 3.12 The network services paradigm.

The Collaborative Application (Groupware) Paradigm

In this model for computer-supported cooperative work, processes participate in a collaborative session as a group. Each participating process may contribute input to part or all of the group. Processes may do so using multicasting to send data to all or part of the group, or they may use virtual **sketchpads** or **whiteboards**, which allow each participant to read and write data to a shared display. The two categories of the groupware paradigms are illustrated in Figure 3.13.

To implement the auctioning system using the message-based groupware paradigm, the auctioneer initiates a group, to be joined by all interested participants. At the onset of the session, the auctioneer multicasts a message announcing the start. During the session, each bid is multicast to all participants so that each

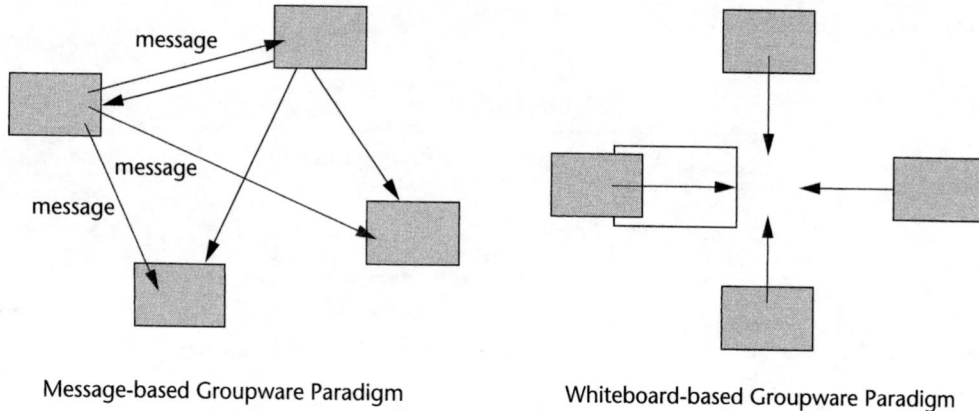

Message-based Groupware Paradigm   Whiteboard-based Groupware Paradigm

Figure 3.13 The collaborative applications paradigm.

may independently assess the status of the auction. Finally, the auctioneer terminates the session by multicasting a message announcing the outcome.

It is not hard to see how the whiteboard paradigm can be applied to our auctioning system. The auctioneer and the participants share a virtual whiteboard. The auctioneer starts the bidding process by writing an announcement to the whiteboard. Subsequently, each participant may place a bid by writing to the whiteboard. Eventually, the auctioneer terminates the session by writing a final announcement.

The collaborative paradigm is the basis of a large number of existing groupware programs such as Lotus QuickPlace [lotus.com, 21]. Application program interfaces supporting the message-based shareware paradigm include the Java multicast API and the Java Shared Data Toolkit (JSDT) [java.sun.com, 18]. The whiteboard paradigm is the basis for a number of applications such as the SMART Board [smarttech.com, 19], NetMeeting [microsoft.com, 20], and Groove [groove.net, 27]. The Notification Service Transfer Protocol (NSTP) has been proposed as "an infrastructure for building synchronous groupware. It is based on the idea of a coordinating notification server that is independent of any given synchronous groupware application. NSTP is intended in some ways to be the synchronous analog of Hypertext Transfer Protocol (HTTP)" [Day, Patterson, and Mitchell, 28].

3.4 Trade-offs

As illustrated in our discussion, a given application can be implemented using any of the paradigms. Given the large number of paradigms and tools available, how does a software developer decide on the most appropriate one for the task at hand?

Level of Abstraction

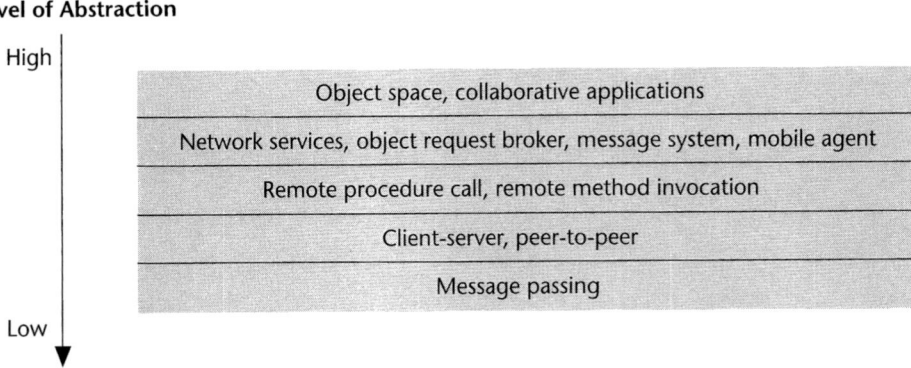

Figure 3.14 The paradigms and levels of abstraction.

To answer the question, one must be aware of the trade-offs between the different approaches. Suffice it to say that each paradigm or tool has some advantage over another. Each advantage, however, may be offset by some disadvantage. In the following paragraphs we will look at some of the issues that should be considered.

Level of Abstraction versus Overhead

Figure 3.14 depicts the paradigms we looked at and their relative levels of abstraction. At the lowest levels are the most basic paradigms: *message passing* and *client server*. At the highest level are *object spaces* and *collaborative computing*, which provide the most abstraction. The development of a highly complex application may be greatly aided by a tool that offers a high level of abstraction. But abstraction comes at a price: *overhead*.

Consider the *Remote Method Invocation* paradigm, for example. As you will see in Chapter 8, in order to provide the remote method abstraction, software modules known as *stubs* and *skeletons* need to be present at run time to handle the details of interprocess communications. The run-time support and additional software modules require additional system resources and execution time. Thus, all things being equal, an application written using RMI will require more system resources and will have a longer run time than will one written using the socket API. For this reason, the socket API may be the most appropriate for an application that calls for a fast response time or for a system with minimum resources. On the other hand, RMI or other tools that offer more abstraction may allow an application to be developed more rapidly, and hence may be more appropriate if response time and resource consumption are not a concern.

Scalability

The complexity of a distributed application increases significantly, possibly exponentially, as the number of participants (processes or objects) increases. Consider our example application, the auctioning system. As described, the auctioneer must manage the addresses of the participants so that it may announce the start and end of the session. Furthermore, the auctioneer needs to repeatedly contact individual participants to inform them of the latest highest bid. Using message passing, the developer must provide the coding to manage the addresses and to contact the participants individually. The complexity grows as the number of participants increases.

With a toolkit based on a high-level paradigm such as *object spaces* or a *publish/subscribe message system*, the complexity of managing the participants is handled by the system. An application thus implemented can accommodate an increase in the number of participants with no additional complexity.

Mobile-agent is another paradigm that allows an application to scale well, since the number of participating hosts can increase without any significant impact on the complexity of a program based on the paradigm.

Cross-Platform Support

Paradigms, being abstract models, are inherently platform independent. Toolkits based on paradigms, on the other hand, may be platform dependent, and many are. In order to provide the generality, a tool that supports heterogeneous platforms necessarily incurs complexity, compared to one that supports a single platform. For the same reason, the programming syntax also tends to be more cumbersome.

Many of the Java technologies, including Java RMI API and JavaSpaces, by choice run on Java virtual machines only. As a result, if these technologies are employed, all participants in an application must be written in the Java language. Likewise, COM/DCOM technologies are deployable on Microsoft platforms only.

By contrast, CORBA is an architecture designed for cross-platform support; hence tools based on the architecture can support programs written in different languages and can also support processes running on different platforms.

Beyond these trade-offs, there are software-engineering issues that should be considered when you are choosing a tool. Some of these are

- The maturity and stability of the tool
- The fault tolerance provided by the tool
- The availability of developer tools
- Maintainability
- Code reuse

Summary

This chapter looked at a wide range of paradigms for distributed applications. The paradigms presented were

- Message passing
- Client-server
- Peer-to-peer
- Message system
  - Point-to-point
  - Publish/subscribe
- Remote procedure call
- Distributed objects
  - Remote method invocation
  - Object request broker
  - Object space
- Mobile agents
- Network services
- Collaborative applications

To varying degrees, these paradigms provide abstraction that insulates the developers from the detail of interprocess communication and event synchronization, allowing the programmer to concentrate on the bigger picture of the application itself.

In choosing a paradigm or a tool for an application, there are trade-offs that should be considered, including overhead, scalability, cross-platform support, and software engineering issues.

Exercises

1. Consider the implementation of a simple chat room where participants converge in a virtual meeting place and exchange messages among all who are present in the room.

   Explain how you might apply each of the paradigms discussed in the chapter to your implementation.

   Compare the adequacy of the paradigms for this application. From the point of view of the programmer, which of the paradigms seem(s) the most natural? Which seem(s) the least natural?

2. Consider the trade-offs that we looked at.

   a. Can you think of any additional trade-offs?

   b. Compare and contrast the strengths and weaknesses of each of the paradigms that we looked at in terms of these trade-offs.

3. Consider the paradigms that we looked at. For each, describe an application for which you think the paradigm is appropriate. Explain.

4. Many of the paradigms that we looked at involve *middleware*, a software module that serves as an intermediary among the participants of an application.

   a. Consider the publish/subscribe message system model. How does the middleware in the paradigm allow *publish/subscribe*?

   b. How might a middleware program allow *cross-platform support*?

   c. How might a middleware program provide asynchronous interprocess communication?

   d. Which of the paradigms involves middleware? Explain.

5. Suppose you are building a software system for an organization to track expense records. Using the system, each employee may submit an expense request online, and subsequently receive an approval or denial online. An employee may also submit a record for an expense that has been incurred. Without going into specifics, choose a paradigm for the system, justify your choice, and describe how you would apply the paradigm to the application.

References

1. David J. Barnes. *Object-Oriented Programming*. Upper Saddle River, NJ: Prentice Hall, 1999.

2. Douglas E. Comer and David L. Stevens. *Internetworking with TCP/IP*, Vol. 3: *Client-Server Programming and Applications*. Upper Saddle River, NJ: Prentice Hall, 2001.

3. Elliotte Rusty Harold. *Java Network Programming*. Sebastopol, CA: O'Reilly, 1997.

4. Welcome to Jini.org!, *http://www.jini.org/*

5. Alan Dickman. *Designing Applications with Msmq: Message Queuing for Developers*. Reading, MA: Addison-Wesley, 1998.

6. IBM MQ Series Family home page, *http://www-4.ibm.com/software/ts/mqseries/*

7. John Wetherill, Messaging Systems and the Java™ Message Service, *http://developer.java.sun.com/developer/technicalArticles/Networking/messaging/*

8. RFC1831: Remote Procedure Call Protocol Specification Version 2, August 1995, *http://www.ietf.org/rfc/rfc1831.txt*

9. DCE1.1; Remote Procedure Call, Open Group Standard, Document Number C706 August 1997, *http://www.opennc.org/public/pubs/catalog/c706.htm*

10. The Object Management Group homepage, *http://www.corba.org/*

11. Thomas J. Mowbray and Ron Zahavi. *The Essential CORBA*. New York, NY: Wiley, 1995.

12. The Community Resource for Jini Technology, *http://jini.org/*

13. D'Agents: Mobile Agents at Dartmouth College, *http://agent.cs.dartmouth.edu/*

14. TACOMA—Operating system support for agents, *http://www.tacoma.cs.uit.no/*

15. JavaSpaces™ Technology, *http://java.sun.com/products/javaspaces/*

16. Concordia's welcome page, *http://www.meitca.com/HSL/Projects/Concordia/Welcome.html*

17. IBM Aglets Software Development Kit, *http://www.trl.ibm.co.jp/aglets/*

18. Java Shared Data Toolkit User Guide, *http://java.sun.com/products/java-media/jsdt/2.0/jsdt-guide/introduction.doc.html#15891* and *http://java.sun.com/products/java-media/jsdt/2.0/jsdt-guide/jsdtTOC.fm.html*

19. SMART Board Interactive Whiteboard, Software Features, *http://www.smarttech.com/products/smartboard/software.asp*

20. NetMeeting Home, *http://www.microsoft.com/windows/netmeeting/*

21. IBM Lotus Software—QuickPlace, *http://lotus.com/*

22. Microsoft Message Queueing, *http://msdn.microsoft.com/library/psdk/msmq/msmq_overview_4ilh.htm*

23. Java socket API, *http://java.sun.com/producsts/jdk/1.2/docs/api/index.html*

24. Winsock Development Information, *http://www.sockets.com/*

25. The World Wide Web Consortium (W3C), Simple Object Access Protocol (SOAP), *http://www.w3.org/TR/SOAP/*

26. The XNSORG homepage, *http://www.xns.org/*

27. Groove homepage, *http://www.groove.net/*

28. Mark Day, John F. Patterson, David Mitchell, The Notification Service Transfer Protocol (NSTP): Infrastructure for Synchronous Groupware, Lotus Technical Report 96-13, *http://www.scope.gmd.de/info/www6/technical/paper080/paper80.html*

29. jxta.org, *http://www.jxta.org/*, Project JXTA home site.

30. Jabber Software Foundation, *http://www.jabber.org/*, Jabber Software Foundation home site.

## CHAPTER 4

The Socket API

This chapter introduces the first programming facility for implementing inter-process communications: the **socket API**.

As you may recall from Chapter 2, the socket API is a mechanism that provides a low level of abstraction for IPC. Its simplicity is why it is presented at this point. Although application programmers seldom have to code at this level, the understanding of socket API is important for at least two reasons. First, the upper-layer facilities are built on top of the socket API; that is, they are implemented using the operations provided in the socket API. Second, for applications that place a premium on response time or that run on a platform with limited resources, the socket API may be the most appropriate, or may even be the only available, facility for IPC.

4.1 Background

The socket API first appeared in the early 1980s as a program library in a version of the UNIX operating system known as **Berkeley Unix** (BSD 4.2) to provide the functionalities for IPC. Today socket APIs are supported on all major operating systems. On UNIX-based systems such as BSD or Linux, the API is part of the kernel, or core, of the operating system. On personal computer operating systems such as MS-DOS, Windows NT (and its variants), Mac-OS, and OS/2, the API is provided as program libraries. (On Windows systems, the API is known as **Winsock**.) Java, a language designed with network programming in mind, provides the socket API as part of the language's core classes. These APIs all share the same message-passing model and very similar syntax.

In this chapter, we will use the Java socket API as a representative.

Socket is a term borrowed from telephone communications. In the early days of telephony (prior to the twentieth century), a person wishing to make a call to another person had to go through a human operator, who manually established a connection by physically inserting the two ends of a cable into two specific receptacles, each assigned to one of the two parties, on a panel of sockets. Disconnection also had to be carried out by the operator manually. This metaphor was the basis of the socket API for interprocess communications.

4.2 The Socket Metaphor in IPC

Borrowing from the terminology of telephony, the designer of the socket API has provided a programming construct termed a *socket*. A process wishing to communicate with another process must create an instance of such a construct (see Figure 4.1). Unlike early telephony, however, the communication between the parties may be connection-oriented or connectionless. For clarity, we will present the connectionless socket API first.

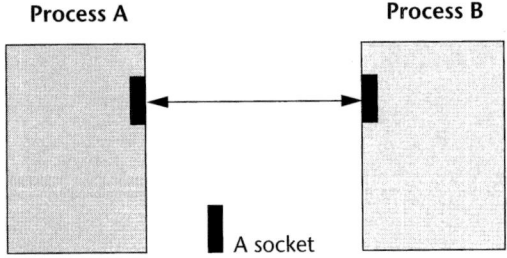

Figure 4.1 The conceptual model of the socket API.

4.3 The Datagram Socket API

As you may recall from Chapter 1 of this book or elsewhere, there are two key protocols at the transport layer of the Internet architecture: User Datagram Protocol (**UDP**) and Transmission Control Protocol (**TCP**).

In the parlance of data networks, a *packet* is a unit of data transmitted over the network. Each packet contains the data (the payload) and some control information (the header), which includes the destination address.

The **User Datagram Protocol** (UDP) allows a packet to be transported (that is, to be sent or received at the transport layer) using connectionless communication. The data packet thus transported is called a **datagram**. In accordance with connectionless communication, each datagram transported is individually addressed and routed, and may arrive at the receiver in any order. For example, if process1 on host A sends messages transported in datagrams m_1, m_2, successively to process 2 running on host B, the datagrams may be transported over the network via different routes, and they may arrive at the receiving process in either of the two orders: m_1–m_2 or m_2–m_1.

The **Transmission Control Protocol** (TCP) is connection-oriented and transports a stream of data over a logical connection established between the sender and the receiver. By virtue of the connection, data sent from a sender to a receiver can be guaranteed to be received in the same order that they were sent. For example, if process 1 on host A sends messages transported in m_1, m_2, successively to process 2 running on host B, the receiving process may assume that the messages will be delivered to it in the order m_1–m_2 and not m_2–m_1.

The Java socket API, as with all other socket APIs, provides socket programming constructs that make use of either the UDP or TCP protocol. Sockets that use UDP for transport are known as **datagram sockets**, while sockets that use TCP are termed **stream sockets**. Because of their relative simplicity, we will first look at datagram sockets.

The Connectionless Datagram Socket

It may surprise you, but datagram sockets can support both connectionless and connection-oriented communication at the application layer (see Figure 4.2). This is so because even though datagrams are sent or received without the notion of connections at the transport layer, the run-time support of the socket API can create and maintain logical connections for datagrams exchanged between two processes, as you will see in the next section.

The **run-time support** of an API is a set of software that is bound to the program during execution in support of the API.

In Java, two classes are provided for the datagram socket API:

1. The *DatagramSocket* class for the sockets
2. The *DatagramPacket* class for the datagrams exchanged

A process wishing to send or receive data using this API must instantiate a *DatagramSocket* object, or a socket in short. Each socket is said to be **bound** to a UDP port of the machine that is local to the process (that is, the machine on which the process is executing). Recall from Chapter 1 that in IPv4 the valid port numbers are 0 through 65,535, with 0 through 1023 reserved for well-known services.

It is highly recommended that you develop the habit of consulting the online Java API documentation [java.sun.com, 1] for the most up-to-date definition of each Java class introduced. You should also check the online API for the exact and current definition of a method or constructor.

To send a datagram to another process (which presumably has instantiated its socket at a local address of, say, host *h* and port *p*), a process must create an object that represents the datagram itself. This object can be created by instantiating a *DatagramPacket* object that carries (1) a reference to a byte array that contains the payload data, and (2) the destination address (the host ID and port number to which the receiver's socket is bound, *h* and *p* in this case.) Once the *DatagramPacket* object is created and loaded with the payload data and destination, the sending process then invokes a call to the *send* method in the *DatagramSocket* object, specifying a reference to the *DatagramPacket* object as an argument.

The **payload data** is so named to differentiate it from the *control data*, which includes the destination address and is also carried in a datagram.

At the receiving process, a *DatagramSocket* object must also be instantiated and bound to a local port; the port number must agree with that specified in the

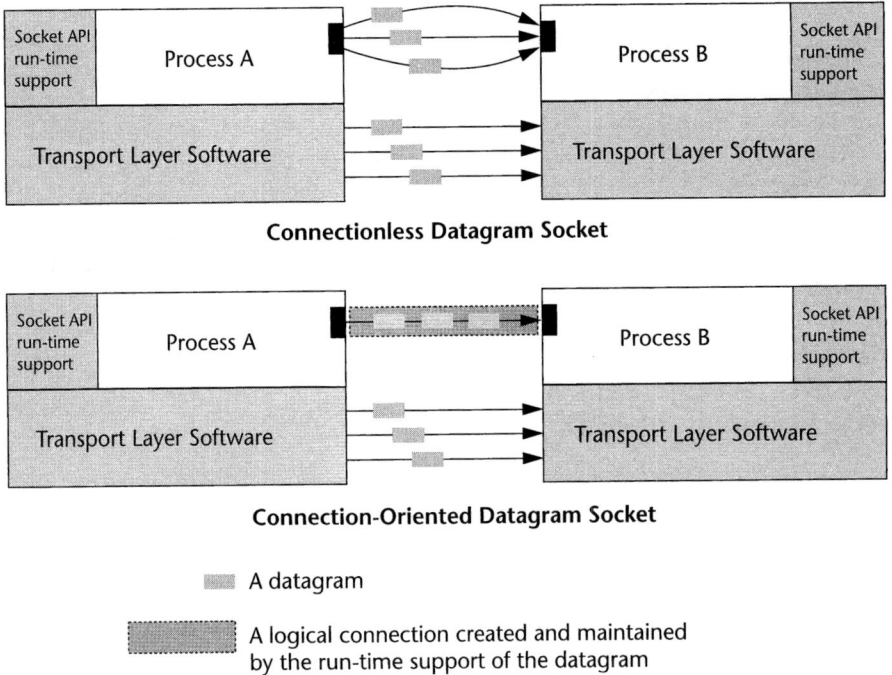

Connectionless Datagram Socket

Connection-Oriented Datagram Socket

A datagram

A logical connection created and maintained by the run-time support of the datagram socket API

Figure 4.2 Connectionless and connection-oriented datagram socket.

datagram packet of the sender. To receive datagrams sent to the socket, the process creates a *DatagramPacket* object that references a byte array and calls a *receive* method in its *DatagramSocket* object, specifying as argument a reference to the *DatagramPacket* object.

Figure 4.3 illustrates the data structures in the programs for the two processes, while Figure 4.4 illustrates the program flow in the two processes.

With connectionless sockets, a socket bound to a process can be used to send datagrams to different destinations. It is also possible for multiple processes to simultaneously send datagrams to the same socket bound to a receiving process, in which case the order of the arrival of these messages will be unpredictable, in accordance with the underlying UDP protocol. Figure 4.5a illustrates a scenario where a process, A, uses a single connectionless socket to communicate with two other processes in a session. For example, A may receive a datagram m_1 from B, followed by a datagram m_2 from C, then m_3, m_4 from B, followed by m_5 from C, and so forth. Alternatively, it is also possible for A to open a separate socket for each of processes B and C, so that datagrams from the two processes can be addressed to and received via the two separate sockets (see Figure 4.5b).

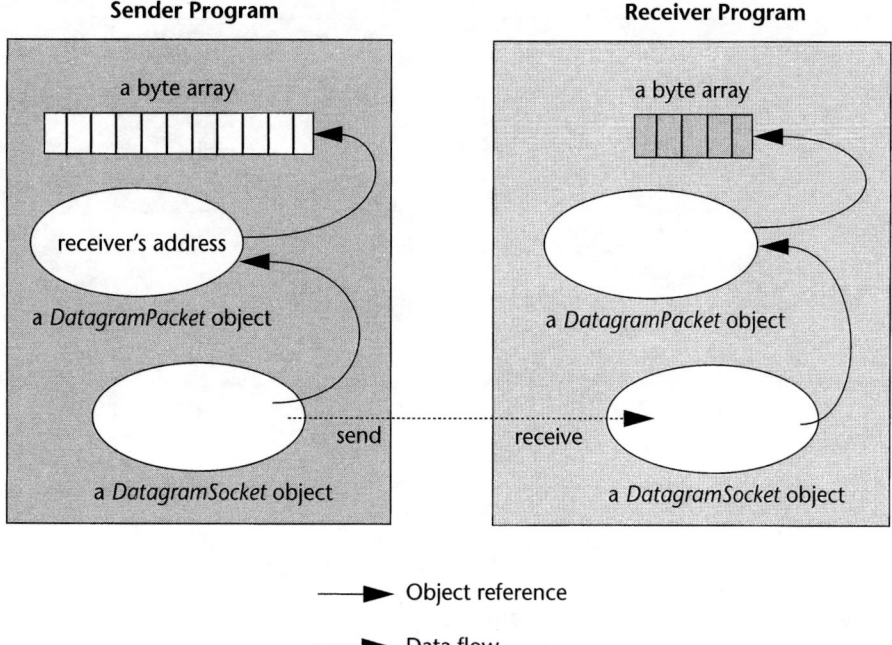

Figure 4.3 The data structures in the sender program and the receiver program.

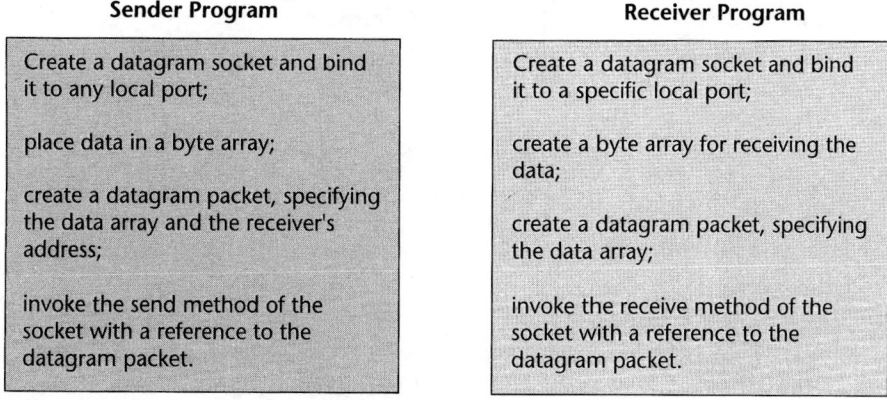

Figure 4.4 The program flow in the sender process and the receiver process.

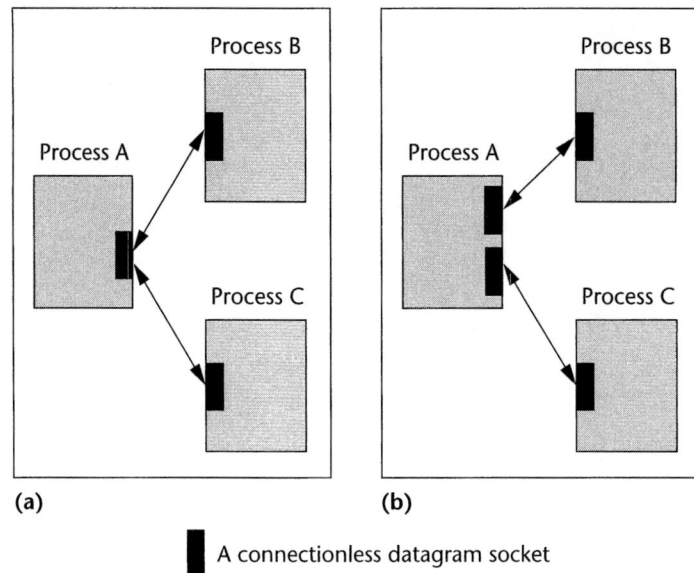

(a)   (b)

▮ A connectionless datagram socket

Figure 4.5 Connectionless datagram sockets.

Table 4.1 summarizes the key methods and constructors for the *DatagramPacket* class, while Table 4.2 summarizes those for the *DatagramSocket* class. Keep in mind that there are many more methods than are presented in this table.

Table 4.1 Key Methods for the *DatagramPacket* class

Method/Constructor	Description
DatagramPacket(byte[ ] buf, int length)	Constructs a datagram packet for receiving packets of length *length*; data received will be stored in the byte array referenced by *buf*
DatagramPacket(byte[ ] buf, int length, InetAddress address, int port) (Note: The *InetAddress* class represents an IP address.)	Constructs a datagram packet for sending packets of length *length* to the socket bound to the specified port number on the specified host; data received will be stored in the byte array referenced by *buf*
DatagramSocket( )	Constructs a datagram socket and binds it to any available port on the local host machine; this constructor can be used for a process that sends data and does not need to receive data

Table 4.2 Key Methods for the *DatagramSocket* class

Method/Constructor	Description
DatagramSocket(int port)	Constructs a datagram socket and binds it to the specified port on the local host machine; the port number can then be specified in a datagram packet destined for this socket.
void close( )	Closes this datagramSocket object
void receive(DatagramPacket p)	Receives a datagram packet using this socket
void send(DatagramPacket p)	Sends a datagram packet using this socket
void setSoTimeout(int timeout)	Sets a timeout in milliseconds for the blocking receive operations issued with this socket

Figure 4.6 illustrates the basic syntax in a pair of programs that communicate using datagram sockets.

```
//Excerpt from a receiver program
DatagramSocket ds = new DatagramSocket(2345);
DatagramPacket dp =
  new DatagramPacket(buffer, MAXLEN);
ds.receive(dp);
len = dp.getLength( );
System.out.Println(len + "bytes received.\n");
String s = new String(dp.getData( ), 0, len);
System.out.println(dp.getAddress( ) +
  "at port" + dp.getPort( ) + "says" + s);
```

```
// Excerpt from the sending process
InetAddress receiverHost =
   InetAddress.getByName("localHost");
DatagramSocket theSocket = new
DatagramSocket( );
String message = "Hello world!";
byte[ ] data = message.getBytes( );
data = theLine.getBytes( );
DatagramPacket thePacket
  = new DatagramPacket(data, data.length,
     receiverHost, 2345);
theSocket.send(theOutput);
```

Figure 4.6 Using the connectionless datagram socket API in programs.

Event Synchronization in Datagram Sockets

In basic socket APIs, whether connection-oriented or connectionless, the *send* operations are **nonblocking** while the *receive* operations are **blocking**. A process will continue with its execution after the issuance of a *send* method call. But a *receive* method call, once invoked in a process, will cause the process to be suspended until a datagram is indeed received. To avoid indefinite blocking, the receiving process may use the *setSoTimeout* method to set a timeout for some interval, say 50 seconds. If no data is received after the timeout period, a Java exception will be thrown (specifically, a *java.io. InterruptedIOException* will occur) and can be caught in the code to handle the situation as appropriate.

Figure 4.7 is an event diagram showing a session of a request-response protocol using datagram sockets.

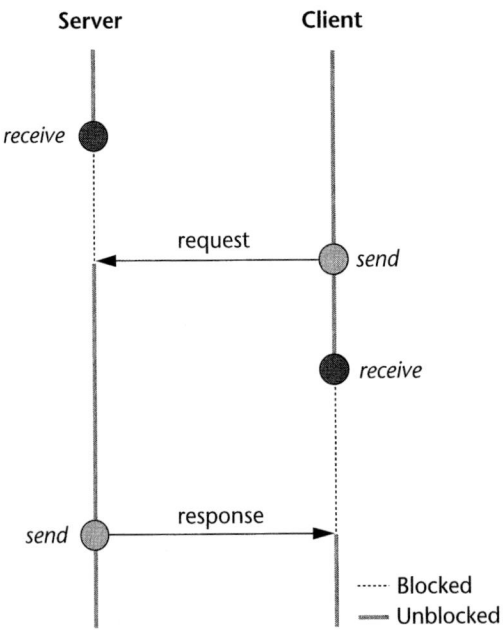

Figure 4.7 Event synchronization with connectionless sockets.

Example 1 Figures 4.8 and 4.9 illustrate the code for two programs that use datagram sockets to exchange a single data string. By design the logic of the programs is as simple as possible to highlight the basic syntax for interprocess communications. Note that the sender creates a datagram packet that contains a destination address (see lines 31 through 33 in Figure 4.8) while the receiver's datagram packet does not carry a destination address (see lines 31 and 32 in Figure 4.9). Note also that the sender's socket is bound to an unspecified port number (see line 28 in Figure 4.8) while the receiver's socket is bound to a specified port number (see line 28 in Figure 4.9) so that the sender may specify this port number in its datagram (see line 33 in Figure 4.8) as the destination. It should also be mentioned that for simplicity the sample programs use rudimentary syntax (lines 37–39 in *Example1Sender* and 38–40 in *Example1Receiver*) to handle exceptions. In an actual application, it is often necessary to handle the exceptions using more refined coding.

Figure 4.8 *Example1Sender.java.*

```
1   import java.net.*;
2   import java.io.*;
3
4   /**
5    *   This example illustrates the basic method calls for connectionless
6    *   datagram socket.
7    *   @author M. L. Liu
8    */
9   public class Example1Sender {
10
11  // An application which sends a message using connectionless
12  // datagram socket.
13  // Three command line arguments are expected, in order:
14  // <domain name or IP address of the receiver>
15  // <port number of the receiver's socket>
16  // <message, a string, to send>
17
18     public static void main(String[ ] args) {
19        if (args.length != 3)
20          System.out.println
21            ("This program requires three command line arguments");
22        else {
23          try {
24            InetAddress receiverHost = InetAddress.getByName(args 0]);
25            int receiverPort = Integer.parseInt(args[1]);
26            String message = args[2];
27
28            // instantiates a datagram socket for sending the data
29            DatagramSocket mySocket = new DatagramSocket( );
30            byte[ ] buffer = message.getBytes( );
31            DatagramPacket datagram =
32              new DatagramPacket(buffer, buffer.length,
33                 receiverHost, receiverPort);
34            mySocket.send(datagram);
35            mySocket.close( );
36          } // end try
37          catch (Exception ex) {
38            ex.printStackTrace( );
39          } // end catch
40        } // end else
41     } // end main
42  } // end class
```

Figure 4.9 *Example1Receiver.java.*

```
1   import java.net.*;
2   import java.io.*;
3
4   /**
5    *  This example illustrates the basic method calls for connectionless
6    *  datagram socket.
7    *  @author M. L. Liu
8    */
9   public class Example1Receiver {
10
11  // An application which receives a message using connectionless
12  // datagram socket.
13  // A command line argument is expected:
14  // <port number of the receiver's socket>
15  // Note: the same port number should be specified in the
16  // command-line arguments for the sender.
17
18    public static void main(String[] args) {
19      if (args.length != 1)
20        System.out.println
21          ("This program requires a command line argument.");
22      else {
23          int port = Integer.parseInt(args[0]);
24        final int MAX_LEN = 10;
25        // This is the assumed maximum byte length of the
26        // datagram to be received.
27        try {
28          DatagramSocket mySocket = new DatagramSocket(port);
29          // instantiates a datagram socket for receiving the data
30          byte[ ] buffer = new byte[MAX_LEN];
31          DatagramPacket datagram =
32            new DatagramPacket(buffer, MAX_LEN);
33          mySocket.receive(datagram);
34          String message = new String(buffer);
35          System.out.println(message);
36          MySocket.close( );
37        } // end try
38        catch (Exception ex) {
39          ex.printStackTrace( );
40        } // end catch
41      } // end else
42    } // end main
43  } // end class
```

Since data is sent in discrete packets in a connectionless manner, there are some anomalies in the behavior of connectionless datagram sockets:

■ If a datagram is sent to a socket that has not yet been created by the receiver, the datagram may be discarded. In other words, the datagram may *not* be saved by the IPC facility in order that it will be delivered to the receiver when it eventually issues a *receive* call. In this case, the data is lost and the *receive* call may result in indefinite blocking. You can experiment with this behavior by starting *Example1Receiver* before running *Example1Sender*.

■ If the receiver specifies a datagram buffer (that is, the byte array associated with the *DatagramPacket* object) with a size *n*, a message received with a byte size exceeding *n* will be truncated. For example, if *Example1Sender* sends a message of 11 bytes, then the last byte in the message (corresponding to the last character) will not show up in the output of *Example1Receiver*, since the receiving datagram buffer size is only 10 bytes long.

Example 2   In Example 1, the communication is simplex; that is, it is one-way, from the sender to the receiver. It is possible to make the communication duplex, or bidirectional. To do so, *Example1Sender* will need to bind its socket to a specific address so that *Example1Receiver* can send datagrams to that address. The sample code in Figures 4.10, 4.11, and 4.12 illustrates how this duplex communication can be carried out. For code modularity, a class called *MyDatagramSocket* (Figure 4.10) is created as a subclass of *DatagramSocket*, with two instance methods for sending and receiving a message respectively. The *Example2SenderReceiver* program (Figure 4.11) instantiates a *MyDatagramSocket* object, then calls its *sendMessage* method, followed by a call to its *receiveMessage* method. The *Example2ReceiverSender* program (Figure 4.12) instantiates a *MyDatagramSocket* object, then calls its *receiveMessage* method, followed by a call to its *sendMessage* method.

Figure 4.10 *MyDatagramSocket.java.*

```
1   import java.net.*;
2   import java.io.*;
3
4   /**
5    *    A subclass of DatagramSocket which contains
6    *    methods for sending and receiving messages
7    *    @author M. L. Liu
8    */
9   public class MyDatagramSocket extends DatagramSocket {
10    static final int MAX_LEN = 10;
11    MyDatagramSocket(int portNo) throws SocketException{
12      super(portNo);
13    }
14    public void sendMessage(InetAddress receiverHost, int receiverPort,
15       String message) throws IOException {
16
17      byte[ ] sendBuffer = message.getBytes( );
18      DatagramPacket datagram =
19        new DatagramPacket(sendBuffer, sendBuffer.length,
20        receiverHost, receiverPort);
21      this.send(datagram);
22    } // end sendMessage
23
```

(continued next page)

```
24    public String receiveMessage( )
25        throws IOException {
26      byte[ ] receiveBuffer = new byte[MAX_LEN];
27      DatagramPacket datagram =
28        new DatagramPacket(receiveBuffer, MAX_LEN);
29      this.receive(datagram);
30      String message = new String(receiveBuffer);
31      return message;
32    } // end receiveMessage
33  } // end class
```

Figure 4.11 *Example2SenderReceiver.java.*

```
1
2  import java.net.*;
3
4  /**
5  *    This example illustrates a process which sends then receives
6  *    using a datagram socket.
7  *    @author M. L. Liu
8  */
9  public class Example2SenderReceiver {
10 // An application which sends then receives a message using
11 // connectionless datagram socket.
12 // Four command line arguments are expected, in order:
13 // <domain name or IP address of the receiver>
14 // <port number of the receiver's datagram socket>
15 // <port number of this process's datagram socket>
16 // <message, a string, to send>
17
18   public static void main(String[ ] args) {
19     if (args.length != 4)
20       System.out.println
21       ("This program requires four command line arguments");
22     else {
23       try {
24         InetAddress receiverHost = InetAddress.getByName(args[0]);
25         int receiverPort = Integer.parseInt(args[1]);
26         int myPort = Integer.parseInt(args[2]);
27         String message = args[3];
28         MyDatagramSocket mySocket = new MyDatagramSocket(myPort);
29         // instantiates a datagram socket for both sending
30         // and receiving data
31         mySocket.sendMessage( receiverHost, receiverPort, message);
32         // now wait to receive a datagram from the socket
33         System.out.println(mySocket.receiveMessage());
34         mySocket.close( );
35       } // end try
36       catch (Exception ex) {
37         ex.printstackTrace();
```

(continued next page)

```
38            } // end catch
39          } // end else
40       } // end main
41
42  } // end class
```

Figure 4.12 *Example2ReceiverSender.java.*

```
1
2   import java.net.*;
3
4   /**
5    *    This example illustrates a process which sends then receives
6    *    using a datagram socket.
7    *    @author M. L. Liu
8    */
9   public class Example2ReceiverSender {
10  // An application which sends then receives a message using
11  // connectionless datagram socket.
12  // Four command line arguments are expected, in order:
13  //    <domain name or IP address of the receiver>
14  //    <port number of the receiver's datagram socket>
15  //    <port number of this process's datagram socket>
16  //    <message, a string, to send>
17
18     public static void main(String[ ] args) {
19        if (args.length != 4)
20          System.out.println
21            ("This program requires four command line arguments");
22        else {
23          try {
24            InetAddress receiverHost = InetAddress.getByName(args[0]);
25            int receiverPort = Integer.parseInt(args[1]);
26            int myPort = Integer.parseInt(args[2]);
27            String message = args[3];
28            // instantiates a datagram socket for both sending
29            // and receiving data
30            MyDatagramSocket mySocket = new MyDatagramSocket(myPort);
31            // First wait to receive a datagram from the socket
32            System.out.println(mySocket.receiveMessage());
33            // Now send a message to the other process.
34            mySocket.sendMessage( receiverHost, receiverPort, message);
35            mySocket.close( );
36          } // end try
37          catch (Exception ex) {
38            ex.printStackTrace( );
39          }// end catch
40        } // end else
41     } // end main
42
43  } // end class
```

It is also possible for multiple processes to engage in connectionless communication in this manner; that is, you can add a third process that also has a datagram socket so that it too can send to and receive from the other processes.

In the exercises you will have an opportunity to experiment with the sample code to enhance your understanding of the connectionless datagram socket API.

Connection-Oriented Datagram Socket API

Next we will study how to use datagram sockets for connection-oriented communications. It should be mentioned here that it is uncommon to employ datagram sockets for connection-oriented communication; the connection provided by this API is rudimentary and typically insufficient for applications. Stream-mode sockets, which will be introduced later in this chapter, are more typical and more appropriate for connection-oriented communication.

Table 4.3 describes two methods of the *DatagramSocket* class for making and for terminating a connection. A connection is made for a socket by specifying the address of a remote socket. Once such a connection is made, the socket is dedicated to exchanging datagram packets with the remote socket. On a *send* operation, if the datagram's address does not match the socket address at the other end, an *IllegalArgumentException* will be thrown. If data is sent to the socket from a source other than the connected remote socket, the data will be ignored. Thus, once a connection is attached to a datagram socket, that socket will not be available for communication with any other socket until the connection is terminated. Note that the connection is unilateral; that is, it is enforced on only one side. The socket on the other side is free to send data to and receive data from other sockets, unless it commits to a connection to this socket.

Table 4.3 Method Calls for a Connection-Oriented Datagram Socket

Method/Constructor	Description
void connect(InetAddress address, int port)	Creates a logical connection between this socket and a socket at the remote address and port
void disconnect( )	Terminates the current connection, if any, from this socket

Example 3 Code sample *Example3*, shown in Figures 4.13 and 4.14 illustrates the syntax of using connection-oriented datagram sockets. In Figure 4.13, *Example3Sender.java*, a connection is created between the datagram socket of the sender process and that of the receiving process. Note that the connection is made at both sides. Once a connection is mutually established, each process is committed to using its socket for IPC with the other process. (This does not prohibit either process from creating another connection using another socket,

however.) In the example, the sender sends 10 copies of the same messages successively via the connection. In the receiver process, each of the 10 messages received is immediately displayed. The receiver process then sends a single message back to the sender process to illustrate that the connection allows bidirectional communication.

Figure 4.13 *Example3Sender.java.*

```
1  import java.net.*;
2
3
4  /**
5  *   This example illustrates the basic syntax for connection-oriented
6  *   datagram socket.
7  *   @author M. L. Liu
8  */
9  public class Example3Sender {
10
11 // An application which uses a connection-oriented datagram
12 // socket to send multiple messages, then receives one.
13 // Four command line arguments are expected, in order:
14 // <domain name or IP address of the receiver>
15 // <port number of the other process' datagram socket>
16 // <port number of this process's datagram socket>
17 // <message, a string, to send>
18
19   public static void main(String[] args) {
20     if (args.length != 4)
21       System.out.println
22       ("This program requires four command line arguments");
23     else {
24       try {
25         InetAddress receiverHost = InetAddress.getByName(args[0]);
26         int receiverPort = Integer.parseInt(args[1]);
27         int myPort = Integer.parseInt(args[2]);
28         String message = args[3];
29         // instantiates a datagram socket for the connection
30         MyDatagramSocket mySocket = new MyDatagramSocket(myPort);
31         // make the connection
32         mySocket.connect(receiverHost, receiverPort);
33         for (int i=0; i<10; i++)
34           mySocket.sendMessage( receiverHost, receiverPort, message);
35         // now receive a message from the other end
36         System.out.println(mySocket.receiveMessage( ));
37         // terminate the connection, then close the socket
38         mySocket.disconnect( );
39         mySocket.close( );
40       } // end try
41       catch (Exception ex) {
42         ex.printStackTrace( );
43       } // end catch
44     } // end else
45   } // end main
46 } // end class
```

Figure 4.14 *Example3Receiver.java.*

```
1  import java.net.*;
2
3
4  /**
5  *   This example illustrates the basic syntax for connection-oriented
6  *   datagram socket.
7  *   @author M. L. Liu
8  */
9  public class Example3Receiver {
10
11 // An application which uses a connection-oriented datagram
12 // socket to receive multiple messages, then sends one.
13 // Four command line arguments are expected, in order:
14 // <domain name or IP address of the sender>
15 // <port number of the sender's datagram socket>
16 // <port number of this process's datagram socket>
17 // <message, a string, to send>
18
19   public static void main(String[ ] args) {
20     if (args.length != 4)
21       System.out.println
22       ("This program requires four command line arguments");
23     else {
24       try {
25         InetAddress senderHost = InetAddress.getByName(args[0]);
26         int senderPort = Integer.parseInt(args[1]);
27         int myPort = Integer.parseInt(args[2]);
28         String message = args[3];
29         // instantiates a datagram socket for receiving the data
30         MyDatagramSocket mySocket = new MyDatagramSocket(myPort);
31         // make a connection with the sender's socket
32         mySocket.connect(senderHost, senderPort);
33         for (int i=0; i<10; i++)
34           System.out.println(mySocket.receiveMessage( ));
35         // now send a message to the other end
36         mySocket.sendMessage( senderHost, senderPort, message);
37         mySocket.close( );
38       } // end try
39       catch (Exception ex) {
40         ex.printStackTrace( );
41       } // end catch
42     } // end else
43   } // end main
44 } // end class
```

This concludes our introduction to datagram sockets. We will have occasion to revisit it in later chapters, but for now we will turn our attention to another model of the socket API: the stream-mode socket API.

4.4 **The Stream-Mode Socket API**

Whereas the datagram socket API supports the exchange of **discrete** units of data (that is, datagrams), the stream-mode socket API provides a model of data transfer based on the **stream-mode I/O** of the Unix operating systems. By definition, a stream-mode socket supports connection-oriented communication only.

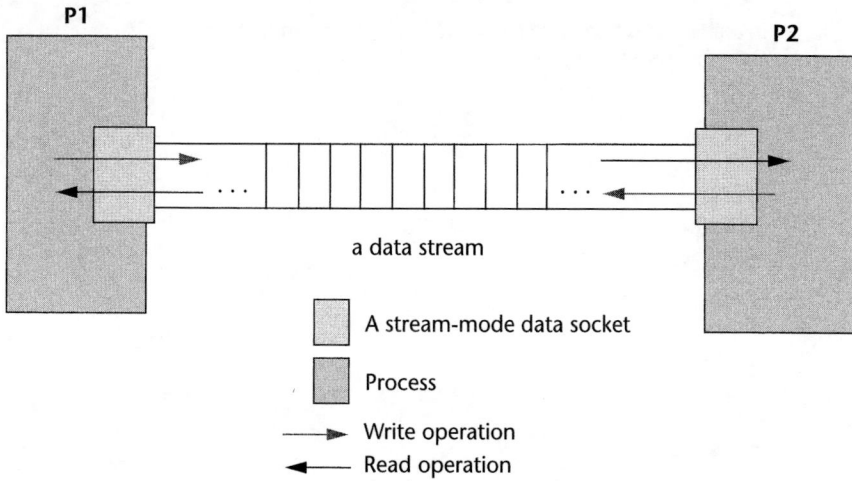

Figure 4.15 Using a stream-mode socket for data transfer.

In stream-mode input-output, data is transferred using the concept of a continuous data stream flowing from a source to a destination (also called a *sink*). Data is inserted, or written, into a stream by a process that controls the source, and data is extracted, or read, from the stream by a process attached to the destination. Figures 4.15 and 4.16 illustrate the concept of a data stream. Note that the continuous nature of a stream allows data to be inserted and extracted from the stream at different rates.

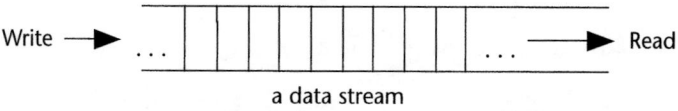

The units of data written and read need not match.
For example, 100 bytes of data written using one *write* operation
can be read using an operation reading 20 bytes, followed by another
read operation using 80 bytes.

Figure 4.16 Stream-mode I/O.

The stream-mode socket API (Figure 4.17) is an extension of the stream-mode I/O model. Using the API, each of two processes individually creates a stream-mode socket. A connection between the sockets is then formed. Data, as a stream of characters, are written into the sender's socket, which can then be read by the receiver via its socket. This is similar to the connection-oriented datagram socket API that we have already studied, except for the difference in the discrete nature of the data transported in datagram sockets.

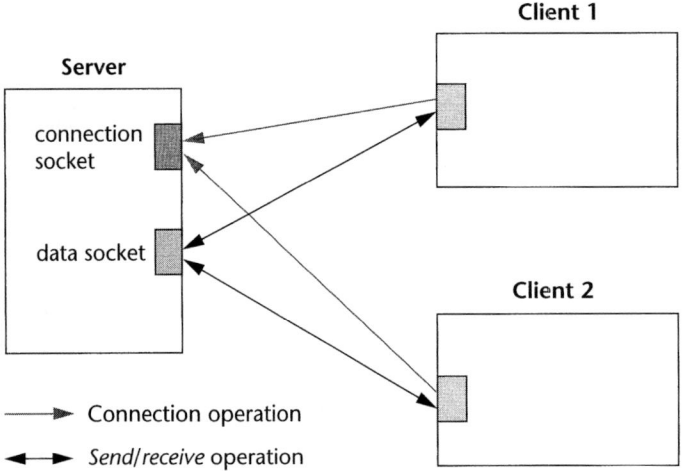

A server uses two sockets: one for accepting connections, another for send/receive.

Figure 4.17 The stream-mode socket API.

In Java, the stream-mode socket API is provided with two classes: *ServerSocket* and *Socket*. The term *Server* comes from the client-server paradigm, for which the API was designed. (Recall that the client-server paradigm was introduced in Chapter 3; it will be studied in detail in Chapter 5.) The syntax of the API is intertwined with the client-server paradigm. For now we will study the API independent of that paradigm.

With the stream-mode socket API, there are two types of sockets:

■ The first type of sockets, provided via the *ServerSocket* class, is for accepting connections. For clarity we will refer to them in this chapter as **connection sockets**.

■ The other type of sockets, provided via the *Socket* class, is for data exchange. For clarity, we will refer to them in this chapter as **data sockets**.

Using this API, a process known as the **server** establishes a connection socket and then listens for connection requests from other processes. Connection requests are accepted one at a time. When a connection is accepted, a data socket is created for the connection. Through the data socket, the server process can read from and/or write to the data stream. When the communication session between the two processes is over, the data socket is closed, and the server is free to accept the next connection request via the connection socket.

A process that wishes to communicate with the server is known as a **client**. A client creates a socket; then, via the server's connection socket, it makes a request to the server for a connection. Once the request is accepted, the client's socket is connected to the server's data socket so that the client may proceed to read from and/or write to the data stream. When the communication session between the two processes is completed, the data socket is closed.

Operations and Event Synchronization

There are two main classes in the stream socket API: the *ServerSocket* class and the *Socket* class. The *ServerSocket* class is for the establishment of connections, while the *Socket* class is for the transfer of data. The key methods and constructors for the two classes are listed in Tables 4.4 and 4.5, respectively.

Table 4.4 Key Methods and Constructors of the *ServerSocket* (connection socket) Class

Method/Constructor	Description
ServerSocket(int port)	Creates a server socket on a specified port.
Socket accept( ) *throws IOException*	Listens for a connection to be made to this socket and accepts it. The method blocks until a connection is made.
void close( ) *throws IOException*	Closes this socket.
void setSoTimeout(int timeout) *throws SocketException*	Sets a timeout period (in milliseconds) so that a call to *accept( )* for this socket will block for only this amount of time. If the timeout expires, a *java.io.InterruptedIOException* is raised.

Table 4.5 Key Methods and Constructors of the *Socket* (data socket) Class

Method/Constructor	Description
Socket(InetAddress address, int port)	Creates a stream socket and connects it to the specified port number at the specified IP address.
void close( ) *throws IOException*	Closes this socket.
InputStream getInputStream( ) *throws IOException*	Returns an input stream so that data may be read from this socket.
OutputStream getOutputStream( ) *throws IOException*	Returns an output stream so that data may be written to this socket.
void setSoTimeout(int timeout) *throws SocketException*	Sets a timeout period for blocking so that a *read( )* call on the InputStream associated with this socket will block for only this amount of time. If the timeout expires, a *java.io.InterruptedIOException* is raised.

For event synchronization, the following operations are blocking:

- Accept (accepting a connection). If no request is waiting, the server process will be suspended until a request for connection arrives.
- Reading from the input stream associated with a data socket. If the amount of data requested is not currently present in the data stream, the reading process will be blocked until a sufficient amount of data has been written into the data stream.

You may have noticed that specific *read* and *write* methods are not provided. The reason is that you are expected to use methods associated with *InputStream* and *OutputStream* classes to perform these operations, as you will soon see.

Figure 4.18 illustrates the program flow in a connection listener and a connection requestor.

Example 4 Figures 4.19 and 4.20 illustrate the basic syntax for stream-mode sockets. *Example4ConnectionAcceptor*, as the name implies, accepts connections by establishing a *Serversocket* object at a specified port (say 12345). *Example4ConnectionRequestor* creates a *Socket* object, specifying as arguments the host name and port number (12345 in this case) of the *Acceptor*. Once the connection has been accepted by the *Acceptor*, a message is written to the socket's data stream by the *Acceptor*. At the *Requestor*, the message is read from the data stream and displayed.

Connection Listener (Server)	Connection Requester (Client)
Create a connection socket and listen for connection requests; accept a connection; create a data socket for reading from or writing to the socket stream; get an input stream for reading to the socket; read from the stream; get an output stream for writing to the socket; write to the stream; close the data socket; close the connection socket.	Create a data socket and request a connection; get an output stream for writing to the socket; write to the stream; get an input stream for reading to the socket; read from the stream; close the data socket.

Figure 4.18 Program flow in a connection listener and a connection requestor.

Figure 4.19 *Example4ConnectionAcceptor.java.*

```
1   import java.net.*;
2   import java.io.*;
3
4   /**
5   *    This example illustrates the basic syntax for stream-mode
6   *    socket.
7   *    @author M. L. Liu
8   */
9   public class Example4ConnectionAcceptor {
10
11  // An application that accepts a connection and receives a message
        using stream-mode socket.
12  // Two command line arguments are expected, in order:
13  // <port number for the the Server socket used in this process>
14  // <message, a string, to send>
15
16    public static void main(String[] args) {
17      if (args.length != 2)
18        System.out.println
19          ("This program requires three command line arguments");
```

(continued next page)

```
20       else {
21         try {
22             int portNo = Integer.parseInt(args[0]);
23             String message = args[1];
24             // instantiates a socket for accepting connection
25             ServerSocket connectionSocket = new ServerSocket(portNo);
26  /**/     System.out.println("now ready accept a connection");
27             // wait to accept a connecion request, at which
28             // time a data socket is created
29             Socket dataSocket = connectionSocket.accept();
30  /**/     System.out.println("connection accepted");
31             // get an output stream for writing to the data socket
32             OutputStream outStream = dataSocket.getOutputStream();
33             // create a PrinterWriter object for character-mode output
34             PrintWriter socketOutput =
35               new PrintWriter(new OutputStreamWriter(outStream));
36             // write a message into the data stream
37             socketOutput.println(message);
38             //The ensuing flush method call is necessary for the data to
39             // be written to the socket data stream before the
40             // socket is closed.
41             socketOutput.flush();
42  /**/     System.out.println("message sent");
43             dataSocket.close( );
44  /**/     System.out.println("data socket closed");
45             connectionSocket.close( );
46  /**/     System.out.println("connection socket closed");
47         } // end try
48         catch (Exception ex) {
49             ex.printStackTrace( );
50         } // end catch
51       } // end else
52     } // end main
53 } // end class
```

Figure 4.20 *Example4ConnectionRequestor.java.*

```
1  import java.net.*;
2  import java.io.*;
3
4  /**
5  *   This example illustrates the basic syntax for stream-mode
6  *   socket.
7  *   @author M. L. Liu
8  */
9  public class Example4ConnectionRequestor {
10
11 // An application that requests a connection and sends a message
      using stream-mode socket.
12 // Two command line arguments are expected:
13 // <host name of the connection accceptor>
14 // <port number of the connection acceptor>
```

(continued next page)

```
15       public static void main(String[] args) {
16          if (args.length != 2)
17            System.out.println
18            ("This program requires two command line arguments");
19          else {
20            try {
21               InetAddress acceptorHost = InetAddress.getByName(args[0]);
22               int acceptorPort = Integer.parseInt(args[1]);
23               // instantiates a data socket
24               Socket mySocket = new Socket(acceptorHost, acceptorPort);
25  /**/       System.out.println("Connection request granted");
26               // get an input stream for reading from the data socket
27               InputStream inStream = mySocket.getInputStream();
28               // create a PrinterWriter object for character-mode output
29               BufferedReader socketInput =
30               new BufferedReader(new InputStreamReader(inStream));
31  /**/       System.out.println("waiting to read");
32               // read a line from the data stream
33               String message = socketInput.readLine( );
34  /**/       System.out.println("Message received:");
35               System.out.println("\t" + message);
36               mySocket.close( );
37  /**/       System.out.println("data socket closed");
38            } // end try
39            catch (Exception ex) {
40               ex.printStackTrace( );
41            } // end catch
42          } // end else
43       } // end main
44     } // end class
```

There are a number of noteworthy points in this example:

1. Because we are dealing with a data stream, we can use Java's *PrinterWriter* class (line 15, Figure 4.19) for writing to a socket and *BufferedReader* (line 29, Figure 4.20) for reading from a stream. The methods used with these classes are the same as for writing a line of text to the screen or reading a line of text from the keyboard.

2. Although the example shows the *Acceptor* as the sender of data and the *Requestor* as the receiver, the roles can easily be reversed. In that case the *Requestor* will use *getOutputStream* to write to the socket, while the *Acceptor* will use *getInputStream* to read from the socket.

3. In fact, either process can both read from and write to the stream by invoking both *getInputStream* and *getOutputStream*, as illustrated in Example 5 later in this chapter.

4. Although the example reads and writes one line at a time (using the methods *readLine( )* and *println( )* respectively), it is also possible to read and write part of a line instead (using *read( )* and *print( )* respectively). However, for text-based protocols where messages are exchanged in text, reading and writing one line at a time is the norm.

5. When using *PrinterWriter* to write to a socket stream, it is necessary to use a *flush( )* call to "flush the stream" to ensure that all the data is written from a data buffer into the stream as soon as possible, such as before the socket is abruptly closed (see line 41 in Figure 4.19).

Figure 4.21 shows the event diagram for the execution of the programs of Example 4.

The *ConnectionAcceptor* process starts its execution first. The process is suspended when the blocking *accept* method is called, then unsuspended when it receives the connection request from the *Requestor*. Upon resuming execution, the *Acceptor* writes a message to the socket before closing both the data socket and connection socket.

The execution of the *ConnectionRequestor* proceeds as follows: A *Socket* object is instantiated, and an implicit *connect* request is issued to the *Acceptor*. Although the *connect* request is nonblocking, data exchange via the connection cannot proceed until the connection is *accepted* by the process at the other end. Once the connection is accepted, the process invokes a *read* operation to read a message from the socket. Because the *read* operation is blocking, the process is suspended once again until the data for the message is received, whereupon the process *closes* the socket and processes the data.

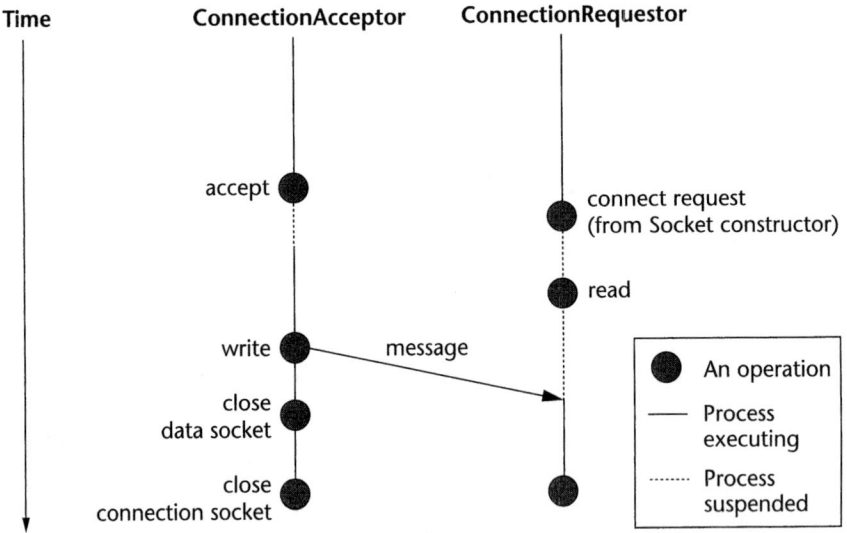

Figure 4.21 *Example4* event diagram.

Diagnostic messages (marked with /**/) have been inserted into the programs so that you may visually observe the progress of the execution of the two programs as they are run.

To allow the separation of the application logic and service logic in the programs, we employ a subclass that hides the details of the data sockets. Figure 4.22 shows the code listing of the *MyStreamSocket* class, which provides methods for reading from and writing to a data socket.

Figure 4.22 *MyStreamSocket.java*, a subclass derived from the Java *Socket* class.

```
1   import java.net.*;
2   import java.io.*;
3
4   /**
5    *   A wrapper class of Socket which contains
6    *   methods for sending and receiving messages.
7    *   @author M. L. Liu
8    */
9   public class MyStreamSocket extends Socket {
10     private Socket socket;
11     private BufferedReader input;
12     private PrintWriter output;
13
14     MyStreamSocket(String acceptorHost,
15       int acceptorPort ) throws SocketException,
16         IOException{
17       socket = new Socket(acceptorHost, acceptorPort );
18       setStreams( );
19     }
20
21     MyStreamSocket(Socket socket) throws IOException {
22       this.socket = socket;
23       setStreams( );
24     }
25
26     private void setStreams( ) throws IOException{
27       // get an input stream for reading from the data socket
28       InputStream inStream = socket.getInputStream();
29       input =
30         new BufferedReader(new InputStreamReader(inStream));
31       OutputStream outStream = socket.getOutputStream();
32       // create a PrinterWriter object for character-mode output
33       output =
34         new PrintWriter(new OutputStreamWriter(outStream));
35     }
36
37     public void sendMessage(String message)
38       throws IOException {
39       output.println(message);
40       //The ensuing flush method call is necessary for the data to
41       // be written to the socket data stream before the
42       // socket is closed.
43       output.flush();
44     } // end sendMessage
```

(continued next page)

```
45
46    public String receiveMessage( )
47      throws IOException {
48      // read a line from the data stream
49      String message = input.readLine( );
50      return message;
51    } //end receiveMessage
52
53    public void close( )
54      throws IOException {
55      socket.close( );
56    }
57  } //end class
```

Example 5 Figures 4.23 and 4.24 are revisions of the source files presented in Figures 4.19 (*ConnectionAcceptor*) and 4.20 (*ConnectionRequestor*), respectively, modified to use the *MyStreamSocket* class instead of the Java class *Socket*.

Figure 4.23 *Example5 ConnectionAcceptor.java.*

```
1   import java.net.*;
2   import java.io.*;
3
4   /**
5    *    This example illustrates the basic syntax for stream-mode
6    *    socket.
7    *    @author M. L. Liu
8    */
9   public class Example5ConnectionAcceptor {
10
11  // An application which receives a message using stream-mode socket
12  // Two command line arguments are expected, in order:
13  // <port number for the the Server socket used in this process>
14  // <message, a string, to send>
15
16    public static void main(String[] args) {
17      if (args.length != 2)
18        System.out.println
19          ("This program requires three command line arguments");
20      else {
21        try {
22          int portNo = Integer.parseInt(args[0]);
23          String message = args[1];
24          // instantiates a socket for accepting connection
25          ServerSocket connectionSocket = new ServerSocket(portNo);
26  /**/    System.out.println("now ready accept a connection");
27          // wait to accept a connecion request, at which
28          // time a data socket is created
```

(continued next page)

```
29              MyStreamSocket dataSocket =
30                 new MyStreamSocket(connectionSocket.accept());
31  /**/        System.out.println("connection accepted");
32              dataSocket.sendMessage(message);
33
34  /**/        System.out.println("message sent");
35              dataSocket.close( );
36  /**/        System.out.println("data socket closed");
37              connectionSocket.close( );
38  /**/        System.out.println("connection socket closed");
39          } // end try
40          catch (Exception ex) {
41             ex.printStackTrace( );
42          } // end catch
43       } // end else
44    } // end main
45 } // end class
```

Figure 4.24 *Example5ConnectionRequestor.java.*

```
1  import java.net.*;
2  import java.io.*;
3
4  /**
5  *   This example illustrates the basic syntax for stream-mode
6  *   socket.
7  *   @author M. L. Liu
8  */
9  public class Example5ConnectionRequestor {
10
11 // An application which sends a message using stream-mode socket.
12 // Two command line arguments are expected:
13 //
14 // <host name of the connection accceptor>
15 // <port number of the connection accceptor>
16
17   public static void main(String[] args) {
18      if (args.length != 2)
19         System.out.println
20         ("This program requires two command line arguments");
21      else {
22         try {
23            String acceptorHost = args[0];
24            int acceptorPort = Integer.parseInt(args[1]);
25         // instantiates a data socket
26            MyStreamSocket mySocket =
27               new MyStreamSocket(acceptorHost, acceptorPort);
28 /**/ System.out.println("Connection request granted");
29            String message = mySocket.receiveMessage( );
30 /**/ System.out.println("Message received:");
```

(continued next page)

```
31                  System.out.println("\t" + message);
32                  mySocket.close( );
33  /**/ System.out.println("data socket closed");
34          } // end try
35          catch (Exception ex) {
36              ex.printStackTrace( );
37          }
38      } // end else
39    } // end main
40  } // end class
```

Using the *MyStreamSocket* subclass, it is much more convenient to perform input and output on the socket, as you will be asked to do in one of the exercises at the end of this chapter.

This concludes our introduction to the stream-mode socket API. We will revisiting this facility in the next chapter.

4.5 Sockets with Nonblocking I/O Operations

As mentioned, the APIs introduced in this chapter are basic socket APIs, which provide asynchronous (nonblocking) *send* operations and synchronous (blocking) *receive* operations. Using these APIs, a process that reads from a socket is subject to blocking. To maximize concurrency, threads can be used so that a read operation is performed in a waiting thread while a separate thread remains active for processing other tasks. However, in some applications that require extensive use of threads, the overhead incurred can be detrimental to the performance or, worse yet, the viability, of the application. Alternatively, there are socket APIs that provide nonblocking I/O operations. Using such an API, neither *send* nor *receive* will result in blocking, and, as explained in Chapter 2, it is necessary for the receiving process to use a listener to be notified of the arrival of the data. Asynchronous sockets are available with Winsock, and, as of version 1.4, Java also provides a new I/O package, **java.nio (NIO)**, that offers sockets with nonblocking I/O operations. The syntax for the new package is considerably more complex than that for the basic API. Interested readers are encouraged to look into [java.sun.com, 6].

4.6 Secure Socket API

Although the details are beyond the scope of this book, you should be aware that **secure socket** APIs exist, which are socket APIs enhanced with data security measures.

Using conventional socket APIs, data is transmitted as bit streams over network links. The bit streams, if intercepted by means of tools such as network protocol analyzers, can be decoded by someone who has knowledge of the data rep-

A protocol analyzer is a tool that allows data packets to be captured and analyzed for network troubleshooting.

THE JAVA SECURE SOCKET EXTENSIONS

Dr. Dobb's Journal, February 2001
Authenticating and encrypting connections
By Kirby W. Angell
Reprinted with the permission of *Dr. Dobb's Journal*

You sit at your computer, marveling at your distributed Java application. Your code creates *Socket* and *ServerSocket* objects like crazy, sending data across the Internet. It is a sight to behold—until you realize that anyone can intercept the data being read, masquerade as one of your applications, and fill your system with bogus data.

As soon as you start looking into authenticating and encrypting the connections between applications, you find that you have entered a complex area. When dealing with encryption, you have to worry about many things—not just which algorithm you plan to use. Attacks to your system can involve the algorithm, protocol, passwords, and other factors you might not even consider.

Luckily, most of the messy details of authenticating and encrypting traffic between two socket-based applications have been worked out in the Secure Sockets Layer (SSL) specification. Sun Microsystems has an implementation of SSL in its Java Secure Socket Extension (JSSE; http://java.sun.com/security/) package. JSSE and the Java Run-Time Environment (JRE) provide most of the tools necessary to implement SSL within your Java application if your Java app is a client communicating with HTTPS servers. Since the JSSE documentation and tools are mostly geared toward this end, it takes some work to figure out how to use the toolset within an application where you need to create both the client and server sides of the connection.

resentation of the data exchanged. Hence it is risky to use sockets to transmit sensitive data, such as credit information and authentication data. To address the problem, protocols have been introduced to secure the data transmitted using socket APIs. Some of the well-known protocols are described in the following paragraphs.

The Secure Socket Layer

Secure Sockets Layer (SSL) [developer.netscape.com, 2] *was* a protocol developed by the Netscape Communications Corporation for transmitting private documents over the Internet. (This description of SSL is based on the definition provided by http://webopedia.internet.com.) An SSL API has methods or functions similar to the socket API, except that data is **encrypted** before it is transmitted over an SSL connection. SSL is supported by modern browsers. When run with the SSL protocol selected, these browsers will transmit encrypted data using the SSL socket API. Many Web sites also use the protocol to obtain confidential user information, such as credit card numbers. By convention, the URL of a Web page that requires an SSL connection starts with **https:** instead of **http:**.

The Java Secure Socket Extension

The Java™ Secure Socket Extension (JSSE) is a set of Java packages that enable secure Internet communications. It implements a version of SSL and TLS (Transport Layer Security) [ietf.org, 5] protocols and includes functionalities for data encryption, server authentication, message integrity, and optional client authentication. Using JSSE [java.sun.com, 3; Angell, 4], developers can provide for the secure passage of data between two processes.

The JSEE API features syntax similar to the Java connection-oriented socket API that we introduced in this chapter.

Summary

In this chapter, we introduced the basic socket application program interface for interprocess communication.

The socket API is widely available as a programming facility for IPC at a relatively low level of abstraction.

Using the Java socket APIs, we introduced two types of sockets:

- The datagram sockets, which use the User Datagram Protocol (UDP) at the transport layer to send and receive discrete data packets known as datagrams.
- The stream-mode socket, which uses the Transport Layer Protocol (TCP) at the transport layer to send and receive data using a data stream.

Key points of the Java datagram socket API:

- It supports both connectionless communication and connection-oriented communication.
- Each process must create a *DatagramSocket* object to send or receive datagrams.
- Each datagram is encapsulated in a *DatagramPacket* object.
- In connectionless communication, a datagram socket can be used to send to or receive from any other datagram socket; in connection-oriented communication, a datagram socket can only be used to send to or receive from the datagram socket attached to the other end of the connection.
- Data for a datagram are placed in a byte array; if a byte array of insufficient length is provided by a receiver, the data received will be truncated.
- The *receive* operation is blocking; the *send* operation is nonblocking.

Key points of the Java stream-mode socket API:

- It supports connection-oriented communication only.

- A process plays the role of connection acceptor and creates a connection socket using the *ServerSocket* class. It then accepts connection requests from other processes.

- A process (a connection requestor) creates a data socket using the *Socket* class, and a connection request is implicitly issued to the ConnectionRequestor.

- When a connection request is granted, the ConnectionAcceptor creates a data socket, of the *Socket* class, to send and receive data to/from the connection requestor. The ConnectionRequestor can also send and/or receive data to/from the ConnectionAcceptor using its data socket.

- The *receive* (read) and the connection-*accept* operations are blocking; the *send* (write) operation is nonblocking.

- The reading and writing of data into the socket of the data stream are decoupled: they can be performed in different data units.

There are socket APIs that provide nonblocking I/O operations, including Winsock and Java NIOS. The syntax of these APIs is more complex, and the use of a listener is needed to handle *blocking* operations.

Data transmitted over a network using sockets are subject to security risks. For sensitive data, it is recommended that secure sockets be employed. Available secure socket APIs include the Secure Socket Layer (SSL) and Java's Secure Socket Extension (JSSE). Secure socket APIs have methods that are similar to the connection-oriented socket APIs.

Exercises

1. In your own words, write a few sentences to explain each of the following terms:

   a. API (application programmer's interface)

   b. The socket API

   c. Winsock

   d. Connection-oriented communication compared with connectionless communication

2. Process 1 sends three messages successively to process 2.
   What is the possible order in which the messages may arrive at process 2 if

   a. connectionless socket is used to send each message?

   b. connection-oriented socket is used to send each message?

3. In the *setSoTimeout* method for the *datagramSocket* (or other socket classes), what happens if the timeout period is set to 0? Does it mean that the timeout happens immediately (since the period is 0)? Consult the online Java API to find the answer.

4. Write a Java code fragment that may appear in a main method to open a datagram socket for receiving a datagram of up to 100 bytes, timing out in 5 seconds. If a timeout does occur, a message "timed out on receive" should be displayed on screen.

5. This exercise guides you through experiments with connectionless datagram socket using code sample *Example1*.

   As a start, it is recommended that you run both programs on one machine, referring to the host name of that machine as "localhost." For example, you may enter the command "java Example1Sender localhost 12345 hello" to execute *Example1Sender*. Optionally, you may repeat the exercises by running the programs on separate machines, assuming that you have access to such machines.

   a. Compile the .*java* files. Then run the two programs by (i) executing the receiver, then (ii) executing the sender, taking care to specify the appropriate command-line arguments in each case. The message sent should not exceed the maximum length allowed in the receiver (that is, 10 characters). Describe the outcome of the run. *Note*: To help you track the run outcomes, it is recommended that you execute each application in a separate window on your screen, preferably sizing and positioning the windows so that you can see the displays side by side.

   b. Rerun the applications from part a, this time reversing the order of steps (i) and (ii). Describe and explain the outcome.

   c. Repeat part a, this time sending a message of length greater than the maximum length allowed (say "01234567890"). Describe and explain the outcome.

Note: To help you track the run outcomes, it is recommended that you execute each application in a separate window on your screen, preferably sizing and positioning the windows so that you can see the displays side by side.

d. Add code in the receiving process so that the blocking for *receive* will time out after 5 seconds. Compile. Start the receiver process but not the sender process. What is the outcome? Describe and explain.

e. Modify the original *Example1* code so that the receiver loops indefinitely to repeatedly receive then display the data received. Recompile. Then (i) start the receiver, (ii) execute the sender, sending a message "message1", and (iii) in another window, start another instance of the sender, sending a message "message2." Does the receiver receive both messages? Capture the code and output. Describe and explain the outcome.

f. Modify the original *Example1* code so that the sender uses the same socket to send the same message to two different receivers. Start the two receivers first, then the sender. Does each receiver receive the message? Capture the code and output. Describe and explain the outcome.

g. Modify the original *Example1* code so that the sender uses two different sockets to send the same message to two different receivers. Start the two receivers first, then the sender. Does each receiver receive the message? Capture the code and output. Describe and explain the outcome.

h. Modify the code from the last step so that the sender sends repeatedly, suspending itself for 3 seconds between each send. (Recall that in Chapter 1 we saw how to use *Thread.sleep( )* to suspend a process for a specified time interval.) Modify the receiver so that it loops to repeatedly receive then display the data received. Compile and run the programs for a few minutes before terminating the programs (by entering the keystroke sequence "control-c"). Describe and explain the outcome.

i. Modify the original *Example1* code so that the sender also receives a message from the receiver. You should need only one socket in each process. Compile, run, and turn in your code; be sure to modify your comments accordingly.

6. This exercise guides you through the experiment with connectionless datagram socket via code sample *Example2*.

a. Draw a UML class diagram to illustrate the relationship between the classes *DatagramSocket*, *MyDatagramSocket*, *Example2SenderReceiver*, and *Example2ReceiverSender*. You need not supply the attributes and methods of the *DatagramSocket* class.

b. Compile the .java files. Then start *Example2ReceiverSender*, followed by *Example2SenderReceiver*. An example of the commands for running the programs is:

```
java Example2ReceiverSender localhost 20000 10000 msg1
java Example2SenderReceiver localhost 10000 20000 msg2
```

Describe the outcome. Why is the order of the execution of the two processes important?

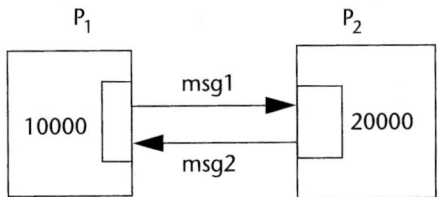

c. Modify the code so that the *senderReceiver* process sends then receives repeatedly, suspending itself for 3 seconds between each iteration. Recompile and repeat the run. Do the same with the *receiverSender*. Compile and run the programs for a few minutes before terminating the programs (by entering the keystroke sequence "control-c"). Describe and explain the outcome.

7. This exercise guides you through experiments with a connection-oriented datagram socket using code sample *Example3*.

a. Compile and run the source files for *Example3*. Describe the outcome of the run. Sample commands for running the two programs are

```
java Example3Receiver localhost 20000 10000 msg1
java Example3Sender localhost 10000 20000 msg2
```

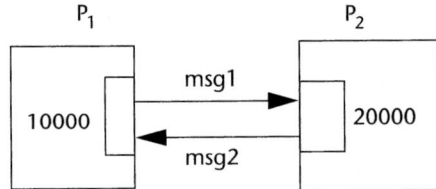

b. Modify the code in *Example3Sender.java* so that the *connect* method call specifies a port number different from the port number of the receiver's socket. (You can do so simply by adding 1 to the receiver port number in the connect method call.) When you rerun the programs (after recompiling the source files) the sender process will now attempt to send datagrams whose destination address does not match the address specified with the receiver's connection. Describe and explain the outcome of the run.

c. Rerun the original programs. This time start a second sender process, specifying the same receiver address. Sample commands for starting the three processes are

```
java Example3Receiver localhost 1000 2000 msg1
java Example3Sender localhost 2000 1000 msg2
java Example3Sender localhost 2000 3000 msg3
```

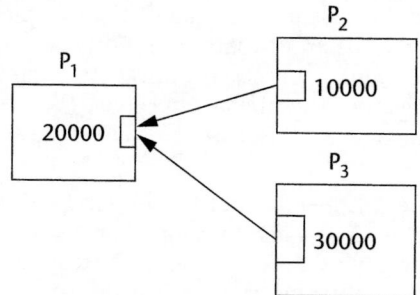

Start the three processes in quick succession so that the second sender process will try to establish a connection to the receiver process when the latter's socket is already connected to that of the first sender process. Describe and explain the outcome of the run.

8. This exercise guides you through experiments with a connection-oriented stream-mode socket using code samples *Example4* and *Example5*.

a. Compile and run *Example4*.java*. (*Note*: We use * as a wildcard character, so that Example4*.java refers to the files whose names start with "Example4" and end with ".java.") Start the *Acceptor* first, then the *Requestor*. Sample commands to do so are:

```
Java Example4ConnectionAcceptor 12345 Good-day!
Java Example4ConnectionRequestor localhost 12345
```

Describe and explain the outcome.

b. Repeat the last step but reverse the order of the programs' execution:

```
Java Example4ConnectionRequestor localhost 12345
Java Example4ConnectionAcceptor 12345 Good-day!
```

Describe and explain the outcome.

c. Add a time delay of 5 seconds in the *ConnectionAcceptor* process just before the message is written to the socket, then repeat part a. This will have the effect of keeping the *Requestor* blocked on reading for 5 extra seconds so that you can observe the blocking visually. Show a trace of the output of the processes. Do the diagnostic messages displayed on the screen agree with the event diagram in Figure 4.21?

d. Modify *Example4*.java* so that the *ConnectionAcceptor* uses *print( )* to write one character at a time to the socket before issuing a *printlin( )* to write an end-of-line. Recompile and run the programs. Is the message received in its entirety? Explain.

e. Compile and run *Example5*.java*. Start the *Acceptor* first, then the *Requestor*. Sample commands to do so are

```
Java Example5ConnectionAcceptor 12345 Good-day!
Java Example5ConnectionRequestor localhost 12345
```

Since the code is logically equivalent to Example4*, the outcome should be the same as that of part a. Modify *Example5*.java* so that the *ConnectionAcceptor* process becomes the message sender and the *ConnectionRequestor* the message receiver. (You may wish to remove the diagnostic messages.) Hand in an event diagram, the program listings, and run outcome.

f. Modify *Example5*.java* so that the *ConnectionRequestor* sends a replying message to the *ConnectionAcceptor* after receiving a message from the *Acceptor*. The replying message should be displayed by the *Acceptor*. Hand in an event diagram, the program listings, and run outcome.

9. Are there socket APIs that provide nonblocking I/O (read and write) operations? Name some. What are the advantages of using such an API over using the basic socket APIs presented in this chapter?

10. Look into the Java NIOS in JDK1.4. Write a report describing how nonblocking socket I/O can be used in a Java program. Provide code samples to illustrate your description.

11. What is a secure socket API? Name some of the secure socket protocols and an API that provides secure sockets. Write a report describing how a secure socket can be used in a Java program. Provide code samples to illustrate your description.

References

1. Java 2 Platform v1.4 API Specification, *http://java.sun.com/j2se/1.4/docs/api/index.html*

2. Introduction to SSL, *http://developer.netscape.com/docs/manuals/security/sslin/contents.htm*

3. Java(TM) Secure Socket Extension, *http://java.sun.com/products/jsse/*

4. Kirby W. Angell, "The Java Secure Socket Extensions," *Dr. Dobb's Journal*, February 2001. *http://www.ddj.com/articles/2001/0102/0102a/0102a.htm?topic=security*

5. The TLS Protocol, RFC2246, *http://www.ietf.org/rfc/rfc2246.txt*

6. New I/O APIs, *http://java.sun.com/j2se/1.4/docs/guide/nio/index.html, java.sun.com*

CHAPTER **5**

The Client-Server Paradigm

In this chapter we will explore the client-server paradigm in detail. We will also make use of our knowledge of socket APIs to look at the implementation of sample client-server applications.

5.1 Background

The term *client-server* has multiple meanings in computing. It can refer to a **network architecture** where the computers on a network function in different roles in order to share resources. In a **client-server architecture**, a computer is called a *server* if it is dedicated to managing resources such as printers or files so that other computers, called *clients*, can access those resources through the server. The client-server architecture, although related to the client-server paradigm, is not the subject of this chapter.

In distributed computing, the client-server paradigm refers to a model for network applications where processes play one of two different roles: a **server process**, also called a **server** for short, is dedicated to managing access to some network service, while **client processes**, called **clients** for short, access the server to obtain a network service. Note that in client-server architecture, the terms *client* and *server* refer to **computers**, while in the client-server distributed computing paradigm, the terms refer to **processes**. In this book, when the term *client-server* is used, it is used to refer to the distributed-computing paradigm.

Figure 5.1 illustrates the concept of the client-server model. A **server process** runs on a network-connected computer, which we will refer to as the **server host**, to manage a network service provided by that host. Note that it is possi-

> **Network architecture** refers to how computers are interconnected in a network. The term is not to be confused with the abstract network architecture models (the OSI model and the Internet model), which we explored in Chapter 1.

133

ble for the server host to provide other network services that are managed by other server processes. A user, typically one using another computer, which we will call the **client host**, makes use of a **client process** to access a particular service. It is possible for other client processes (possibly for other services) to run on the client host at the same time, but the appropriate client process must be used to access a particular service.

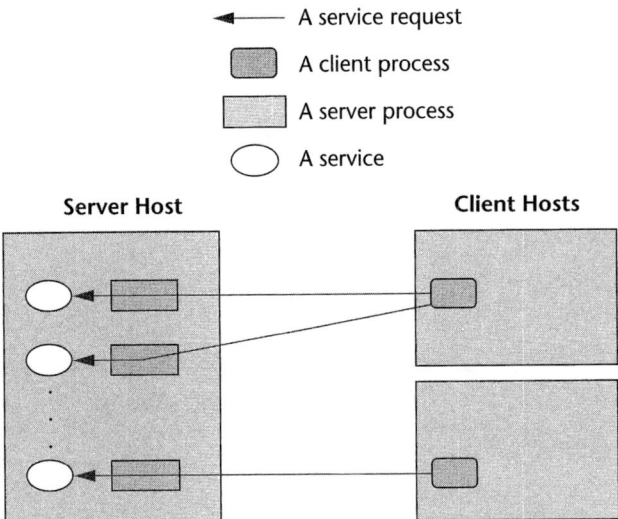

Figure 5.1 The client-server distributed computing paradigm.

The client-server model is designed for providing network services, which were, and still are, the most popular application of distributed computing. By *network service* we mean a service provided to allow network users to share resources. Such resources may be as trivial as the time of day or as complex as the files in the file system of the server host or data from a database system. Over the years, many such network services have been standardized on the Internet: **telnet**, which allows remote logon to a server host; *ftp*, for sending and receiving files from a server host; *Daytime*, which provides a timestamp obtained from a server host; and the *World Wide Web*, for fetching web contents via a server host.

5.2 Client-Server Paradigm Issues

Whereas the concept of the paradigm is simple, in actual implementation there are a number of issues that must be addressed. These issues are discussed in this section.

A Service Session

In the context of the client-server model, we will use the term **session** to refer to the interaction between the server and one client. As shown in Figure 5.1, the service managed by a server may be accessed by multiple clients who want to use the service, sometimes concurrently. Each client, when serviced by the server, engages in a separate and independent session with the server, during which the client conducts a dialog with the server until the client has obtained the service it desires.

Figure 5.2 illustrates the execution flow of the server process. Once started, a network server process runs indefinitely, looping continuously to accept requests for sessions from clients. For each client, the server conducts a service session.

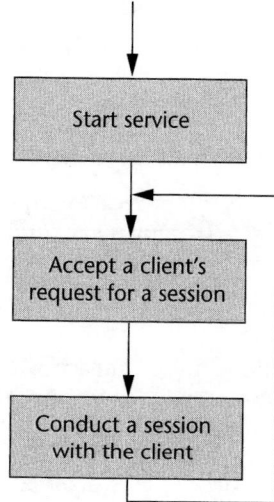

Figure 5.2 The execution flow of the server process.

The Protocol for a Service

A protocol is needed to specify the rules that must be observed by the client and the server during a session of the service. Such rules include specifications on matters such as (1) how the service is to be located, (2) the sequence of inter-process communications, and (3) the representation and interpretation of data exchanged.

Locating the Service

On a UNIX system, you may look at a file named "services" in the /etc/directory, i.e., /etc/services to look up these port assignments.

A mechanism must be available to enable a client process to locate a server for a given service. In the simplest scheme, the service location is static and can be identified using the address of the server process, in terms of the host name and protocol port number assigned to the server process. This is the scheme used for Internet services, where each Internet service is assigned to a specific port number. In particular, a well-known service such as FTP, HTTP, or telnet is assigned a default port number that is reserved on each Internet host for that service. For example, the FTP service is assigned two port numbers: TCP 20 and 21. HTTP is assigned to the TCP port 80.

At a higher level of abstraction, a service may be identified using a logical name registered with a directory or a registry. The logical name will need to be mapped to the physical location of the server process. If the mapping is performed at run time (that is, when a client process is run), then it is possible for the service's location to be dynamic, in which case the service is said to be **location transparent**.

Interprocess Communications and Event Synchronization

In the client-server model, the interaction of the processes follows a **request-response** pattern (see Figure 5.3). During a service session, a client makes a request to the server, which replies with a response. The client may make a subsequent request, followed by a reply from the server. This pattern may repeat indefinitely until the session is concluded.

For each request issued, a client must wait for the reply from the server before it can proceed further. For example, one of the simplest network services is the *Daytime* service, whereby a client process simply obtains a timestamp (the time of day on the server host) from the server process. Translated into plain English, the dialog during a service session of this protocol proceeds as follows:

Client: Hello, <client address> here. May I have a timestamp please?
Server: Here it is: (timestamp follows).

Likewise, the dialog in a World Wide Web session proceeds as follows:

Client: Hello, <client address> here.
Server: Okay. I am a Web server and speak protocol HTTP 1.0.
Client: Great, please get me the Web page index.html at the root of your document tree.
Server: Okay, here's what's in the page (contents follow).

The dialog in each session follows a pattern prescribed in the protocol specified for the service. For example, the Internet *Daytime* service supports the protocol specified in Internet RFC 867 [Postel, 1]. Any implementation of either the

Client   **Server**

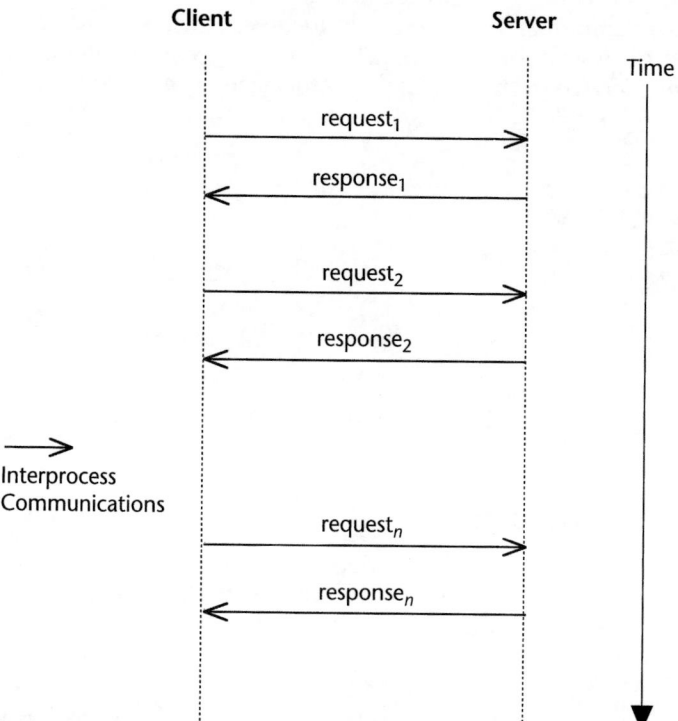

Figure 5.3 The request-response pattern of interprocess communications in the client-server model.

client or server program for this service is expected to adhere to the specification for the protocol, including how the dialog of each session should proceed. Among other things, the specification defines (1) the sequence of interprocess communications between the client and the server, (2) the syntax and semantics of each request and response, and (3) the action expected of each side upon receiving a particular request or response.

Syntax refers to the grammar and spelling of a message. **Semantics** refers to the interpretaton or meanings of the message.

Again, using the simple *Daytime* service as an example, the protocol specifies the following:

■ There is no need for any syntax in the request from the client, as its contact with the server automatically implies a request for time.

■ The response is a timestamp as a character string formatted according to the specification of the protocol. (On a humorous note: This is not unlike a parent who, upon receiving a phone call from an offspring attending college, immediately replies, "Okay, the money is on the way.")

A sequence diagram is a good way to document interprocess communications during a service session. Figure 5.4 shows the sequence diagram for a session of the *Daytime* service. Note that the only message exchanged is the timestamp.

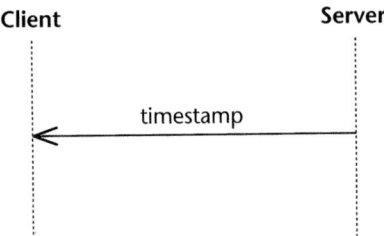

Figure 5.4 The client-server distributed computing paradigm.

Data Representation

The choice of data representation depends on the nature and the needs of the protocol. For a simple service such as *Daytime*, using a text-mode representation is logical, as described in RFC 867 [Postel, 1]:

```
Daytime Syntax

   There is no specific syntax for the daytime. It is recommended that
   it be limited to the ASCII printing characters, space, carriage
   return, and line feed. The daytime should be just one line.

   One popular syntax is
      Weekday, Month Day, Year Time-Zone
      Example:
         Tuesday, February 22, 1982 17:37:43-PST
```

In this specification, the formatting, or syntax, of the timestamp is left up to the implementer.

Choosing a text-mode data representation for a protocol has the advantage of allowing the dialog to be readable by humans, as standard text-mode I/O can be used to display the data exchanged.

5.3 Software Engineering for a Network Service

We are now ready to look at how to construct the software needed for providing a network service.

There are two sets of software involved: one for the client process, the other for the server process. The set of software needed on the client host to support a service or application, including the client program and its run-time support, is sometimes referred to as the **client-side** software, as opposed to the **server-side** software, which includes the server program and all the run-time support that it needs. Assuming that the protocol is well defined and understood, it is possible for the software of both sides (client and server) to be developed separately and independently.

We will use the *Daytime* protocol as an example of the development process for a network service.

Software Architecture

In Chapter 1 we introduced a three-layer software architecture of network applications, wherein the functionalities of each application can be divided into three layers: presentation, application, and service. Accordingly, the software architecture of an application built using the client-server model, or a client-server application, can be described as follows:

- **Presentation layer.** On the server side, a user interface (UI) is needed to allow the server process to be started; typically, a command-line execution is sufficient. On the client side, a user interface needs to be provided by the client process. Using such an interface, a user on the client host may request the service and receive the response from the server. In our sample code, we will use a text-mode user interface for simplicity, but a graphic user interface (GUI) or a Web page can be used instead. In Chapter 9 we will look at how to build a Web page that accepts and displays data.

- **Application logic layer.** On the server side, the time of day needs to be obtained from the system and sent to the client host. On the client side, the request from the user will need to be forwarded to the server, and the response from the server will need to be displayed to the user.

- **Service layer.** The services required to support the application are (1) on the client side, a readout of the server host's clock (for the timestamp); and (2) on both sides, an IPC mechanism.

The functionalities of the three layers must be present in the combined software. Some of the functionalities belong in the client, some in the server. For large-scale applications, it is advisable to design the software so that the functionalities of the three layers are encapsulated in separate software modules. See Figure 5.5.

Every computer has a clock, and most programming languages provide an API for obtaining a reading of the clock.

Client-Side Software   **Server-Side Software**

Presentation logic	Presentation logic
Application logic	Application logic
Service logic	Service logic

Figure 5.5 Software architecture for a client-server application.

IPC Mechanism

Consider the IPC mechanism that we will use in the application logic; the mechanism chosen will affect how the applications transmit data.

Given the limited repertoire of IPC mechanisms that we have learned so far, we have a choice of using (1) a connectionless datagram socket, (2) a connection-oriented datagram socket, or (3) a stream-mode socket.

With proper software architecture, the details of the IPC mechanism will be completely hidden from the presentation logic and will affect only the application logic in the syntax of the IPC commands.

Let's start by looking at a code sample that uses the connectionless datagram socket. We will subsequently see how our software architecture allows us to adapt the software to the connection-oriented stream-mode socket API.

Do not be alarmed by the large number of Java classes used in the example. Each class is straightforward and represents a software module that implements a layer of the logic in the software architecture.

Daytime Client-Server Using Connectionless Datagram Socket

Client-Side Software

Presentation Logic Figure 5.6 presents the class *DaytimeClient1.java*, which encapsulates the client-side presentation logic; that is, it provides the interface for a user of the client process. You will note that the code in this class is concerned solely with obtaining input (the server address) from the user and displaying the output (the timestamp) to the user. To obtain the timestamp, a method call to a "helper" class, *DaytimeClientHelper1.java*, is issued. This method hides the details of the application logic and the underlying service logic. As a result, the programmer of *DaytimeClient1.java* need not be aware of which socket types are used for the IPC.

Application Logic The *DaytimeClientHelper1.java* class (Figure 5.7) encapsulates the client-side application logic. This module performs the IPC for sending a request and receiving a response using a subclass of the *DatagramSocket*, *myClientDatagramSocket*. Note that the details of using datagram sockets are hidden from this module. In particular, this module does not need to deal with the byte array that carries the payload data.

Service Logic The *MyClientDatagramSocket.java* (Figure 5.8) class provides the details of IPC service, in this case using the datagram socket API.

There are at least two significant advantages to separating the three layers of logic into different software modules:

▪ Each module can be developed by people with special skills to focus on a module for which they have expertise. Software engineers who are skilled in user interface may concentrate on developing the modules for the presentation logic, while those specializing in application logic and service logic may focus on developing the other modules.

▪ The separation allows modifications to be made to the logic at one layer without requiring changes to be made at the other layers. For example, the user interface can be changed from text mode to graphical mode without necessitating changes in the application logic or the service logic. Likewise, changes made in the application logic should be transparent to the presentation layer.

Figure 5.9 is a UML class diagram describing the classes used in the implementation of the *DaytimeClient1* program.

Server-Side Software

Presentation Logic Typically, there is very little presentation logic on the server side. In this case, the only user input is for the server port, which, for simplicity, is handled using a command-line argument.

Application Logic The *DaytimeServer1.java* class (Figure 5.10) encapsulates the server-side application logic. This module executes in a forever loop, waiting for a request from a client and then conducting a service session for that client. The module performs the IPC for receiving a request and sending a response using a subclass of the *DatagramSocket*, *myServerDatagramSocket*. Note that the details of using datagram sockets are hidden from this module. In particular, this module does not need to deal with the byte array for carrying the payload data.

Service Logic The *MyServerDatagramSocket* class (Figure 5.11) provides the details of the IPC service, in this case using the datagram socket API. This class is similar to the *MyClientDatagram* class, with the exception that the *receiveMessage* method returns an object of the *DatagramMessage* class (Figure 5.12), which contains the sender's address in addition to the message itself. The sender's address is needed by the server in order for the server to send a request to the client. This is an idiosyncrasy of the connectionless socket: The server has no way of knowing where to send a reply otherwise. The methods employed to obtain the sender's address from a datagram received are *getAddress* and *getHost*, whose descriptions are shown in Table 5.1. These two methods were not mentioned in the last chapter when the datagram socket API was introduced.

Table 5.1 The *getAddress* and *getPort* Methods of DatagramPacket Class

Method	Description
public InetAddress getAddress( )	Returns the IP address of the remote host from a socket from which the datagram was received.
public int getPort( )	Returns the port number on the remote host from a socket from which the datagram was received.

Figure 5.6 *DaytimeClient1.java.*

```
1  import java.io.*;
2
3
4  /**
5  * This module contains the presentation logic of a DaytimeClient.
6  * @author M. L. Liu
7  */
8  public class DaytimeClient1 {
9    public static void main(String[] args) {
10     InputStreamReader is = new InputStreamReader(System.in);
11     BufferedReader br = new BufferedReader(is);
12     try {
13       System.out.println("Welcome to the Daytime client.\n" +
14         "What is the name of the server host?");
15       String hostName = br.readLine( );
16       if (hostName.length() == 0) // if user did not enter a name
17         hostName = "localhost"; // use the default host name
18       System.out.println("What is the port number of the server
                  host?");
19       String portNum = br.readLine();
20       if (portNum.length () == 0)
21         portNum = "13"; // default port number
22         System.out.println("Here is the timestamp received from the server"
23           + DaytimeClientHelper1.getTimestamp(hostName, portNum));
24     } // end try
25     catch (Exception ex) {
26       ex.printStackTrace( );
27     } // end catch
28   } // end main
29 } // end class
```

Figure 5.7 *DaytimeClientHelper1.java.*

```
1
2  import java.net.*;
3
4  /**
5   * This class is a module which provides that application logic
6   * for a Daytime Client.
7   * @author M. L. Liu
8   */
9  public class DaytimeClientHelper1 {
10
11    public static String getTimestamp(String hostName,
12       String portNum) {
13
14      String timestamp = "";
15      try {
16        InetAddress serverHost = InetAddress.getByName(hostName);
17        int serverPort = Integer.parseInt(portNum);
18        // instantiates a datagram socket for both sending
19        // and receiving data
20        MyDatagramSocket mySocket = new MyDatagramSocket();
21        mySocket.sendMessage( serverHost, serverPort, "");
22        // now receive the timestamp
23        timestamp = mySocket.receiveMessage();
24        mySocket.close( );
25
26      } // end try
27      catch (Exception ex) {
28        ex.printStackTrace( );
29      } // end catch
30      return timestamp;
31    } // end main
32  } // end class
```

*It is better software practice for this method to throw an exception in case of errors caused by the socket method calls; this is not done here to avoid the complexity of creating yet another class for the exceptions.

Figure 5.8 *MyClientDatagramSocket.java.*

```
1  import java.net.*;
2  import java.io.*;
3
4  /**
5  * A subclass of DatagramSocket which contains
6  * methods for sending and receiving messages
7  * @author M. L. Liu
8  */
9  public class MyClientDatagramSocket extends DatagramSocket {
10    static final int MAX_LEN = 100;
11    MyDatagramSocket( ) throws SocketException{
12      super( );
13    }
14
15    MyDatagramSocket(int portNo) throws SocketException{
16      super(portNo);
17    }
18
19    public void sendMessage(InetAddress receiverHost,
20        int receiverPort, String message) throws IOException {
21      byte[ ] sendBuffer = message.getBytes( );
22      DatagramPacket datagram =
23        new DatagramPacket(sendBuffer, sendBuffer.length,
24      receiverHost, receiverPort);
25      this.send(datagram);
26    } // end sendMessage
27
28    public String receiveMessage( )
29        throws IOException {
30      byte[ ] receiveBuffer = new byte[MAX_LEN];
31      DatagramPacket datagram =
32        new DatagramPacket(receiveBuffer, MAX_LEN);
33      this.receive(datagram);
34      String message = new String(receiveBuffer);
35      return message;
36    } //end receiveMessage
37  } //end class
```

Presentation Logic

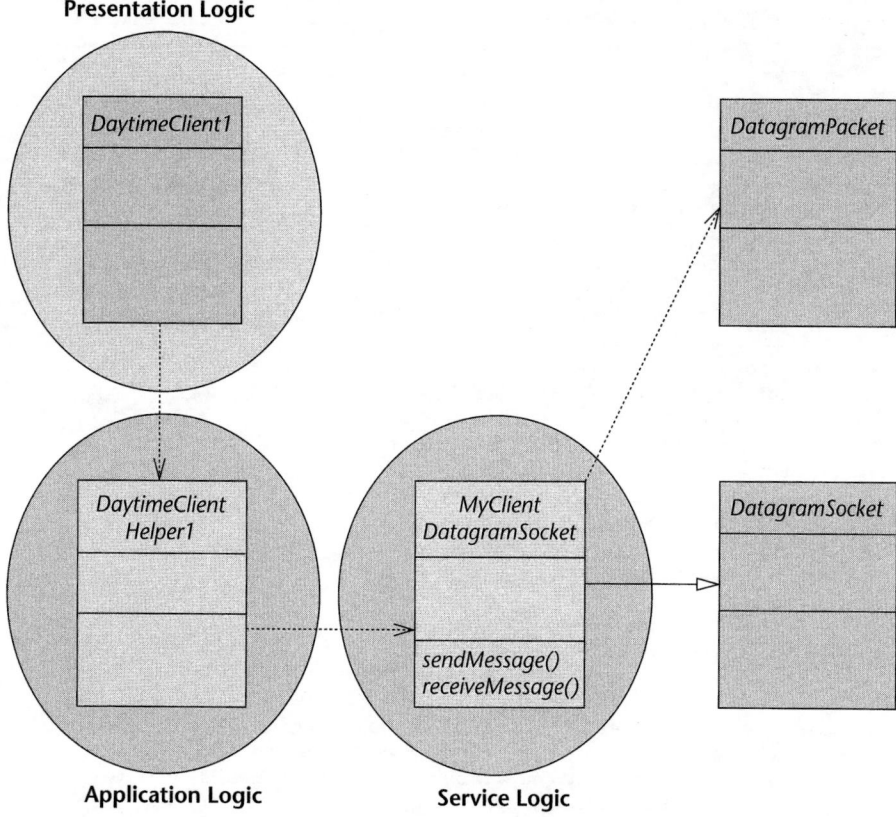

Figure 5.9 UML class diagram for *DayTimeClient1* (not all attributes are shown).

Figure 5.10 *DaytimeServer1.java.*

```
 1  import java.io.*;
 2  import java.util.Date; // for obtaining a timestamp
 3
 4  /**
 5   * This module contains the application logic of a Daytime server
 6   * which uses a connection datagram socket for interprocess
 7     communication.
 8   * A command-line argument is required to specify the server port.
 9   * @author M. L. Liu
10   */
10  public class DaytimeServer1 {
11    public static void main(String[] args) {
12      int serverPort = 13; // default port
13      if (args.length == 1 )
14        serverPort = Integer.parseInt(args[0]);
15      try {
16        // instantiates a datagram socket for both sending
17        // and receiving data
18        MyServerDatagramSocket mySocket =
            new MyServerDatagramSocket(serverPort);
19        System.out.println("Daytime server ready.");
20        while (true) { // forever loop
21          DatagramMessage request =
              mySocket.receiveMessageAndSender();
22          System.out.println("Request received");
23          // The message received is unimportant; it is the sender's
24          // address that we need in order to reply.
25          // Now obtain the timestamp from the local system.
26          Date timestamp = new Date ( );
27          System.out.println("timestamp sent:" +
              timestamp.toString());
28          // Now send the reply to the requestor
29          mySocket.sendMessage(request.getAddress( ),
30            request.getPort( ), timestamp.toString( ));
31        } //end while
32      } // end try
33      catch (Exception ex) {
34        ex.printStackTrace( );
35      } // end catch
36    } // end main
37  } // end class
```

Figure 5.11 *MyServerDatagramSocket.java.*

```
1  import java.net.*;
2  import java.io.*;
3
4
5  /**
6  * A subclass of DatagramSocket which contains
7  * methods for sending and receiving messages
8  * @author M. L. Liu
9  */
10 public class MyServerDatagramSocket extends DatagramSocket {
11    static final int MAX_LEN = 100;
12    MyServerDatagramSocket(int portNo) throws SocketException{
13      super(portNo);
14    }
15    public void sendMessage(InetAddress receiverHost,
16        int receiverPort,
17        String message)
18        throws IOException {
19      byte[ ] sendBuffer = message.getBytes( );
20      DatagramPacket datagram =
21        new DatagramPacket(sendBuffer, sendBuffer.length,
22      receiverHost, receiverPort);
23      this.send(datagram);
24    } // end sendMessage
25
26    public String receiveMessage( )
27        throws IOException {
28      byte[ ] receiveBuffer = new byte[MAX_LEN];
29      DatagramPacket datagram =
30        new DatagramPacket(receiveBuffer, MAX_LEN);
31      this.receive(datagram);
32      String message = new String(receiveBuffer);
33      return message;
34    } //end receiveMessage
35
36    public DatagramMessage receiveMessageAndSender( )
37        throws IOException {
38      byte[ ] receiveBuffer = new byte[MAX_LEN];
39      DatagramPacket datagram =
40        new DatagramPacket(receiveBuffer, MAX_LEN);
41      this.receive(datagram);
42      // create a DatagramMessage object, to contain message
43      // received and sender's address
44      DatagramMessage returnVal = new DatagramMessage( );
45      returnVal.putVal(new String(receiveBuffer),
46        datagram.getAddress( ),
47        datagram.getPort( ));
48      return returnVal;
49    } //end receiveMessage
50 } //end class
```

Figure 5.12 *DatagramMessage.java*

```
1   import java.net.*;
2   /**
3    * A class to use with MyServerDatagramSocket for
4    * returning a message and the sender's address
5    * @author M. L. Liu
6    */
7   public class DatagramMessage{
8      private String message;
9      private InetAddress senderAddress;
10     private int senderPort;
11     public void putVal(String message, InetAddress addr, int port) {
12        this.message = message;
13        this.senderAddress = addr;
14        this.senderPort = port;
15     }
16
17     public String getMessage( ) {
18        return this.message;
19     }
20
21     public InetAddress getAddress( ) {
22        return this.senderAddress;
23     }
24
25     public int getPort( ) {
26        return this.senderPort;
27     }
28  } // end class
```

Figure 5.13 is a UML class diagram describing the classes used in the implementation of the *DaytimeServer1* program.

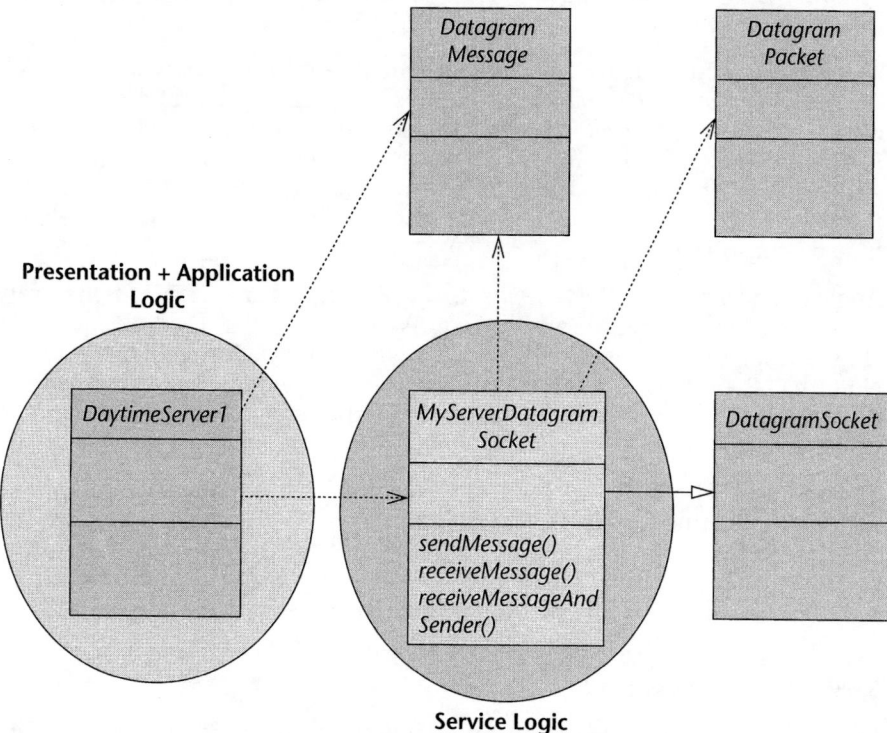

Figure 5.13 UML class diagram for *DayTimeServer1* (not all attributes are shown).

Daytime Client-Server Using Stream-Mode Socket

In the previous section we have seen how the *Daytime* service can be implemented using the connectionless datagram socket for the IPC mechanism.

Suppose we wish to implement the same service using the connection-oriented datagram socket instead. Since this change primarily affects the service logic only, we should need to make extensive modifications only to the Java classes at the service logic layer, as we shall see in this section. The application logic, specifically the *Helper* class, will need to be adjusted accordingly.

Client-Side Software

Presentation Logic Figure 5.14 presents the Java class *DaytimeClient2*, which is the same as *DaytimeClient1* except for a change in the name of the "helper" class, *DaytimeClientHelper2*. (In fact, *DaytimeClient2* can be exactly the same as *DaytimeClient1* if we simply replace the body of the class *DaytimeClientHelper1* with that of *DaytimeClientHelper2*.) The *getTimestamp* method in *DaytimeClientHelper2* now uses the stream-mode socket API, but the details are transparent to *DaytimeClient2*.

Application Logic The *DaytimeClientHelper2* class (Figure 5.15), which encapsulates the client-side application logic, is similar to the *DaytimeClientHelper1* class, except that a stream-mode socket is used instead of a datagram socket. Note that there is now no need for the client to send a null message (which bears the return address) for a request, since the return address is encapsulated in the connection.

Service Logic The *MyStreamSocket* class (Figure 5.17) provides the details of the IPC service, in this case using the stream-mode socket API. The *MyStreamSocket* class is a **wrapper class** in that it "wraps around" the Socket class (that is, it contains an instance variable that is a reference to a *Socket* object) and provides methods for sending a message to and receiving a message from a socket.

Server-Side Software

Presentation Logic The code for *DaytimeServer2* is identical to that of *DaytimeServer1*. The only user input is for the server port, which, for simplicity, is handled using a command-line argument.

Application Logic The code for *DaytimeServer2* (Figure 5.16) uses the stream-mode socket API to accept a connection. The Socket reference returned (for the data socket) is then used to instantiate a *MyStreamSocket* object, whose *sendMessage* method is employed to transmit a timestamp to the client at the other end of the connection.

Service Logic The same wrapper class used for the client, *MyStreamSocket* (Figure 5.17), is used in our server as well, as it contains the necessary methods for stream-mode IPC. Note that a different class or even mechanism for providing the service logic is possible if the server software were developed independently of the client software.

To reiterate, in switching to use the stream-mode socket API, the only modules that required significant modifications are those that provide the service logic on either side.

Figure 5.14 *DaytimeClient2.java.*

```
1   import java.io.*;
2
3
4   /**
5   * This module contains the presentaton logic of a DaytimeClient.
6   * @author M. L. Liu
7   */
8   public class DaytimeClient2 {
9     public static void main(String[ ] args) {
10      InputStreamReader is = new InputStreamReader(System.in);
11      BufferedReader br = new BufferedReader(is);
12      try {
13        System.out.println("Welcome to the Daytime client.\n" +
14          "What is the name of the server host?");
15        String hostName = br.readLine();
16        if (hostName.length( ) == 0) // if user did not enter a name
17          hostName = "localhost"; // use the default host name
18        System.out.println("Enter the port number of the server host.");
19        String portNum = br.readLine();
20        if (portNum.length() == 0)
21          portNum = "13"; // default port number
22        System.out.println("The timestamp received from the server"
23          + DaytimeClientHelper2.getTimestamp(hostName, portNum));
24      } // end try
25      catch (Exception ex) {
26        ex.printStackTrace( );
27      } // end catch
28    } // end main
29  } // end class
```

Figure 5.15 *DaytimeClientHelper2.java.*

```
1
2   import java.net.*;
3
4   /**
5    * This class is a module which provides that application logic
6    * for a Daytime Client which uses stream-mode socket for IPC.
7    * @author M. L. Liu
8    */
9   public class DaytimeClientHelper2 {
10
11     public static String getTimestamp(String hostName,
12       String portNum) throws Exception {
13
14
15       String timestamp = "";
16
17       int serverPort = Integer.parseInt(portNum);
18       // instantiates a stream mode socket and wait to make a
19       // connection to the server port
20  /**/ System.out.println("Connection request made");
21       MyStreamSocket mySocket =
22         new MyStreamSocket(hostName, serverPort);
23       // now wait to receive the timestamp
24       timestamp = mySocket.receiveMessage();
25       mySocket.close( ); // disconnect is implied
26       return timestamp;
27     } // end
28   } // end class
```

Figure 5.16 *DaytimeServer2.java*

```
1   import java.io.*;
2   import java.net.*;
3   import java.util.Date; // for obtaining a timestamp
4
5   /**
6    * This module contains the application logic of a Daytime server
7    * which uses connection-oriented datagram socket for IPC.
8    * A command-line argument is required to specify the server port.
9    * @author M. L. Liu
10   */
11  public class DaytimeServer2 {
12    public static void main(String[] args) {
13      int serverPort = 13; // default port
14      if (args.length == 1 )
15        serverPort = Integer.parseInt(args[0]);
```

(continued next page)

```
16      try {
17        // instantiates a stream socket for accepting
18        // connections
19        ServerSocket myConnectionSocket =
20          new ServerSocket(serverPort);
21        System.out.println("Daytime server ready.");
22        while (true) { // forever loop
23          // wait to accept a connection
24  /**/    System.out.println("Waiting for a connection.");
25          MyStreamSocket myDataSocket = new MyStreamSocket
26          (myConnectionSocket.accept( ));
27          // Note: there is no need to read a request - the
28          // request is implicit.
29  /**/    System.out.println("A client has made connection.");
30          Date timestamp = new Date ( );
31  /**/    System.out.println("timestamp sent: "+ timestamp.toString());
32          // Now send the reply to the requestor
33          myDataSocket.sendMessage(timestamp.toString( ));
34          myDataSocket.close( );
35        } //end while
36      } // end try
37      catch (Exception ex) {
38        ex.printStackTrace( );
39      }
40    } //end main
41  } // end class
```

Figure 5.17 *MyStreamSocket.java.*

```
1   import java.net.*;
2   import java.io.*;
3
4   /**
5   * A wrapper class of Socket which contains
6   * methods for sending and receiving messages
7   * @author M. L. Liu
8   */
9   public class MyStreamSocket extends Socket {
10    private Socket socket;
11    private BufferedReader input;
12    private PrintWriter output;
13
14    MyStreamSocket(String acceptorHost,
15        int acceptorPort ) throws SocketException,
16        IOException{
17      socket = new Socket(acceptorHost, acceptorPort );
18      setStreams( );
19
20    }
```

(continued next page)

```
21
22    MyStreamSocket(Socket socket) throws IOException {
23       this.socket = socket;
24       setStreams( );
25    }
26
27    private void setStreams( ) throws IOException{
28       // get an input stream for reading from the data socket
29       InputStream inStream = socket.getInputStream();
30       input =
31          new BufferedReader(new InputStreamReader(inStream));
32       OutputStream outStream = socket.getOutputStream();
33       // create a PrinterWriter object for character-mode output
34       output =
35          new PrintWriter(new OutputStreamWriter(outStream));
36    }
37
38    public void sendMessage(String message)
39         throws IOException {
40       output.println(message);
41       // The ensuing flush method call is necessary for the data to
42       // be written to the socket data stream before the
43       // socket is closed.
44       output.flush();
45    } // end sendMessage
46
47    public String receiveMessage( )
48         throws IOException {
49       // read a line from the data stream
50       String message = input.readLine( );
51       return message;
52    } //end receiveMessage
53
54 } //end class
```

Figures 5.18 and 5.19 are the UML class diagrams describing the class relations in *DaytimeClient2* and *DaytimeServer2*, respectively.

You have now seen a network service based on the *Daytime* protocol implemented in two different ways, one (*Daytime*1) using a connectionless IPC mechanism, the other (*Daytime*2) using a connection-oriented mechanism. A server, such as *DaytimeServer1*, that uses a connectionless IPC mechanism is called a **connectionless server**. One such as *DaytimeServer2* can be called a **connection-oriented server**.

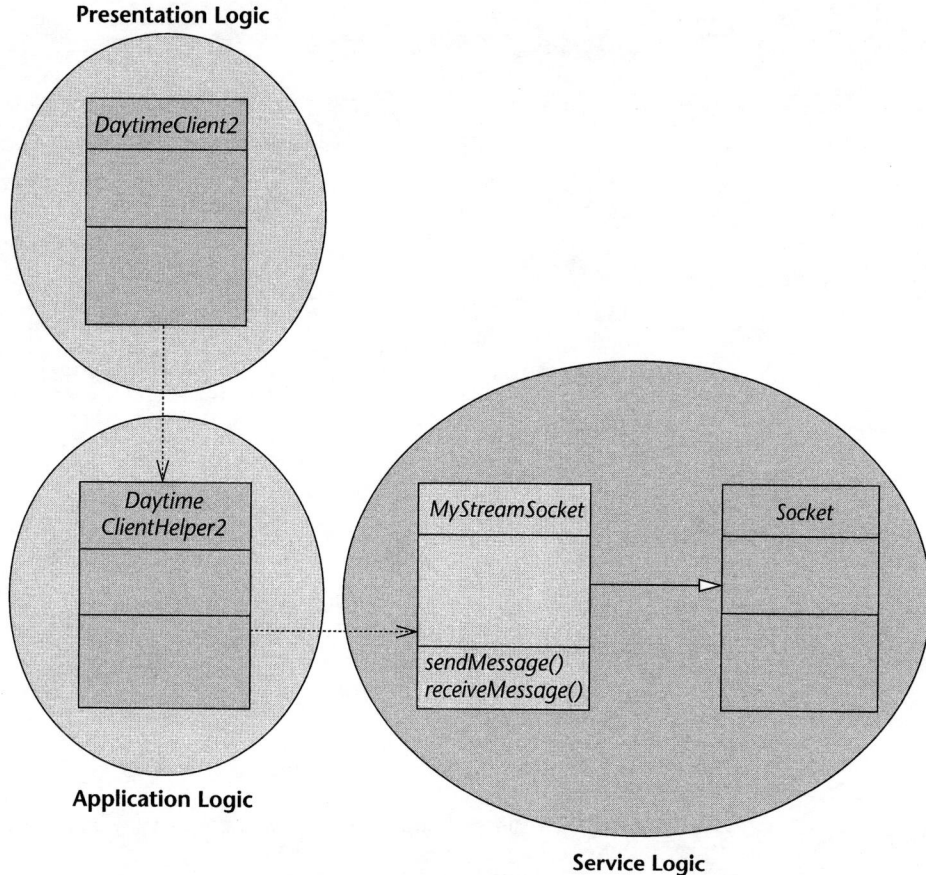

Figure 5.18 UML class diagram for *DaytimeClient2* (not all attributes are shown).

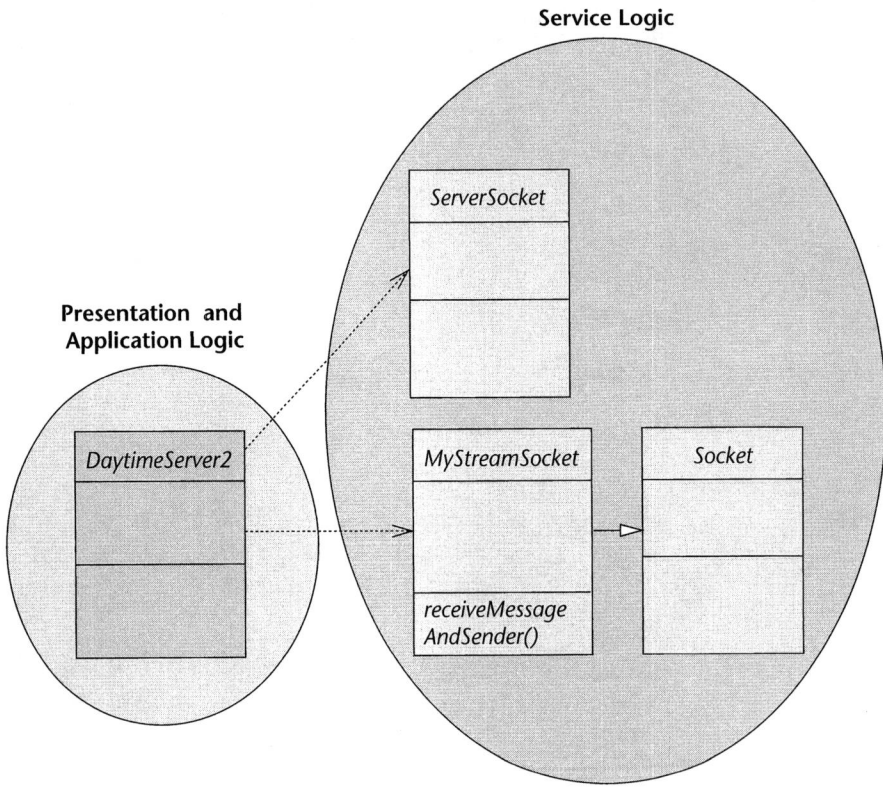

Figure 5.19 UML class diagram for *DaytimeServer2* (not all attributes are shown).

Testing a Network Service

Because of its inherent complexity, network software is notoriously difficult to test. Even a simple network service such as *Daytime* poses a challenge to novices. Following is some advice that you may find helpful:

- Use the three-layered software architecture and modularize each layer on both the client and the server sides.

A **stub** is a method defined with minimal code to allow the program to compile and run initially.

- Use an incremental or stepwise approach in developing each module. Starting with stubs for each method, compile and test a module each time after you put in additional details.

- Develop the client first. It is sometimes useful to employ an *Echo* server (to be introduced in the following section) that is known to be correct and that uses a compatible IPC mechanism to test the client independently of the server. Doing so allows you to develop the client separately from the server.

▧ Use diagnostic messages (similar to those embedded in the sample code presented in this chapter) throughout the source code to report the progress of the program during run time.

▧ Test the client-server suite on a single machine before running the programs on separate machines.

The *Daytime* client-server examples are useful as an introduction to the development of a network service. The simplicity of the protocol is such that each service session involves merely one round of message exchange between the two processes. We will next move on to look at a more complex protocol where the notion of a service session is more significant.

5.4 **Connection-Oriented and Connectionless Servers**

The Internet protocol *Echo* [Postel, 2] is the basis for a well-known Internet service. The *Echo* protocol simply allows a client to send one text line to the server at a time, receiving an echo of each line from the server. In practice, the protocol is useful in that a default *Echo* server (which runs on port 7) on any Internet host can be used as a temporary surrogate server when a software engineer is developing a client for another protocol. For educational purposes, the protocol is interesting in that it can entail multiple rounds of data exchange between a client and a server. Once again, we will look at two implementations of the service: one using a connectionless server, the other a connectionless server.

Connectionless *Echo* Client-Server

Figures 5.20 through 5.22 present an implementation of the *Echo* service using the connectionless datagram socket API.

The *Echo* Client

The presentation logic for the client is encapsulated in the *EchoClient1* class (see Figure 5.20), which provides the user interface for prompting for the server information and then, using a loop, for the text lines to send to the *Echo* server. The sending of the text string and receiving of the echo in return is handled by a method, *getEcho*, of the *EchoClientServer1* (Figure 5.22) class. The *EchoClientHelper1* class (Figure 5.21) provides the application logic for the client. An instance of this class is created by each client process (Figure 5.20), which holds the address of the server host as well as a reference to the socket used by the client for IPC. The *getEcho* method uses the socket to send a line to and then receive a line from the server. Finally, the *close* method closes the socket.

The *Echo* Server

EchoServer1.java (Figure 5.22) combines the presentation logic and application logic for the server. In each iteration of the forever loop, the server reads a line from the socket and then writes the line back to the socket, addressing the reply to the sender. Since there is no connection involved, it is possible for the server to interact with different clients in successive iterations, resulting in interleaved concurrent service sessions. Figure 5.23 illustrates a scenario wherein two concurrent clients of this implementation, A and B, interleave their interactions with an instance of *EchoServer1*.

Figure 5.20 *EchoClient1.java.*

```
1   import java.io.*;
2
3   /**
4    * This module contains the presentation logic of an Echo Client.
5    * @author M. L. Liu
6    */
7   public class EchoClient1 {
8      static final String endMessage = ".";
9      public static void main(String[ ] args) {
10        InputStreamReader is = new InputStreamReader(System.in);
11        BufferedReader br = new BufferedReader(is);
12        try {
13          System.out.println("Welcome to the Echo client.\n" +
14            "What is the name of the server host?");
15          String hostName = br.readLine();
16          if (hostName.length() == 0) // if user did not enter a name
17            hostName = "localhost"; // use the default host name
18          System.out.println("Enter the port number of the server host.");
19          String portNum = br.readLine( );
20          if (portNum.length() == 0)
21            portNum = "7"; // default port number
22          EchoClientHelper1 helper =
23            new EchoClientHelper1(hostName, portNum);
24          boolean done = false;
25          String message, echo;
26          while (!done) {
27            System.out.println("Enter a line to receive an echo back
                from the server, "
28              + "or a single peroid to quit.");
29            message = br.readLine( );
30            if ((message.trim()).equals endMessage){
31              done = true;
32              helper.done( );
33            }
34            else {
35              echo = helper.getEcho( message);
36              System.out.println(echo);
37            }
```

(continued next page)

```
38       } // end while
39     } // end try
40     catch (Exception ex) {
41       ex.printStackTrace( );
42     }
43   } //end main
44 } // end class
```

Figure 5.21 *EchoClientHelper1.java.*

```
1  import java.net.*;
2  import java.io.*;
3
4  /**
5   * This class is a module which provides the application logic
6   * for an Echo client using connectionless datagram socket.
7   * @author M. L. Liu
8   */
9  public class EchoClientHelper1 {
10   private MyClientDatagramSocket mySocket;
11   private InetAddress serverHost;
12   private int serverPort;
13
14   EchoClientHelper1(String hostName, String portNum)
15     throws SocketException, UnknownHostException {
16     this.serverHost = InetAddress.getByName(hostName);
17     this.serverPort = Integer.parseInt(portNum);
18     // instantiates a datagram socket for both sending
19     // and receiving data
20     this.mySocket = new MyClientDatagramSocket();
21   }
22
23   public String getEcho( String message)
24     throws SocketException, IOException {
25     String echo = "";
26     mySocket.sendMessage( serverHost, serverPort, message);
27     // now receive the echo
28     echo = mySocket.receiveMessage();
29     return echo;
30   } // end getEcho
31
32   public void done( ) throws SocketException {
33     mySocket.close( );
34   } // end done
35
36 } // end class
```

Figure 5.22 *EchoServer1.java.*

```
1  import java.io.*;
2
3
4  /**
5   * This module contains the application logic of an echo server
6   * which uses a connectionless datagram socket for interprocess
7   * communication.
8   * A command-line argument is required to specify the server port.
9   * @author M. L. Liu
10  */
11  public class EchoServer1 {
12    public static void main(String[] args) {
13      int serverPort = 7; // default port
14      if (args.length == 1 )
15        serverPort = Integer.parseInt(args[0]);
16      try {
17        // instantiates a datagram socket for both sending
18        // and receiving data
19        MyServerDatagramSocket mySocket =
20          newMyServerDatagramSocket(serverPort);
21        System.out.println("Echo server ready.");
22        while (true) { // forever loop
23          DatagramMessage request =
            mySocket.receiveMessageAndSender();
24          System.out.println("Request received");
25          String message = request.getMessage( );
26          System.out.println("message received: "+ message);
27          // Now send the echo to the requestor
28          mySocket.sendMessage(request.getAddress( ),
29            request.getPort( ), message);
30        } //end while
31      } // end try
32      catch (Exception ex) {
33        ex.printStackTrace( );
34      }
35    } //end main
36  } // end class
```

Connection-Oriented *Echo* Client-Server

Figures 5.24 through 5.26 present an implementation of an *Echo* service client and a server using the stream-mode socket API. Again, the implementation of the presentation logic (in *EchoClient2* and *EchoServer2*) is unchanged from *Echo*1*, but the application logic (in *EchoClientHelp2* and *EchoServer2*) as well as the service logic (in *MyStreamSocket*) are different (since stream-mode socket is used instead of datagram socket).

Note that in *EchoClientHelper2* the connection to the server is performed in the constructor, while each round of message exchange is provided via the *getEcho*

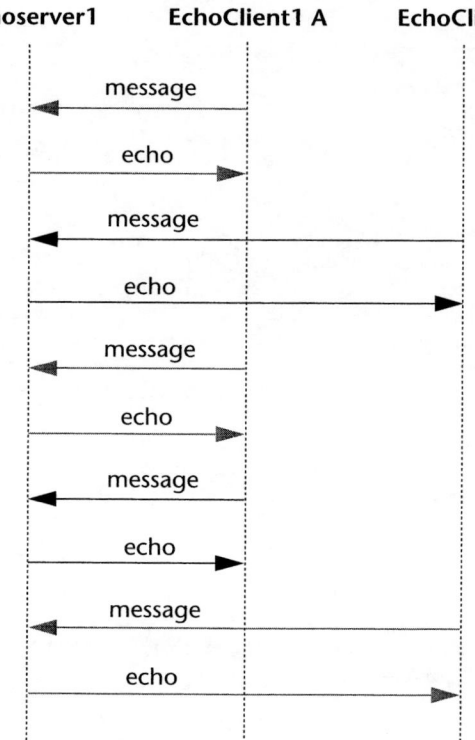

Figure 5.23 A sequence diagram illustrating two interleaved sessions with *EchoServer1*.

method. A method, *done*, is used to transmit the end-of-session message (containing a single period) to the server before the client-side socket is closed.

In *EchoServer2*, a connection socket is first created to accept connections. For each connection accepted, the server continually receives a message and echoes it via the data socket attached to the connection, until the end-of-session message is received. At the end of the session, the data socket for the current client is closed, and the connection is terminated. The server then waits to accept another connection.

Throughout a session, the server maintains its connection with the client and exchanges data with the connected client via a data socket dedicated to that client. If another client connects to the server while it is already occupied with a session, the client will not be able to exchange data with the server until the server has completed the current session. Figure 5.27 shows the sequence diagram of two sessions conducted when client 2 attempts to connect to the server while client 1 is being served. Note that there is no interleaving of the sessions in this case.

Figure 5.24 *EchoClient2.java.*

```
1  import java.io.*;
2
4  /**
5   * This module contains the presentation logic of an Echo Client.
6   * @author M. L. Liu
7   */
8  public class EchoClient2 {
9    static final String endMessage = ".";
9    public static void main(String[ ] args) {
10     InputStreamReader is = new InputStreamReader(System.in);
11     BufferedReader br = new BufferedReader(is);
12     try {
13       System.out.println("Welcome to the Echo client.\n" +
14         "What is the name of the server host?");
15       String hostName = br.readLine( );
16       if (hostName.length() == 0) // if user did not enter a name
17         hostName = "localhost"; // use the default host name
18       System.out.println("What is the port number of the server host?");
19       String portNum = br.readLine();
20       if (portNum.length() == 0)
21         portNum = "7"; // default port number
22       EchoClientHelper2 helper =
23         new EchoClientHelper2(hostName, portNum);
24       boolean done = false;
25       String message, echo;
26       while (!done) {
27         System.out.println("Enter a line to receive an echo back
28           from the server, " + "or a single period to quit.");
29         message = br.readLine( );
30         if ((message.trim( )).equals (".")){
31           done = true;
32           helper.done( );
33         }
34         else {
35           echo = helper.getEcho( message);
36           System.out.println(echo);
37         }
38       } // end while
39     } // end try
40     catch (Exception ex) {
41       ex.printStackTrace( );
42     } // end catch
43   } // end main
44 } // end class
```

Figure 5.25 *EchoClientHelper2.java.*

```
1
2   import java.net.*;
3   import java.io.*;
4
5   /**
6    * This class is a module which provides the application logic
7    * for an Echo client using stream-mode socket.
8    * @author M. L. Liu
9    */
10  public class EchoClientHelper2 {
11
12     static final String endMessage = ".";
13     private MyStreamSocket mySocket;
14     private InetAddress serverHost;
15     private int serverPort;
16
17     EchoClientHelper2(String hostName,
18        String portNum) throws SocketException,
19        UnknownHostException, IOException {
20
21        this.serverHost = InetAddress.getByName(hostName);
22        this.serverPort = Integer.parseInt(portNum);
23        //Instantiates a stream-mode socket and wait for a connection.
24        this.mySocket = new MyStreamSocket(hostName,
25           this.serverPort);
26 /**/ System.out.println("Connection request made");
27     } // end constructor
28
29     public String getEcho( String message) throws SocketException,
30        IOException {
31        String echo = "";
32        mySocket.sendMessage( message);
33        // now receive the echo
34        echo = mySocket.receiveMessage();
35        return echo;
36     } //end getEcho
37
38     public void done( ) throws SocketException,
39        IOException{
40        mySocket.sendMessage(endMessage);
41        mySocket.close( );
42     } // end done
43  } // end class
```

Figure 5.26 *EchoServer2.java.*

```
 1  import java.io.*;
 2  import java.net.*;
 3
 4  /**
 5   * This module contains the application logic of an echo server
 6   * which uses a stream-mode socket for interprocess communication.
 7   * A command-line argument is required to specify the server port.
 8   * @author M. L. Liu
 9   */
10  public class EchoServer2 {
11    static final String endMessage = ".";
12    public static void main(String[] args) {
13      int serverPort = 7; // default port
14      String message;
15
16      if (args.length == 1 )
19        serverPort = Integer.parseInt(args[0]);
20      try {
21        // instantiates a stream socket for accepting
22        // connections
23        ServerSocket myConnectionSocket =
24          new ServerSocket(serverPort);
25 /**/   System.out.println("Daytime server ready.");
26        while (true) { // forever loop
27          // wait to accept a connection
28 /**/     System.out.println("Waiting for a connection.");
29          MyStreamSocket myDataSocket = new MyStreamSocket
30            (myConnectionSocket.accept( ));
31 /**/     System.out.println("connection accepted");
32          boolean done = false;
33          while (!done) {
34            message = myDataSocket.receiveMessage( );
35 /**/       System.out.println("message received: "+ message);
36            if ((message.trim()).equals (endMessage)){
37              // Session over; close the data socket.
38 /**/         System.out.println("Session over.");
39              myDataSocket.close( );
40              done = true;
41            } // end if
42            else {
43              // Now send the echo to the requestor
44              myDataSocket.sendMessage(message);
45            } // end else
46          } // end while !done
47        } // end while forever
48      } // end try
49      catch (Exception ex) {
50        ex.printStackTrace( );
51      } end catch
52    } // end main
51  } // end class
```

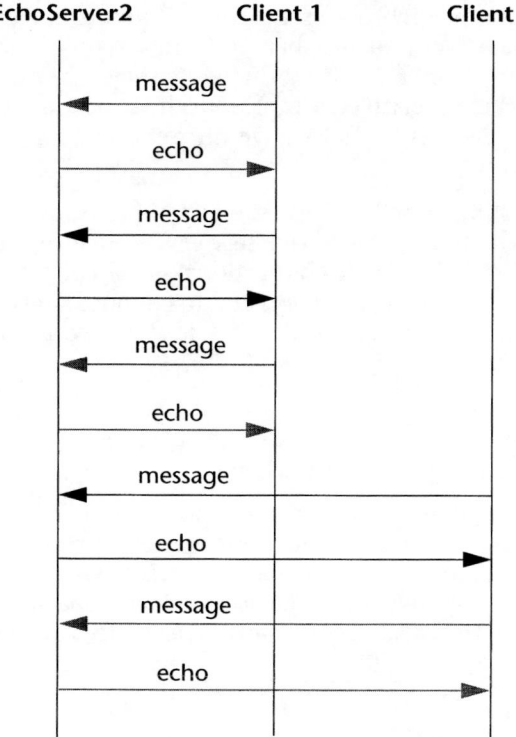

Figure 5.27 *EchoServer2* will not allow interleaved sessions.

5.5 Iterative Server and Concurrent Server

As you can see, with a connection-oriented server such as *DaytimeServer2* and *EchoServer2*, there is no overlapping of client sessions, since the server is limited to exchanging data with a client whose connection it has accepted (but has not disconnected). Such a server is said to be an **iterative server**, since it services one client at a time. When requesting service from a popular iterative server, a client will be blocked until all preceding clients have been served. The result can be a significant blocking time if the service sessions are lengthy, such as in the case of a file transfer protocol. Suppose each session can be expected to last t time units, and that n clients have requested connection at a given time. Disregarding other delays for the sake of simplicity, the next client who requests connection can expect to be blocked for at least $n*t$ time units. If t is large, the latency will be unacceptable.

The solution to this problem is to introduce concurrency to the server, resulting in a **concurrent server**. A concurrent server is capable of conducting multiple client sessions in parallel. A concurrent server can be provided using threads or,

As discussed in Chapter 1, on a system with a single CPU, concurrent execution is effected with time-sharing of the CPU and hence the concurrency is not real.

alternatively, using asynchronous IPC operations. (Concurrent programming using threads was discussed in Chapter 1, and asynchronous IPC operations were discussed in Chapter 2.) Using threads is the conventional technique and has the virtue of being relatively simple. But the scale and performance requirement of modern-day applications have, in some cases, made using asynchronous IPC necessary.

In this presentation, we will discuss the technique of using threads to build a concurrent server. Similar to iterative servers, a concurrent server uses a single connection socket to listen for connections. But a concurrent server creates a new thread to accept each connection and to conduct a service session with the connected client; the thread is terminated upon the conclusion of the session.

Figures 5.28 and 5.29 present the concurrent server and the thread class it uses. The *run* method of the thread class carries out the logic for a client session. Note that no change is needed in the code on the client side: *EchoClient2* can be used to access *EchoServer3* with no change.

Figure 5.30 shows the sequence diagram for two concurrent sessions. It may be of interest for you to compare the sequence diagram with the two presented before (Figures 5.23 and 5.27). With a concurrent server, a client will not have to wait long for its connection to be accepted; the only latency the client will experience will be that resulting from its own service session.

Figure 5.28 *EchoServer3.java.*

```
1   import java.io.*;
2   import java.net.*;
3
4
5   /**
6    * This module contains the application logic of an echo server
7    * that uses a stream-mode socket for interprocess communication.
8    * Unlike EchoServer2, this server services clients concurrently.
9    * A command-line argument is required to specify the server port.
10   * @author M. L. Liu
11   */
12  public class EchoServer3 {
13    public static void main(String[] args) {
14      int serverPort = 7; // default port
15      String message;
16
17      if (args.length == 1 )
18        serverPort = Integer.parseInt(args[0]);
19      try {
20        // instantiates a stream socket for accepting
21        // connections
22        ServerSocket myConnectionSocket =
23          new ServerSocket(serverPort);
```

(continued next page)

```
24  /**/     System.out.println("Daytime server ready.");
25           while (true) { // forever loop
26              // wait to accept a connection
27  /**/        System.out.println("Waiting for a connection.");
28              MyStreamSocket myDataSocket = new MyStreamSocket
29                (myConnectionSocket.accept( ));
30  /**/        System.out.println("connection accepted");
31              // Start a thread to handle this client's sesson
32              Thread theThread =
33                new Thread(new EchoServerThread(myDataSocket));
34              theThread.start();
35              // and go on to the next client
36           } // end while forever
37        } // end try
38        catch (Exception ex) {
39           ex.printStackTrace( )
40        } // end catch
41     } // end main
42  } // end class
```

Figure 5.29 *EchoServerThread.*

```
1
2   import java.io.*;
3   /**
4   * This module is to be used with a concurrent Echo server.
5   * Its run method carries out the logic of a client session.
6   * @author M. L. Liu
7   */
8   class EchoServerThread implements Runnable {
9     static final String endMessage = ".";
10    MyStreamSocket myDataSocket;
11
12    EchoServerThread(MyStreamSocket myDataSocket) {
13       this.myDataSocket = myDataSocket;
14    } // end constructor
15
16    public void run( ) {
17      boolean done = false;
18      String message;
19      try {
20        while (!done) {
21           message = myDataSocket.receiveMessage( );
22  /**/     System.out.println("message received: "+ message);
23           if ((message.trim()).equals (endMessage)){
24             //Session over; close the data socket.
25  /**/       System.out.println("Session over.");
26             myDataSocket.close( );
27             done = true;
28           } //end if
```

(continued next page)

```
29              else {
30                  // Now send the echo to the requestor
31                  myDataSocket.sendMessage(message);
32              } // end else
33          } // end while !done
34      } // end try
35      catch (Exception ex) {
36          System.out.println("Exception caught in thread: " + ex);
37      } // end catch
38  } // end run
39 } // end class
```

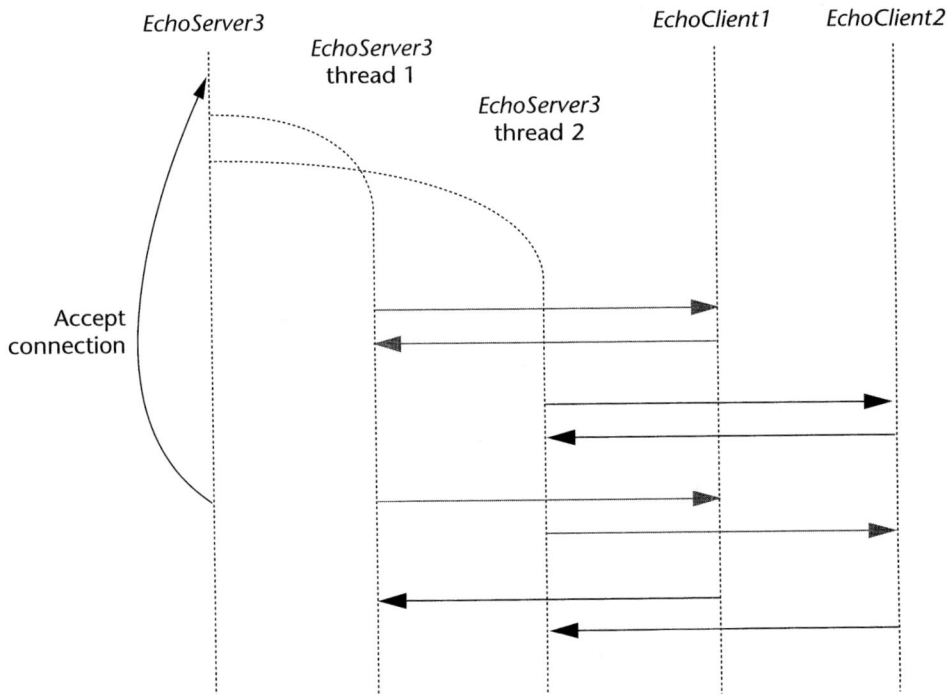

Figure 5.30 *EchoServer3* supports concurrent client sessions.

Concurrent servers are the norm in modern network services. Although iterative servers are acceptable for all but the simplest protocols, studying servers of this type is still a good learning experience.

5.6 Stateful Servers

Both the *Daytime* protocol and the *Echo* protocol belong in a category of protocols known as **stateless protocols**, as opposed to **stateful protocols**. A protocol is *stateless* if no state information needs to be maintained by the server. Such is the case with the *Daytime* protocol, where the server merely sends a timestamp obtained from the system to each client; and also with the *Echo* protocol, where the protocol only requires that the server echo each message it receives. In either protocol, the task performed by the server is independent of its state, such as how long the server has been in service or which client it is serving.

A stateless server is one that provides a service according to a stateless protocol and hence does not have to maintain any state information, as in the case of the *Daytime* server or the *Echo* server. A **stateful server**, as the name implies, is one that must maintain some state information in order to provide its service.

What exactly is meant by state information? There are two types: global state information and session state information.

Global State Information

This type of information is maintained by the server for all the clients throughout the lifetime of a server. For example, suppose a protocol, which we will call the *counter* protocol (not a standard Internet protocol), requires that a server maintain a counter, initialized to 0. Each time the server is contacted by a client, it increments the counter by 1 and sends the current value of the counter to the client. To provide such a service, the server must have the value of the counter placed in some storage where it can be retrieved and updated throughout the execution of the server. For a simple counter, the storage may be implemented using a variable of primitive data type in Java. For more complex state information, the storage may be implemented using a file, a database, or other mechanisms. Figure 5.31 shows the code for a server that services the *counter* protocol. Note that a static variable is used to maintain the counter whose update is synchronized for mutual exclusion. The client program is shown in Figures 5.32 and 5.33.

Figure 5.31 *CounterServer1.java.*

```java
1  import java.io.*;
2
3  /**
4   * This module contains the application logic of a Counter server
5   * which uses a datagram socket for interprocess communication.
6   * A command-line argument is required to specify the server port.
7   * @author M. L. Liu
8   */
9  public class CounterServer1 {
10
11     /* state information */
12     static into counter = 0;
13
14     public static void main(String[] args) {
15        int serverPort = 12345; // default port
16        if (args.length == 1 )
17           serverPort = Interger.parseInt(args[0]);
18        try {
19           // instantiates a datagram socket for both sending
20           // and receiving data
21           MyServerDatagramSocket mySocket =
22              new MyServerDatagramSocket(serverPort);
23  /**/   System.out.println("Counter server ready.");
24        while (true) { // forever loop
25           DatagramMessage request =
26              mySocket.receiveMessageAndSender();
27           System.out.println("Request received");
28           // The message received is unimportant; it is the sender's
29           // address that we need in order to reply.
30           // No increment the counter, then send its value to the client.
31           increment();
32  /**/     System.out.println("counter sent "+ counter);
33           // Now send the reply to the requestor
34           mySocket.sendMessage(request.getAddress(),
35              request.getPort(), String.valueOf(counter));
36        } // end while
37        } // end try
38        catch (Exception ex) {
39           ex.printStackTrace( );
40        } // end catch
41     } // end main
42
43     static private synchronized void increment(){
44        counter++;
45     }
46
47  } // end class
```

Figure 5.32 *CounterClient1.java.*

```
1  import java.io.*;
2
3
4  /**
5  * This module contains the presentation logic of a counter Client.
6  * @author M. L. Liu
7  */
8  public class CounterClient1 {
9    public static void main(String[] args) {
10     InputStreamReader is = new InputStreamReader(System.in);
11     BufferedReader br = new BufferedReader(is);
12     try {
13       System.out.println("Welcome to the Daytime client.\n" +
14         "What is the name of the server host?");
15       String hostName = br.readLine();
16       if (hostName.length() == 0) // if user did not enter a name
17         hostName = "localhost"; // use the default host name
18       System.out.println("What is the port number of the server host?");
19       String portNum = br.readLine();
20       if (portNum.length() == 0)
21         portNum = "12345"; // default port number
22       System.out.println("Counter received from the server: "
23         + CounterClientHelper1.getCounter(hostName, portNum));
24     } // end try
25     catch (Exception ex) {
26       ex.printStackTrace( );
27     }
28   } //end main
29 } // end class
```

Figure 5.33 *CounterClientHelper1.java.*

```
1
2  import java.net.*;
3
4  /**
5   * This class is a module that provides the application logic
6   * for a Counter Client.
7   * @author M. L. Liu
8   */
9  public class CounterClientHelper1 {
10
11     public static int getCounter(String hostName,
12         String portNum)
13         {
14       int counter = 0;
15       String message = "";
16       try {
17         InetAddress serverHost =
18           InetAddress.getByName(hostName);
19         int serverPort = Integer.parseInt(portNum);
20         // instantiates a datagram socket for both sending
21         // and receiving data
22         MyDatagramSocket mySocket = new MyDatagramSocket();
23         mySocket.sendMessage( serverHost, serverPort, "");
24         // now receive the counter value
25         message = mySocket.receiveMessage();
26  /**/   System.out.println("Message received: " + message);
27         counter = Integer.parseInt(message.trim());
28         mySocket.close( );
29       } // end try
30       catch (Exception ex) {
31         ex.printStackTrace( );
32       } // end catch
33       return counter;
34     } // end main
35  } // end class
```

Session State Information

For some protocols or applications, there is a need to maintain information specific to a client session.

Consider a network service such as *ftp*. A file is typically transferred to blocks, requiring several rounds of data exchanges to complete the file transfer. The state information of each session includes:

1. the name of the file being used

2. the current block number

3. the action (get, put, etc) being performed on the file

There are at least two schemes to maintain the session state data.

Stateless Server. In one scheme, the session state information may be maintained by the client so that each request contains the session state information, allowing the server to service each request in accordance with the state data sent in the request. The dialog during a session will then proceed roughly as follows:

> Client: Please send me block 1 of the file *foo* in directory *someDir*.
> Server: Okay. Here is that block of the file.
> Client: Please send me block 2 of the file *foo* in directory *someDir*.
> Server: Okay. Here is that block of the file.
> ...
> Client: Please send me block *n* of the file *foo* in directory *someDir*.
> Server: Okay. Here is that block of the file.

By requiring the client to maintain the session data, this scheme allows the server to process each request in the same manner, and thereby reduces the complexity of its application logic. Such a server is known as a **stateless server**.

Stateful Server. In the second scheme, the session state information may be maintained by the server, in which case the dialog during a session may proceed roughly as follows:

> Client: Please send me the file *foo* in directory *someDir*.
> Server: Okay. Here is block 0 of the file foo.
> Client: Got it.
> Server: Okay. Her is block 1 of the file foo.
> Client: Got it.
> ...
> Server: Okay. Here is block 2 of the file foo.
> Client: Got it.

With this scheme, the server keeps track of the progress of the session by maintaining the session state. Such a server is known as a **stateful server**. Figure 5.34 illustrates the difference between a stateless server and a stateful server.

Stateful servers are more complex to design and implement. In addition to the logic required for maintaining state data, provisions must be made to safeguard the state information in the event that a session is disrupted. If a stateful server host fails temporarily in the midst of a session, it is important for the ongoing session to resume in the correct state. Otherwise, it is possible for the client to, in our example, receive the wrong block of the file after the session recovers from the failure.

Another example of a stateful protocol is one for a shopping cart application. Each session must maintain state data that keeps track of the identity of the shopper and the cumulative contents of the shopping cart.

In actual implementation, a server may be stateless, stateful, or a hybrid. In the last case, the state data may be distributed between the server as well as the client. Which type of server is employed is a design issue.

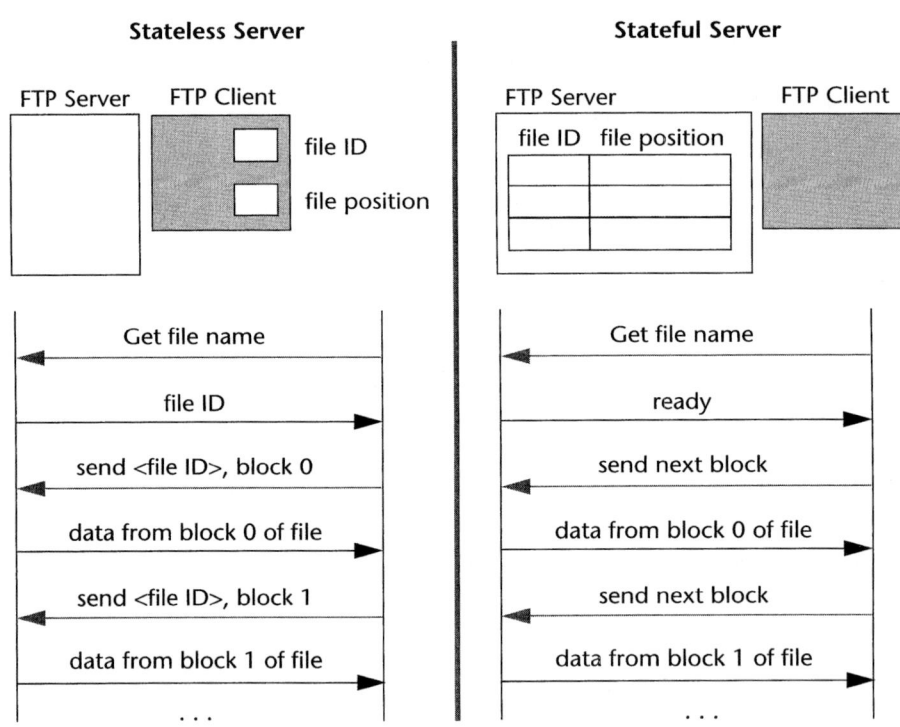

Figure 5.34 The difference between a stateless server and a stateful server.

INTERNET SOCIETY

Press release (excerpt)
The "North Star" Who Defined the Internet
Reprinted by permission of the Internet Society (http://www.isoc.org/internet/)

Reston, VA—October 19, 1998. The Internet Community mourns the loss of a leader and the first individual member of the Internet Society. Jonathan B. Postel passed away on Friday, October 16th. For thirty years, Postel served all Internet users in a variety of key roles, although few outside the technical community may know his name. Long before there were any books written about the Internet, there was only a series of technical documents known as the "Request For Comments" or RFC series. Jon edited and organized these materials, which helped to set the Internet's first standards.

"Jon has been our North Star for decades, burning brightly and constantly, providing comfort and a sense of security while all else changed," said Vint Cerf, current chairman of the board of the Internet Society. "He was Internet's Boswell and its technical conscience. His loss will be sorely felt, not only for his expertise, but because the community has lost a dear and much-loved friend."

Postel began his networking career in 1969 while a graduate student at UCLA working on the now-famous ARPANET project (precursor to the Internet) as a research assistant to Professor Leonard Kleinrock who said, "Jon's key contributions to our work during those critical formative days of the ARPANET is largely unrecognized. As we broke new ground at the birthplace of the Internet in 1969, I remember Jon as a deeply dedicated, brilliant young programmer on our team. It was a frontier at that time, and Jon was truly a pioneer with a vision. It was in those days that he became editor of the 'Request for Comments' series, which

continues to this day. Jon's dedication to the growth and health of the Internet continued from those heady times throughout the rest of his life. And for this, he sought neither recognition nor praise. Jon's passing is a tragic loss which will be felt by all those whose lives have been touched by the Internet, but especially by those of us who traveled the road with this quiet gentle man these many many years."

For many years, Postel was the Internet Assigned Numbers Authority (IANA) which oversees the allocation and assignment of domain names and Internet addresses. Ultimately, the task grew large enough that he acquired a small staff to assist in this work. His early recognition of the importance of careful documentation seems truly clairvoyant with today's hindsight. All the technical work on the ARPANET and later, the Internet, as well as the theory and practice behind the administration of names and addresses, is collected for historians today largely because of Jon's dedication. At a time when the network was only an experiment, Jon Postel was fully committed to providing a safe and secure haven for the information that makes it possible for the Internet to function.

He was directly responsible for the management of the .US domain name. Additionally, he served as a member of the Internet Architecture Board from its inception in 1983 continuously through the present. Postel had many other roles including a key part in the founding of the Internet Society. He also founded the Los Nettos network service in the Los Angeles area.

Postel offered something rarely found at any time: quiet, competent and continuous stewardship. He regarded his responsibilities as a kind of public trust. He never received any personal benefit from the exploding business of the Internet, choosing instead to stay outside of the business frenzy, the Initial Public Offerings and other paraphernalia of Wall Street.

Postel's friend and graduate school colleague, Stephen D. Crocker, led the development of the host protocols for the ARPANET. Crocker started the RFC series and Jon instantly volunteered to edit them. "The unthinkable has happened. We've all lost a great friend and major pillar of support and sanity in our peculiar, surrealistic world," said Crocker. "To those of us involved in the human 'network' of engineers who design and develop the Internet, he was one of the key people who kept the network running. He worked tirelessly and selflessly. He was always there."

"I can't believe he's gone, Jon was a hero to me and to many others on the Internet. What a mediator he was: always smiling and ready to consider a new idea, with no agenda of his own other than to further the Greater Good of the Internet around the World," said Jean Armour Polly, former Internet Society Trustee.

While working on the ARPANET at UCLA, Postel pursued a Ph.D. research program under the direction of Professors David Farber at UC Irvine and Gerald Estrin at UCLA. Professor Farber reminisces: "Jon was my second Ph.D. student. I was his primary thesis advisor along with Jerry Estrin and I remember with fond memories the months spent closely working with Jon while his eager mind developed the ideas in back of what was a pioneering thesis that founded the area of protocol verification. Since I was at UC Irvine and Jon at UCLA we used to meet in the morning prior to my ride to UCI at a Pancake House in Santa Monica for breakfast and the hard work of developing a thesis. I gained a great respect for Jon then and 10 pounds of weight."

Jerry Estrin recalls Jon Postel as a wonderfully fine, gentle, unselfish human being who truly cared about people and his professional contributions. "In the 1970s, he was fearless in trying to apply an emerging graph model to verification of complex ARPANET protocols. I will not forget Jon coming to me during a graduate seminar and gently asking if I could refrain from pipe smoking during class. He showed the same foresight about the toxic effects of smoking as he did about the positive potential impact of computer networks."

Postel served in many positions in his long connection with the Internet. He worked with industry legend Doug Engelbart at SRI International in Menlo Park, CA, where he became a strong supporter of the oNLine System (NLS), a predecessor in many respects to the World Wide Web, including the hyperlink feature so familiar to us today. He moved to the Washington area to support the Advanced Research Projects Agency for a time and then came to USC Information Sciences Institute where he became a permanent star in the Internet heavens, guiding all Internauts as they explored the expanding ocean the Internet has become.

Postel was elected to the Board of Trustees of the Internet Society in 1993 and re-elected to a second three-year term in 1996. In the last two years, he worked tirelessly to help facilitate the migration of the US Government-funded IANA and general Domain Name management system into a non-profit, international, private sector enterprise. Shortly before his death, the Internet Corporation for Assigned Names and Numbers (ICANN) was incorporated and has been proposed as the successor to the US Government-funded system that has served the Internet community for nearly 30 years.

Remembrances of Jon Postel by those who knew him or knew of him may be found on ISOC's web site, http://www.isoc.org/postel/.

Summary

This chapter has introduced you to the client-server paradigm in distributed computing. Topics covered include

- The difference between the client-server system architecture and the client-server distributed computing paradigm
- A definition of the paradigm and an explanation of why it is widely adopted in network services and network applications
- The issues of service sessions, protocols, service location, interprocess communications, data representation, and event synchronization in the context of the client-server paradigm
- The three-tier software architecture of client-server applications: presentation logic, application logic, and service logic
- Connectionless server versus connection-oriented server
- Iterative server versus concurrent server and the effect on a client session
- Stateful server versus stateless server
- For the stateful server, global state information versus session state information.

Exercises

1. In the context of distributed computing, describe the client-server paradigm. Why is this paradigm especially appropriate for network services?

2. Describe the three-tier software architecture for client-server software. Briefly explain the functionalities of each layer on each side. Why is it advantageous to encapsulate the logic of separate layers in separate software modules?

3. This exercise deals with *DaytimeServer1* and *DaytimeClient1*, which use connectionless datagram sockets. For this set of exercises, it is sufficient for you to run the client and server processes on one machine and specify the host name as "localhost."

   a. Why is it necessary for the server to use the *receiveMessageAndSender* method to accept the client's request instead of using the *receiveMessage* method?

   b. Compile *Daytime*1.java* ("javac Daytime*1.java"). Then run the programs:

      i. by starting the client first, then the server (don't forget to specify a port number as a command-line argument). What happened? Describe and explain.

      ii. by starting the server first (don't forget to specify a port number as a command-line argument), then the client. What happened? Describe and explain.

   c. Modify the *MAX_LEN* constant in *MyClientDatagramSocket.java* to 10. Recompile and run, starting the server first. Observe the message received by the client. Describe and explain the outcome.

   d. Restore the original value of *MAX_LEN*. Recompile and rerun the programs, starting the server first. Start another client, preferably from a different machine. Describe and explain the outcome. Draw a time-event diagram describing the event sequencing of the interactions between the server and the two clients.

4. This exercise includes *DaytimeServer2* and *DaytimeClient2*, which use stream sockets.

   a. In your own words, describe the difference between this set of classes and the classes for *Daytime*1*.

   b. Compile *Daytime*2.java* (javac Daytime*2.java). Then run the programs:

      i. by starting the client first, then the server (don't forget to specify a port number as a command-line argument). What happened? Describe and explain.

      ii. by starting the server first (don't forget to specify a port number as a command-line argument), then the client. What happened? Describe and explain.

c. To experiment with the effect of a connection, add a delay (by using *Thread.sleep(3000)*) in *Daytime2Server.java* after a connection is accepted and before a timestamp is obtained from the system. Adding the delay has the effect of artificially lengthening each service session by 3 seconds. Recompile and start the server, then start two clients in separate screens on your system. How long did it take for the second client to make a connection with the server? Describe and explain, keeping in mind that the server is iterative.

5. Assuming that our implementation is correct, you should be able to use either of the two *DaytimeClients* from the examples presented (Figures 5.6 and 5.14) to obtain a timestamp from any Internet host that provides the standard *Daytime* service at TCP/UDP port 13. Try to do so with an Internet host that you know, using both *DaytimeClient1* and *DaytimeClient2*. Be aware that some systems will refuse access to the *Daytime* service on port 13 for security reasons. Describe your experiment and outcomes, keeping in mind that most existing *Daytime* service servers were implemented years ago using the C language.

6. This exercise uses *EchoServer1* and *EchoClient1*, which use connectionless datagram sockets for the *Echo* service.

   Compile *Echo*1.java (javac Echo*1.java)*. Then:

   a. Run the programs by starting the server first (don't forget to specify a port number as a command-line argument), then the client. Conduct a session and observe the diagnostic messages displayed on both sides. Describe your observations of the sequence of events.

   b. With the server running, start two clients in separate windows. Can you conduct the two client sessions in parallel? Describe and explain your observations. Do your observations agree with the sequence diagram in Figure 5.23?

   c. You may wonder what happens when a client sends data to a connectionless server that is already busy serving another client. To experiment: Add a delay of 10 seconds (10,000 milliseconds) in the server before the echo is sent. Then repeat part b. Describe and explain your observations. Is the data from the second client received by the server?

7. This exercise deals with *EchoServer2* and *EchoClient2*. Recall that *EchoServer2* is connection-oriented and iterative.

   Compile *Echo*2.java (javac Echo*2.java)*. Then:

   a. Run the programs by starting the server first (don't forget to specify a port number as a command-line argument), then the client. Conduct a session and observe the diagnostic messages displayed on both sides. Describe your observations of the sequence of events.

   b. With the server running, start two clients in separate windows. Can you conduct the two client sessions in parallel? Describe and explain your observations. Do your observations agree with the sequence diagram in Figure 5.27?

8. This exercise deals with *EchoServer3*. Recall that *EchoServer3* is connection-oriented and concurrent.

   Compile *Echo*3.java*. Then:

   a. Run the programs by starting the server *EchoServer3* first (don't forget to specify a port number as a command-line argument), then the client *EchoClient2*. Conduct a session and observe the diagnostic messages displayed on both sides. Describe your observations of the sequence of events.

   b. With the server running, start two clients in separate windows. Can you conduct the two client sessions in parallel? Describe and explain your observations. Do your observations agree with the sequence diagram in Figure 5.30?

9. In your own words, describe the differences, from a client's point of view, between an iterative server and a concurrent server for a service such as *Echo*, which involves multiple rounds of message exchanges. Your description should address (i) the software logic (recall the three-layer software architecture), and (ii) the run-time performance (in terms of the delay or latency experienced by a client).

10. This exercise deals with stateful servers that maintain global state information.

    a. Compile *CounterServer1.java* and *CounterClient1.java* ("javacCounter*.java"). Run the server then a client several times. Does the counter increase with each client?

    b. Modify *CounterServer1.java* and *CounterClient1.java* so that the counter increases by 2 with each client. Rerun the client and server and check the outcomes.

    c. Provide the code for a connection-oriented server and client for the *counter* protocol.

11. Using the three-tier software architecture presented in this chapter, design and implement a client-server suite for the following protocol (it is not a well-known service): Each client sends a name to the server. The server accumulates the names received from successive clients (by appending each, with a newline character, '/n', to a static string). Upon receiving a name, the server sends the names it has collected to the client. The client then displays all the names it receives from the server. Figure 5.38 below illustrates the sequence diagram of the protocol with 3 concurrent client sessions.

    a. Is this server a stateful server? If so, what kind of state information (global or session) does it maintain?

    b. Create one or more of the following suites for the protocol:

       i. Connectionless server and client

       ii. Connection-oriented, iterative server and client

iii. Connection-oriented, concurrent server and client

For each suite, hand in: (A) program listings, and (B) a description of how the three-tier architecture is realized using separate software modules (Java classes).

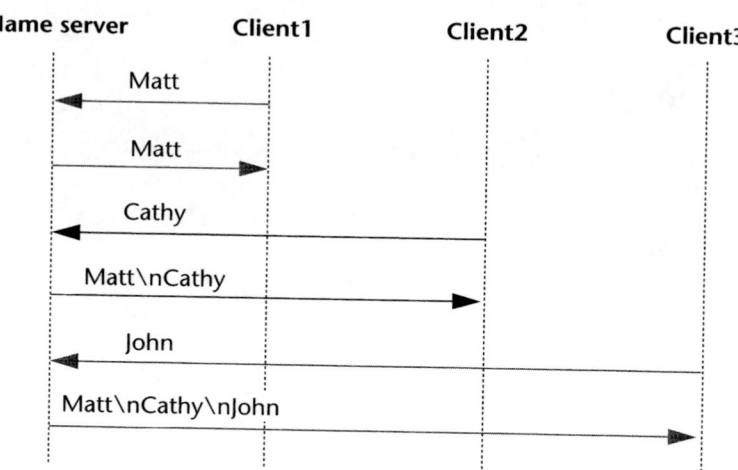

Figure 5.35 A sequence diagram of the protocol showing three concurrent client sessions.

12. Consider the following protocol, which we will call the *countdown* protocol. Each client contacts the server with an initial message that specifies an integer value n. The client then loops to receive n messages from the server, with the messages bearing the values n, $n–1$, $n–2$, ..., 1 successively.

    a. Is this server a stateful server? If so, what kind of state information (global or session) does it maintain?

    b. Create one or more of the following suites for this protocol:

       i. Connectionless server and client

       ii. Connection-oriented, iterative server and client

       iii. Connection-oriented, concurrent server and client

          For each suite, hand in: (A) program listings, and (B) a description of how the three-tier architecture is realized using separate software modules (Java classes).

13. Consider a network service as follows: A client prompts for an integer n entered on the keyboard and sends it to the server, then receives from the server a string containing the value $n+1$.

    a. Write an implementation-independent specification for the protocol, with description of (1) the sequence of events (using a sequence diagram), and (2) data representation.

b. Provide the code for three versions of a client-server suite:
- Connectionless (using datagram packets)
- Connection-oriented (using stream sockets) and iterative server
- Connection-oriented (using stream sockets) and concurrent server

References

1. Jon Postel, The DayTime Protocol, RFC 867, *http://www.ietf.org/rfc/rfc0867.txt?number=867*

2. Jon Postel, The Echo Protocol, RFC 862, *http://www.ietf.org/rfc/rfc0862.txt?number=862*

## CHAPTER 6

Group Communication

In previous chapters, we have presented interprocess communications (IPC) as the exchange of information between two processes. In this chapter, we will look at IPC among a group of processes, or **group communication**.

6.1 Unicasting versus Multicasting

In the IPC we have presented so far, data is sent from a source process, the sender, to one destination process, the receiver. This form of IPC can be called **unicasting**, the sending of information to a single receiver, as opposed to **multicasting**, the sending of information to multiple receivers. Unicasting provides one-to-one IPC; multicasting supports one-to-many IPC. See Figure 6.1.

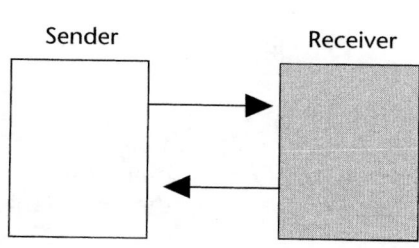

One-to-One Communication, or Unicast

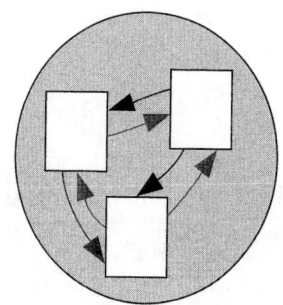

Group Communication, or Multicast

Figure 6.1 Unicast IPC and multicast IPC.

184 **CHAPTER 6** Group Communication

Replication of a service refers to maintaining duplicates of that service. A common technique for enhancing the availability of a service in the presence of failures is to duplicate the data and the supporting system for that service.

Fault tolerance refers to the ability of an application to tolerate failures to some extent.

Whereas the majority of network services and network applications use unicasting for IPC, multicasting is useful for applications such as instant messages, groupware, online conferences, and interactive learning, and it can be used for applications such as a real-time online auction. Multicasting is also useful in the replication of services for fault tolerance.

In an application or network service that makes use of multicasting, a set of processes forms a group, called a **multicast group**. Each process in a group can send and receive messages. A message sent by any process in the group can be received by each participating process in the group. A process may also choose to leave a multicast group.

In an application such as online conferencing, a group of processes interoperate using multicasting to exchange audio, video, and/or text data.

As before, our discussion will concentrate on the service layer, specifically the IPC mechanism, for the application.

6.2 An Archetypal Multicast API

An application program interface that supports multicasting must provide the following primitive operations:

- **Join.** The join operation allows a process to join a specific **multicast group**. A process that has joined a multicast group is a **member** of the group and is entitled to receive all messages addressed to the group. A process may be a member of one or more multicast groups at any one time. Note that for this and other multicast operations, a naming scheme is needed to uniquely identify a multicast group.
- **Leave.** This operation allows a process to stop participating in a multicast group. A process that has left a multicast group is no longer a member of the group and is thereafter not entitled to receive any multicast addressed to the group, although the process may remain a member of other multicast groups.
- **Send.** The send operation allows a process to send a message to all processes currently participating in a multicast group.
- **Receive.** The receive operation allows a member process to receive messages sent to a multicast group.

In section 6.5 we will look at Java's multicast API and sample programs using the API, at which time you will see how these primitive operations are provided using Java syntax. Before we do that, however, let's explore some of the interesting issues specific to multicasting. These issues arise from the **one-to-many** nature of multicasting.

6.3 Connectionless versus Connection-Oriented Multicast

A basic multicast mechanism is connectionless. The reason is obvious if you consider the one-to-many nature of multicasting. In a group of n processes, if a connection is to be established between a sender and every other process in the group, a total of $n-1$ connections will be needed. Moreover, each of the n processes may potentially be a sender, so that each process must maintain a connection with every other process, resulting in a total of $n * (n - 1)$ or roughly n^2 connections. If $n-1$ is large, the sheer number of such connections will become prohibitively expensive.

Moreover, connectionless IPC is appropriate for a common type of multicast applications: applications where audio or video data is transmitted among processes in real time. (By saying that the data is transmitted in real time, we mean that the latency between sending and receiving should be close to zero.) When audio or video data is transmitted, the reduction in **latency** provided by connectionless communication outweighs the advantages offered by connection-oriented communication. When data for animation is sent, for example, it is more acceptable for a receiver to experience a distortion in the image of an occasional frame (a likely occurrence with connectionless communication) than a frequent, perceptible delay between consecutive frames (a likely occurrence with connection-oriented communication).

Latency refers to the delay in data transmission.

6.4 Reliable Multicasting versus Unreliable Multicasting

When a multicast message is sent by a process, the run-time support of the multicast mechanism is responsible for delivering the message to each process currently in the multicast group. As each participating process may reside on a separate host, the delivery of these messages requires the cooperation of mechanisms running independently on those systems. Due to factors such as failures of network links, defects in network hosts, routing delays, and differences in software and hardware, the time between when a unicast message is sent and when it is received may vary among the recipient processes. While the differences in message delivery to individual hosts may be insignificant if the machines are localized geographically, this may not be the case if the hosts are dispersed over a wide-area network.

Moreover, a message may never be received by one or more of the processes at all, owing to errors and/or failures in the network, the machines, or the run-time support.

Whereas some applications, such as video conferencing, can tolerate an occasional miss or misordering of messages, there are applications—such as database applications—for which such anomalies are unacceptable.

Therefore, when employing a multicasting mechanism for an application, it is important that you choose one with the characteristics appropriate for your application. Otherwise, measures will need to be provided in the logic of the application in order to handle the anomalies that may occur in message delivery. For that reason, it is useful to classify multicasting mechanisms in terms of their characteristics of message delivery.

Unreliable Multicasting

At its most basic, a multicast system will make a good-faith attempt to deliver messages to each participating process, but the delivery of the correct message to each process is not guaranteed. Thus any message sent by a process may be received by zero or more processes. In the best case, the message, in its correct form, is received by all processes. In the worst case, the message may be received by no process correctly. In other cases, the message may be received by some but not all processes, or the message may be received by some processes in a corrupted form, or more than once. Such a system is said to provide **unreliable multicasting**.

Reliable Multicasting

A multicast system that guarantees that each message is eventually delivered correctly to each process in the group is said to provide **reliable multicasting**. In such a system, each message sent by a process can be assumed to be delivered in a noncorrupted form to all processes in the group eventually.

The definition of reliable multicasting requires that each participating process receives *exactly one copy* of each message sent. Yet the definition places *no* restriction on the order in which the messages are delivered to each individual process: Each process may receive the messages in any permutation of the order in which those messages were sent. For applications where the order of message delivery is significant, it is helpful to further classify reliable multicast systems as described below.

Unordered

An unordered reliable multicast system guarantees the safe delivery of each message, but it provides *no guarantee* of the delivery order of the messages.

For example, suppose three processes P_1, P_2, and P_3 have formed a multicast group. Further suppose that three messages, m_1, m_2, and m_3, have been sent to the group. Then an unordered reliable multicast system may deliver the messages to each of the three processes in any of the 3! (factorial of 3)= 6 permutations (m_1-m_2-m_3, m_1-m_3-m_2, m_2-m_1-m_3, m_2-m_3-m_1, m_3-m_1-m_2, m_3-m_2-m_1).

Note that it is possible for each participant to receive the messages in an order different from the order of messages delivered to other participants. In our example, it is possible for the messages to be delivered to P_1 in the order m_1-m_2-m_3, for the messages to be delivered to P_2 in the order m_2-m_1-m_3, and for the messages to be delivered to P_3 in the order m_1-m_3-m_2. Of course, it is also possible for the messages to be delivered to P_1, P_2, and P_3 in the same order, say m_1-m_2-m_3, but we cannot make that assumption about an application if it employs an unordered multicast mechanism.

FIFO Multicasting

A system that guarantees that the delivery of the messages adheres to the following condition is said to provide **FIFO** (first in-first out) or **send-order** multicast:

> *If process P sent messages m_i and m_j, in that order, to a multicast group, then each process in the multicast group will be delivered the messages m_i and m_j, in that order.*

To illustrate this definition, let's look at an example. Suppose P_1 sends messages m_1, m_2, and m_3, in that order, to a multicast group G. Then, with FIFO multicasting, each process in G is guaranteed to have those messages delivered in that same order: m_1, m_2, then m_3. Note that this definition places no restriction on the delivery order among messages sent by different processes. To illustrate the point, let's use a simplified example of a multicast group of two processes: P_1 and P_2. Suppose P_1 sends messages m_{11} then m_{12}, while P_2 sends messages m_{21} then m_{22}. Then a FIFO multicast system can deliver the messages to each of the two processes in any of the following orders:

m_{11}-m_{12}-m_{21}-m_{22}, m_{11}-m_{21}-m_{12}-m_{22}, m_{11}-m_{21}-m_{22}-m_{12},
m_{21}-m_{11}-m_{12}-m_{22}, m_{21}-m_{11}-m_{22}-m_{12}, m_{21}-m_{22}-m_{11}-m_{12}.

Note that while the messages sent by P_1 must be delivered to each process in the order of the sequence m_{11}-m_{12}, and the messages sent by P_2 must be delivered in the order of the sequence m_{21}-m_{22}, the two sequences can interleave in any manner.

Causal-Order Multicasting

A multicast system is said to provide **causal** multicasting if its message delivery satisfies the following criterion:

> *If message m_i causes (results in) the occurrence of message m_j, then m_i will be delivered to each process prior to m_j. Messages m_i and m_j are said to have a **causal** or **happen-before** relationship, denoted $m_i \rightarrow m_j$.*

The happen-before relationship is transitive: if $m_i \rightarrow m_j$ and $m_j \rightarrow m_k$, then $m_i \rightarrow m_j \rightarrow m_k$. In this case, a causal-order multicast system guarantees that these three messages will be delivered to each process in the order of m_i, m_j, then m_k.

As an illustration, suppose three processes—P_1, P_2, and P_3—are in a multicast group. P_1 sends a message m_1, to which P_2 replies with a multicast message m_2. Since m_2 is triggered by m_1, the two messages share a causal relationship of $m_1 \rightarrow m_2$. Suppose the receiving of m_2 in turn triggers a multicast message m_3 sent by P_3, that is, $m_2 \rightarrow m_3$. The three messages then share the causal relationship of $m_1 \rightarrow m_2 \rightarrow m_3$. A causal-order multicast message system ensures that these three messages will be delivered to each of the three processes in the order m_1-m_2-m_3. Note that in this case there is no restriction on the order of message delivery if the multicast system were FIFO instead of causal.

As a variation of the previous example, suppose P_1 multicasts message m_1, to which P_2 replies with a multicast message m_2, and independently P_3 replies to m_1 with a multicast message m_3. The three messages now share these causal relationships: $m_1 \rightarrow m_2$ and $m_1 \rightarrow m_3$. A causal-order multicast system can deliver these messages to the participating processes in either of the following orders:

m_1-m_2-m_3

m_1-m_3-m_2

In this example, it is not possible for the messages to be delivered to any of the processes in any other permutation of the three messages, such as m_2-m_1-m_3 or m_3-m_1-m_2. The first of these violates the causal relationship $m_1 \rightarrow m_2$, while the second permutation violates the causal relationship $m_1 \rightarrow m_3$.

Atomic Order Multicasting

In an **atomic-order multicast system**, all messages are guaranteed to be delivered to each participant in the *exact same order*. Note that the delivery order does not have to be FIFO or causal, but it must be the same for each process.

Example:

P_1 sends m_1, P_2 sends m_2, and P_3 sends m_3.

An atomic system will guarantee that the messages will be delivered to each process in only one of the six orders: m_1-m_2-m_3, m_1-m_3-m_2, m_2-m_1-m_3, m_2-m_3-m_1, m_3-m_1-m_2, m_3-m_2-m_1.

Example:

P_1 sends m_1, then m_2.

P_2 replies to m_1 by sending m_3.

P_3 replies to m_3 by sending m_4.

Although atomic multicasting imposes no ordering on these messages, the sequence of events dictates that P_1 must deliver m_1 before sending m_2. Likewise, P_2 must receive m_1, then m_3, while P_3 must receive m_3 before m_4. Hence any atomic delivery order must preserve the order m_1-m_3-m_4. The remaining message m_2 can, however, be interleaved with these messages in any manner. Thus an atomic multicast will result in the messages being delivered to each of the processes in one of the following orders: m_1-m_2-m_3-m_4, m_1-m_3-m_2-m_4, or m_1-m_3-m_4-m_2. For example, the messages may be delivered to each process in this order: m_1-m_3-m_2-m_4.

6.5 The Java Basic Multicast API

At the transport layer, the basic multicast supported by Java is an extension of the User Datagram Protocol (UDP), which, as you recall, is connectionless and unreliable. At the network layer of the network architecture, multicast packets are transmitted across networks using Internet multicast routing [cisco.com, 5] supported by routers (known as mrouters) capable of multicast routing in addition to unicast routing. Multicasting on a local network (one interconnected without a router) is carried out using multicasting supported by the local area network protocol (such as Ethernet multicasting). The routing and delivery of multicast messages are topics beyond the scope of this book. Fortunately, such matters are transparent to an application programmer using a multicast API.

For the basic multicast API, Java provides a set of classes that are closely related to the datagram socket API classes that we looked at in Chapter 4. There are three major classes in the API, the first three of which we have already seen in the context of datagram sockets.

1. *InetAddress.* In the datagram socket API, this class represents the IP address of the sender or receiver. In multicasting, this class can be used to identify a multicast group (as explained in the "IP Multicast Addresses" section below).

2. *DatagramPacket.* As with datagram sockets, an object of this class represents an actual datagram; in multicasting, a *DatagramPacket* object represents a packet of data sent to all participants or received by each participant in a multicast group.

3. *MulticastSocket.* The *MulticastSocket* class is derived from the *DatagramSocket* class, with additional capabilities for joining and leaving a multicast group. An object of the multicast datagram socket class can be used for sending and receiving IP multicast packets.

IP Multicast Addresses

Recall that in the Java unicast socket API, a sender identifies a receiver by specifying the host name of the receiving process as well as the protocol port to which the receiving process is bound.

Consider for a moment what a multicast sender needs to address. Instead of a single process, a multicast datagram is meant to be received by all the processes that are currently members of a specific multicast group. Hence each multicast datagram needs to be addressed to a multicast group instead of an individual process.

The Java multicast API uses the Internet Protocol (IP) multicast addresses for identifying multicast groups.

In IPv4, a multicast group is specified by (1) a class D IP address *combined with* (2) a standard UDP port number. (Note that in IPv6 multicast addressing is significantly different; see [faqs.org, 4] for details.) Recall from Chapter 1 that Class D IP addresses are those with the prefix bit string of 1110, and hence these addresses are in the range of 224.0.0.0 to 239.255.255.255, inclusive. Excluding the four prefix bits, there are $32 - 4 = 28$ remaining bits, resulting in an address space size of 2^{28}; that is, approximately 268 million class D addresses are available, although the address 224.0.0.0 is reserved and should not be used by any application. IPv4 multicast addresses are managed and assigned by the Internet Assigned Numbers Authority (IANA) [rfc-editor.org, 3].

An application that uses the Java multicast API must specify at least one multicast address for the application. To select a multicast address for an application, there are the following options:

1. Obtain a permanently assigned static multicast address from IANA. Permanent addresses are limited to global, well-known Internet applications, and their allocations are highly restricted. A list of the currently assigned addresses can be found in [iana.org, 2]. Following is a sample of some of the most interesting of the assigned addresses:

```
224.0.0.1 All Systems on this Subnet
224.0.0.11 Mobile-Agents
224.0.1.16 MUSIC-SERVICE
224.0.1.17 SEANET-TELEMETRY
224.0.1.18 SEANET-IMAGE
224.0.1.41 gatekeeper
224.0.1.84 jini-announcement
224.0.1.85 jini-request
224.0.1.115 Simple Multicast
224.0.6.000-224.0.6.127 Cornell ISIS Project
224.0.7.000-224.0.7.255 Where-Are-You
224.0.8.000-224.0.8.255 INTV
224.0.9.000-224.0.9.255 Invisible Worlds
224.0.11.000-224.0.11.255 NCC.NET Audio
224.0.12.000-224.0.12.063 Microsoft and MSNBC
224.0.17.000-224.0.17.031 Mercantile & Commodity Exchange
224.0.17.064-224.0.17.127 ODN-DTV
224.0.18.000-224.0.18.255 Dow Jones
224.0.19.000-224.0.19.063 Walt Disney Company
224.0.22.000-224.0.22.255 WORLD MCAST
224.2.0.0-224.2.127.253 Multimedia Conference Calls
```

2. Choose an arbitrary address, assuming that the combination of the chosen random address and port number will not likely be in use.

3. Obtain a transient multicast address at run time; such an address can be received by an application through the Session Announcement Protocol [faqs.org, 6].

Option 3 is beyond the scope of this chapter. For our examples and exercises, we will make use of the static address 224.0.0.1, with an equivalent domain name ALL-SYSTEMS.MCAST.NET, for processes running on all machines on the local area network, such as those in your laboratory. Alternatively, we may use an arbitrary address that presumably has not been assigned, such as a number in the range of 239.*.*.* (for example, 239.1.2.3).

In the Java API, a *MulticastSocket* object is bound to a port address such as 3456, and methods of the object allow for the joining and leaving of a multicast address such as 239.1.2.3.

Joining a Multicast Group

To join a multicast group at IP address *m* and UDP port *p*, a *MulticastSocket* object must be instantiated with *p*, then the object's *joinGroup* method can be invoked, specifying the address *m*:

```
// join a Multicast group at IP address 239.1.2.3 and port 3456
InetAddress group = InetAddress.getByName("239.1.2.3");
MulticastSocket s = new MulticastSocket(3456);
s.joinGroup(group);
```

Sending to a Multicast Group

A multicast message can be sent using syntax similar to that for the datagram socket API. Specifically, a datagram packet must be created with the specification of a reference to a byte array containing the data, the length of the array, the multicast address, and a port number. The *send* method of the *MulticastSocket* object (inherited from the *DatagramSocket* class) can then be invoked to send the data.

It is not necessary for a process to join a multicast group in order to send messages to it, although it must do so in order to receive the messages. When a message is sent to a multicast group, all processes that have joined the multicast group, which may include a sender, can be expected (but not guaranteed) to receive the message.

The following code segment illustrates the syntax for sending to a multicast group.

```
String msg = "This is a multicast message.";
InetAddress group = InetAddress.getByName("239.1.2.3");
MulticastSocket s = new MulticastSocket(3456);
s.joinGroup(group); // optional
DatagramPacket hi = new DatagramPacket(msg.getBytes( ),
  msg.length( ), group, 3456);
s.send(hi);
```

Receiving Messages Sent to a Multicast Group

A process that has joined a multicast group may receive messages sent to the group using syntax similar to that for receiving data through a datagram socket API. The following code segment illustrates the syntax for receiving messages sent to a multicast group.

```
byte[] buf = new byte[1000];
InetAddress group = InetAddress.getByName("239.1.2.3");
MulticastSocket s = new MulticastSocket(3456);
s.joinGroup(group);
DatagramPacket recv = new DatagramPacket(buf, buf.length);
s.receive(recv);
```

Leaving a Multicast Group

A process may leave a multicast group by invoking the *leaveGroup* method of a *MulticastSocket* object, specifying the multicast address of the group:

```
s.leaveGroup(group);
```

Setting the "Time-to-Live"

The run-time support for a multicast API often employs a technique known as message propagation, whereby a packet is propagated from a host to a neighboring host in an algorithm that, when executed properly, will eventually deliver the message to all the participants. Under some anomalous circumstances, however, it is possible that the algorithm that controls the message propagation does not terminate properly, resulting in a packet circulating in the network indefinitely. This phenomenon is undesirable, as it causes unnecessary overhead on the systems and the network. To avoid this occurrence, it is recommended that a "time-to-live" parameter be set with each multicast datagram. The time-to-live (**ttl**) parameter, when set, limits the count of network links, or hops, to which the packet will be forwarded on the network.

In the Java API, this parameter can be set by invoking the *setTimeToLive* method of the sender's *MulticastSocket*, as follows:

```
String msg = "Hello everyone!";
InetAddress group = InetAddress.getByName("224.0.0.1");
MulticastSocket s = new MulticastSocket(3456);
s.setTimeToLive(1); // set time-to-live to 1 hop - a count appropriate
                    // for multicasting to local hosts
DatagramPacket hi = new DatagramPacket(msg.getBytes( ),
  msg.length( ),group, 3456);
s.send(hi);
```

The value specified for the *ttl* must be in the range $0 \leq ttl \leq 255$; an *IllegalArgumentException* will be thrown otherwise.

The recommended *ttl* settings are [Harold, 12]

▪ 0 if the multicast is restricted to processes on the same host

▪ 1 if the multicast is restricted to processes on the same subnet

▪ 32 if the multicast is restricted to processes on the same site

▪ 64 if the multicast is restricted to processes on the same region

▪ 128 if the multicast is restricted to processes on the same continent

▪ 255 if the multicast is unrestricted

Example 1 Figures 6.2 and 6.3 show the coding for a simple example multicast application, presented here primarily to illustrate the syntax of the API. When run, each receiver process (Figure 6.3) subscribes to the multicast group 239.1.2.3 at port 1234 and listens for a message. The sender process (Figure 6.2), on the other hand, is not a member of the multicast group (although it can be); it sends a single message to the multicast group 239.1.2.3 at port 1234 before closing its multicast socket.

Figure 6.2 *Example1Sender.java.*

```
1   import java.io.*;
2   import java.net.*;
3
4   /**
5    *  This example illustrates the basic syntax for basic multicast.
6    *  @author M. L. Liu
7    */
8   public class Example1Sender {
9
10  // An application which uses a multicast socket to send
11  // a single message to a multicast group.
12  // The message is specified as a command-line argument.
13
14    public static void main(String[ ] args) {
15       MulticastSocket s;
16       InetAddress group;
17       if (args.length != 1)
18         System.out.println
19           ("This program requires a command line argument");
20       else {
21         try {
22           // create the multicast socket
23           group = InetAddress.getByName("239.1.2.3");
24           s = new MulticastSocket(3456);
25           s.setTimeToLive(32); // restrict multicast to processes
26                                // running on hosts at the same site.
27           String msg = args[0];
```

(continued next page)

```
28            DatagramPacket packet =
29              new DatagramPacket(msg.getBytes(), msg.length(),
30                group, 3456);
31            s.send(packet);
32            s.close( );
33          }
34          catch (Exception ex) { // here if an error has occurred
35            ex.printStackTrace( );
36          } // end catch
37        } //end else
38      } // end main
39    } // end class
```

Figure 6.3 *Example1Receiver.java.*

```
1  import java.io.*;
2  import java.net.*;
3
4
5  /**
6  * This example illustrates the basic syntax for basic multicast.
7  * @author M. L. Liu
8  */
9  public class Example1Receiver {
10
11 // An application that joins a multicast group and
12 // receives a single message sent to the group.
13   public static void main(String[ ] args) {
14     MulticastSocket s;
15     InetAddress group;
16     try {
17        // join a Multicast group and wait to receive a message
18        group = InetAddress.getByName("239.1.2.3");
19        s = new MulticastSocket(3456);
20        s.joinGroup(group);
21        byte[] buf = new byte[100];
22        DatagramPacket recv = new DatagramPacket(buf, buf.length);
23        s.receive(recv);
24        System.out.println(new String(buf));
25        s.close( );
26     }
27     catch (Exception ex) { // here if an error has occurred
28        ex.printStackTrace( );
29     } // end catch
30   } // end main
31 } // end class
```

Example 2 As another illustration of the Java multicast API, we present an example where each process in a multicast group sends a message, and, independently, each process also displays all of the messages it receives as a member of the multicast group.

Example2SenderReceiver.java (Figure 6.4) is the code for the example. In the main method, a thread is spawned to receive and display the messages (see line 39). To ensure that each process is ready to receive, a pause is imposed (see lines 40–43) before the process is allowed to send its message.

Figure 6.4 *Example2SenderReceiver.java.*

```
1   // This program illustrates sending and receiving using multicast
2
3   import java.io.*;
4   import java.net.*;
5   /**
6   * This example illustrates using multithreads to send and
7   * receive multicast in one process.
8   * @author M. L. Liu
9   */
10  public class Example2SenderReceiver{
11
12  // An application which uses a multicast socket to send
13  // a single message to a multicast group, and a separate
14  // thread which uses another multicast socket to receive
15  // messages sent to the same group.
16  // Three command-line arguments are expected:
17  // <multicast IP address>,<multicast port>,<message>
18
19    public static void main(String[ ] args) {
20
21      InetAddress group = null;
22      int port = 0;
23      MulticastSocket socket = null;
24      String characters;
25      byte[] data = null;
26
27      if (args.length !=3)
28        System.out.println("Three command-line arguments are
             expected.")
29      else {
30        try {
31          group = InetAddress.getByName(args[0]);
32          port = Integer.parseInt(args[1]);
33          characters = args[2];
34          data = characters.getBytes();
35          DatagramPacket packet =
36            new DatagramPacket(data, data.length, group, port);
```

(continued next page)

```
37          Thread theThread =
38             new Thread(new ReadThread(group, port));
39          theThread.start();
40          System.out.println("Hit return when ready to send:");
41          InputStreamReader is = new InputStreamReader(System.in);
42          BufferedReader br = new BufferedReader(is);
43          br.readLine();
44          socket = new MulticastSocket(port);
45          socket.setTimeToLive(1);
46          socket.send(packet);
47          socket.close( );
48       }
49       catch (Exception se) {
50          se.printStackTrace( );
51       } // end catch
52    } // end else
53  } // end main
54
55 } // end class
```

Figure 6.5 *ReadThread.java.*

```
1  import java.net.*;
2  import java.io.*;
3  /**
4   * This class is to be used with Example2SenderReceiver for
5   * reading multicast messages while the main thread sends
6   * a multicast message. Each message read is echoed on the
7   * screen.
8   * @author M. L. Liu
9   */
10 class ReadThread implements Runnable {
11
12   static final int MAX_LEN = 30;
13   private InetAddress group;
14   private int port;
15
16   public ReadThread(InetAddress group, int port) {
17     this.group = group ;
18     this.port = port;
19   }
20
21   public void run( ) {
22
23     try {
24
25       MulticastSocket socket = new MulticastSocket(port);
26       socket.joinGroup(group);
27       while (true) {
28         byte[ ] data = new byte[MAX_LEN];
```

(continued next page)

```
29              DatagramPacket packet =
30                 new DatagramPacket(data, data.length, group, port);
31              socket.receive(packet);
32              String s = new String(packet.getData());
33              System.out.println(s);
34          } // end while
35        } // end try
36        catch (Exception exception) {
37           exception.printStackTrace( );
38        } // end catch
39      } // end run
40
41   } //end class
```

The Java basic multicast API and similar mechanisms can be employed to provide support for an application's service logic. Note that an application may use a combination of unicasting and multicasting for its IPC.

An application that makes use of multicasting is sometimes called a **multicast-aware** application.

For those who are interested in a chat room implemented using multicast, (see reference [Hughes, 7]).

6.6 Reliable Multicast API

The Java multicast API that we have explored in this chapter is an extension of the datagram socket API. As a result, it shares a key characteristic of datagrams: unreliable delivery. In particular, messages are not guaranteed to be delivered to any of the receiving processes. Hence, the API provides **unreliable multicasting**. But keep in mind that in your exercises, if you run your processes on one host or on hosts on one subnet, you are not likely to observe any loss of messages or scrambling in the delivery order of the messages. These anomalies are more likely when the participating hosts are remotely connected, due to network failures or routing delays.

As mentioned, there are applications for which unreliable multicasting is unacceptable. For such applications, there are a number of available packages that provide reliable multicast API, some of which include

- **The Java Reliable Multicast Service (JRM Service)** [Rosenzweig, Kadansky, and Hanna, 8; Bischof, 9] is a package that enhances the Java basic multicast API by providing the capabilities for a receiver to repair multicast data that are lost or damaged, as well as security measures to protect data privacy.
- The **Totem** system [alpha.ece.ucsb.edu, 10], developed by the University of California, Santa Barbara, "provides reliable, totally ordered delivery of messages to processes within process groups on a single local-area network, or over multiple local-area networks interconnected by gateways."

▦ TASC's **Reliable Multicast Framework (RMF)** [tascnets.com, 11] provides reliable and send-ordered (FIFO) multicasting.

The use of these packages is beyond the scope of this book. Interested readers are encouraged to consult the references for further details.

Summary

This chapter provides an introduction to the use of group communication in distributed computing.

▦ Multicasting differs from unicasting: Unicasting is one-to-one communication, while multicasting is one-to-many communication.

▦ An archetypal multicast API must provide operations for joining a multicast group, leaving a multicast group, sending to a group, and receiving multicast messages sent to a group.

▦ Basic multicasting is connectionless and unreliable; in an unreliable multicast system, messages are not guaranteed to be safely delivered to each participant.

▦ A reliable multicast system ensures that each message sent to a multicast group is delivered correctly to each participant. Reliable multicasts can be further categorized by the order of message delivery they support:

  ● Unordered multicasting may deliver the messages to each participant in any order.

  ● FIFO multicasting preserves the order of messages sent by each sender.

  ● Causal multicasting preserves causal relationships among the messages.

  ● Atomic multicasting delivers the messages to each participant in the same order.

▦ IP multicast addressing uses a combination of a Class D address and a UDP port number. Class D IP addresses are managed and assigned by IANA. A multicast application may use a static Class D address, a transient address obtained at run time, or an arbitrarily unassigned address.

▦ The Java basic multicast API provides unreliable multicasting. A *MulticastSocket* is created with the specification of a port number. The *joinGroup* and *leaveGroup* methods of the *MulticastSocket* class can be invoked to join or leave a specific multicast group. *Send* and *receive* methods can be invoked to send and receive a multicast datagram. The *DatagramPacket* class is also needed to create the datagrams.

▦ There are existing packages that provide reliable multicasting, including the Java Reliable Multicast (JRM) Service.

Exercises

1. Suppose a multicast group currently has two member processes, P_1 and P_2, participating. Suppose P_1 multicasts m_{11}, then m_{12}; P_2 multicasts m_{21}, then m_{22}. Further assume that no message is lost in delivery.

   a. Theoretically, in how many different orders can all four messages be delivered to each process if the messages are unrelated?

   b. Theoretically, in how many different orders can all the messages be delivered to each process if the messages are casually related as $m_{11} \rightarrow m_{21} \rightarrow m_{12} \rightarrow m_{22}$?

   c. What are the possible orders of message delivery of each process if the messages are unrelated and the multicast is FIFO, causal, and atomic?

   d. What are the possible orders of message delivery of each process if the messages are causally related as $m_{11} \rightarrow m_{21} \rightarrow m_{12} \rightarrow m_{22}$ and the multicast is FIFO, causal, *and* atomic?

2. Suppose the following events take place in chronological order in a multicast group participated by three processes P_1, P_2, and P_3:

   P_1 multicasts m_1.

   P_2 responds to m_1 by multicasting m_2.

   P_3 multicasts m_3 spontaneously.

   P_1 responds to m_3 by multicasting m_4.

   P_3 responds to m_2 by multicasting m_5.

   P_2 multicasts m_6 spontaneously.

   For each of the following scenarios, state in the corresponding entry in the table below whether the scenario is permitted or not by that mode of multicasting.

   a. All processes are delivered m_1, m_2, m_3, m_4, m_5, m_6, in that order.

   b. P_1 and P_2 are each delivered m_1, m_2, m_3, m_4, m_5, m_6.

      P_3 is delivered m_2, m_3, m_1, m_4, m_5, m_6.

   c. P_1 is delivered m_1, m_2, m_5, m_3, m_4, m_6.

      P_2 is delivered m_1, m_3, m_5, m_4, m_2, m_6.

      P_3 is delivered m_3, m_1, m_4, m_2, m_5, m_6.

   d. P_1 is delivered m_1, m_2, m_3, m_4, m_5, m_6

      P_2 is delivered m_1, m_4, m_2, m_3, m_6, m_5.

      P_3 is delivered m_1, m_3, m_6, m_4, m_2, m_5.

   e. P_1 is delivered m_1, m_2, m_3, m_4, m_5, m_6.

      P_2 is delivered m_1, m_3, m_2, m_5, m_4, m_6.

      P_3 is delivered m_1, m_2, m_6, m_5, m_3, m_4.

     f. P_1 is delivered m_2, m_1, m_6.

       P_2 is delivered m_1, m_2, m_6.

       P_3 is delivered m_6, m_2, m_1.

    g. No message is delivered to any of the processes.

Scenario	Reliable Multicasting	FIFO Multicasting	Causal Multicasting	Atomic Multicasting
a.				
b.				
c.				
d.				
e.				
f.				
g.				

3. This exercise is based on *Example1* presented in this chapter.

   a. Compile the *Example1*.java* programs. Then execute them in each of the following sequences. Describe and explain the outcome of each:

     i. Start two or more receiver processes first, then a sender process with a message of your choice.

     ii. Start a sender process with a message of your choice first, then two or more receiver processes.

   b. Based on *Example1Receiver.java*, create a program, *Example1aReceiver.java*, that joins a multicast group of a different IP address (e.g., 239.1.2.4) but the same port. Compile *Example1aReceiver.java*. Start two or more *Example1Receiver* processes first, then an *Example1aReceiver* process, and then a sender process with a message of your choice. Does the *Example1aReceiver* process receive the message? Describe and explain the outcome.

   c. Based on *Example1Receiver.java*, create a program, *Example1bReceiver.java*, that joins a multicast group of the same IP address but a different port. Compile *Example1bReceiver.java*. Start two or more *Example1Receiver* processes first, then an *Example1bReceiver* process, and then a sender process with a message of your choice. Does the *Example1bReceiver* process receive the message? Describe and explain the outcome.

d. Based on *Example1Sender.java*, create a program, *Example1SenderReceiver.java*, that joins the multicast group, sends a message, then listens for (receives) a multicast message before closing the multicast socket and exiting. Compile the program, then start two or more receiver processes before starting the *SenderReceiver* process. Describe the outcome. Turn in the listing of *SenderReceiver.java*.

e. Based on *Example1Sender.java*, create a program, *Example1bSender.java*, that sends a message to the multicast address of the program *Example1bReceiver.java*. Compile the program, then start an *Example1Receiver* process, an *Example1bReceiver* process, an *Example1Sender* process, then an *Example1bSender* process. Describe and explain the message(s) received by each process.

f. Based on *Example1Receiver.java* and *Example1bReceiver.java*, create a program, *Example1cReceiver.java*, that uses two threads (including the main thread). Each thread joins one of the two multicast groups and receives, then displays, one message before leaving the group. You may find the sample *ReadThread.java* useful.

Compile and run *Example1cReceiver.java*, then start an *Example1Sender* process, followed by an *Example1bSender* process. Does the receiver process display both messages? Turn in the program listings of *Example1cReceiver.java* and its thread class.

4. This exercise is based on Example 2 presented in this chapter.

a. Compile *Example2SenderReceiver.java*, then start two or more processes of the program, specifying with each a unique message. Example commands are as follows:

```
java Example2SenderReceiver 239.1.2.3 1234 msg1
java Example2SenderReceiver 239.1.2.3 1234 msg2
java Example2SenderReceiver 239.1.2.3 1234 msg3
```

In this example, each of the three processes should display on screen the messages msg1, msg2, and msg3. Be sure to start all processes before allowing each one to send its message. Describe the run outcomes.

b. Modify *Example2SenderReceiver.java* so that each process sends its message ten times. Compile and run. Describe the run outcomes and hand in the program listings.

5. Write your own multicast application. Write an application such that multiple processes use group communication to carry out an election. There are two candidates: Jones and Smith. Each process multicasts its vote in a message that identifies itself and its vote. Each process keeps track of the vote count for each candidate, including its own. At the end of the election (when everyone in the group has voted), each process tallies the votes independently and displays the outcome on its screen (e.g., Jones 10, Smith 5).

Hand in the listings of your application and answer these questions:

a. How does your design allow the participants to join a multicast group?

b. How does your design synchronize the onset of the election so that every process is ready to receive any vote cast by a member in the group?

c. In your run, do the independent tallies agree with each other? Can you assume that the tallies will always agree with each other? Explain.

References

1. Java 2 Platform SE v1.3.1: Class MulticastSocket, *http://java.sun.com/j2se/1.3/docs/api/java/net/MulticastSocket.html*

2. IANA multicast-addresses, *http://www.iana.org/assignments/multicast-addresses*

3. RFC 3171, IANA Guidelines for IPv4 Multicast Address Allocation, *http://www.rfc-editor.org/rfc/rfc3171.txt*

4. RFC 2375–IPv6 Multicast Address Assignments, *http://www.faqs.org/rfcs/rfc2375.html*

5. Cisco–Multicast Routing, *http://www.cisco.com/warp/public/614/17.html*

6. RFC 2974–Session Announcement Protocol, *http://www.faqs.org/rfcs/rfc2974.html*

7. Merlin Hughes, Multicast the Chatwaves–JavaWorld, October 1999, *http://www.javaworld.com/javaworld/jw-10-1999/jw-10-step_p.html*

8. Phil Rosenzweig, Miriam Kadansky, and Steve Hanna, *The Java Reliable Multicast Service: A Reliable Multicast Library, http://www.sun.com/research/techrep/1998/smli_tr-98-68.pdf*

9. Hans-Peter Bischof, *JRMS Tutorial*, Department of Computer Science, Rochester Institute of Technology, *http://www.cs.rit.edu/~hpb/JRMS/Tutorial/*

10. Robust Distributed Systems for Real-Time Applications, *http://alpha.ece.ucsb.edu/project_totem.html*

11. Reliable Multicast Framework (RMF), *http://www.tascnets.com/newtascnets/Software/RMF/*, Litton TASC.

12. Elliotte Rusty Harold, *Java Network Programming*, Sebastopol, CA: O'Reilly Press, 2000.

## CHAPTER 7

Distributed Objects

Until now we have confined our attention to using the message-passing paradigm in distributed computing. Using the message-passing paradigm, processes exchange data and, by observing mutually agreed upon protocols, collaborate to accomplish desirable tasks. Application program interfaces based on this paradigm, such as the Java unicast and multicast socket APIs, provide the abstraction that hides the details of lower-layer network communications and allows us to write code that performs IPC using relatively simple syntax. This chapter introduces a paradigm that offers further abstraction, distributed objects.

7.1 Message Passing versus Distributed Objects

The message-passing paradigm is a natural model for distributed computing in the sense that it mimics interhuman communications. It is an appropriate paradigm for network services where processes interact with each other through the exchange of messages. But the abstraction provided by this paradigm may not meet the needs of some complex network applications for the following reasons:

■ Basic message passing requires that the participating processes be **tightly coupled.** Throughout their interaction, the processes must be in direct communication with each other. If communication is lost between the processes (owing to failures in the communication link, in the systems, or in one of the processes), the collaboration fails. As an example, consider a session of the *Echo* protocol: If the communication between the client and the server is disrupted, the session cannot continue.

▪ The message-passing paradigm is **data-oriented**. Each message contains data marshaled in a mutually agreed upon format, and each message is interpreted as a request or response according to the protocol. The receiving of each message triggers an action in the receiving process.

For example, in the *Echo* protocol, the receiving of a message from process *p* elicits in the *Echo* server this action: a message containing the same data is sent to *p*. In the same protocol, the receiving of a message from the *Echo* server by process *p* triggers this action: a new message is solicited from the user, and the message is sent to the *Echo* server.

Whereas the data orientation of the paradigm is appropriate for network services and simple network applications, it is inadequate for complex applications involving a large mix of requests and responses. In such an application, the task of interpreting the messages can become overwhelming.

The **distributed object paradigm** is a paradigm that provides abstractions beyond those of the message-passing model. As its name implies, the paradigm is based on objects that exist in a distributed system. In object-oriented programming, supported by an object-oriented programming language such as Java, objects are used to represent an entity that is significant to an application. Each object encapsulates

▪ the **state** or data of the entity—in Java, such data is contained in the **instance variables** of each object;
▪ the **operations** of the entity, through which the state of the entity can be accessed or updated—in Java, these are the **methods**.

To illustrate, consider objects of the *DatagramMessage* class presented in Figure 5.12 (in Chapter 5). Each object instantiated from this class contains three state data items: a message, the sender's address, and the sender's port number. In addition, each object contains three operations: (1) a method *putVal*, which allows the values of these data items to be modified, (2) a *getMessage* method, which allows the current value of the message to be retrieved, and (3) a *getAddress* method, which allows the sender's address to be retrieved.

Although we have used objects such as *DatagramMessage* in previous chapters, those are **local** objects instead of **distributed** objects. Local objects are objects whose methods can only be invoked by a **local process**, a process that runs on the same computer on which the object exists. A distributed object is one whose methods can be invoked by a **remote process**, a process running on a computer connected via a network to the computer on which the object exists. In a distributed object paradigm, network resources are represented by distributed objects. To request service from a network resource, a process invokes one of its operations or methods, passing data as parameters to the method. The method is executed on the remote host, and the response is sent back to the requesting process as a return value. Compared to the message-passing paradigm, the distributed objects paradigm is **action-oriented**: The focus is on the invocation of the operations, while the data passed takes on a secondary role (as parameters and return values). Although less intuitive to human beings, the distributed-object paradigm is more natural to object-oriented software development.

Figure 7.1 illustrates the paradigm. A process running in host *A* makes a method call to a distributed object residing on host *B*, passing with the call the data for the arguments, if any. The method call invokes an action performed by the method on host *A*, and a return value, if any, is passed from host *A* to host *B*. A process that makes use of a distributed object is said to be a **client process** of that object, and the methods of the object are called **remote methods** (as opposed to local methods, or methods belonging to a local object) to the client process.

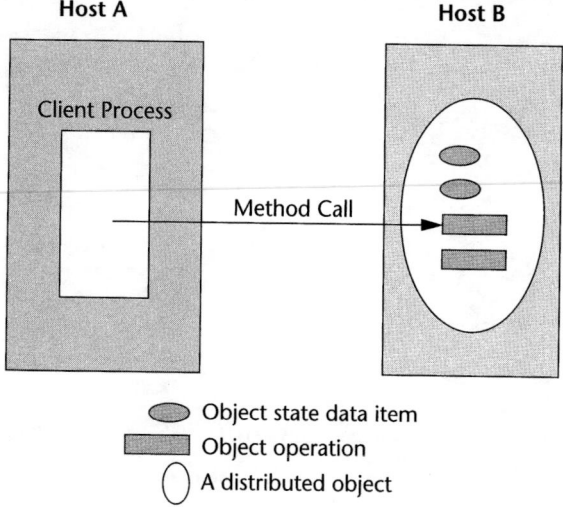

Figure 7.1 The distributed objects paradigm.

In the rest of the chapter, we will present an archetypal facility that supports the distributed object paradigm; then we will explore a sample facility: the **Java Remote Method Invocation (RMI)**.

7.2 An Archetypal Distributed Object Architecture

The premise behind a distributed object system is to minimize the programming differences between remote method invocations and local method calls, thereby allowing remote methods to be invoked in an application using syntax similar to that used for local method invocations. In actuality, there are differences, because remote method invocations involve communication between independent processes, and hence issues such as data marshaling and event synchronization need to be addressed. Such differences are encapsulated in the architecture.

Figure 7.2 presents an archetypal architecture for a facility that supports the distributed objects paradigm.

A distributed object is provided, or **exported**, by a process, here called the **object server**. A facility, here called an **object registry**, or **registry** for short, must be present in the system architecture in order for the distributed object to be registered.

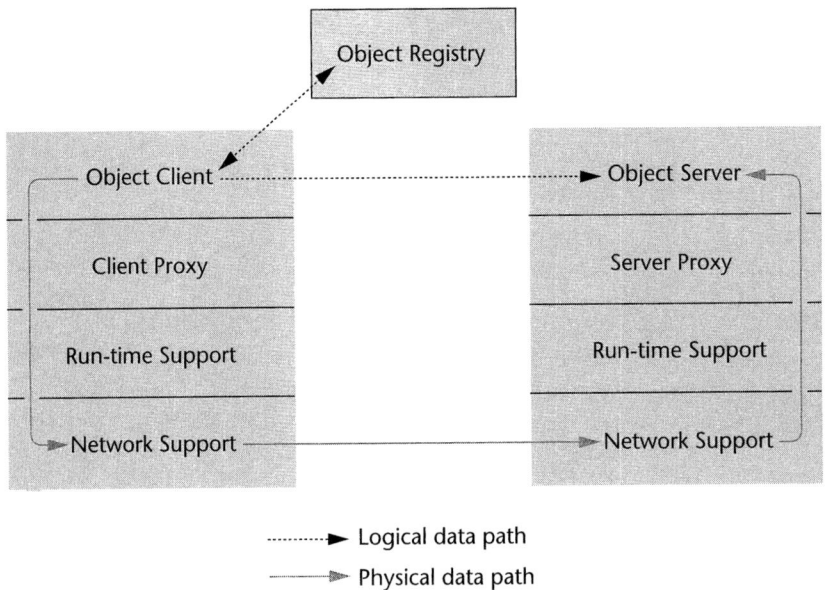

Logical data path

Physical data path

Figure 7.2 An archetypal distributed object system.

In programming language, a reference is a "handle" for an object; it is a representation through which an object can be located in the computer where the object resides.

The term proxy, in the context of distributed computing, refers to a software component that serves as an intermediary between other software components.

To access a distributed object, a process, the **object client**, looks up the registry for a **reference** to the object. This reference is used by the object client to make calls to the methods of the remote object, or **remote methods**. Logically, the object client makes a call directly to a remote method. In reality, the call is handled by a software component, called a **client proxy**, which interacts with the software on the client host to provide the **run-time support** for the distributed object system. The run-time support is responsible for the interprocess communication needed to transmit the call to the remote host, including the marshaling of the argument data that needs to be transmitted to the remote object.

A similar architecture is required on the server side, where the run-time support for the distributed object system handles the receiving of messages and the unmarshaling of data, and forwards the call to a software component called the **server proxy**. The server proxy interfaces with the distributed object to invoke the method call locally, passing in the unmarshaled data for the arguments. The method call triggers the performance of some tasks on the server host. The outcome of the execution of the method, including the marshaled data for the return value, is forwarded by the server proxy to the client proxy, via the run-time support and network support on both sides.

7.3 **Distributed Object Systems**

The distributed object paradigm has been widely adopted in distributed applications, for which a large number of toolkits based on the paradigm are available. Among the most well known of such toolkits are

- Java Remote Method Invocation (RMI),
- systems based on the Common Object Request Broker Architecture (CORBA),
- the Distributed Component Object Model (DCOM), and
- toolkits and APIs that support the Simple Object Access Protocol (SOAP).

Of these, the most straightforward is the Java RMI [java.sun.com/products, 7; java.sun.com/doc, 8; developer.java.sun.com, 9; java.sun.com/marketing, 10], which we will discuss in this chapter in detail. CORBA [corba.org, 1] and its implementations are the subjects of Chapter 9. SOAP [w3.org, 2] is a Web-based protocol and will be introduced in Chapter 11 when we discuss Web-based applications. DCOM [microsoft.com, 3; Grimes, 4] is beyond the scope of this textbook; interested readers should consult the references.

It is not possible to cover all of the existing distributed object facilities, and it is safe to say that toolkits supporting the paradigm will continue to emerge. Familiarizing yourself with the Java RMI API should provide the fundamentals and prepare you for learning the details of similar facilities.

7.4 **Remote Procedure Calls**

Remote Method Invocation (RMI) has its origin in a paradigm called **Remote Procedure Call**.

Procedural programming predates object-oriented programming. In procedural programming a procedure or a function is a control structure that provides the abstraction for an action. The action of a function is invoked by a function call. To allow for variability, a function call may be accompanied by a list of data, known as arguments. The value or the reference of each argument is said to be passed to the function, and it may determine the action actualized by the function. The conventional procedure call is a call to a procedure residing in the same system as the caller, and thus the procedure call can be termed a **local procedure call**.

In the remote procedure call model, a procedure call is made by one process to another, possibly residing in a remote system, with data passed as arguments. When a process receives a call, the actions encoded in the procedure are executed, the caller is notified of the completion of the call, and a return value, if any, is transmitted from the callee to the caller. Figure 7.3 illustrates the RPC paradigm.

Based on the RPC model, a number of application programming interfaces have emerged. These APIs provide remote procedure calls using syntax and semantics resembling those of local procedure calls. To mask the details of interprocess communications, each remote procedure call is transformed by a tool called **rpc-gen** to translate a local procedure call directed to a software module commonly termed a **stub** or, more formally, a **proxy**. Via the proxy, messages representing the procedure call and its arguments are passed to the remote machine.

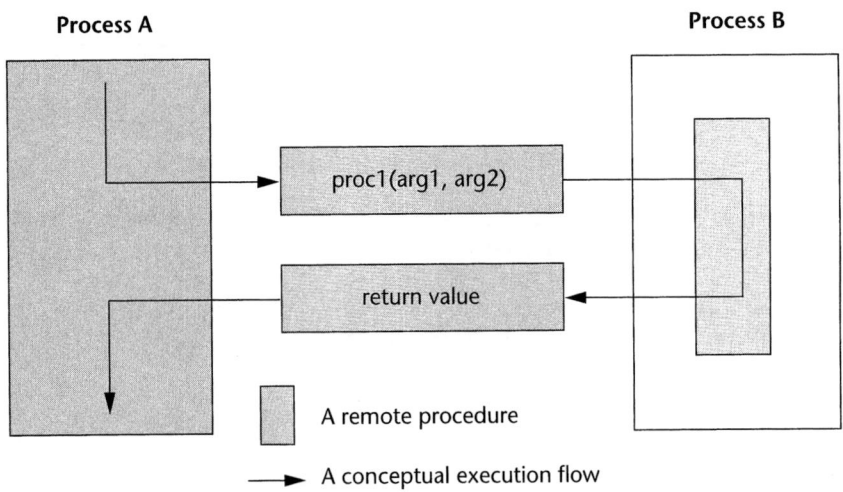

Figure 7.3 The Remote Procedure Call paradigm.

At the other end, a proxy receives the message and transforms it to a local procedure call to the remote procedure. Figure 7.4 illustrates the behind-the-scenes transformation of a remote procedure call into local procedure calls and the intervening message passing.

Note that a proxy is employed on either side to provide the run-time support needed for the interprocess communications, carrying out the necessary data marshaling and socket calls.

Since its introduction in the early 1980s, the Remote Procedure Call model has been widely in use in network applications. There are two prevalent APIs for this paradigm. One, the **Open Network Computing Remote Procedure Call** [ietf.org, 5], evolved from the RPC API that originated from Sun Microsystems, Inc., in the early 1980s. The other well-known API is the **Open Group Distributed Computing Environment** (DCE) RPC [opennc.org, 6]. Both APIs provide a tool, **rpcgen**, for transforming remote procedure calls to local procedure calls to the stub.

In spite of its historical significance, we will not study RPC in detail for the following reasons:

■ RPC, as its name implies, is procedure-oriented. RPC APIs employ syntax for procedural or function calls. Hence they are more suitable to programs written in a procedural language such as C. They are, however, not appropriate

Host A

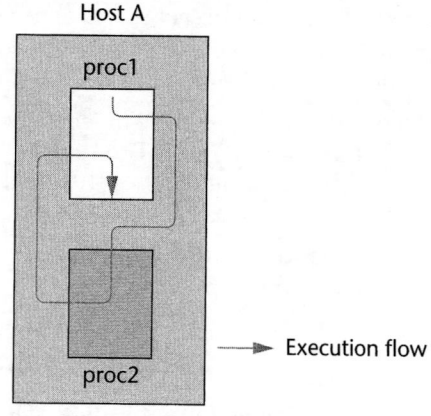

→ Execution flow

A Local Procedure Call

1. proc1 on Host A makes a call to proc2 on Host B.
2. The run-time support maps the call to a call to the proxy on Host A.
3. The proxy marshals the data and makes an IPC call to a proxy on Host B.

7. The proxy receives the return value, unmarshals the data, and forwards the return value to proc1, which resumes its execution flow.

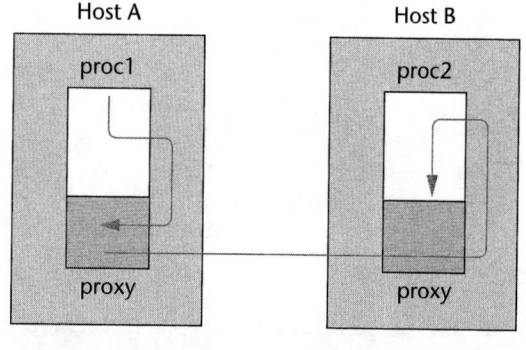

4. The proxy on Host B unmarshals the data received and issues a call to proc2.
5. The code in proc2 is executed and returns to the proxy on Host B.
6. The proxy marshals the return value and makes an IPC call to the proxy on Host A.

A Remote Procedure Call
(the return execution path is not shown)

Figure 7.4 Local Procedure Call versus Remote Procedure Call.

for programs written in Java, the object-oriented language we have adopted for this book.

■ In lieu of RPC, Java provides the **Remote Method Invocation** API, which is object-oriented and has a syntax that is more accessible than RPC.

7.5 **Remote Method Invocation**

Remote Method Invocation (RMI) is an object-oriented implementation of the Remote Procedure Call model. It is an API for Java programs only, but its relative simplicity makes this API a good starting point for students learning to use distributed objects in network applications.

Using RMI, an object server exports a remote object and registers it with a directory service. The object provides remote methods, which can be invoked in client programs.

Syntactically, a remote object is declared with a **remote interface**, an extension of the Java interface. The remote interface is implemented by the object server. An object client accesses the object by invoking its methods, using syntax similar to local method invocations.

In the rest of this chapter we will explore in detail the Java RMI API.

7.6 The Java RMI Architecture

Figure 7.5 illustrates the architecture of the Java RMI API. As with RPC APIs, Java RMI architecture calls for proxy software modules to provide the run-time support needed to transform the remote method invocations to local method calls, and to handle the details for the underlying interprocess communications. In this architecture, three abstraction layers are present on both the client side and the server side. We will look at the two sides separately.

Client-Side Architecture

1. The **Stub layer**. A client process's remote method invocation is directed to a proxy object, known as a **stub**. The stub layer lies beneath the application layer and serves to intercept remote method invocations made by the client program; then it forwards them to the next layer below, the Remote Reference Layer.

2. The **Remote Reference layer** interprets and manages references made from clients to the remote service objects and issues the IPC operations to the next layer, the transport layer, to transmit the method calls to the remote host.

3. The **Transport layer** is TCP based and therefore connection-oriented. This layer and the rest of the network architecture carry out the IPC, transmitting the data representing the method call to the remote host.

Server-Side Architecture

Skeleton, the server-side proxy, is "deprecated" (outdated) since Java 1.2. Its functionalities are replaced by the use of a technique known as "reflection." For our discussion, we will continue to include the skeleton in the architecture as a conceptual presence.

Conceptually, the server-side architecture also involves three abstraction layers, although the implementation varies depending on the Java release.

1. The **Skeleton layer** lies just below the application layer and serves to interact with the stub layer on the client side. Quoting from [java.sun.com/products, 7],

   "The skeleton carries on a conversation with the stub; it reads the parameters for the method call from the link, makes the call to the remote service implementation object, accepts the return value, and then writes the return value back to the stub."

2. The **Remote Reference layer**. This layer manages and transforms the remote reference originating from the client to local references that are understandable to the Skeleton layer.

3. The **Transport layer**. As with client-side architecture, this layer is the connection-oriented transport layer, that is, the TCP in the TCP/IP network architecture.

Object Registry

The RMI API makes it possible for a number of directory services to be used for registering a distributed object. One such directory service is the **Java Naming and Directory Interface** (JNDI), which is more general than the RMI registry that we will use in this chapter in the sense that it can be used by applications that do not use the RMI API. The RMI registry, *rmiregistry*, a simple directory service, is provided with the Java Software Development Kit (SDK). The RMI Registry is a service whose server, when active, runs on the **object server's host machine**, by convention and by default on the TCP port 1099.

The Java SDK is what you download to your machine to obtain the use of the Java class libraries and tools such as the java compiler *javac*.

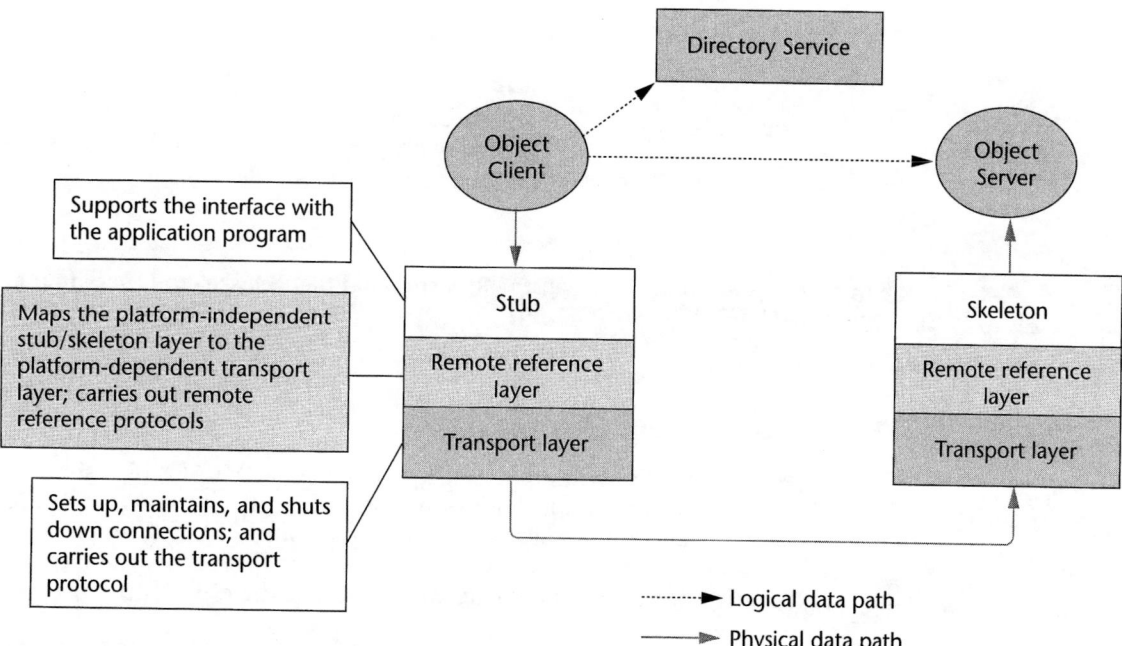

Figure 7.5 The Java RMI architecture.

Logically, from the point of view of the software developer, the remote method invocations issued in a client program interact directly with the remote objects in a server program, in the same manner that a local method call interacts with a local object. Physically, the remote method invocations are transformed to calls to the stubs and skeletons at run time, resulting in data transmission across the network link. Figure 7.6 is a time-event diagram describing the interaction between the stub and the skeleton.

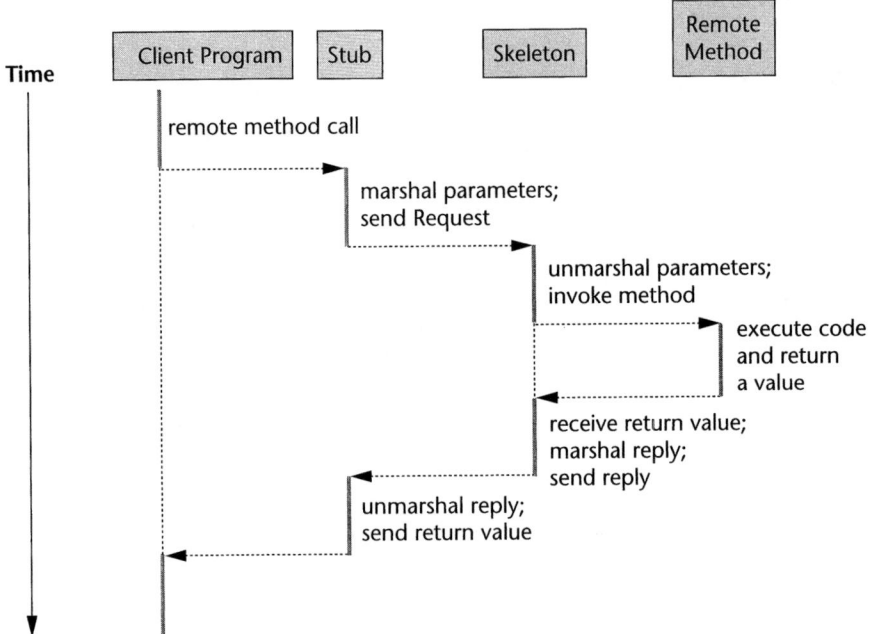

Figure 7.6 Interactions between the RMI stub and the RMI skeleton (based on a diagram in [java.sun.com/docs, 8]).

7.7 The API for the Java RMI

In this section we will introduce a subset of the Java RMI API. (For simplicity, the presentation in this chapter does not cover **security managers**, the use of which is highly recommended for all RMI applications. Security managers are covered in section 8.3 of the next chapter.) There are three areas to be covered: the **remote interface**, the **server-side software**, and the **client-side software**.

The Remote Interface

In the RMI API, the starting point of creating a distributed object is a Java **remote interface**. A Java interface is a class that serves as a template for other classes: It contains declarations, or signatures, of methods whose implementations are to be supplied by classes that realize the interface.

A Java remote interface is an interface that inherits from the Java **Remote** class, which allows the interface to be implemented using RMI syntax. Other than the Remote extension and the RemoteException that must be specified with each method signature, a remote interface has the same syntax as a regular or local Java interface. A sample remote interface illustrating the basic syntax is presented in Figure 7.7.

Figure 7.7 A sample Java remote interface.

```
1  // file: SomeInterface.java
2  // to be implemented by a Java RMI server class.
3
4  import java.rmi.*
5
6  public interface SomeInterface extends Remote {
7     // signature of first remote method
8     public String someMethod1( )
9        throws java.rmi.RemoteException;
10    // signature of second remote method
11    public int someMethod2( float someParameter)
12       throws java.rmi.RemoteException;
13    // signature of other remote methods may follow
14 } // end interface
```

In this example, an interface called *SomeInterface* is declared. The interface extends the Java *Remote* class (line 6), making it a remote interface.

Contained within the block enclosed between curly braces (lines 6–14) are the signatures for two **remote methods**, here named *someMethod1* (lines 8–9) and *someMethod2* (lines 11–12), respectively.

As declared, *someMethod1* requires no arguments to be passed (hence the empty parameter list following the method name) and returns a *String* object. The method *someMethod2* requires an argument value of *float* type and returns a value of *int* type.

Note that a serializable object, such as a *String* object or an object of another class, can be an argument, or it can be returned by the remote method. A copy of the item (specifically, a deep copy of the object), be it a primitive type or an object, is passed to the remote method. A return value is handled likewise, but in the opposite direction.

The *java.rmi.Remote Exception* must be listed in the *throws* clause (lines 9 and 12) of each method signature. An exception of this type is raised when errors occur during the processing of a Remote Method Invocation, and the exception is required to be handled in the method caller's program. Causes of such exceptions include errors that may occur during interprocess communications, such as access failures and connection failures, as well as problems unique to remote method invocations, including errors resulting from the object, the stub, or the skeleton not being found.

A serializable object is an object of a class that is serializable, so that the object can be data marshaled for transmission over a network.

The Server-Side Software

An object server is an object that provides the methods of and the interface to a distributed object. Each object server must (1) implement each of the remote methods specified in the interface, and (2) register an object that contains the implementation with a directory service. It is recommended that the two parts be provided as separate classes, as illustrated below.

The Remote Interface Implementation

A class that implements the remote interface should be provided. The syntax is similar to a class that implements a local interface. Figure 7.8 shows a template of the implementation.

Figure 7.8 Sample syntax for a remote interface implementation.

```
1   import java.rmi.*;
2   import java.rmi.server.*;
3
4   /**
5    * This class implements the remote interface SomeInterface.
6    */
7
8   public class SomeImpl extends UnicastRemoteObject
9       implements SomeInterface {
10
11      public SomeImpl( ) throws RemoteException {
12          super( );
13      }
14
15      public String someMethod1( ) throws RemoteException {
16          // code to be supplied
17      }
18
19      public int someMethod2( ) throws RemoteException {
20          // code to be supplied
21      }
22
23  } //end class
```

The import statements (lines 1–2) are needed for the *UnicastRemoteObject* and the *RemoteException* classes referred to in the code.

The heading of the class (line 8) must specify that (1) it is a subclass of the Java *UnicastRemoteObject* class, and (2) it implements a specific remote interface, named *SomeInterface* in the template. (*Note*: A *UnicastRemoteObject* supports unicast RMI, that is, RMI using unicast IPC. Presumably, a *MulticastRemoteObject* class can also be made available, which supports RMI using multicast IPC.)

A constructor for the class (lines 11–13) should be defined. The first line of the code should be a statement (a *super( )* call) that invokes the base class's constructor. Additional code may appear in the constructor, if needed.

The definition of each remote method should then follow (lines 15–21). The heading of each method should match its signature in the interface file.

Figure 7.9 is a UML diagram for the *SomeImpl* class.

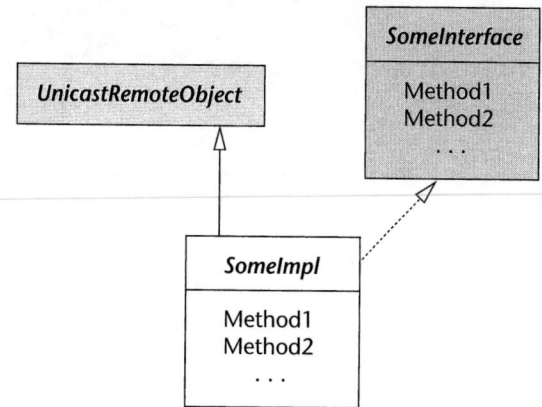

Figure 7.9 The UML class diagram for *SomeImpl*.

Stub and Skeleton Generations

In RMI, a distributed object requires a proxy each for the object server and the object client, known as the object's skeleton and stub, respectively. These proxies are generated from the implementation of a remote interface using a tool provided with the Java SDK: the RMI compiler **rmic**. To invoke this tool, the command, which can be issued at either a UNIX system prompt or a Windows command prompt, is as follows:

```
rmic <class name of the remote interface implementation>
```

For example:

```
rmic SomeImpl
```

If the compilation is successful, two proxy files will be generated, each prefixed with the implementation class name *SomeImpl_skel.class* and *SomeImpl_stub.class*, for example.

The stub file for the object, as well as the remote interface file, must be shared with each object client: These files are required for the client program to compile. A copy of each file may be provided to the object client side manually (that is, by placing a copy of the file in an appropriate directory on the client side).

In addition, the Java RMI has a feature called **stub downloading**, which allows a stub file to be obtained by a client dynamically. Stub downloading will be covered in Chapter 8, where we will investigate some advanced topics in RMI.

The Object Server

The object server class instantiates and exports an object of the remote interface implementation. Figure 7.10 shows a template for the object server class.

Figure 7.10 Sample syntax for an object server.

```
1   import java.rmi.*;
2   import java.rmi.server.*;
3   import java.rmi.registry.Registry;
4   import java.rmi.registry.LocateRegistry;
5   import java.net.*;
6   import java.io.*;
7
8   /**
9    * This class represents the object server for a distributed
10   * object of class SomeImpl, which implements the remote
11   * interface SomeInterface.
12   */
13
14  public class SomeServer {
15    public static void main(String args[]) {
16      String portNum, registryURL;
17      try{
18        // code for port number value to be supplied
19        SomeImpl exportedObj = new SomeImpl( );
20        startRegistry(RMIPortNum);
21        // register the object under the name "some"
22        registryURL = "rmi://localhost:" + portNum + "/some";
23        Naming.rebind(registryURL, exportedObj);
24        System.out.println("Some Server ready.");
25      }// end try
26      catch (Exception re) {
27        System.out.println(
28        "Exception in SomeServer.main: " + re);
29      } // end catch
30    } // end main
31
32    // This method starts a RMI registry on the local host, if it
33    // does not already exist at the specified port number.
34    private static void startRegistry(int RMIPortNum)
35        throws RemoteException{
36      try {
37        Registry registry = LocateRegistry.getRegistry(RMIPortNum);
38        registry.list( );
39        // The above call will throw an exception
40        // if the registry does not already exist
41      }
```

(continued on next page)

```
42         catch (RemoteException ex) {
43            // No valid registry at that port.
44            System.out.println(
45               "RMI registry cannot be located at port "
46               + RMIPortNum);
47            Registry registry =LocateRegistry.createRegistry(RMIPortNum);
48            System.out.println(
49               "RMI registry created at port " + RMIPortNum);
50         } // end catch
51      } // end startRegistry
52
53   } // end class
```

In the following paragraphs we will look at the various parts of this template.

Creating an Object of the Remote Interface Implementation On line 19, an object of the **implementation** class of the remote interface is created; the reference to this object will subsequently be **exported**.

Exporting the Object Lines 20–23 in the template code export the object. To export the object, its reference must be registered with a directory service. As has already been mentioned, in this chapter we will use the *rmiregistry* service provided with the Java SDK. An *rmiregistry* server overseeing an RMI registry must be running on the object server host to provide this functionality.

Each RMI registry maintains a list of exported objects and supports an interface for looking up these objects. A registry may be shared by all object servers running on the same host. Alternatively, an individual server process may create and use its own registry if desired, in which case multiple *rmiregistry* servers may run at different port numbers on the host, each overseeing a separate list of exported objects.

On a production system, there should be an *rmiregistry* server running at all times, presumably at default port number 1099. For our code samples, we will not assume that the RMI Registry is always available, but we will instead make provisions in our code to start a copy of the server on demand and at a port of your choosing, so that each student may use a separate copy of the registry in his/her experiment in order to avoid name collisions.

A name collision occurs if an attempt is made to export an object under a name that coincides with the name of an object already in the registry.

In our object server template, the static method *startRegistry( )* (lines 34–51) is provided in the program to start up an RMI Registry server, if it is not currently running, at a user specified port number (line 20):

```
startRegistry(RMIPortNum);
```

In a production system where the default RMI registry server is used and where it can be assumed to be constantly running, the *startRegistry* call—and hence the *startRegistry* method itself—can be omitted.

In our object server template, the code for exporting an object (lines 22–23) is as follows:

```
// register the object under the name "some"
registryURL = "rmi://localhost:" + portNum + "/some";
Naming.rebind(registryURL, exportedObj);
```

The *Naming* class provides methods for storing and obtaining references from the registry. In particular, the *rebind* method allows an object reference to be stored in the registry with a URL in the form of

```
rmi://<host name>:<port number>/<reference name>
```

The *rebind* method will overwrite any reference in the registry bound with the given reference name. If the overwriting is not desirable, there is also a *bind* method.

The host name should be the name of the server, or simply "localhost.". The reference name is a name of your choice and should be unique in the registry.

The sample code first checks to see if an RMI registry is currently running at the default port. If not, an RMI registry is activated.

Alternatively, an RMI registry can be activated by hand using the *rmiregistry* utility, which comes with the Java Software Development Kit (SDK), by entering the following command at the system prompt:

```
rmiregistry <port number>
```

where the port number is a TCP port number. If no port number is specified, port number 1099 is assumed.

When an object server is executed, the exporting of the distributed object causes the server process to begin to listen and wait for clients to connect and request the service of the object. An RMI object server is a concurrent server: Each request from an object client is serviced using a separate thread of the server. Since invocations of remote methods may be executed concurrently, it is important that the implementation of a remote object is thread-safe. Readers may wish to review the discussion on "Concurrent Programming" in section 1.5 in Chapter 1.

The Client-Side Software

The program for the client class is like any other Java class. The syntax needed for RMI involves locating the RMI registry in the server host and looking up the remote reference for the server object; the reference then can be cast to the remote interface class and the remote methods invoked. A template for an object server is presented in Figure 7.11.

The Import Statements   The import statements (lines 1–4) are needed in the code in order for the program to compile.

Figure 7.11 Template for an object client.

```
1  import java.io.*;
2  import java.rmi.*;
3  import java.rmi.registry.Registry;
4  import java.rmi.registry.LocateRegistry;
5
6  /**
7   * This class represents the object client for a distributed
8   * object of class SomeImpl, which implements the remote
9   * interface SomeInterface.
10 */
11
12 public class SomeClient {
13   public static void main(String args[ ]) {
14     try {
15       int RMIPort;
16       String hostName;
17       String portNum;
18       // Code for obtaining hostName and RMI Registry port
19       // to be supplied.
20
21       // Look up the remote object and cast its reference
22       // to the remote interface class--replace "localHost" with
23       // the appropriate host name of the remote object.
24       String registryURL =
25         "rmi://localhost:" + portNum + "/some";
26       SomeInterface h =
27         (SomeInterface)Naming.lookup(registryURL);
28       // invoke the remote method(s)
29       String message = h.method1( );
30       System.out.println(message);
31       // method2 can be invoked similarly
32     } // end try
33     catch (Exception ex) {
34       ex.printStackTrace( );
35     } // end catch
36   } // end main
37   // Definition for other methods of the class, if any.
38 } // end class
```

Looking Up the Remote Object   The code on lines 24–27 are for looking up the remote object in the registry. The *lookup* method of the *Naming* class is used to retrieve the object reference, if any, previously stored in the registry by the object server. Note that the retrieved reference should be cast to the remote interface (*not* its implementation) class.

```
String registryURL = "rmi://localhost:" + portNum + "/some";
SomeInterface h = (SomeInterface)Naming.lookup(registryURL);
```

Invoking the Remote Method The remote interface reference can be used to invoke any of the methods in the remote interface, as on lines 29–30 in the example:

```
String message = h.method1( );
System.out.println(message);
```

Note that the syntax for the invocation of the remote methods is the same as for local methods.

7.8 A Sample RMI Application

Figures 7.12 through 7.15 comprise the complete listing of a sample RMI application, Hello. The server exports an object that contains a single remote method, *sayHello*. As you study the code, try to identify the different parts we discussed in the previous section.

Figure 7.12 *HelloInterface.java.*

```
 1  // A simple RMI interface file - M. Liu
 2  import java.rmi.*;
 3
 4  /**
 5   * This is a remote interface.
 6   * @author M. L. Liu
 7   */
 8
 9  public interface HelloInterface extends Remote {
10  /**
11   * This remote method returns a message.
12   * @para name - a string containing a name.
13   * @return a String message.
14   */
15    public String sayHello(String name)
16       throws java.rmi.RemoteException;
17
18    }
```

Figure 7.13 *HelloImpl.java.*

```
1  import java.rmi.*;
2  import java.rmi.server.*;
3
4  /**
5  * This class implements the remote interface
6  * HelloInterface.
7  * @author M. L. Liu
8  */
9
10 public class HelloImpl extends UnicastRemoteObject
11 implements HelloInterface {
12
13   public HelloImpl() throws RemoteException {
14     super( );
15   }
16
17   public String sayHello(String name)
18       throws RemoteException {
19     return "Hello, World!" + name;
20   }
21 } // end class
```

Figure 7.14 *HelloServer.java.*

```
1  import java.rmi.*;
2  import java.rmi.server.*;
3  import java.rmi.registry.Registry;
4  import java.rmi.registry.LocateRegistry;
5  import java.net.*;
6  import java.io.*;
7
8  /**
9  *  This class represents the object server for a distributed
10 *  object of class Hello, which implements the remote interface
11 *  HelloInterface.
12 *  @author M. L. Liu
13 */
14
15 public class HelloServer {
16   public static void main(String args[ ]) {
17     InputStreamReader is = new InputStreamReader(System.in);
18     BufferedReader br = new BufferedReader(is);
19     String portNum, registryURL;
```

(continued on next page)

```
20        try{
21          System.out.println("Enter the RMIregistry port number:");
22          portNum = (br.readLine()).trim();
23          int RMIPortNum = Integer.parseInt(portNum);
24          startRegistry(RMIPortNum);
25          HelloImpl exportedObj = new HelloImpl();
26          registryURL = "rmi://localhost:" + portNum + "/hello";
27          Naming.rebind(registryURL, exportedObj);
28  /**/    System.out.println
29  /**/    ("Server registered. Registry currently contains:");
30  /**/    // list names currently in the registry
31  /**/    listRegistry(registryURL);
32          System.out.println("Hello Server ready.");
33        }// end try
34        catch (Exception re) {
35          System.out.println("Exception in HelloServer.main: " + re);
36        } // end catch
37    } // end main
38
39    // This method starts an RMI registry on the local host, if it
40    // does not already exist at the specified port number.
41    private static void startRegistry(int RMIPortNum)
42        throws RemoteException{
43      try {
44          Registry registry = LocateRegistry.getRegistry(RMIPortNum);
45          registry.list( ); // This call will throw an exception
46          // if the registry does not already exist
47      }
48      catch (RemoteException e) {
49          // No valid registry at that port.
50  /**/    System.out.println
51  /**/       ("RMI registry cannot be located at port "
52  /**/       + RMIPortNum);
53          Registry registry =
54            LocateRegistry.createRegistry(RMIPortNum);
55  /**/    System.out.println(
56  /**/       "RMI registry created at port " + RMIPortNum);
57        } // end catch
58    } // end startRegistry
59
60    // This method lists the names registered with a Registry object
61    private static void listRegistry(String registryURL)
62        throws RemoteException, MalformedURLException {
63      System.out.println("Registry " + registryURL + " contains: ")
64      String [ ] names = Naming.list(registryURL);
65      for (int i=0; i < names.length; i++)
66        System.out.println(names[i]);
67    } // end listRegistry
68
69  } // end class
```

Figure 7.15 *HelloClient.java.*

```
1   import java.io.*;
2   import java.rmi.*;
3
4   /**
5   * This class represents the object client for a distributed
6   * object of class Hello, which implements the remote interface
7   * HelloInterface.
8   * @author M. L. Liu
9   */
10
11  public class HelloClient {
12
13      public static void main(String args[ ] ) {
14          try {
15              int RMIPort;
16              String hostName;
17              InputStreamReader is = new InputStreamReader(System.in);
18              BufferedReader br = new BufferedReader(is);
19              System.out.println("Enter the RMIRegistry host namer:");
20              hostName = br.readLine();
21              System.out.println("Enter the RMIregistry port number:");
22              String portNum = br.readLine();
23              RMIPort = Integer.parseInt(portNum);
24              String registryURL =
25                  "rmi://" + hostName+ ":" + portNum + "/hello";
26              // find the remote object and cast it to an interface object
27              HelloInterface h =
28                  (HelloInterface)Naming.lookup(registryURL);
29              System.out.println("Lookup completed " );
30              // invoke the remote method
31              String message = h.sayHello("Donald Duck");
32              System.out.println("HelloClient: " + message);
33          } // end try
34          catch (Exception e) {
35              System.out.println("Exception in HelloClient: " + e);
36          } // end catch
37      } // end main
38  } // end class
```

Once you understand the basic structure of the sample RMI application we have just presented, you should be able to use the syntax in the template to build any RMI application by replacing the presentation and application logic; the service logic (using RMI) is invariant.

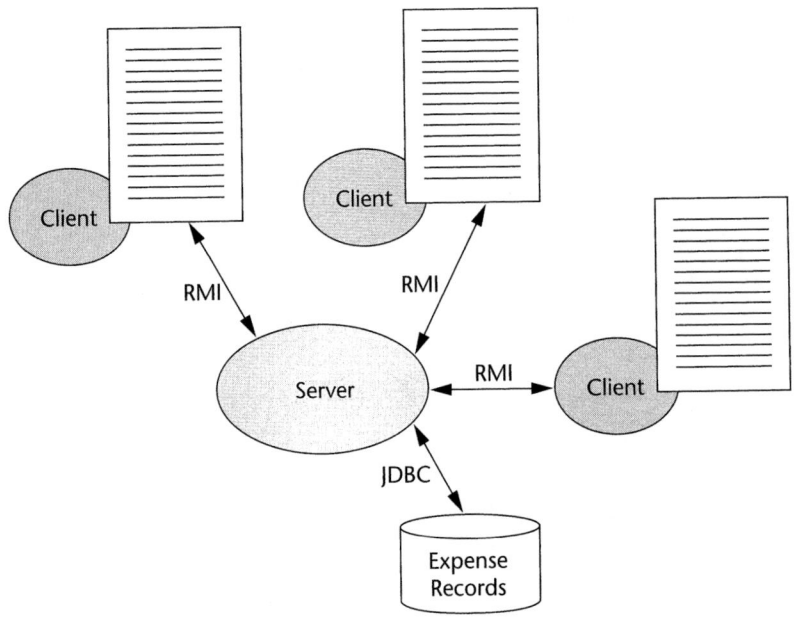

Figure 7.16 A sample RMI application.

The RMI technology is a good candidate for a software component at the service layer. A sample industrial application is the expense report system for an enterprise, shown in Figure 7.16 and described in [java.sun.com/marketing, 8]. In the illustrated application, the object server provides remote methods that allow the object clients to look up or update the data in an expense records database. Programs that are clients of the object provide the application or business logic for processing the data and the presentation logic for the user interface.

The Java RMI facility is rich in features. This chapter has presented a very basic subset of those features, as an illustration of a distributed object system. Some of the more interesting advanced features of RMI will be introduced in the next chapter.

7.9 Steps for Building an RMI Application

Having looked at the various aspects of the RMI API, we now conclude with a description of the step-by-step procedure for building an RMI application so that you can experiment with the paradigm. We describe the algorithm for doing so on both sides of the object server and the object client. Keep in mind that in a production environment it is likely that the development of software on the two sides may proceed independently.

The algorithm is phrased in terms of an application named *Some*. The steps will apply to any application by replacing the name *Some* with the name of the application.

Algorithm for Developing the Server-Side Software

1. Open a directory for all the files to be generated for this application.
2. Specify the remote server interface in *SomeInterface.java*. Compile and revise it until there is no more syntax error.
3. Implement the interface in *SomeImpl.java*. Compile and revise it until there is no more syntax error.
4. Use the RMI compiler ***rmic*** to process the implementation class and generate the stub file and skelton file for the remote object:

   ```
   rmic SomeImpl
   ```

   The files generated can be found in the directory as *SomeImpl_Skel.class* and *SomeImpl_Stub.class*. Steps 3 and 4 should be repeated each time a change is made to the interface implementation.
5. Create the object server program *SomeServer.java*. Compile and revise it until there is no more syntax error.
6. Activate the object server

   ```
   java SomeServer
   ```

Algorithm for Developing the Client-Side Software

1. Open a directory for all the files to be generated for this application.
2. Obtain a copy of the remote interface class file. Alternatively, obtain a copy of the source file for the remote interface, and compile it using ***javac*** to generate the interface class file.
3. Obtain a copy of the stub file for the implementation of the interface *SomeImpl_Stub.class*.
4. Develop the client program *SomeClient.java* and compile it to generate the client class.
5. Activate the client.

   ```
   java SomeClient
   ```

Figure 7.17 illustrates the placement of the various files for an application on the client side and the server side. The remote interface class and the stub class files for each remote object must be present on the object client host, along with the object client class. On the server side are the interface class, the object server class, the interface implementation class, and the stub class for the remote object.

Object Client Host

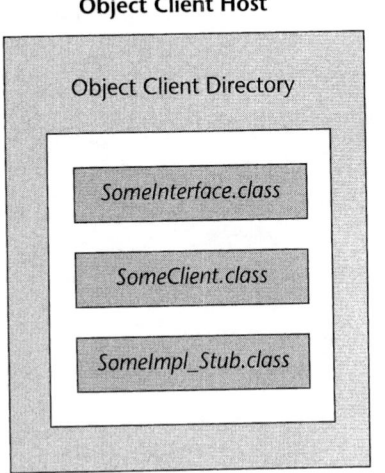

Object Server Host

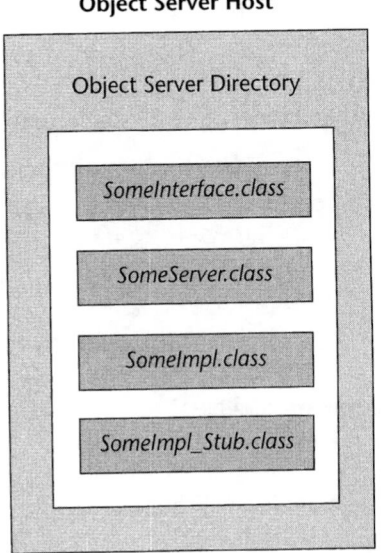

Figure 7.17 Placement of files for an RMI application.

7.10 Testing and Debugging

As with any form of network programming, the tasks of testing and debugging concurrent processes are nontrivial. It is recommended that you adhere to the following incremental steps in developing an RMI application:

1. Build a template for a minimal RMI program. Start with a remote interface containing a single method signature, its implementation using a stub, a server program that exports the object, and a client program with just enough code that invokes the remote method. Test the template programs on one host until the remote method can be made successfully.

2. Add one signature at a time to the interface. With each addition, modify the client program to invoke the added method.

3. Fill in the definition of each remote method, one at a time. Test and thoroughly debug each newly added method before proceeding with the next one.

4. After all remote methods have been thoroughly tested, develop the client application using an incremental approach. With each increment, test and debug the programs.

5. Distribute the programs on separate machines. Test and debug.

7.11 Comparison of RMI and Socket APIs

The Remote Method Invocation API, as representative of the distributed object paradigm, is an efficient tool for building network applications. It can be used in lieu of the socket API (representing the message-passing paradigm) to build a network application rapidly. However, you should be aware that the gain in convenience is not without its drawbacks.

Some of the trade-offs between the RMI API and the socket API are enumerated below:

■ The socket API works closely with the operating system and hence has less execution overhead. RMI requires additional software support, including the proxies and the directory service, which inevitably incur run-time overhead. For applications that require high performance, the socket API may remain the only viable solution.

■ On the other hand, the RMI API provides the abstraction that eases the task of software development. Programs developed with a higher level of abstraction are more comprehensible and hence easier to debug.

■ Because it operates at a lower layer, a socket API is typically platform and language independent. The same may not be true with RMI. The Java RMI, for example, requires Java-specific run-time supports. As a result, an application implemented using Java RMI must be written in Java and can only run on Java platforms.

The choice of an appropriate paradigm and an appropriate API is a key decision in the design of an application. Depending on the circumstances, it is possible for one paradigm or API to be used in some parts of an application, while another paradigm or API is used elsewhere in the application.

In software engineering, a prototype is an initial version put together quickly to demonstrate the user interface and functionalities of a proposed application.

Because of the relative ease with which network applications can be developed using RMI, RMI is a good candidate for the rapid development of a prototype for an application.

7.12 Food for Thought

The model of distributed object-oriented computing presented in this chapter is based on the vision that, from the programmer's point of view, there is no essential distinction between local objects and remote objects. Although this vision is widely accepted as the basis of distributed object systems, it is not without its detractors. The authors of [research.sun.com, 11], for one, argue that this vision, though convenient, is inappropriate because it ignores the inherent differences between local and remote objects. Exercise 11 at the end of the chapter asks you to look into this argument.

Summary

This chapter introduced you to the distributed object paradigm. Following is a summary of the key points:

- The distributed object paradigm is at a higher level of abstraction than the message-passing paradigm.
- Using the paradigm, a process invokes methods of a remote object, passing in data as arguments and receiving a return value with each call, using syntax similar to local method calls.
- In a distributed object system, an object server provides a distributed object whose methods can be invoked by an object client. Each side requires a proxy that interacts with the system's run-time support to perform the necessary IPC. Additionally, an object registry must be available to enable distributed objects to be registered and looked up.
- Among the best-known distributed object system protocols are the Java Remote Method Invocation (RMI), the Distributed Component Object Model (DCOM), the Common Object Request Broker Architecture (CORBA), and the Simple Object Access Protocol (SOAP).
- Java RMI is representative of distributed object systems. Some of the topics related to RMI covered are:
  - The architecture of the Java remote method invocation API includes three architecture layers on both the client side and the server side. On the client side, the stub layer accepts a remote method invocation and transforms it into messages to the server side. On the server side, the skeleton layer receives the messages and transforms them to a local method call to the remote method. A directory service such as JNDI or the RMI Registry can be used for the object registry.
  - The software for an RMI application includes a remote interface, server-side software, and client-side software. The syntax and recommended algorithms for developing the software were presented.
- Some trade-offs between the socket API and the Java RMI API were discussed.

Exercises

1. Compare and contrast the message-passing paradigm with the distributed object paradigm.

2. Compare and contrast a local procedure call with a remote procedure call.

3. Describe the Java RMI architecture. What is the role of the RMI Registry?

4. Consider a simple application where a client sends two integer values to a server, which sums the values and returns the sum to the client.

   a. Describe how you would implement the application using the socket API. Describe the messages exchanged and the actions triggered by each message.

   b. Describe how you would implement the application using the RMI API. Describe the interface, the remote methods, and the remote method invocations in the client program.

5. This exercise makes use of the *Hello* example.

   a. Open a directory for this exercise. Place the source files for the *Hello* example in the directory.

   b. Compile *HelloInterface.java* and *HelloImpl.java*.

   c. Use *rmic* to compile *HelloImpl*. Check the folder to see that the proxy classes are generated. What are their names?

   d. Compile *HelloServer.java*. Check the contents of your folder.

   e. Run the server, specifying a random port number for the RMI Registry. Check the messages displayed, including the list of names currently in the registry. Do you see the name under which the server registered the remote object (as specified in the program)?

   f. Compile and run *HelloClient.java*. When prompted, specify "localhost" for the host name and the RMI registry port number you previously specified. What happened? Explain.

   g. Run the client program on a separate machine. Were you successful?

6. Open a new folder. Copy all the source files of the *Hello* example to the folder. Add code in the *sayHello* method of *HelloImpl.java* so that there is a 5-second delay before the method returns. This has the effect of artificially lengthening the latency for each invocation of the method. Compile and start the server.

   In separate screens, start two or more clients. Observe the sequence of events displayed on the screens. Can you tell if the method calls are executed by the object server concurrently or iteratively? Explain.

7. Open a new folder. Copy all the source files of the *Hello* example to the folder. Modify the *sayHello* method so that an argument, a name string, is passed in as an argument, and the return string is the string "Hello!" concatenated with the name string.

   a. Show the code modifications.

   b. Recompile and run the server and then the client. Describe and explain what happened.

   c. Run *rmic* again to generate the new proxies for the modified interface, and then run the server and the client.

   Hand in the source listings and a script of the run outcomes.

8. Use RMI to implement a *Daytime* server and client suite.

9. Using RMI, write an application for a prototype opinion poll system. Assume that only one issue is being polled. Respondents may choose *yes, no, or don't care*. Write a server application to accept the votes, keep the tally (in transient memory), and provide the current counts to those who are interested.

   a. Write the interface file first. It should provide remote methods for accepting a response to the poll, providing the current counts (e.g., "10 yes, 2 no, 5 don't care") only when the client requests it.

   b. Design and implement a server to (i) export the remote methods, and (ii) maintain the state information (the counts). Note that the updates of the counts should be protected with mutual exclusion.

   c. Design and implement a client application to provide a user interface for accepting a response and/or a request, and to interact with the server appropriately via remote method invocations.

   d. Test your application by running two or more clients on different machines (preferably on different platforms).

   e. Hand in listings of your files, which should include your source files (the interface file, the server file(s), the client file(s)), and a README file that explains the contents and interrelationship of your source files and the procedure for running your work.

10. Create an RMI application for conducting an election. The server exports two methods:

    ▪ *castVote*, which accepts as a parameter a string containing a candidate's name (Gore or Bush), and returns nothing, and

    ▪ *getResult*, which returns, in an *int* array, the current count for each candidate.

    Test your application by running all processes on one machine. Then test your application by running the client and server on *separate* machines.

    Turn in the source code for the remote interface, the server, and the client.

11. Read reference [research.sun.com, 11]. Summarize the reasons why the authors find fault with the distributed object model, which minimizes the programming differences between local and remote object invocations. Do you agree with the authors? What might be an alternative model for distributed objects that addresses the authors' complaints? (*Hint*: Look into the Jini Network Technology [sun.com, 12].)

References

1. Object Management Group. Welcome to the OMG's CORBA Website, *http://www.corba.org/*

2. World Wide Web Consortium. SOAP Version 1.2 Part 0: Primer, *http://www.w3.org/TR/soap12-part0/*

3. Distributed Component Object Model (DCOM)—Downloads, Specifications, Samples, Papers, and Resources for Microsoft DCOM, *http://www.microsoft.com/com/tech/DCOM.asp*, Microsoft.

4. Richard T. Grimes. *Professional DCOM Programming*. Chicago, IL: Wrox Press, Inc., 1997.

5. RFC 1831: Remote Procedure Call Protocol Specification Version 2, August 1995, *http://www.ietf.org/rfc/rfc1831.txt*

6. The Open Group, DCE 1.1: Remote Procedure Call, *http://www.opennc.org/public/pubs/catalog/c706.htm*

7. Java™ Remote Method Invocation, *http://java.sun.com/products/jdk/rmi*

8. RMI—The Java Tutorial, *http://java.sun.com/docs/books/tutorial/rmi/*

9. Introduction to Distributed Computing with RMI, *http://developer.java.sun.com/developer/onlineTraining/rmi/RMI.html*

10. Java Remote Method Invocation—Distributed Computing for Java, *http://java.sun.com/marketing/collateral/javarmi.html*

11. Jim Waldo, Geoff Wyant, Ann Wollrath, and Sam Kendall. A Note on Distributed Computing, Report TR-94-29, Sun Microsystems Laboratories, 1994, *http://research.sun.com/research/techrep/1994/smli_tr-94-29.pdf*

12. Jini Network Technology, An Executive Overview, white paper. Sun Microsystems, Inc., 2001, *http://www.sun.com/software/jini/whitepapers/jini-execoverview.pdf*

CHAPTER **8**

Advanced RMI

In the last chapter, Java RMI was introduced as an example of a distributed object system. By design, only the most basic features of RMI were presented there, although we mentioned that the API has a rich collection of features. Chapter 8 may be omitted if you are not interested in exploring RMI further. However, the use of security managers (see section 8.3) is highly recommended for all RMI applications.

In this chapter we will look at some of RMI's more interesting advanced features, namely, **stub downloading**, **security manager**, and **client callback**. Although these features are not inherent to the distributed object paradigm, they are helpful mechanisms and can be useful to application developers. Studying these topics also provides a chance to reinforce your understanding of the distributed object paradigm in general, and the RMI API in particular.

8.1 Client Callback

Consider an RMI application where participating processes must be notified by an object server when a certain event occurs. As examples, participants in a chat room need to be notified when a new participant has entered the chat room, and must processes participating in a real-time online auction are to be notified when the bidding starts. Such a feature is also useful in a network game where the players need to be informed of the updated state of the game. Within the framework of the basic RMI API presented in the previous chapter, it is not possible for the server to initiate a call to the client to transmit some information when the information becomes available, since a remote method call is unidirectional (from the client to the server). One way to accomplish the transmission of such information is for each client process to **poll** the object server by repeatedly invoking a remote method, say *HasBiddingStarted*, until the method returns true:

```
ServerInterface h =
  (ServerInterface)Naming.lookup(registryURL);
while (!(h.HasBiddingStarted( )) {;}
  // start bidding
```

Polling is indeed a technique employed in many network programs. But it is a very costly technique in terms of system resources, as each remote method invocation takes up a separate thread on the server host, along with the system resources that its execution entails. A more efficient technique is known as **callback**: It allows each object client interested in the occurrence of an event to register itself with the object server so that the server may initiate a remote method invocation to the object clients when the awaited event occurs. Figure 8.1 compares the two techniques: polling and callback.

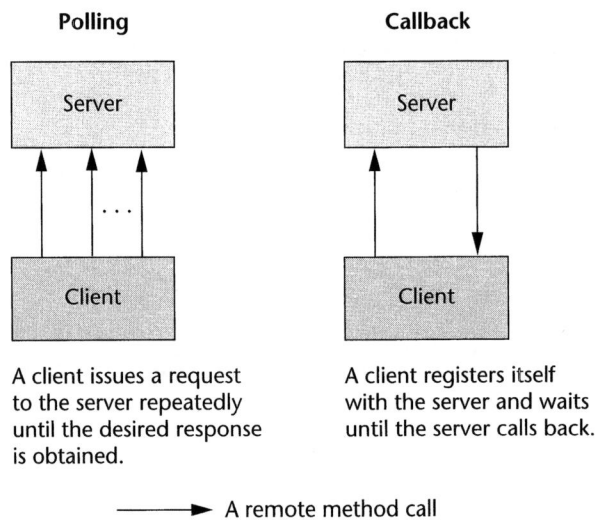

A client issues a request to the server repeatedly until the desired response is obtained.

A client registers itself with the server and waits until the server calls back.

————► A remote method call

Figure 8.1 Polling versus callback.

In RMI, **client callback** is a feature that allows an object client to register itself with a remote object server for **callbacks** so that the server may issue a remote method invocation to the client when an awaited event occurs. Note that with client callbacks, the remote method invocations are now two-way, or duplex— from the client to the server, and vice versa. Since the basic RMI API, introduced in the previous chapter, allows only remote method invocations issued by a client to an object server, clearly additional syntax is necessary to support client callbacks.

When an object server makes a callback, the roles of the two processes are reversed: The object server becomes a client of the object client so that the object server may initiate a remote method invocation to the object client.

Figure 8.2 illustrates the architecture for RMI with client callback. Compared with the architecture for basic RMI, two sets of proxies are now required. One set is required for the server remote interface, as in the basic RMI architecture. The other set of proxies is for an additional interface, the client remote interface. The client remote interface provides a remote method that can be invoked by the server for the callback.

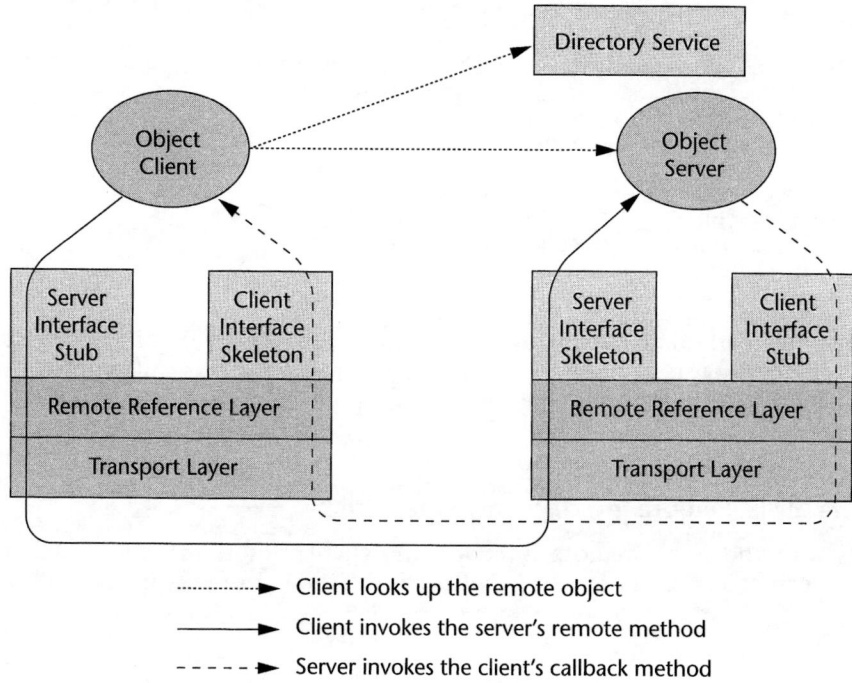

Figure 8.2 The architecture of RMI with client callback.

As an illustration, we will augment the *Hello* application presented in the previous chapter so that each client object will register with the server for callback and then will be notified subsequently whenever another client object registers for callback with the object server.

Client-Side Augmentation for Client Callback

For the callback, the client must provide a remote method that allows the server to notify it of the awaited event. It can do so in a manner similar to the remote methods provided by the object server. We will explain the syntax in the subsections that follow.

The Client Remote Interface

Recall that the object server provides a remote interface that declares the remote methods that an object client may invoke. For the callback, a similar remote interface will need to be provided by the object client. We will call this interface the client remote interface (for example, *CallbackClientInterface*), as opposed to the server remote interface (for example, *CallbackServerInterface*). The client remote interface should contain at least one method to be invoked by the server for the callbacks. The client remote interface for our example is as follows:

```
public interface CallbackClientInterface
    extends java.rmi.Remote{

  // This remote method is invoked by a callback
  // server to make a callback to a client which
  // implements this interface.
  // The parameter is a string containing information for the
  // client to process upon being called back.
  // This method returns a message to the server.
  public string notifyMe(String message)
    throws java.rmi.RemoteException;

} // end interface
```

Here the method *notifyMe* is to be invoked by the server when it makes the callbacks, passing as argument a string. Upon receiving the callback, the client makes use of the string it receives to compose a string that it returns to the server.

The Client Remote Interface Implementation

As with the server remote interface, the client remote interface needs to be implemented in a class, called *CallbackClientImpl* in our example, as follows:

```
import java.rmi.*;
import java.rmi.server.*;
public class CallbackClientImpl extends UnicastRemoteObject
  implements CallbackClientInterface {
  public CallbackClientImpl() throws RemoteException {
    super( );
  }
  public string notifyMe(String message){
    String returnMessage = "Call back received: " + message;
    System.out.println(returnMessage);
    return returnMessage;
  }
} // end CallbackClientImpl class
```

In this example the callback method *notifyMe* simply displays the string returned from the server, and returns a string to the server.

As with the server remote interface, the compiler **rmic** should be applied to the implementation of the client remote interface to generate the proxies needed at run time.

Augmentation to the Client Class

In the object client class, code needs to be added for the client to instantiate an object of the remote client interface implementation. A reference to the object is then registered with the server using a remote method provided by the server (see the next section, "Server-Side Augmentations for Client Callback"). A sample of the code that needs to be added to the client class is as follows:

```
CallbackServerInterface h =
  (CallbackServerInterface)Naming.lookup(registryURL);
CallbackClientInterface callbackObj =
  new CallbackClientImpl();
// register for callback
h.registerForCallback(callbackObj);
```

Figures 8.3 through 8.5 present the code for the client-side software for the modified *Hello* application.

Figure 8.3 *CallbackClientInterface.java* for the modified *Hello* application.

```
1   import java.rmi.*;
2
3   /**
4    *  This is a remote interface for illustrating RMI
5    *  client callback.
6    *  @author M. L. Liu
7    */
8
9   public interface CallbackClientInterface
10       extends java.rmi.Remote{
11      // This remote method is invoked by a callback
12      // server to make a callback to a client that
13      // implements this interface.
14      // @message a string containing information for the
15      // client to process upon being called back.
16
17      public void notifyMe(String message)
18         throws java.rmi.RemoteException;
19
20   } // end interface
```

Figure 8.4 *CallbackClientImpl.java* for the modified *Hello* application.

```
1   import java.rmi.*;
2   import java.rmi.server.*;
3
4   /**
5    * This class implements the remote interface
6    * CallbackClientInterface.
7    * @author M. L. Liu
8    */
```

(continued next page)

```
 9
10  public class CallbackClientImpl extends UnicastRemoteObject
11      implements CallbackClientInterface {
12
13    public CallbackClientImpl() throws RemoteException {
14      super( );
15    }
16
17    public string notifyMe(String message){
18      String returnMessage = "Call back received: " + message;
19      System.out.println(returnMessage);
20        return returnMessage;
21    }
22
23  } // end CallbackClientImpl class
```

Figure 8.5 *CallbackClient.java* for the modified *Hello* application.

```
 1  import java.io.*;
 2  import java.rmi.*;
 3
 4  /**
 5   * This class represents the object client for a
 6   * distributed object of class CallbackServerImpl,
 7   * which implements the remote interface
 8   * CallbackServerInterface. It also accepts callbacks
 9   * from the server.
10   *
11   *
12   *
13   * @author M. L. Liu
14   */
15
16  public class CallbackClient {
17
18    public static void main(String args[]) {
19      try {
20        int RMIPort;
21        String hostName;
22        InputStreamReader is =
23          new InputStreamReader(System.in);
24        BufferedReader br = new BufferedReader(is);
25        System.out.println(
26          "Enter the RMIRegistry host namer:");
27        hostName = br.readLine();
28        System.out.println(
29          "Enter the RMIRegistry port number:");
30        String portNum = br.readLine();
31        RMIPort = Integer.parseInt(portNum);
32        System.out.println(
33          "Enter how many seconds to stay registered:");
```

(continued on next page)

```
34          String timeDuration = br.readLine();
35          int time = Integer.parseInt(timeDuration);
36          String registryURL =
37             "rmi://localhost:" + portNum + "/callback";
38          // find the remote object and cast it to an
39          // interface object
40          CallbackServerInterface h =
41             (CallbackServerInterface)Naming.lookup(registryURL);
42          System.out.println("Lookup completed " );
43          System.out.println("Server said " + h.sayHello());
44          CallbackClientInterface callbackObj =
45             new CallbackClientImpl();
46          // register for callback
47          h.registerForCallback(callbackObj);
48          System.out.println("Registered for callback.");
49          try {
50             Thread.sleep(time * 1000);
51          }
52          catch (InterruptedException ex){ // sleep over
53             h.unregisterForCallback(callbackObj);
54             System.out.println("Unregistered for callback.");
55          }
56       } // end try
57       catch (Exception e) {
58          System.out.println(
59             "Exception in CallbackClient: " + e);
60       }
61    } // end main
62 } // end class
```

Server-Side Augmentations for Client Callback

On the server side, a remote method needs to be provided to allow a client to register for callback. In the simplest case, the method signature may be analogous to this sample:

```
public void registerForCallback(
   // You may choose a method name of your choice.
   CallbackClientInterface callbackClientObject
) throws java.rmi.RemoteException;
```

A reference to an object that implements the client remote interface (*CallbackClientInterface, not CallbackClientImpl*) is accepted as an argument. A companion method *unregisterForCallback* may also be provided to allow a client to cancel the registration (so that it will no longer receive callbacks). The implementation of these methods, along with a local method *doCallbacks*—for performing the callbacks—is presented in Figure 8.7. Figure 8.6 shows the server interface file augmented with the additional method signatures. Figure 8.8 shows the code for the object server, which is unchanged from the version presented in the last chapter.

Figure 8.6 *CallbackServerInterface.java* for the modified *Hello* application.

```
1  import java.rmi.*;
2
3  /**
4  * This is a remote interface for illustrating RMI
5  * client callback.
6  * @author M. L. Liu
7  */
8
9  public interface CallbackServerInterface extends Remote {
10
11    public String sayHello( )
12      throws java.rmi.RemoteException;
13
14      // This remote method allows an object client to
15      // register for callback
16      // @param callbackClientObject is a reference to the
17      //   object of the client; to be used by the server
18      //   to make its callbacks
19
20    public void registerForCallback(
21        CallbackClientInterface callbackClientObject)
22      throws java.rmi.RemoteException;
23
24      // This remote method allows an object client to
25      // cancel its registration for callback
26
27    public void unregisterForCallback(
28        CallbackClientInterface callbackClientObject)
29      throws java.rmi.RemoteException;
30  }
```

Figure 8.7 *CallbackServerImpl.java* for the modified *Hello* application.

```
1  import java.rmi.*;
2  import java.rmi.server.*;
3  import java.util.Vector;
4
5  /**
6  * This class implements the remote interface
7  * CallbackServerInterface.
8  * @author M. L. Liu
9  */
10
11  public class CallbackServerImpl extends UnicastRemoteObject
12      implements CallbackServerInterface {
13
14    private Vector clientList;
15
16
```

(continued on next page)

```
17   public CallbackServerImpl() throws RemoteException {
18     super( );
19     clientList = new Vector();
20   }
21
22   public String sayHello( )
23       throws java.rmi.RemoteException {
24     return("hello");
25   }
26
27   public void registerForCallback(
28       CallbackClientInterface callbackClientObject)
29       throws java.rmi.RemoteException{
30     // store the callback object into the vector
31     if (!(clientList.contains(callbackClientObject))) {
32       clientList.addElement(callbackClientObject);
33       System.out.println("Registered new client ");
34       doCallbacks();
35     } // end if
36   }
37
38   // This remote method allows an object client to
39   // cancel its registration for callback
40   // @param id is an ID for the client; to be used by
41   // the server to uniquely identify the registered client.
42   public synchronized void unregisterForCallback(
43       CallbackClientInterface callbackClientObject)
44       throws java.rmi.RemoteException{
45     if (clientList.removeElement(callbackClientObject)) {
46       System.out.println("Unregistered client ");
47     } else {
48       System.out.println(
49         "unregister: clientwasn't registered.");
50     }
51   }
52
53   private synchronized void doCallbacks( )
         throws java.rmi.RemoteException {
54     // make callback to each registered client
55     System.out.println(
56       "**************************************\n" +
57       "Callbacks initiated --");
58     for (int i = 0; i < clientList.size(); i++) {
59       System.out.println("doing "+ i +"-th callback\n");
60       // convert the vector object to a callback object
61       CallbackClientInterface nextClient =
62         (CallbackClientInterface)clientList.elementAt(i);
63       // invoke the callback method
64       nextClient.notifyMe("Number of registered clients="
65         + clientList.size());
66     }// end for
67     System.out.println("*******************************\n"
68       + "Server completed callbacks --");
69   }// end doCallbacks
70
71 }// end CallbackServerImpl class
```

The *registerForCallback* and *unregisterForCallback* methods modify a common data structure (the *Vector* object containing references to callback clients). Since invocations of these methods may be executed concurrently, it is important that these methods be protected with mutual exclusion. In this example, mutual exclusion is provided through the use of synchronized method.

Figure 8.8 *CallbackServer.java* for the modified *Hello* application.

```java
1  import java.rmi.*;
2  import java.rmi.server.*;
3  import java.rmi.registry.Registry;
4  import java.rmi.registry.LocateRegistry;
5  import java.net.*;
6  import java.io.*;
7
8  /**
9   * This class represents the object server for a distributed
10  * object of class Callback, which implements the remote
11  * interface CallbackInterface.
12  * @author M. L. Liu
13  */
14
15 public class CallbackServer {
16   public static void main(String args[ ]) {
17     InputStreamReader is =
18       new InputStreamReader(System.in);
19     BufferedReader br = new BufferedReader(is);
20     String portNum, registryURL;
21     try{
22       System.out.println(
23         "Enter the RMIregistry port number:");
24       portNum = (br.readLine()).trim();
25       int RMIPortNum = Integer.parseInt(portNum);
26       startRegistry(RMIPortNum);
27       CallbackServerImpl exportedObj =
28         new CallbackServerImpl( );
29       registryURL =
30         "rmi://localhost:" + portNum + "/callback";
31       Naming.rebind(registryURL, exportedObj);
32       System.out.println("Callback Server ready.");
33     }// end try
34     catch (Exception re) {
35       System.out.println(
36         "Exception in HelloServer.main: " + re);
37     } // end catch
38   } // end main
39
40   // This method starts an RMI registry on the local host, if
41   // it does not already exist at the specified port number.
42   private static void startRegistry(int RMIPortNum)
43       throws RemoteException{
44     try {
45       Registry registry =
46         LocateRegistry.getRegistry(RMIPortNum);
47       registry.list( );
48       // This call will throw an exception
49       // if the registry does not already exist
50     }
```

(continued next page)

```
51        catch (RemoteException e) {
52          // No valid registry at that port.
53          Registry registry =
54            LocateRegistry.createRegistry(RMIPortNum);
55        }
56    } // end startRegistry
57
58  } // end class
```

It is necessary for the server to employ a data structure to maintain a list of the client interface references registered for callbacks. In the sample code, a *Vector* object is used for this purpose, but you may substitute any appropriate data structure of your choice. Each call to *registerForCallback* results in a reference being added to the vector, while each call to *unregisterForCallback* results in the removal of a reference from the vector.

In the example, the server makes a callback (via the *doCallbacks* method) whenever a call is made to *registerForCallback*, whereupon the number of currently registered clients is reported to the client via callbacks. In other applications, the callbacks can be triggered by other events and may be made in an event handler.

In our sample, a client unregisters itself after a specified period of time. In actual applications, the cancellation of registration may occur at the end of a client session (such as a chat room session, a game session, or an auction session).

Steps for Building an RMI Application with Client Callback

In the following pages we present a revised description of the step-by-step procedure for building an RMI application, allowing for client callback.

Algorithm for Developing the Server-Side Software

1. Open a directory for all the files to be generated for this application.
2. Specify the remote server interface in *CallbackServerInterface.java*. Compile it until there is no more syntax error.
3. Implement the interface in *CallbackServerImpl.java*. Compile it until there is no more syntax error.
4. Use the RMI compiler *rmic* to process the implementation class and generate the stub file and skeleton file for the remote object:

   ```
   rmic CallbackServerImpl
   ```

   The files generated can be found in the directory as *CallbackServerImpl_ Skel.class* and *CallbackServerImpl_Stub.class*. Steps 3 and 4 should be repeated each time a change is made to the interface implementation.
5. Obtain a copy of the client remote interface class file. Alternatively, obtain a copy of the source file for the remote interface and compile it using *javac* to generate the interface class file *CallbackClientInterface.class*.

6. Create the object server program *SomeServer.java*. Compile it until there is no more syntax error.

7. Obtain a copy of the client remote interface stub file *CallbackClientImpl_Stub.class*.

8. Activate the object server

```
java SomeServer
```

Algorithm for Developing the Client-Side Software

1. Open a directory for all the files to be generated for this application.

2. Specify the remote client interface in *CallbackClientInterface.java*. Compile it until there is no more syntax error.

3. Implement the interface in *CallbackClientImpl.java*. Compile it until there is no more syntax error.

4. Use the RMI compiler *rmic* to process the implementation class *CallbackClientImpl.class* and generate the stub file *CallbackClientImpl_Stub.class* and skeleton file *CallbackClientImpl_Skel.class* for the remote object:

```
rmic CallbackClientImpl
```

The files generated can be found in the directory as *CallbackClientImpl_Skel.class* and *CallbackClientImpl_Stub.class*. Steps 3 and 4 should be repeated each time a change is made to the interface implementation.

5. Obtain a copy of the server remote interface class file. Alternatively, obtain a copy of the source file for the remote interface and compile it using *javac* to generate the interface class file.

6. Create the object client program *CallbackClient.java*. Compile it until there is no more syntax error.

7. Obtain a copy of the server remote interface stub file *CallbackServerImpl_Stub.class*. Activate the client.

```
java SomeClient
```

Figure 8.9 illustrates the files needed on the two sides, for an application that makes use of client callback. (As was mentioned in the last chapter, as of Java 1.2 the use of skeleton classes is no longer required in RMI applications. The functionalities of skeleton classes are replaced by the use of a technique known as **reflection**.

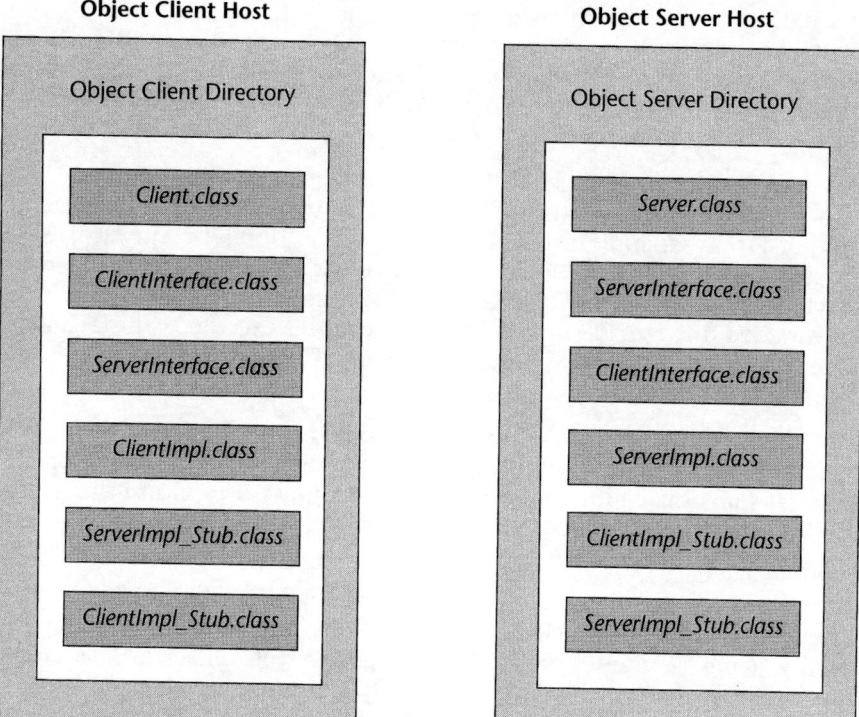

Figure 8.9 File placements for an RMI application with client callback.

8.2 Stub Downloading

In the architecture of a distributed object system, a proxy is required to interact with an object client's remote method call. In Java RMI, this proxy is the server remote interface stub. In the previous chapter we discussed how the server remote interface proxies (both the stub and the skeleton) can be generated by applying the RMI compiler *rmic* to the implementation of the server remote interface. The stub class thus generated will need to be present on the client host at run time for a client object program to execute. This can be arranged by manually placing the stub class file in the same package or directory of the object client program.

In Java, a **package** is a declared set of related classes, interfaces, or other packages.

Java RMI provides a mechanism that allow stubs to be made available to the client dynamically [developer.java.sun.com, 2]. Using **dynamic stub downloading**, a copy of the stub class does not need to be present on the client host. Instead, it can be transmitted from a Web server to the client host when the client is activated, on demand.

Stub downloading makes use of "the ability to dynamically download Java software from any Uniform Resource Locator (URL) to a Java virtual machine (JVM) running in a separate process, usually on a different physical system" [java.sun.com/products, 1]. Using stub downloading, a stub class is filed by the object developer with a Web server as a Web document, which can then be **downloaded** (using HTTP) when an object client is executed, in the same manner as the downloading of **applets**. The use of HTTP to download applets will be discussed in Chapter 11.

As before, a server exports an object by contacting the RMI registry and registering a remote reference to the object, specifying a symbolic name for the reference. If stub dowloading is desired, the server must also inform the registry of the URL where the stub class is filed. The mechanics of the steps involved will be presented in a later section.

Also as before, a client that wishes to invoke a remote method of an exported object contacts the RMI registry on the server host to retrieve the remote reference by name. Without stub downloading, the stub object (a Java class file) must be placed on the client host manually and must be locatable by the Java Virtual Machine. If stub downloading is in use (that is, if the object server has made all the necessary arrangements described in the previous paragraph), then the stub class is obtained dynamically from an HTTP server so that it can interact with the object client and the RMI run-time support. The downloaded stub class is not persistent, meaning that it will not be stored permanently on the client host, but will instead be deallocated by the system when the client session is over. In the absence of Web caching, each execution of the client class will require that the stub be re-downloaded from the Web server.

Web caching is a technique that employs caching to avoid repeated downloading of the same document.

Figure 8.10 illustrates the interaction among the object client, the object server, and the RMI registry when stub downloading is involved. We will soon discuss the algorithms for running an application using stub downloading. Before we do that, we must present a related topic: the RMI security manager.

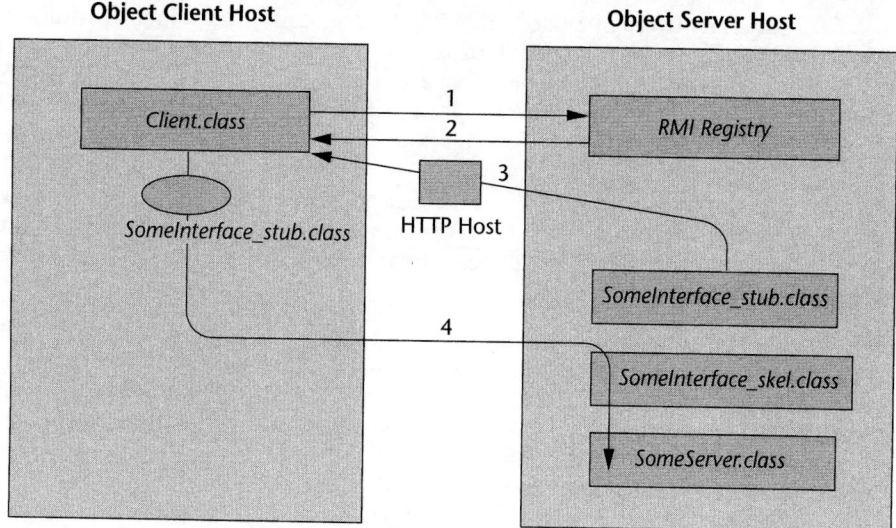

1. Client looks up the interface object in the RMI Registry on the server host.

2. The RMI Registry returns a remote reference to the interface object.

3. If the interface object's stub is not on the client host and if it is so arranged by the server, the stub is downloaded from an HTTP server.

4. Via the server stub, the client process interacts with the skeleton of the interface object to access the methods in the server object.

Figure 8.10 Stub downloading.

8.3 RMI Security Manager

Although stub downloading is a helpful feature, its use introduces a concern for system security. Such a concern is not unique to RMI but is associated with object downloading in general. When an object such as an RMI stub is transferred from a remote host, its execution subjects the local host to potential malicious attacks. Since a downloaded object originates from a foreign source, the execution of its code, if unrestricted, may potentially wreak havoc on the local host, resulting in damages similar to those caused by a "computer virus" [cert.org, 3].

To counter the threats posed by a downloaded stub, Java provides a *RMISecurityManager* class. An RMI program may instantiate an object of this class. Once instantiated, the object oversees all security-sensitive actions that arise during the execution of the program. These actions include the accessing of local files and the making of network connections, since such actions may result in undesirable modification of local resources or misuse of network resources. In particular, the RMI run-time support requires that a server process install a **security manager** before it can export any object that requires stub downloading, and that a client process install a security manager before it can download a stub.

Although the notion of security manager was not introduced in the last chapter, its use is recommended in all RMI applications, regardless of whether stub downloading is involved. By default, an RMI security manager is very restrictive: it allows no file access and allows connections to the originating host only. (This access restriction is imposed on applet downloading as well.) This restriction, however, will prevent an RMI object client from contacting the **RMI registry** of the object server host and will also prevent it from downloading a stub. It is possible to relax these restrictions by installing a special file known as a **security policy file**, whose syntax specifies what type of restrictions a security manager, including RMI security managers, should enforce. By default, there is a **systemwide** security policy file installed in a special directory of each Java-enabled system. The restrictions specified in the system security policy file—the default restrictions previously mentioned—will be those enforced by the security manager unless you override it by specifying an alternate policy file. Alternatively, a security policy file can be specified for a specific application so that restrictions may be imposed on a per application basis. For your exercises, it is recommended that you specify a security file with each application that you run so that you may have control over the restrictions imposed on your application only, without affecting the restrictions imposed on others. On some systems, you may not have the access privilege to modify the systemwide Java security policy file.

Now we will describe how to make use of an RMI security manager in an RMI application.

Instantiation of a Security Manager in an RMI Program

The *RMISecurityManager* is a class provided by Java, and can be instantiated in both the object client and the object server in a statement such as the following:

```
System.setSecurityManager(new RMISecurityManager( ));
```

This statement should appear before the code for accessing the RMI registry. Figures 8.11 and 8.12 illustrate the *Hello* examples, presented in the previous chapter, augmented with the instantiation of a security manager.

Figure 8.11 *HelloServer.java*, which installs a security manager.

```
1  import java.rmi.*;
2  import java.rmi.server.*;
3  import java.rmi.registry.Registry;
4  import java.rmi.registry.LocateRegistry;
5  import java.net.*;
6  import java.io.*;
7
8  /**
9   * This class represents the object server for a distributed
10  * object of class Hello, which implements the remote
11  * interface HelloInterface. A security manager is
12  * installed to safeguard stub downloading.
13  * @author M. L. Liu
14  */
15
16 public class HelloServer {
17   public static void main(String args[]) {
18     InputStreamReader is =
19       new InputStreamReader(System.in);
20     BufferedReader br = new BufferedReader(is);
21     String portNum, registryURL;
22     try{
23       System.out.println(
24         "Enter the RMIregistry port number:");
25       portNum = (br.readLine()).trim();
26       int RMIPortNum = Integer.parseInt(portNum);
27
28       // start a security manager - this is needed if
29       // stub downloading is in use for this application
30       System.setSecurityManager(
31         new RMISecurityManager());
32
33       startRegistry(RMIPortNum);
34       HelloImpl exportedObj = new HelloImpl();
35       registryURL =
36         "rmi://localhost:" + portNum + "/hello";
37       Naming.rebind(registryURL, exportedObj);
38       System.out.println(
39         "Server registered. Registry contains:");
40       // list names currently in the registry
41       listRegistry(registryURL);
42       System.out.println("Hello Server ready.");
43     }// end try
44     catch (Exception re) {
45       System.out.println(
46         "Exception in HelloServer.main: " + re);
47     } // end catch
48   } // end main
49
```

(continued on next page)

```
50    // This method starts a RMI registry on the local host,
51    // if it doesn't already exist at the specified port number
52    private static void startRegistry(int RMIPortNum)
53          throws RemoteException{
54      try {
55        Registry registry =
56          LocateRegistry.getRegistry(RMIPortNum);
57        registry.list( ); // This call will throw an
58        //exception if the registry does not already exist
59      }
60      catch (RemoteException e) {
61        // No valid registry at that port.
62        System.out.println(
63          "RMI registry cannot be located at port "
64          + RMIPortNum);
65        Registry registry =
66          LocateRegistry.createRegistry(RMIPortNum);
67        System.out.println(
68          "RMI registry created at port " + RMIPortNum);
69      }
70    } // end startRegistry
71
72    //This method lists the names registered with a Registry
73    private static void listRegistry(String registryURL)
74        throws RemoteException, MalformedURLException {
75      System.out.println(
76        "Registry " + registryURL + " contains: ");
77      String [ ] names = Naming.list(registryURL);
78      for (int i=0; i < names.length; i++)
79        System.out.println(names[i]);
80    } //end listRegistry
81
82  } // end class
```

Figure 8.12 *HelloClient.java*, which installs a security manager.

```
1  import java.io.*;
2  import java.rmi.*;
3
4  /**
5  * This class represents the object client for a
6  * distributed object of class Hello, which implements
7  * the remote interface HelloInterface. A security
8  * manager is installed to safeguard stub downloading.
9  * @author M. L. Liu
10 */
11
12 public class HelloClient {
13
14   public static void main(String args[]) {
15     try {
```

(continued next page)

```
16          int RMIPort;
17          String hostName;
18          InputStreamReader is =
19            new InputStreamReader(System.in);
20          BufferedReader br = new BufferedReader(is);
21          System.out.println(
22            "Enter the RMIRegistry host namer:");
23          hostName = br.readLine();
24          System.out.println(
25            "Enter the RMIregistry port number:");
26          String portNum = br.readLine();
27          RMIPort = Integer.parseInt(portNum);
28
29          // start a security manager - this is needed if stub
30          // downloading is in use for this application.
31          System.setSecurityManager(new RMISecurityManager());
32
33          String registryURL =
34            "rmi://localhost:" + portNum + "/hello";
35          // find the remote object and cast it to an
36          // interface object
37          HelloInterface h =
38            (HelloInterface)Naming.lookup(registryURL);
39          System.out.println("Lookup completed " );
40          // invoke the remote method
41          String message = h.sayHello();
42          System.out.println("HelloClient: " + message);
43        } // end try
44        catch (Exception e) {
45          System.out.println(
46            "Exception in HelloClient: " + e);
47        }
48      } //end main
49  }//end class
```

The Syntax of a Java Security Policy File

A Java security policy file is a text file containing code that specifies the granting of specific permissions. Following is a typical *java.policy* file for an RMI application.

```
grant {
  // Allows RMI clients to make socket connections to the
  // public ports on any host.
  // If you start the RMIregistry on a port in this range, you
  // will not incur a resolve access violation.
  // permission java.net.SocketPermission "*:1024-65535",
  //    "connect,accept,resolve";
  // Permits socket access to port 80, the default HTTP port -
  // needed by client to contact an HTTP server for stub
  // downloading
  permission java.net.SocketPermission "*:80", "connect";
};
```

For your exercises, it is recommended that a copy of this file be filed under the name *java.policy* in the same directory for the application at both the object client host and the object server host.

When activating the client, use a command option to specify that the client process should be allowed the privileges defined in the policy file, as follows:

```
java -Djava.security.policy=java.policy SomeClient
```

Likewise, the server should be activated as follows:

```
java -Djava.security.policy=java.policy SomeServer
```

These two commands assume that the policy file is named *java.policy* and is available in the current directory on both the server side and the client side.

A full discussion of Java security policy, including an explanation of the syntax used in the file, can be found in [java.sun.com/marketing, 4].

Specifying Stub Downloading and a Security Policy File

1. If the stub is to be downloaded from an HTTP server, transfer the stub class to an appropriate directory on that HTTP server, for example, directory **stubs** on host *www.mycompany.com*, and make sure that the access permission to the file is set to world-readable.

2. When activating the server, specify the following command options:

```
java -Djava.rmi.server.codebase=<URL>
  -Djava.security.policy=
  <full directory path to a security policy file>
```

where

<URL> is the URL for the directory that contains the stub class; for example, http://www.mycompany.com/stubs/

Note the forward slash at the end of the URL, which indicates that the URL leads to a directory, not a file.

<full directory path to java security policy file> specifies the security policy file for this application; for example, java.security, if the file java.security is in the current directory.

For example,

```
java -Djava.rmi.server.codebase=http://www.mycompany.com/stubs/
-Djava.security.policy= java.security HelloServer
```
(all on one line)

will start the *HelloServer* and allow stub downloading from the *stubs* directory on the *www.mycompany.com* Web server.

Figure 8.13 illustrates the set of files needed for an RMI application and the placement of these files, assuming dynamic stub downloading. (For simplicity, we assume that the application does not use client callback. You may add the files for client callback if desired.)

On the server side, the files are the class files for the server, the remote interface, the interface implementation (generated by *javac*), the stub class (generated by *rmic*), the skeleton class (generated by *rmic*), and the application's security policy file. On the client side, the files needed are the client class, the server remote interface class, and the application's security policy file. Finally, the stub class file needs to be stored on the HTTP host from which the stub is to be downloaded.

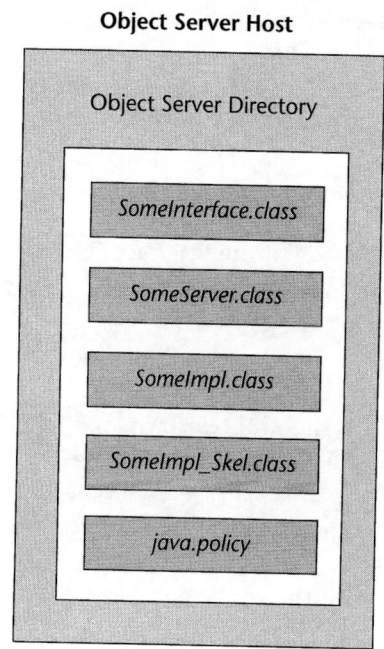

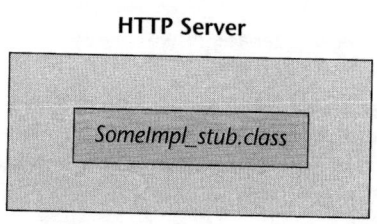

Figure 8.13 RMI file placements for an application that uses stub downloading.

Algorithms for Building an RMI Application, Allowing for Stub Downloading

Following is a description of the step-by-step procedure for building an RMI application, taking into consideration the use of stub downloading. Again, for simplicity we have left out the details for client callbacks.

Algorithm for Developing the Server-Side Software

1. Open a directory for all the files to be generated for this application.

2. Specify the remote server interface in *SomeInterface.java*. Compile the program until there is no more syntax error.

3. Implement the interface in *SomeImpl.java*. Compile the program until there is no more syntax error.

4. Use the RMI compiler *rmic* to process the implementation class and generate the stub file and skeleton file for the remote object:

   ```
   rmic SomeImpl
   ```

   The files generated can be found in the directory as *SomeImpl_Skel.class* and *SomeImpl_Stub.class*. Steps 3 and 4 should be repeated each time a change is made to the interface implementation.

5. Create the object server program *SomeServer.java*. Compile it until there is no more syntax error.

6. If stub downloading is desired, copy the stub class file to an appropriate directory on the HTTP host.

7. If the RMI registry is used and if it has not already been activated, activate a RMI registry. For example:

   ```
   rmiregistry <port number, 1099 by default>
   ```

   Alternatively, the activation may be coded in the object server program.

8. Make up a Java security policy file called *java.policy* (or a name of your choice) for the application, and place it in an appropriate directory or in the current direct directory.

9. Activate the server, specifying (1) the codebase if stub downloading is desired, and (2) the security policy file.

   ```
   Java –Djava.rmi.server.codebase=http://somehost.someU.edu/stubs/
   -djava.security.policy=java.policy
   ```

   This command is supposed to be all on one line, although you may use a line continuation character ('\') on a UNIX system. It is recommended that you put the command in an executable text file (such as *runServer.bat* on a Windows system or *runServer* on a UNIX system) and run the file to start the server.

For the *Hello* application, the *runServer.bat* file contains this line:

```
java—Djava.security.policy=java.policy
-Djava.rmi.server.codebase=http://www.csc.calpoly.edu/~mliu/stubs/
HelloServer
```

Again, there should be *no* line breaks in the file.

Object Client-Side Algorithm for Developing the Client-Side Software

1. Open a directory for all the files to be generated for this application.
2. Obtain a copy of the remote interface class file *SomeInterface.class*. Alternatively, obtain a copy of the source file *SomeInterface.java* for the remote interface, and compile it using *javac* to generate the interface class file.
3. Develop the client program *SomeClient.java*, and compile it to generate the client class.
4. If stub downloading is not desired, obtain a copy of the stub class file (say *SomeImpl_Stub.class*) and place it in the current directory.
5. Make up a java security policy file *java.policy* for the application, and place it in an appropriate directory or the current direct directory.
6. Activate the client, specifying the security policy file.

```
Java -Djava.security.policy=java.policy SomeClient
```

This command is supposed to be all on one line, although you may use a line continuation character ('\') on a UNIX system. It is recommended that you put the command in an executable text file (such as *runClient.bat* on a Windows system or *runClient* on a UNIX system) and run the file to start the client.

For the *Hello* application, the *runClient.bat* file contains this line:

```
java -Djava.security.policy=java.policy HelloClient
```

Again, there should be *no* line breaks in the file.

If client callback is required, the additional steps described in "Steps for Building an RMI Application with Client Callback," the section presented earlier in this chapter, can be inserted into the algorithm.

Summary

In this chapter we looked at a number of advanced features of the Java RMI API. Although these features are not inherently part of the distributing objects paradigm, they are interesting and useful for some applications.

Client Callback

■ Client callback is useful for an application where the clients desire to be notified by the server of the occurrence of some event.

■ Client callback allows an object server to make a remote method invocation to a client via a reference to a client remote interface.

■ To provide client callback, the client-side software supplies a remote interface, instantiates an object that implements the interface, and passes to the server a reference to the object. The object server collects these client references in a data structure. When the awaited event occurs, the object server invokes a callback method (defined in the client remote interface) to pass data to the appropriate clients.

■ Two sets of stub and skeletons are needed: one for the server remote interfaces and the other for the client remote interface.

Stub Downloading and Security Manager

■ Stub downloading allows a stub class to be loaded to an object client at run time.

■ Stub downloading requires the setting of the *java.rmi.server.codebase* property when the server is initiated: The property should be set to a directory on an HTTP server where a copy of the stub class is stored and is world accessible.

■ Stub downloading requires the installation of an RMI security manager in both the client class and the server class.

■ For stub downloading, the use of a security manager is necessary since the execution of an object downloaded from an unknown machine may potentially introduce a threat to the client computer.

■ A security manager oversees access restrictions specified in a Java security policy file, which can be a systemwide policy file or a policy file applied to an individual application only.

■ A sample security policy file suitable for RMI applications was presented in the chapter.

■ For security protection, the use of security managers is recommended in all RMI applications, regardless of whether stub downloading is involved.

Exercises

1. In the context of Java RMI, what is client callback? Why is it useful?

2. Try out the *Callback* program sample on one or more machines.

   a. Open a folder (called *callback*) for this exercise. Create two subfolders—call them *Server* and *Client*, respectively—on your PC. Copy the source files to the *Server* folder and the *Client* folder respectively.

   b. Follow the algorithms presented in the chapter to set up and run the object server and an object client. Write a report describing your actions and the outcomes.

   c. Start a few more clients in quick succession. Report your actions and the outcomes.

   d. Copy the *callback* folder into a new folder. Modify the source files in the new folder so that the server will notify a client only when *exactly three* clients are currently registered for callback. Show changes made in the source files.

   e. Returning to the *callBack* folder, start a server and a client each, specifying a lifetime of 600 seconds for the client. While the client is waiting for call-back, abort the client process by entering Ctrl-C. Quickly start a new client process so that the server will attempt a callback to all registered clients. Report what you observe.

      Make changes to the source code so that the problem you observed does not occur. Describe the changes you made to the programs. Hand in the modified source listings.

3. In an exercise for the last chapter, you used RMI to write an application for a prototype opinion poll system. Modify that application so that each client provides the user interface for a respondent to cast a vote. In addition, the current tally of the poll will be displayed on the client screen *whenever* a new vote has been cast (either by this client or by some other).

   Turn in listings of your source files, including all interface files. A demonstration of the programs in the laboratory is recommended.

4. In the context of Java RMI, what is stub downloading? Why is it useful?

5. Experiment with stub downloading using the sample presented in section 8.3 of this chapter. You should be able to find the files in the *stubDownload* folder of the program samples.

   a. Open a folder (called *stubDownload*) for this exercise. Create two subfolders on your PC and call them *Server* and *Client*, respectively. Copy the RMI *Hello* sample files to the respective folder.

   b. Compile the files. Use *rmic* to generate the stub and skeleton files in the *Server* folder. Copy the stub class to the *Client* folder.

c. Start a server from the *Server* folder without specifying stub downloading (that is, without setting the codebase property when running the Java interpreter). Then start a client from the *Client* folder. Check to see that they work as expected.

d. In the *Client* folder, delete the *HelloImpl_Stub.class* file. Start a client again. You should get a notification of exceptions from Java run time due to the absence of the stub class.

e. Back in the *Server* folder, copy the *HelloImpl_Stub.class* file to a Web server to which you have access, in a directory called *stubs* (or a name of your choice).

   Where applicable, set the access protection to the stubs directory and the stub file so that they are world readable. Start a server from the *Server* folder, this time specifying stub downloading (that is, setting the codebase property to allow downloading from the directory where you filed the stub class).

f. Back in the *Client* folder, try running the client again. If stub downloading functions as expected, then the client should work this time.

g. Try duplicating the *Client* folder and starting other clients on different systems in similar fashion, using stub downloading in each case.

Write a report describing your experiment.

6. Repeat the exercise on the *Callback* sample. This time, the client should be able to download the server stub dynamically, while the server should be able to obtain the client stub dynamically.

   It is recommended that you first experiment with the clients and the server using a local copy of the stub files. Then delete the server stub from the client folder, and try running the client with stub downloading. Subsequently, delete the client stub from the server folder, and try running the server with stub downloading. Write a report describing your experiment.

References

1. Dynamic Code Downloading Using RMI, *http://java.sun.com/products/jdk/1.2/docs/guide/rmi/codebase.html*

2. Introduction to Distributed Computing with RMI, *http://developer.java.sun.com/developer/onlineTraining/rmi/RMI.html*

3. CERT(r) Coordination Center, CERT/CC Computer Virus Resources, *http://www.cert.org/other_sources/viruses.html*

4. Java Remote Method Invocation—Distributed Computing for Java, *http://java.sun.com/marketing/collateral/javarmi.html*

Internet Applications

By far the best known distributed application is the **World Wide Web** (WWW), or **the Web** for short. Technically, the Web is a distributed system of HTTP servers and clients, more commonly known as Web servers and Web browsers. This chapter looks at a number of Internet protocols. These protocols are of interest not only for practical reasons but also because they provide a case study of how protocols evolve over time in response to usage demands.

Prior to the emergence of the Web, the user community of the Internet was largely made up of researchers and academics who used network services such as electronic mail and file transfer to exchange data.

The World Wide Web originated with Tim Berners-Lee [w3.org/People, 4] in late 1990 for CERN, the European Particle Physics Laboratory in Geneva, Switzerland [public.Web.cern.ch, 6]. A proposal for a "universal hypertext system" was submitted in November 1990 by Tim Berners-Lee and Robert Cailliau for a "universal hypertext system." Since the original proposal, the growth of the World Wide Web has been extraordinary (see Figure 9.1); the Web has expanded far beyond the research and academic community into all sectors worldwide, including commerce and private homes. The continued development of Web technology is currently coordinated by the World Wide Web Consortium (W3C) [w3.org, 11].

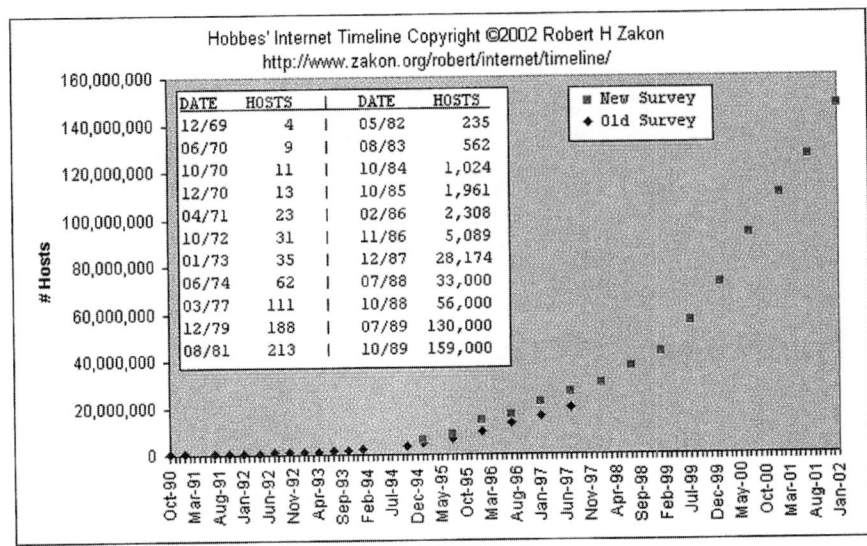

Figure 9.1 The growth of the WWW [zakon.org, 1] (reprinted by permission).

In the 1960s, Doug Engelbart, inventor of the mouse device, prototyped an "oNLine System" (NLS) that supports hypertext browsing and editing, and Ted Nelson coined the word hypertext [w3.org/History.html, 2].

The genius of the World Wide Web is that it combines three important and well-established computing technologies:

1. **Hypertext documents. Hypertext** documents predate the WWW and are documents in which chosen words or phrases, typically highlighted, can be marked as links to other documents, so that a user is able to access the linked documents by clicking with a mouse on the highlighted text.

2. **Network-based information retrieval.** Network-based information retrieval allows documents to be retrieved over a network. Prior to the emergence of the WWW, the **File Transfer Protocol** (FTP) [ietf.org, 12] service was the most widely used service for such information retrieval.

3. **Standard Generalized Markup Language (SGML).** In 1986 a new ISO standard (ISO 8879) [iso.org, 3] was released, allowing documents to be "marked up" with tags so that they can be displayed in a uniform format on any platform, independent of the presentation mechanics.

Combining the three concepts, the World Wide Web makes it possible for a document to be marked up with the **Hypertext Markup Language (HTML)** so that a linked document can be automatically fetched from a remote computer on the Internet and displayed on a local computer.

At its most basic, the World Wide Web is a client-server application based on a protocol named the **Hypertext Transfer Protocol (HTTP)** [faqs.org, 8], which we have already briefly visited in earlier chapters. A Web server is a connection-oriented server that implements HTTP. By default, an HTTP server runs at the well-known port 80. A user runs a World Wide Web client (colloquially referred to as a *browser*) on a local computer. The client interacts with a Web server according to the HTTP, specifying a document to be fetched. If the document is located by the server in its directory, the document's contents are returned to the client, which presents those contents to the user.

The popularity of the Web was such that, reportedly, the load of the first Web server host, *info.cern.ch*, rose by a factor of 10 each year between 1991 and 1994.

9.1 HTML

The Hypertext Markup Language (HTML) [archive.ncsa.uiuc.edu, 14] is a markup language used to create documents that can be retrieved using the World Wide Web. HTML is based on SGML, with semantics that are appropriate for representing information of a wide range of document types. HTML markup can represent hypertext news, mail, documentation, and hypermedia; menus of options; database query results; simple structured documents with in-line graphics; and hypertext views of existing bodies of information. Figure 9.2 illustrates a sample text file, a Web page, written in HTML.

Figure 9.2 Sample HTML code.

```
<HTML>
<HEAD>
<TITLE>A Sample Web Page</TITLE>
</HEAD>
<HR>
<BODY>
<center>
<H1>My Home Page</H1>
<IMG SRC="/images/myPhoto.gif">
<b>Welcome to Kelly's page!</b>
<p>
<! A list of hyperlinks follows.>
<a href="/doc/myResume.html"> My resume</a>.
<p>
<a href="http://www.someUniversity.edu/">My university<a>
</center>
<HR>
</BODY>
</HTML>
```

9.2 XML—The Extensible Markup Language

Whereas HTML is a language that allows a document to be marked up for the presentation or display of the information contained in a document, the **Extensible Markup Language** (XML) [w3.org/XML, 15] allows a document to be marked up for structured information. Also based on SGML, XML uses tags to describe the information contained in a document. Figure 9.3 presents a very simple XML code sample [java.sun.com, 16] that describes the structured information representing a message. The tags in this example identify the message as a whole, the destination and sender addresses, the subject, and the text of the message.

Since its introduction in 1998, XML has become widely deployed in distributed computing. It is used in protocols such as SOAP (simple object access protocol) for Web-based remote procedure calls and Jabber [jabber.org, 26] for instant messages.

Figure 9.3 Sample XML code.

```
<message>
  <to>you@yourAddress.com</to>
  <from>me@myAddress.com</from>
  <subject>This is a message</subject>
  <text>
    Hello world!
  </text>
</message>
```

9.3 HTTP

Originally conceived for fetching and displaying text files, **HTTP** [w3.org/Protocols/HTTP/HTTP2.html, 7; ietf.org, 10; w3.org/Protocols/HTTP/AsImplemented.html, 17] has been extended to allow the transferring of Web contents of virtually unlimited types. As such, it is regarded as the **transport protocol** on the Web.

The first version of HTTP, **HTTP/0.9**, was a simple protocol for raw data transfer. The most widely used HTTP version is **HTTP/1.0**, which was a draft [w3.org/Protocols/HTTP/AsImplemented.html, 17] proposed by Tim Berners-Lee in 1991 but has no formal specification, although its "common usage" is described in RFC1945 [faqs.org, 8]. Since then, an improved protocol, known as HTTP/1.1, has been developed and often adopted. **HTTP/1.1** [ietf.org, 10] is a far more extensive protocol than HTTP/1.0, but the basics of the protocol are well represented in the simpler HTTP/1.0. In the rest of this section, we will present the essence of HTTP/1.0 and point out some of the key differences between HTTP/1.0 and HTTP/1.1. For simplicity, only a subset of the protocol will be introduced in this chapter.

The basic HTTP is a **connection-oriented, stateless, request-response protocol**. An HTTP server, or Web server, runs on TCP port 80 by default. HTTP clients, colloquially called Web browsers, are processes that implement HTTP to interact with a Web server to retrieve documents phrased in HTML, whose contents are displayed according to the documents' markups.

In HTTP/1.0 each connection allows only one round of request-response: a client obtains a connection and issues a request; the server processes the request, issues a response, and closes the connection thereafter. Figure 9.4, which you have already seen previously in Chapter 2, is an event diagram describing an HTTP/1.0 session.

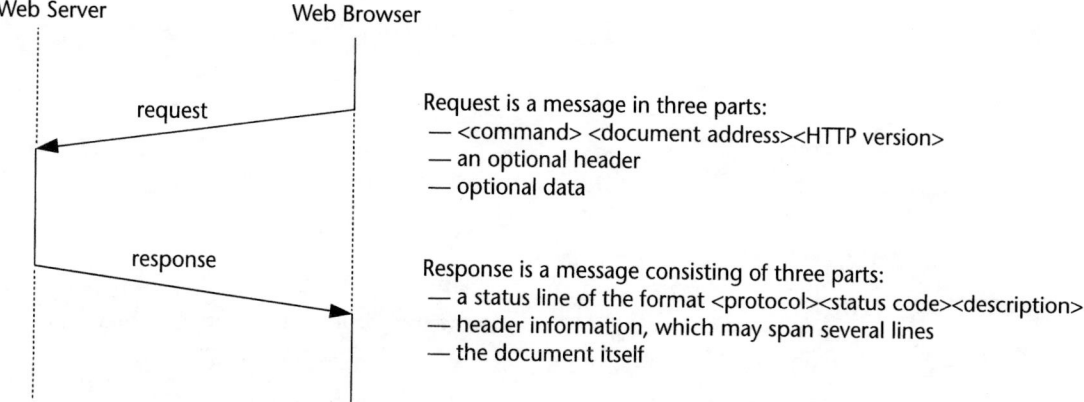

Figure 9.4 An event diagram for the Hypertext Transfer Protocol.

HTTP is a **text-based request-response protocol**. The requests and responses are character strings. Each request and response is composed of these parts, in order:

1. The **request/response** line
2. A **header section**
3. A blank line
4. The **body**

Next we will describe each of the three parts: first, the request, and then the response.

The Client Request

A client request is sent to the server after the client has established a connection to the server.

The Request Line

A request line takes the following form:

```
<HTTP method><space><Request-URI><space><protocol specification>\r\n
```

where

- *<HTTP method>* is the name of a method defined for the protocol (to be described),
- *<Request-URI>* is the URI of a Web document or, more generally, a Web object,
- *<protocol specification>* is a specification of the protocol observed by the client, and
- *<space>* is a space character.

An example request line is as follows:

```
GET /index.html HTTP/1.0
```

The *<HTTP method>* in a client request is a reserved word that specifies an operation of the server that the client desires. Some of the key client request methods are listed below:

- *GET*—for retrieving the contents of a Web object referenced by the specified URI
- *HEAD*—for retrieving a header from the server only, not the object itself
- *POST*—used to send data to a process on the server host
- *PUT*—used to request the server to store the contents enclosed with the request to the server machine in the file location specified by the URI

The *<Request-URI>* is the Uniform Resource Identifier, first introduced in Chapter 1, and it takes the form

```
/<directory path name>.../<directory path name>/<file name>
```

The *<protocol specification>* specifies the protocol (name and version) that the client assumes, for example, HTTP/1.0.

Request Header

The request line is optionally followed by a request header. According to [faqs.org, 8], "The request header fields allow the client to pass additional information about the request, and about the client itself, to the server. These fields act as request modifiers, with semantics equivalent to the parameters on a programming language method (procedure) invocation."

A header is composed of one or more lines, each line in the form of

```
<keyword>: <value>\r\n
```

Some of the keywords and values that may appear in a request header are

- **Accept**—specifies the content-types acceptable by the client.
- **User-Agent**—specifies the type of browser.
- **Connection**—"Keep-Alive" can be specified to request that the server does not immediately close a connection after sending a response.
- **Host**—host name of the server.

An example request header is as follows:

```
Accept: */*
Connection: Keep-Alive
Host: www.someU.edu
User-Agent: Generic
```

Request Body

A request optionally ends with a request body, which contains data that needs to be transferred to the server in association with the request. For example, if the *POST* method is specified in the request line, then the body contains data to be passed to the target process. (This is an important feature and will become clearer when we discuss CGI and servlets.)

Following are some examples of a complete client request:

Example 1

```
GET / HTTP/1.1
<blank line>
```

Example 2

```
HEAD / HTTP/1.1
Accept: */*
Connection: Keep-Alive
Host: somehost.com
User-Agent: Generic
<blank line>
```

Example 3

```
POST /cgi/myServer.cgi HTTP/1.0
Accept: */*
Connection: Keep-Alive
Host: somehost.com
User-Agent: Generic
Content-type: application/x-www-form-urlencoded
Content-length: 11
<blank line>
Name=donald&email=donald@someU.edu
```

The Server Response

In response to a request received from a client, the HTTP server sends a response. Similar to the request, an HTTP response is composed of these parts, in order:

1. The response or status line

2. A header section

3. A blank line

4. The body

The Status Line

The status line takes this form:

```
<protocol><sp><status-code><sp><description>\r\n
```

The following are the status code designations:

```
100-199 Informational
200-299 Client request successful
300-399 Client request redirected
400-499 Client request incomplete
500-599 Server errors
```

Example 1

```
HTTP/1.0 200 OK
```

is a status line sent by a server that runs HTTP/1.0, indicating that the request was processed successfully.

Example 2

```
HTTP/1.1 404 NOT FOUND
```

is a status line sent by a server that runs HTTP/1.1, indicating that the request was not processed successfully because the specified document could not be found.

Response Header

The status line is followed by a response header. A response header is composed of one or more lines; each line takes this form:

```
<keyword>: <value>\r\n
```

There are two types of lines that may appear in a response header:

- **Response header lines.** These header lines return information about the response, the server, and further access to the resource requested, as follows:

```
Age: seconds
Location: URI
Retry-After: date|seconds
Server: string
WWW-Authenticate: scheme realm
```

- **Entity header lines.** These header lines contain information about the contents of the object requested by the client, as follows:

```
Content-Encoding
Content-Length
Content-Type: type/subtype (see MIME)
Expires: date
Last-Modified: date
```

The following is an example response header:

```
Date: Mon, 30 Oct 2000 18:52:08 GMT
Server: Apache/1.3.9 (Unix) ApacheJServ/1.0
Last-modified: Mon, 17 June 2001 16:45:13 GMT
Content-Length: 1255
Connection: close
Content-Type: text/html
```

A comprehensive list of response header lines can be found in [ietf.org, 10]. Some of the more interesting types of header lines follow:

- **Content-Type** specifies the type of the data using the contents type designation of the **MIME** protocol, which we will discuss in a later section.
- **Content-Encoding** specifies the encoding scheme (such as *uuencode* or *base64*) of the data, usually for the purpose of data compression.
- **Content-length** is the length of the contents in the response body in terms of number of bytes.
- The **expiration date** gives the date/time (specified in a format defined with HTTP) after which the Web object should be considered stale.
- The **Last-Modified date** specifies the date that the object was last modified.

uuencode stands for UNIX-to-UNIX encode and was originally an encoding scheme for text contents transferred between UNIX systems. It has since been extended beyond UNIX systems.

Base64 is an encoding scheme for text contents specified with the MIME protocol [faqs.org, 9].

Response Body

The body of the response follows the header and a blank line and contains the contents of the Web object requested.

An example of a complete HTTP server response is shown in Figure 9.5.

Figure 9.5 A sample HTTP server response.

```
HTTP/1.1 200 OK
Date: Sat, 15 Sep 2001 06:55:30 GMT
Server: Apache/1.3.9 (Unix) ApacheJServ/1.0
Last-Modified: Mon, 30 Apr 2001 23:02:36 GMT
ETag: "5b381-ec-3aedef0c"
Accept-Ranges: bytes
Content-Length: 236
Connection: close
Content-Type: text/html

<html>
<head>
<title>My Web page </title>
</head>
<body>
Hello world!
</BODY></HTML>
```

Content Type and MIME

One of the most important header lines returned in a server response is the Content-Type of the object requested. Specification of the content type follows the scheme established in a protocol known as **MIME (Multipurpose Internet Mail Extension)**. Originally used for email, MIME is now widely employed for describing the content of a document sent over a network.

MIME supports a large number and evolving set of predefined content types, specified in the format of **Type/Subtype**. A small subset of the types and subtypes are listed in Table 9.1.

Table 9.1 A Subset of MIME Content Types

Type	Subtype
text	Plain, rich text, html, tab-separated values, xml
message	Email, news
application	Octet-stream (can be used for transferring Java.class files, for example), Adobe-postscript, Mac-binhex40, xml
image	jpeg, gif
audio	basic,midi,mp3
video	mpeg, quicktime

A Basic HTTP Client

To reinforce your understanding of the topics we have explored so far, let us look at a basic HTTP client that you should be able to implement given the knowledge you have learned so far. You undoubtedly have used a commercial Web browser such as Netscape or Internet Explorer to access and view Web objects. Although the presentation logic of these browsers is complex, the service logic is not, as illustrated in the code for our basic HTTP client presented in Figure 9.6. In the code sample, the client uses a connection-oriented socket to send to a Web server a request formulated according to HTTP, and then the client interprets and displays the response returned by the server, line by line.

Figure 9.6 A simple HTTP client written using the socket API.

```
1   // MyStreamSocket is a Java class presented in Chapter 4.
2   import MyStreamSocket;
3   import java.net.*;
4   import java.io.*;
5
6   public class HTTPClient {
7
8   // An application that communicates with an HTTP
9   // server to retrieve the text contents of a Web page.
10  // These command line arguments are expected, in order:
11  // <host name of the HTTP server>
12  // <port number of the HTTP server>
13  // <full path to a Web document on the server host>
14
15    public static void main(String[] args) {
16      if (args.length != 3)
17        System.out.println
18          ("This program requires 3 command line arguments");
19      else {
20        try {
21          InetAddress host =
22            InetAddress.getByName(args[0]);
23          int port = Integer.parseInt(args[1]);
24          String fileName = args[2].trim();
25          String request =
26            "GET " + fileName + " HTTP/1.0\n\n";
27          MyStreamSocket mySocket =
28          new MyStreamSocket(host, port);
29          /**/ System.out.println("Connection made");
30          mySocket.sendMessage(request);
31          // now receive the response from the HTTP server
32          String response;
33          response = mySocket.receiveMessage();
34          // read and display one line at a time
35          while (response != null) {
36            System.out.println(response);
37            response = mySocket.receiveMessage();
38          }
```

(continued on next page)

```
39          }
40          catch (Exception ex) {
41            System.out.println("ERROR : " + ex) ;
42            ex.printStackTrace(System.out);
43          } // end catch
44        } // end else
45      } // end main
46  } // end class
```

Our simple HTTP client opens a connection to an HTTP server specified by the user. Then the client formulates a simple *GET* request, sends the request to the server, and then displays the response it receives from the server. Unlike a commercial browser, our simple browser makes no interpretation of the response but displays the text as it is received.

As a point of interest, the Java API provides a class called *URL* specifically for retrieving data from a Web object identified using a URI. Table 9.2 describes two constructors and a key method for this class, which are used in the code sample presented in Figure 9.7 to implement our simple Web browser.

Table 9.2 Method Calls for a Java URL Object

Method/Constructor	Description
URL(*String spec*)	Creates a *URL* object from the URL name contained in a *String*
URL(*String protocol,String* host, int *port,String file*)	Creates a *URL* object from the specified *protocol, host, port* number, and *file*.
InputStream openStream( )	Opens a connection to this *URL* and returns an *InputStream* for reading from that connection.

Figure 9.7 A simple HTTP client written using the URL class.

```
1  import java.net.*;
2  import java.io.*;
3
4  public class URLBrowser {
5
6  // An application which uses a URL object to retreive
7  // the text contents of a Web page.
8  // These command line arguments are expected, in order:
9  // <host name of the HTTP server>
10 // <port number of the HTTP server>
11 // <full path to a Web document on the server host>
12
13    public static void main(String[] args) {
14      if (args.length != 3)
```

(continued on next page)

```
15        System.out.println
16          ("This program requires 3 command line arguments");
17      else {
18        try {
19          String host = args[0];
20          String port = args[1].trim();
21          String fileName = args[2].trim();
22          String URLString =
23            "http://" + host + ":" + port + fileName;
24          URL theURL = new URL("http", host, port, );
25
26          InputStream inStream = theURL.openStream( );
27          BufferedReader input =
28            new BufferedReader
29            (new InputStreamReader(inStream));
30          String response;
31          response = input.readLine();
32          // read and display one line at a time
33          while (response != null) {
34            System.out.println(response);
35            response = input.readLine();
36          } //end while
37        }
38      catch (Exception ex) {
39          System.out.println("ERROR : " + ex) ;
40          ex.printStackTrace(System.out);
41      } // end catch
42    } // end else
43  } // end main
44 } //end class
```

HTTP, a Connection-Oriented, Stateless Protocol

As specified in [faqs.org, 8], HTTP is a connection-oriented protocol. With HTTP/1.0, a connection to a server is **automatically closed** as soon as the server returns a response. Thus exactly one round of exchange is allowed between a client and a Web server. If a client needs to contact the same server more than once in one session, it must reconnect to the server to reissue another request. This scheme is adequate for the original intent of HTTP for retrieving simple network documents. But it is inefficient for retrieving documents that contain a large number of links to additional objects to be fetched by the server, since fetching each of these links requires a reestablishment of a connection. It is also insufficient for sophisticated Web applications based on HTTP (such as shopping carts). As a result, HTTP/1.0 was extended to allow a request header line *Connection: Keep-Alive* to be issued by a client who wishes to maintain a persistent connection with the server; a cooperating server will keep the connection open after sending a response. In HTTP/1.1, connections are persistent by default. A persistent connection allows multiple requests to be sent over the same TCP connection.

HTTP/1.0 (as well as version 1.1) is also a stateless protocol: the server does not maintain any state information on a client's session. Regardless of whether the connection is kept alive, each request is handled by a server as a new request. As with nonpersistent connections, a stateless protocol is adequate for the original intent of the protocol, but it is not adequate for the more complex applications for which HTTP has been extended.

9.4 Dynamically Generated Web Contents

In the beginning, HTTP was employed to transfer static contents, that is, contents that exist in a constant state, such as a plain text file or an image file. As the Web evolved, applications began to use HTTP for a purpose not originally intended: as an application that allows a browser user to retrieve data based on dynamic information entered during an HTTP session. A typical Web application, such as a shopping cart, requires the fetching of remote data based on data entered by a client at run time. For example, an enterprise application typically allows a user to key in data, which is then used to formulate a query to retreive data from a database; subsequently, the outcome of the query is formatted and displayed to the user. To make such an application Web based, it is desirable to allow a client to submit data during a Web session to retrieve data from the Web server host, to be displayed by the Web browser (as illustrated in Figure 9.8). For that purpose, the basic HTTP was extended and also augmented with additional protocols to support the retrieval of dynamically generated Web contents, that is, contents that do not exist in a constant state, but are instead generated dynamically according to run-time parameters.

In Figure 9.8, dashed lines with arrows represent the data flow between the data source (a database system in this case) and the HTTP server. The dashed lines indicate that the data does not flow directly between the data source and the server. The reason for the indirect data flow is that a general HTTP server does not possess the application logic for fetching the data from the data source. Instead, an **external process** that has the application logic will need to serve as an intermediary. In our example, the external process runs on the server host, accepts input data from the Web server, exercises its application logic to obtain data from the data source, and returns the outcome to the Web server, which transmits the outcome to the client.

The first widely adopted protocol to augment HTTP in supporting run-time-generated Web contents is the **Common Gateway Interface** (CGI) protocol, our next topic. Although rudimentary by comparison to other, more sophisticated protocols that emerged later, CGI is the predecessor of these sophisticated protocols and facilities (such as the Java servlet) that serve similar purposes. Understanding CGI and some of its supplementary protocols is helpful because it prepares us for the study of more advanced protocols and facilities. Today CGI is still widely in use on the Web.

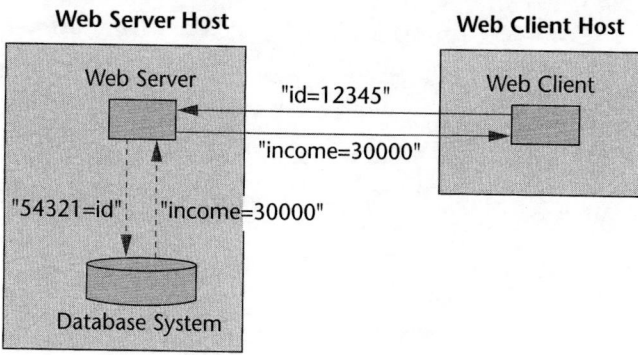

Figure 9.8 Dynamic Web contents.

9.5 **Common Gateway Interface (CGI)**

The **Common Gateway Interface (CGI)** [hoohoo.ncsa.uiuc.edu/cgi/overview. html, 19; hoohoo.ncsa.uiuc.edu/cgi/interface.html, 20; comp.leeds.ac.uk, 21] is a protocol for providing an interface, or a gateway, between an information server and an external process (that is, a process external to the server). Using the CGI protocol, a Web client may specify a program, known as a **CGI script**, as the target Web object in an HTTP request. The Web server fetches the CGI script and activates it as a process, passing to the process input data transmitted by the Web client. The Web script executes and transmits its output to the Web server, which returns the Web-script-generated data as the body of a response to the Web client.

The sequence diagram in Figure 9.9 illustrates the working of an example CGI application. A browser issues a request for a static document *hello.html* (Figure 9.10). The static document is fetched by a Web server, and its content is returned to the browser as the body of the response. The content (whose syntax will be discussed in the next section) contains a specification to a Web script named *hello.cgi*. When a Submit button displayed on the browser screen is pressed by the user, a new request is dispatched to the Web server, specifying *hello.cgi* as the Web object to fetch. Assuming that the object requested is a CGI script and therefore executable, the server initiates an execution of the script, passing to it the input data, if any, from the browser user. In the course of the execution of the CGI script, the content of a Web page is generated as the program's output and is transmitted to the server. Finally, the server sends the dynamically generated Web page to the Web client in the body of a response.

Figure 9.10 presents the Web page *hello.html*. We will discuss the details of the syntax in a later section. For now, please note that a *FORM ACTION* tag specifies the name of the CGI script *hello.cgi*.

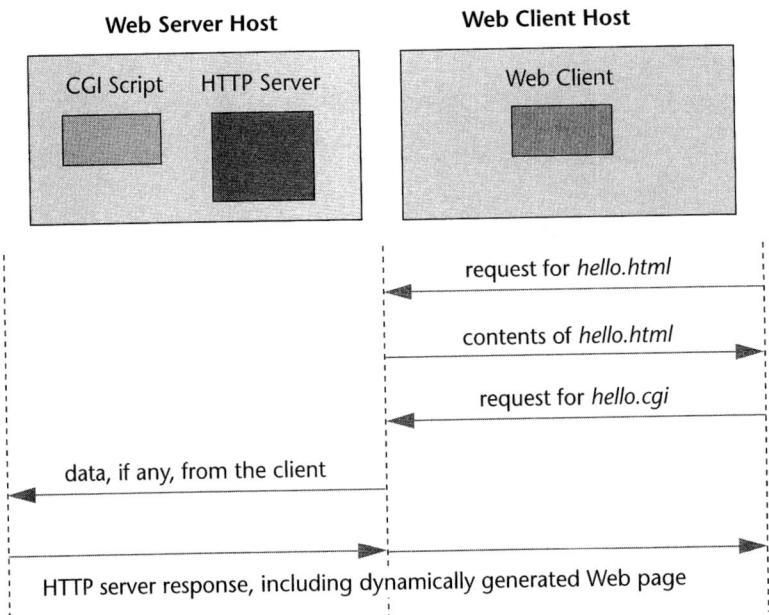

Figure 9.9 The Common Gateway Interface protocol.

Figure 9.10 *Hello.html.*

```
<!Sample Web page for illustrating CGI>
<!Author: M. Liu, 9/15/01>
<HTML>
<HEAD>
<TITLE>A Web page that invokes a Web script</TITLE>
</HEAD>
<BODY>
<H1>This Web page illustrates the use of a Web script</H1>
<P>
<FONT color = green>
This page contains an action tag which specifies a Web script.
Upon retrieving this page from the Web server, the browser
processes the contents and, when the SUBMIT button is pressed,
requests the server to run the script or program specified
with the action tag
</FONT>
<BR>
The script or program is either a run-script written in a
script language such as Perl, or an executable generated
from a source program written in a language such as C/C++
</P>
<HR>
```

(continued on next page)

```
<FORM METHOD="post" ACTION="hello.cgi">
<HR>
Press <input type="submit" value="here"> to submit your query.
</FORM>
<HR>
</BODY>
</HTML>
```

Java is not used for implementing CGI programs. In Chapter 11 we will introduce Java servlets in detail; they are Java programs that are the equivalent of CGI scripts.

Figure 9.11 shows an implementation of *hello.cgi*. The example is written in C. Although you may not be familiar with the C language, its syntax is sufficiently similar to Java that you should be able to follow the code samples in this chapter. A CGI program can be written in any programming language, including interpretive languages (such as Perl, TKL, Python, JavaScript, Visual Basic script), as well as compiled languages (such as C, C++, ADA). For illustration, a version of the program, written in the popular script language Perl, is presented in Figure 9.12. Although you may not be familiar with C, you should recognize the straightforward syntax in this program, which simply outputs the contents of a Web page line by line, starting with a response header line specifying the content type, followed by two new-line characters, then HTML lines, which specify that the "Hello World" message be displayed in blue.

A new-line character is a linefeed, which has an ASCII value of 10.

Figure 9.11 *Hello.cgi*, a C program for a CGI script.

```
/**
 * This C program is for a CGI script which generates
 * the output for a Web page. When displayed by a
 * browser, the message "Hello there!" will be shown
 * in blue.
 */
#include <stdio.h>

main(int argc, char *argv[]) {

  printf("Content-type: text/html%c%c",10,10);
  printf("<font color = blue>");
  printf("<H1>Hello there!</H1>");
  printf("</font>");
}
```

The output lines are transmitted to the Web server, which returns the lines to the client as a response. (Note that no status line is included in the CGI script output: The absence of a status line is interpreted as "status okay" by the browser.)

Figure 9.12 presents the same Web script, written in the interpretive language Perl.

Figure 9.12 *Hello.pl*, a Perl program for a CGI script.

```
#!/usr/local/bin/perl

# The above line must be the first line in the program.
# It specifies that the perl interpreter is to be invoked
# when the script is run. The directory path specified
# should be one that contains the perl interpreter on the
# Web server host.

# Hello.pl
# A simple Perl CGI script

print "Content-type: text/html\n\n";
print "<head>\n";
print "<title>Hello, World</title>\n";
print "</head>\n";
print "<body>\n";
print "<font color = blue>\n";
print "<h1>Hello, World</h1>\n";
print "</font>\n";
print "</body>\n";
```

You may have noticed that the example just presented does not make use of any user input, and the contents of the dynamically generated Web page are predeterminable. This is because the example is provided as an overview of the CGI protocol. In practice, a CGI script is typically invoked by a special kind of Web page known as a Web form (to be described in the next section), which accepts input at run time and invokes a CGI script that makes use of such input.

A Web Form

A Web form [w3.org, 24] is a special kind of Web page that (1) provides a graphical user interface that prompts the user to input data and, (2) when a Submit button on the page is pressed by the user, invokes the execution of an external program on the Web server host. A simple Web form, as displayed on a browser screen, is shown in Figure 9.13.

Figure 9.14 presents the HTML code that generates the Web form. Readers are directed to [ftp.ics.uci.edu,13; archive.ncsa.uiuc.edu, 14] for details of the various tags used in the code.

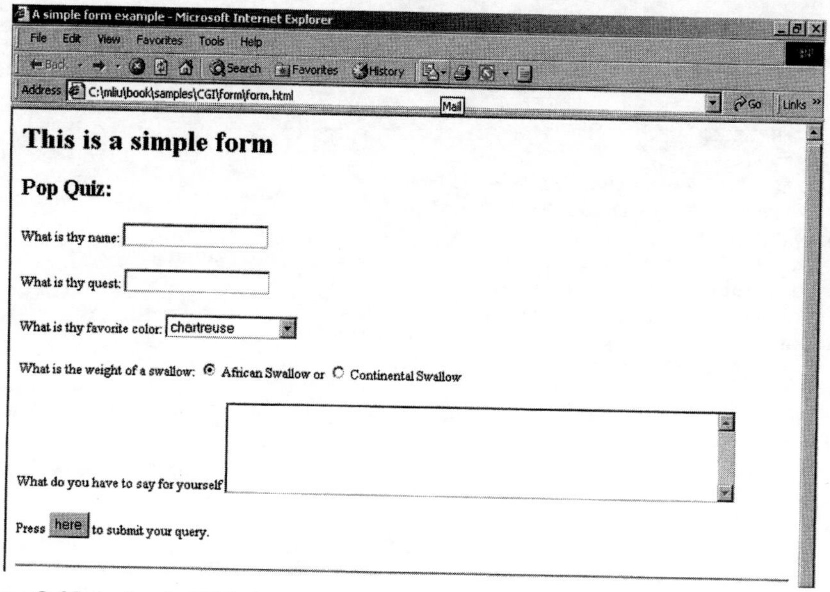

Figure 9.13 A simple Web form.

Figure 9.14 Code for a simple Web form [archive.ncsa.uiuc.edu, 14].

```
1   <HTML>
2   <HEAD>
3   <TITLE>A simple form example</TITLE>
4   </HEAD>
5   <BODY>
6   <H1>This is a simple form</H1>
7   <FORM METHOD="get" ACTION="form.cgi">
8   <H2> Pop Quiz: </H2>
9   What is thy NAME: <INPUT NAME="NAME"><P>
10  What is thy quest: <INPUT NAME="quest"><P>
11  What is thy favorite color:
12  <SELECT NAME="color">
13  <OPTION SELECTED>chartreuse
14  <OPTION>azure
15  <OPTION>puce
16  <OPTION>cornflower
17  <OPTION>olive drab
18  <OPTION>gunmetal
19  <OPTION>indigo2
20  <OPTION>blanched almond
21  <OPTION>flesh
```

(continued on next page)

```
22  <OPTION>ochre
23  <OPTION>opal
24  <OPTION>amber
25  <OPTION>mustard
26  </SELECT>
27  <P>
28  What is the weight of a swallow:
29  <INPUT TYPE="radio" NAME="swallow"
30  VALUE="african" checked> African Swallow or
31  <INPUT TYPE="radio" NAME="swallow" VALUE="continental">
32  Continental Swallow
33  <P>
34  What do you have to say for yourself
35  <TEXTAREA NAME="text" ROWS=5 COLS=60></TEXTAREA>
36  <P>
37  Press <INPUT TYPE="submit" NAME="sButton" VALUE="here">
38  to submit your query.
39  </FORM>
40  <HR>
41  </BODY>
42  </HTML>
```

HTML is not case sensitive—the use of all uppercase letters in a tag is optional.

A relative URL is one based on the directory of the Web page in which the relative URL appears. For example, if the Web page is /someDir/someSubDir/somePage.html, then a relative URL, anotherPage.html, appearing in the page expands to the absolute URL, which would be /someDir/someSubDir/anotherPage.html.

The code that generates a Web form is enclosed between the HTML tags *<FORM>* ... *</FORM>* (see lines 7 and 39 in the example). Within the *<FORM>* tag (see line 7), attributes can be specified to provide additional information related to the CGI protocol, including

- *ACTION=<URL>*

   where *<URL>* is a character string containing the absolute or relative URL of the identification of the external program that is to be initiated by the Web server when the form is submitted; see line 7 in Figure 9.14.

- *METHOD=<a reserved word>*, where the reserved word is a method name, such as *POST* or *GET*, which specifies the manner in which the external program expects to receive from the Web server the collection of data submitted by the user, called the query data. The meaning of these methods will be explained later; see line 7 in Figure 9.14.

In the coding for the form, each of the input items (also called **input elements**) has a *NAME* tag (see lines 9, 10, 12, 29, 31, 35, and 37). For each of these items, the browser user enters or selects a value. The collection of the data for the input items is a character string, called a **query string**, of *name=value* pairs separated by the & character. Each *name=value* pair is encoded using URL-encoding [w3.org, 22; blooberry.com, 23], so that some "unsafe" characters (such as spaces, quotes, %, and &) are mapped to a hexadecimal representation.

For example, the value string "The return is >17%" is encoded "The%20return%20is%20%3E17%25."

Here is an example of a query string for the example form:

```
name=John%20Doe&quest=peace%20on%20earth&color=azure
&swallow=continental&text=The%20return%20is%20%3E17%25
```

The marshaling of the data into a query string, including the encoding of the values, is performed by the browser. When the form is submitted by the user, the query string is passed to the server in the HTTP request, in a manner depending on the *FORM METHOD* specified in the form. In the next section, we will explain how the query string is transmitted to the server and then to the external program.

Query String Processing

Based on the form input, the browser assembles the query string as previously described. The string is transmitted to the Web server, which in turn passes the string on to the external program (the CGI script named in the form). The manner in which the string is transmitted depends on the specification of the *FORM METHOD* in the Web form.

The FORM *GET* Method—Sending the Query String to the Server

If *GET* is specified with the *FORM METHOD* tag, the query string is transmitted to the server in an HTTP request with a *GET* method line previously described in section 9.3. Recall that an HTTP *GET* request specifies a URI for the Web object requested by the client. To accommodate the query string, the syntax for the URI specification was extended to allow the attachment of the query string to the end of the URI (for the CGI script), delimited by the '?' character, as, for example:

```
GET /cgi/hello.cgi?name=John%20Doe&quest=peace HTTP/1.0
```

Since the length of the *GET* request-URI line is limited (owing to the input-buffer size imposed by the machines), the length of the query string that can be appended in this manner is also limited. Hence this method is not suitable if the form needs to send a large amount of data, such as data entered in a text box.

The FORM *POST* Method—Sending the Query String to the Server

If *POST* is specified with the *FORM METHOD* tag, the query string is transmitted to the server in an HTTP request with the *POST* method line previously described in section 9.3. Recall that an HTTP *POST* request is followed by a request body, which holds text contents to be sent to the server. Using the *POST METHOD*, the URI of the CGI script is specified with the *POST* request line, followed by the request header, a blank line, then the query string, as, for example:

```
POST /cgi/hello.cgi HTTP/1.0
Accept: */*
Connection: Keep-Alive
Host: myHost.someU.edu
User-Agent: Generic

name=John%20Doe&quest=peace%20on%20earth&color=azure
```

Since the length of the request body is unlimited, the query string can be of arbitrary length. Hence the *POST* method can be used to send any amount of query data to the server.

The FORM *GET* Method—
Sending the Query String to the External Program

Environment variables
are variables maintained
by the operating system
of the server host.

With the *GET* method the server invokes the CGI script and passes on the query string that it received from the browser, as appended to the URI in the HTTP request. The CGI program, or the external program in general, will receive the encoded form input in an **environment variable** called *QUERY_STRING*. The CGI program retrieves the query string from the environment variable, decodes the character string to obtain the name-value pairs, and makes use of the values of the parameters during the execution of the program to generate output phrased in HTML.

The FORM *POST* Method—
Sending the Query String to the External Program

On most systems, there
is a standard source of
input for a process, typically the keyboard, and
a standard destination
for its output, typically
the screen display.

The server invokes the CGI script and passes on the query string that it received from the browser via the request body. The CGI program, or the external program in general, will receive the encoded form input on the **standard input**. The CGI program reads the query string from the standard input, decodes the character string to obtain the name-value pairs, and uses the parameters during the execution of the program to generate output phrased in HTML.

Encoding and Decoding Query Strings

An associative array is a
data structure for hold-
ing a set of pairs
(key,value).

Whether a query string is obtained from the *QUERY_STRING* environment variable or from the standard input, the CGI program must decode the string and extract the name-value pairs from it, so that the parameters may be used for the program's execution. Because of the popularity of CGI programs, there are a number of existing libraries or classes that provide routines (functions) and methods for this purpose. For example, Perl has easy-to-use procedures in a library called *CGI-lib* for the decoding and extracting of the name-value pairs into a data structure called an *associative array*; and The National Center for Supercomputing Applications (NCSA) provides a library of C routines for the same purpose.

Figure 9.15 presents a CGI program, written in C, for our sample form that specifies *FORM METHOD = GET*. The program uses routines named *getword* and *unescape* (lines 46–49) for decoding and extracting the query string. The resulting name-value pairs are placed in a data structure declared on lines 16–19, and 27, which is effectively an associate array. Note that on line 39 the code makes use of a C routine *getenv* to retrieve the query string from the environment variable *QUERY_STRING*. In this sample, the names and values thus retrieved are simply displayed (lines 51–63).

Figure 9.15 *getForm.c* [hoohoo.ncsa.uiuc.edu, 19].

```
1   /* Author: M. Liu, based on a NCSA CGI tutorial sample.
2   This is the source code for getForm.cgi.
3   It is invoked from getForm.html, and dynamically
4   generates a Web page that displays the name-value
5   pairs obtained from the predecessor form (getForm.html).
6   This program uses the NCSA CGI library for processing
7   a query string obtained via the GET method.
8   */
09  #include <stdio.h>
10  #ifndef NO_STDLIB_H
11  #include <stdlib.h>
12  #else
13  char *getenv();
14  #endif
15
16  typedef struct {
17    char name[128];
18    char val[128];
19  } entry;
20
21  void getword(char *word, char *line, char stop);
22  char x2c(char *what);
23  void unescape_url(char *url);
24  void plustospace(char *str);
25
26  main(int argc, char *argv[]) {
27    entry entries[10000];
28    register int x,m=0;
29    char *cl;
30
31    printf("Content-type: text/html%c%c",10,10);
32
33    if(strcmp(getenv("REQUEST_METHOD"),"GET")) {
34      printf("This script should be referenced
35        with a METHOD of GET.\n");
36      exit(1);
37    }
38
39    cl = getenv("QUERY_STRING");
40    if(cl == NULL) {
41      printf("No query information to decode.\n");
42      exit(1);
43    }
44    for(x=0;cl[0] != '\0';x++) {
45      m=x;
46      getword(entries[x].val,cl,'&');
47      plustospace(entries[x].val);
48      unescape_url(entries[x].val);
49      getword(entries[x].name,entries[x].val,'=');
50    }
```

(continued on next page)

```
51    printf("<BODY bgcolor=\"#CCFFCC\">");
52    printf("<H2>This page is generated
53       dynamically by getForm.cgi.</H2>");
54    printf("<H1>Query Results</H1>");
55    printf("You submitted the following name/value".
56       "pairs:<p>%c",10);
57    printf("<ul>%c",10);
58
59    for(x=0; x <= m; x++)
60       printf("<li> <code>%s = %s</code>%c",
61          entries[x].name, entries[x].val,10);
62    printf("</BODY>");
63    printf("</HTML>");
64  }
```

Figure 9.16 presents a CGI program, written in C, for our sample form that specifies *FORM METHOD = POST*. It uses routines named *makeword* and *unescape* (lines 51–54) for decoding and extracting the query string. The resulting name-value pairs are placed in a data structure declared on lines 18–21 and 31, which is effectively an associate array. Note that the for loop starting on line 49 reads the query string from the standard input, extracts one word at a time, decodes it, and places the names and values in the data structure. In this sample, the names and values thus obtained are simply displayed (lines 56–66).

Figure 9.16 *postForm.c* [hoohoo.ncsa.uiuc.edu, 19].

```
1   /* Author: M. L. Liu, based on an NCSA CGI tutorial sample.
2   This is the source code for postForm.cgi, for the simple
3   form example. It is invoked from postForm.html, and
4   generates a dynamic Web page that displays the name-
5   value-pairs obtained from postForm.html.
6   This program uses the NCSA CGI library for processing a
7   query string obtained via the POST method.
8   */
9   #include <stdio.h>
10  #ifndef NO_STDLIB_H
11  #include <stdlib.h>
12  #else
13  char *getenv();
14  #endif
15
16  #define MAX_ENTRIES 10000
17
18  typedef struct {
19    char *name;
20    char *val;
21  } entry;
22
23  char *makeword(char *line, char stop);
24  char *fmakeword(FILE *f, char stop, int *len);
```

(continued on next page)

```
25  char x2c(char *what);
26  void unescape_url(char *url);
27  void plustospace(char *str);
28
29
30  main(int argc, char *argv[]) {
31    entry entries[MAX_ENTRIES];
32    register int x,m=0;
33    int cl;
34
35    printf("Content-type: text/html%c%c",10,10);
36    if(strcmp(getenv("REQUEST_METHOD"),"POST")) {
37      printf("This script should be referenced ",
38         "with a METHOD of POST.\n");
39      exit(1);
40    }
41    if(strcmp(getenv("CONTENT_TYPE"),
42         "application/x-www-form-urlencoded")) {
43      printf("The query string does not contain ",
44         "URL-encoded data \n");
45      exit(1);
46    }
47    cl = atoi(getenv("CONTENT_LENGTH"));
48
49    for(x=0;cl && (!feof(stdin));x++) {
50      m=x;
51      entries[x].val = fmakeword(stdin,'&',&cl);
52      plustospace(entries[x].val);
53      unescape_url(entries[x].val);
54      entries[x].name = makeword(entries[x].val,'=');
55    }
56    printf("<body bgcolor=\"#FFFF99\">");
57    printf("<H1>Query Results</H1>");
58    printf("You submitted the following name/value pairs:",
59       "<p>%c",10);
60    printf("<ul>%c",10);
61
62    for(x=0; x <= m; x++)
63      printf("<li> <code>%s = %s</code>\n",entries[x].name,
64         entries[x].val);
65    printf("</body>");
66    printf("</html>");
67  }
```

Environment Variables Used with CGI

An **environment variable** is a parameter of a user's working environment on a computer system, such as the default directory path for the system to locate a program invoked by the user or the version of operating system in use. On a computer system, environment variables can be employed across multiple languages and operating systems to provide information specific to an application.

On UNIX systems, the settings of environment variables can be found in a dot file (such as .login or .cshrc) in the home directory of your account. On Windows systems, you can find the settings of environment variables in the control panel.

CGI uses environment variables that are set by the HTTP server to pass information about requests from the server to the external program (CGI script).

Following are some of the key environment variables related to CGI:

- *REQUEST_METHOD*. The method type with which the request was made. For CGI, this is *GET* or *POST*.
- *QUERY_STRING*. If the *GET* method was specified in the form, this variable contains a URL-encoded character string for the form data.
- *CONTENT_TYPE*. The content type of the data, which should be "application/x-www-form-urlencoded" for a query string.
- *CONTENT_LENGTH*. The length of the query string in number of bytes.

9.6 Web Session and Session State Data

During a session of a Web application such as a shopping cart, several HTTP requests are issued, each of which may invoke an external program such as a CGI script. Figure 9.17 illustrates a simplified session of such an application: The first Web form prompts for a customer ID, which is validated by the CGI script *form1.cgi*. The Web script dynamically generates a Web form, denoted *form2.html*. (Note that this file is never written to disk; it merely exists as the output from the Web script directed to the Web server.) The form prompts the customer to fill out a purchase order. The purchase order selected by the user is sent to a second Web script, *form2.cgi*, which dynamically generates yet another transient Web form (*form3.html*), which in turn displays the customer's account data and the contents of the shopping cart. The session may continue in this manner involving yet more additional Web scripts and dynamically generated Web pages until the user terminates the session.

Note that in our example it is necessary for the second CGI script, *form2.cgi*, to know the value of the data item *id* in the query string sent to the first CGI script, *form1.cgi*. That is, *id* is a **session state data** item that needs to be shared among the Web scripts invoked throughout the session. However, since the Web scripts are separate programs executed in independent contexts, they do not share data. Moreover, there is no provision in HTTP or CGI to support session state data, since both of these protocols are stateless and do not support the notion of a session.

Because of the popularity of Internet applications, a variety of mechanisms have emerged to allow the sharing of session data among CGI scripts (and other external programs). These mechanisms can be classified as follows:

- **Server-side facilities.** Since the CGI scripts are executed on the HTTP server host, it is logical to make use of facilities on that host for maintaining session state data.

  For example, secondary storage (file or database) on the server host may be used as a repository of session state data: Each Web script deposits shared state data items in the storage, which can be subsequently retrieved by other scripts. The disadvantage of this scheme is the overhead involved and the

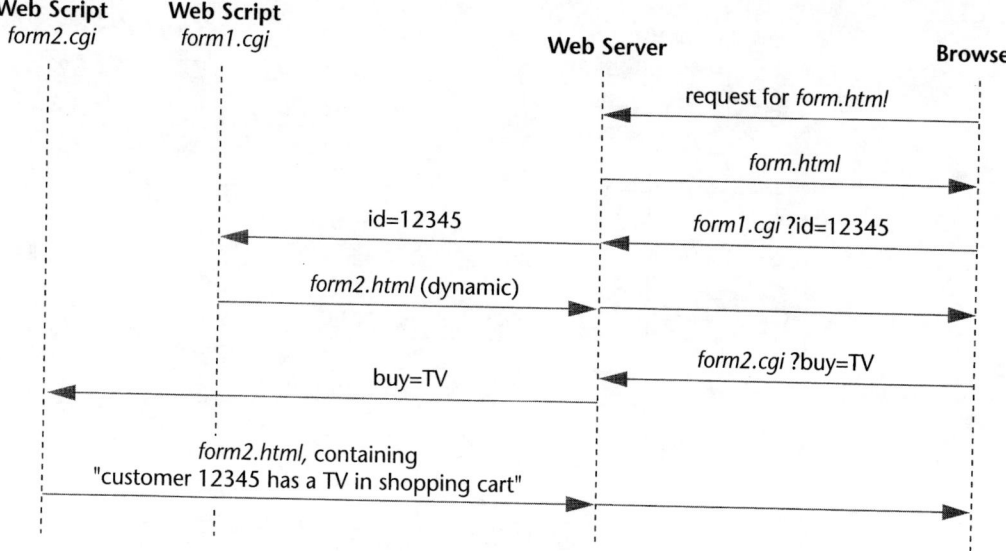

Figure 9.17 A Web session involving multiple external programs.

need for storage management for a potentially large number of concurrent sessions.

Alternatively, the HTTP server may support persistent data objects that may be employed as state data repository. In the Chapter 11, we will look at some of the mechanisms based on this idea.

- **Client-side facilities.** An ingenious idea for managing session state data is to maintain the data with the help of the clients. Since each session is associated with a single client, this scheme allows the state data to be maintained in a decentralized fashion. Specifically, the scheme allows the state data to be passed from a Web script to the client, which in turn passes the data to a subsequent Web script. The data passing can be repeated throughout the duration of the Web session. Figure 9.18 illustrates the idea. The state data item *id* is passed from the first Web script, via the Web server, to the browser. The data item is sent from the Web client to a subsequent CGI script when that script is invoked. In turn, CGI script 2 passes the data items *id* and *buy* to the Web client. In the next round, the browser sends the items to the last CGI script, which contributes an additional item *charge* to the session state data.

In the rest of this chapter, we will look at two schemes that make use of client-side facilities to maintain session data:

- **Hidden form fields.** This scheme embeds session state data in dynamically generated Web forms.
- **Cookies.** This funny-named mechanism uses transient or persistent storage on the client host to hold state data, which is passed in the HTTP request header to Web scripts that require the data.

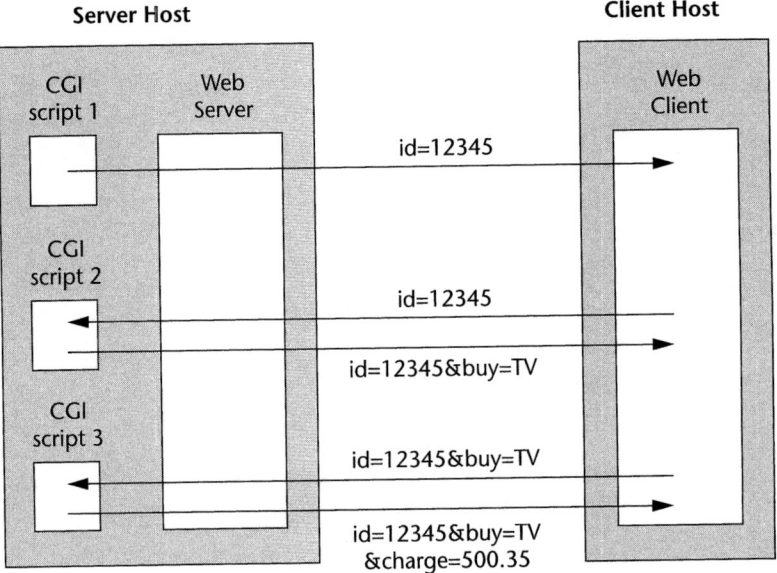

Figure 9.18 Session state data transmitted via the Web client.

Using Hidden Form Fields for Transferring Session State Data

A hidden form field or a **hidden field** is an *INPUT* element in a Web form specified with *TYPE=HIDDEN*. Unlike other *INPUT* elements, a hidden field is *not* displayed by the browser and requires no user input. Rather, the value of the element is the *VALUE* attribute specified with the field, and the name-value of the field is collected by the browser, along with the name-value pairs of other *INPUT* elements, in the query string when the form is submitted.

Figure 9.19 illustrates the use of hidden fields to pass data between Web scripts. The first Web script *form1.cgi* generates the element *<input type=hidden name="id" value="12345">* in the dynamically generated *form2.html*. When presenting *form2.html*, the browser will not display this field. The other input field, not specified as hidden, is displayed to prompt the user for a purchase. When *form2.html* is submitted, the query string *"id=12345&buy=tv"* is sent to the second Web form, *form2.cgi*. When the query string is decoded, the value of the state data item *id* becomes available to *form2.cgi*. Figure 9.20 presents the sequence diagram.

The hidden field is a rudimentary scheme for maintaining session data. It has the merit of simplicity, requiring only the introduction of a new form field element and no additional resources on either the server side or the client side. In the scheme, the HTTP client becomes a temporary repository for the state information, and the session data is sent using the normal mechanisms for transmitting query strings.

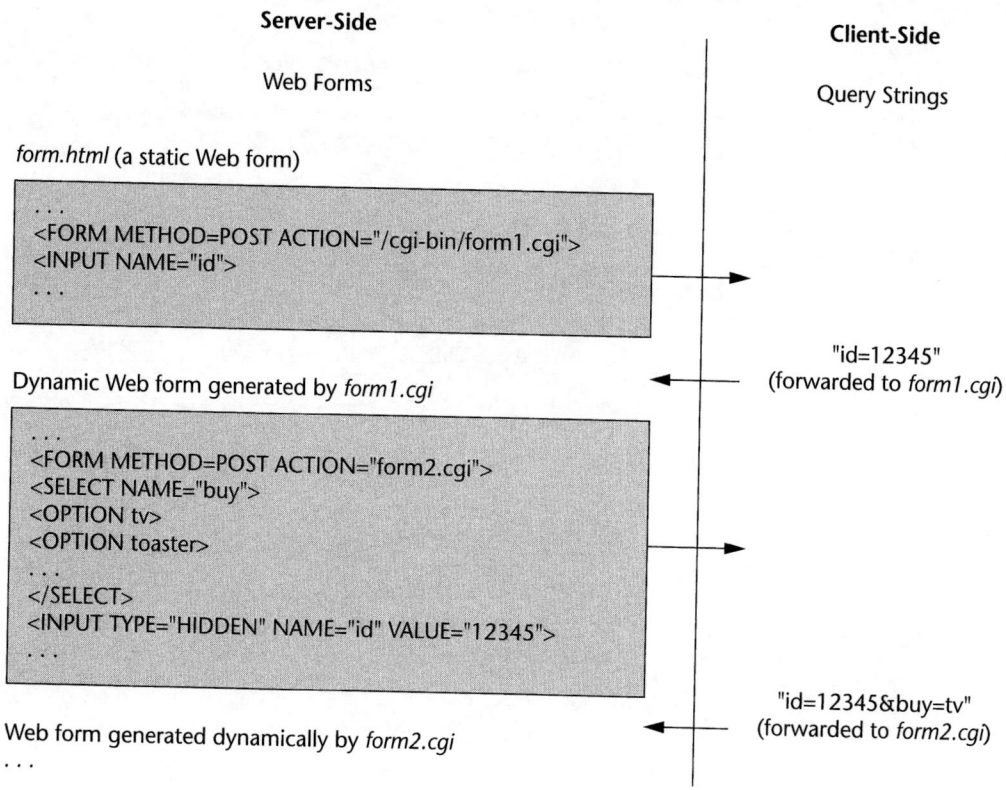

Figure 9.19 Using a hidden form field to pass session data—an overview.

As always, there is a trade-off. The simplicity of the scheme comes at the cost of privacy or security risk, in the sense that the state data transmitted using hidden form field is unprotected. In our example shown in Figure 9.20, the *id* value of a customer is transmitted using a hidden input element. Although such an element is not displayed by the browser, it is embedded in the source code of the dynamically generated Web page *form2.html*, which is plainly viewable by any browser user who exercises the *view source* capability provided by the browser. Hence the scheme allows state data to become exposed, and therefore poses a privacy or security risk. For this reason, hidden fields should not be used to transmit sensitive data such as a social security number or account balances.

Figures 9.21, 9.22, and 9.23 present code samples for the use of hidden form fields to pass state data between CGI scripts. The initial Web form (Figure 9.21) invokes the script *hiddenForm.cgi*, which extracts the name-value pairs in the query string that it receives (lines 43–48 in Figure 9.22), then encloses each pair in a hidden form field in the Web page that it generates (lines 64–66 in Figure 9.22). The hidden field data are included in the query string for the CGI script *hiddenForm2.cgi* (Figure 9.23), which extracts the name-value pairs (lines 40–46) and simply displays them (lines 54–59).

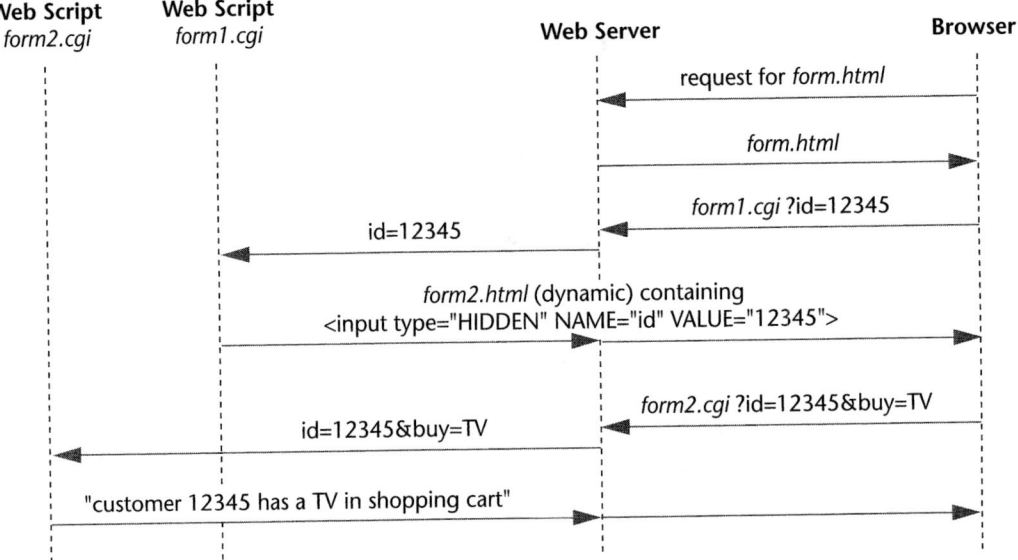

Figure 9.20 Using a hidden form field to pass session data—detailed view.

Figure 9.21 A hidden form fields example: *form.html*.

```
<HTML>
<HEAD>
<TITLE>Hidden form fields example</TITLE>
</HEAD>
<BODY>
<H1>Using hidden form fields for session information</H1>
<P>
This form invokes a CGI script which uses hidden form
fields to pass session data to a subsequently executed
CGI script.
</P>
<HR>
<FORM method="post" action="hiddenForm.cgi">
<H2> Pop Quiz: </H2>
What is your ID: <input name="id"><P>
<P>
Press <input type="submit" value="here"> to submit your query.
</FORM>
<HR>
</BODY>
</HTML>
```

Figure 9.22 A hidden form fields example: *hiddenForm.c*.

```
1   /*  hiddenForm.c - source code for hiddenForm.cgi
2   Author: M. L. Liu.
3   This script dynamically generates a Web page which
4   contains hidden form fields which contain the name-
5   value pairs received in the query string.
6   */
7
8   #include <stdio.h>
9   #ifndef NO_STDLIB_H
10  #include <stdlib.h>
11  #else
12  char *getenv();
13  #endif
14
15  #define MAX_ENTRIES 10000
16
17  typedef struct {
18    char *name;
19    char *val;
20  } entry;
21
22  char *makeword(char *line, char stop);
23  char *fmakeword(FILE *f, char stop, int *len);
24  char x2c(char *what);
25  void unescape_url(char *url);
26  void plustospace(char *str);
27
28
29  main(int argc, char *argv[]) {
30    entry entries[MAX_ENTRIES];
31    register int x,m=0;
32    int cl;
33
34    printf("Content-type: text/html%c%c",10,10);
35    if(strcmp(getenv("REQUEST_METHOD"),"POST")) {
36      printf
37        ("This script should be used with a POST METHOD.\n");
38      exit(1);
39    }
40
41    cl = atoi(getenv("CONTENT_LENGTH"));
42
43    for(x=0;cl && (!feof(stdin));x++) {
44      m=x;
45      entries[x].val = fmakeword(stdin,'&',&cl);
46      plustospace(entries[x].val);
47      unescape_url(entries[x].val);
48      entries[x].name = makeword(entries[x].val,'=');
49    }
```

(continued on next page)

```
50   /* generate a dynamic form which contains hidden form fields */
51   printf("<FORM method=\"post\" action=\"hiddenForm2.cgi\">");
52   printf("<H@>This form was dynamically generated by ",
53      "hiddenForm.cgi</H2>");
54   printf("<H1>Query Results</H1>");
55   printf("You submitted the following name/value pairs:<p>%c",10);
56   printf("<ul>%c",10);
57
58   for(x=0; x <= m; x++)
59     printf("<li> <code>%s = %s</code>%c",entries[x].name,
60        entries[x].val,10);
61   printf("</ul>%c",10);
62
63   /* now put each name-value pair in a hidden form field */
64   for(x=0; x <= m; x++)
65     printf("<INPUT TYPE=\"HIDDEN\" NAME=%s VALUE=%s>\n",,
66        entries[x].name, entries[x].val);
67
68   printf("Press <input type=\"submit\" value=\"here\"> to ",
69      "submit your query.");
70   printf("<HR>");
71   printf("</FORM>");
72   printf("</BODY>");
73   printf("</HTML>");
74
75 }
```

Figure 9.23 A hidden form fields example: *hiddenForm2.c.*

```
 1  */ hiddenForm2.c - source code for hiddenForm2.cgi
 2  Author: M. L. Liu.
 3  This script simply displays the name-value pairs it
 4  receives in the query string, which should include
 5  the name-value pairs that appeared in the hidden-form
 6  of the Web page which invokes this script.
 7  */
 8  #include <stdio.h>
 9  #ifndef NO_STDLIB_H
10  #include <stdlib.h>
11  #else
12  char *getenv();
13  #endif
14
15  #define MAX_ENTRIES 10000
16
17  typedef struct {
18    char *name;
19    char *val;
20  } entry;
21
```

(continued on next page)

```
22  char *makeword(char *line, char stop);
23  char *fmakeword(FILE *f, char stop, int *len);
24  char x2c(char *what);
25  void unescape_url(char *url);
26  void plustospace(char *str);
27
28  main(int argc, char *argv[]) {
29    entry entries[MAX_ENTRIES];
30    register int x,m=0;
31    int cl;
32
33    printf("Content-type: text/html%c%c",10,10);
34    if(strcmp(getenv("REQUEST_METHOD"),"POST")) {
35      printf("This script should use the POST METHOD.\n");
36      exit(1);
37    }
38    cl = atoi(getenv("CONTENT_LENGTH"));
39
40    for(x=0;cl && (!feof(stdin));x++) {
41      m=x;
42      entries[x].val = fmakeword(stdin,'&',&cl);
43      plustospace(entries[x].val);
44      unescape_url(entries[x].val);
45      entries[x].name = makeword(entries[x].val,'=');
46    }
47
48    printf("<H2>This form was dynamically generated by ",
49      "hiddenForm2.cgi</H2>");
50    printf("<H1>Query Results</H1>");
51    printf("You submitted the following name/value pairs:<p>%c",10);
52    printf("<UL>%c",10);
53
54    for(x=0; x <= m; x++)
55      printf("<li> <code>%s = %s</code>%c",entries[x].name,
56        entries[x].val,10);
57    printf("</UL>%c",10);
58    printf("</HTML>");
59    printf("</BODY>");
60  }
```

Using Cookies for Transferring Session State Data

A more sophisticated scheme for session state data repository on the client side is a mechanism known as a **cookie**, named so "for no compelling reason" [ics.uci.edu, 5; home.netscape.com, 25]. However, http://www.webopedia.com claims that "[t]he name cookie derives from Unix objects called magic cookies. These are tokens that are attached to a user or program and change depending on the areas entered by the user or program."

The scheme makes use of an extension of the basic HTTP to allow a server's response to contain a piece of state information for which the client will provide storage in an object. According to [home.netscape.com, 25], "Included in that state object is a description of the range of URLs for which that state is valid. Any future HTTP requests made by the client which fall in that range will include a transmittal of the current value of the state object from the client back to the server."

Each cookie contains a URL-encoded name-value pair, similar to a name-value pair in a query string, for a state data item (for example, id=12345). A CGI script creates a cookie by including a *Set-Cookie* header line as part of the HTTP response that it outputs. When such a response is received by the browser, it creates an object, a cookie, that contains the name-value pair specified for the cookie. Each cookie is stored on the client host, either temporarily or persistently. Subsequently, the name-value pair of the cookie is retrieved and then embedded in a *Cookie* header line in each request sent by the browser to the Web server. Upon encountering a *Cookie* header line, the Web server collects the name-value pairs in a string and places the string in an environment variable named *HTTP_COOKIE*. The format of the *HTTP_COOKIE* string is the same as that for a query string previously described in section 9.5.

Figure 9.24 illustrates the use of cookies. Script *form.cgi* introduces a cookie that contains "id=12345", which is sent to the Web browser in a response header line dynamically generated by *form.cgi*. As a result, a cookie containing "id-12345"

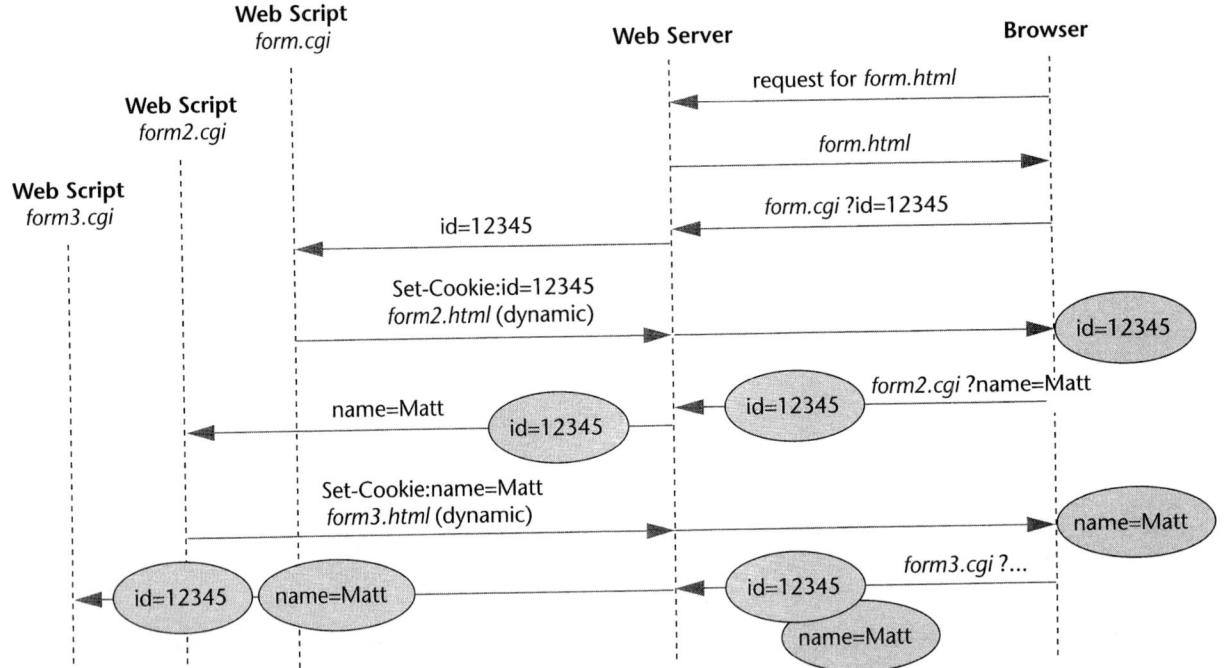

Figure 9.24 Using cookies to pass session data.

is stored on the client host. When a subsequent HTTP request is issued by the browser for *form2.cgi*, the name-value pair (id=12345) is retrieved from the cookie and included in a request header line. Upon receiving the request, the server extracts the name-value string ("id=12345") from the header line and places the string in the environment variable *HTTP_COOKIE*. The Web script *form2.cgi* can then extract the state data (id=12345) from *HTTP_COOKIE*. Note that *form2.cgi* can generate an additional cookie, which, in our example, contains the name-value pair "name=Matt". If a subsequent CGI script is invoked, the name-value pair of each previously created cookie is sent along in the request header. In our example, *form3.cgi* will receive in *HTTP_COOKIE* the state data id=12345 and name=Matt from the two cookies generated by the preceding Web scripts.

Syntax of the Set-Cookie HTTP Response Header Line

The previous description presented a simplified scenario of using cookies to maintain state data. In reality, the *Set-Cookie* header line, used by a CGI script to initiate a cookie, has a rich set of syntax. The following description is based on [home.netscape.com, 25]:

The *Set-Cookie* header line is a string in the following format (keywords are listed in bold):

```
Set-Cookie: NAME=VALUE; expires=DATE;
path=PATH; domain=DOMAIN_NAME; secure
```

The line starts with the keyword "Set-Cookie" and the delimiter colon (:), followed by a list of attributes separated by semicolons. The attributes are explained as follows:

- *NAME=VALUE*. Similar to form input data, this is a URL-encoded name-value pair for the state data to be stored in the cookie created. This is the only required attribute on the *Set-Cookie* header line.

- *expires*=<a date string>. The *expires* attribute specifies a date string that defines the valid lifetime of that cookie. Once the expiration date has been reached, the client host is free to deallocate the cookie, and the state data contained in the cookie can no longer be assumed to be sent to the server in subsequent HTTP requests.

  The date string is formatted as follows:

```
Wdy, DD-Mon-YYYY HH:MM:SS GMT
```

  The time format is based on RFC 822, RFC 850, RFC 1036, and RFC 1123, with the variations that the only legal time zone is GMT, and the separators between the elements of the date must be dashes.

  expires is an optional attribute. If not specified, the cookie will expire when the user's session ends.

- *domain*=<a domain name>. This attribute sets the *domain* for the cookie created. Among the cookies stored on the client host, a browser is supposed to send only cookies whose *domain* attributes are made with the Internet domain name of the host name specified in the URI of the object in the HTTP request (with which the cookie is sent). If there is a "tail match," then the cookie will go through path matching to see if it should be sent. *Tail matching* means that the *domain* attribute is matched against the tail of the fully qualified domain name in the URI. For example, a *domain* attribute of "acme.com" would match host names "anvil.acme.com" as well as "shipping.crate.acme.com." Thus, the name-value pair in the cookie tagged with the *domain* attribute of acme.com will be sent with an HTTP request where the requested object has a URI containing the host name anvil.acme.com (such as anvil.acme.com/index.html) or shipping.crate.acme.com (such as shipping.crate.acme.com/sales/shop.htm).

Only hosts within the specified domain can set a cookie for a domain, and domains must have at least two or three periods in them to prevent domains of the form: ".com", ".edu", and "va.us".

The default value of *domain* is the host name of the server that generated the cookie response. For example, if the server is www.someU.edu, then, if no *domain* attribute is set with a cookie, then the cookie's *domain* is www.someU.edu.

■ *path*=<a path string>. The *path* attribute is used to specify the subset of URIs in a domain for which the cookie is valid. If a cookie has already passed the *domain* matching, then the pathname component of the URI is compared with the *path* attribute, and if there is a *head-match*, the cookie is considered valid and is sent along with the HTTP request. For example, the path "/foo" would match "/foobar" and "/foo/bar.html". The path "/" is the most general path.

If the *path* is not specified, it is assumed that the path is the same as that for the document being described by the header that contains the cookie.

The examples in Table 9.3 illustrate the usage of the Domain attribute and the Path attribute. In the examples, * is a wild card string, representing any string at all.

■ *Secure*. If a cookie is marked "secure," it will be transmitted only if the communications channel with the host is secure, such as HTTPS (HTTP over SSL) servers. If "secure" is not specified, a cookie is considered safe to be sent in the clear over unsecured channels.

Table 9.3 Examples of Cookie Domain Attributes and Cookie Path Attribute Settings

Cookie Domain Attribute	Cookie Path Attribute	The request URI that will cause the name-value pair in the cookie to be sent in the request header.
www.someU.edu	none	*.www.someU.edu/*
www.someU.edu	/	*.www.someU.edu/*
www.someU.edu	/foo	*.www.someU.edu/foo*
www.someU.edu	/foo/foo	*.www.someU.edu/foo/foo*

Syntax of the Cookie HTTP Request Header Line

When requesting a URL from an HTTP server, the browser will match the URI against all cookies stored on the client host [home.netscape.com, 25]. If any matching cookie is found, then a line containing the name/value pairs of all matching cookies will be included in the HTTP request header. The format of the line is as follows:

```
Cookie: NAME₁=VALUE₁; NAME₂=VALUE₂; ...; NAMEₙ=VALUEₙ
```

When such a line is encountered by the HTTP server in the request header, the server extracts the substrings containing the name-value pairs from the line and places the string in an environment variable named *HTTP_COOKIE*. When the CGI script is executed, it may retrieve the state data, as name-value pairs, from the environment variable *HTTP_COOKIE*.

For example,if the following request is sent to the server

```
GET /cgi/hello.cgi?name=John&quest=peace HTTP/1.0
Cookie: age=25
<blank line>
```

then the server will place the string "name=John&quest=peace" in the environment variable *QUERY_STRING* and the string "age=25" in *HTTP_COOKIE* for the invoked CGI script.

Alternatively, if the request is

```
POST /cgi/hello.cgi HTTP/1.0
Cookie: age=25
<blank line>
name=John&quest=peace
```

then the string "name=John&quest=peace" will be sent by the server to the standard input of the CGI script, while the string "age=25" will be placed in environment variable *HTTP_COOKIE*.

The domain and path attributes for the cookies are designed to allow state data to be shared among selective CGI scripts, as illustrated by the following examples (taken directly from [home.netscape.com, 25]):

Example 1: Transaction Sequence

The client requests a document and receives the following response:

```
Set-Cookie: CUSTOMER=WILE_E_COYOTE; path=/; expires=Wednesday, 09-Nov-99
23:12:40 GMT
```

When client requests a URL in path "/" on this server, it sends

```
Cookie: CUSTOMER=WILE_E_COYOTE
```

The client requests a document and receives the following response:

```
Set-Cookie: PART_NUMBER=ROCKET_LAUNCHER_0001; path=/
```

When client requests a URL in path "/" on this server, it sends

```
Cookie: CUSTOMER=WILE_E_COYOTE; PART_NUMBER=ROCKET_LAUNCHER_0001
```

The client receives the following:

```
Set-Cookie: SHIPPING=FEDEX; path=/foo
```

When the client requests a URL in path "/" on this server, it sends

```
Cookie: CUSTOMER=WILE_E_COYOTE; PART_NUMBER=ROCKET_LAUNCHER_0001
```

When the client requests a URL in path "/foo" on this server, it sends the following:

```
Cookie: CUSTOMER=WILE_E_COYOTE; PART_NUMBER=ROCKET_LAUNCHER_0001; SHIP-
PING=FEDEX
```

Example 2: Transaction Sequence

Assume all mappings from the previous example have been cleared.

The client receives the following:

```
Set-Cookie: PART_NUMBER=ROCKET_LAUNCHER_0001; path=/
```

When the client requests a URL in path "/" on this server, it sends

```
Cookie: PART_NUMBER=ROCKET_LAUNCHER_0001
```

The client receives the following:

```
Set-Cookie: PART_NUMBER=RIDING_ROCKET_0023; path=/ammo
```

When the client requests a URL in path "/ammo" on this server, it sends the following:

```
Cookie: PART_NUMBER=RIDING_ROCKET_0023; PART_NUMBER=ROCKET_LAUNCHER_0001
```

Note: There are two name-value pairs named "PART_NUMBER" since there are two cookies that match the path attribute: the "/" and "/ammo".

Sample Code for Using Cookies to Pass State Data

In this section, we introduce a sample set of CGI scripts that make use of cookies. Figure 9.25 shows a static Web form that, when submitted, invokes the CGI script *cookie.cgi*.

The source code for *cookie.cgi* is shown in Figure 9.26. In lines 39–45, the CGI script obtains the query string from the standard input (since the *POST* method was used), extracts the name-value pairs in the query string, and places them in the associative *entry* array. In lines 50–54, each of the name-value pairs from the array is placed in a newly created cookie. For simplicity, no attributes are set with each cookie, so that the lifespan of each cookie will be that of the current Web session. (*Note:* In an actual application, only those name-value pairs that are needed for state data should be placed in cookies.)

Figure 9.25 *Cookie.html.*

```
<TITLE>A simple form which invokes a CGI script that creates cookies
</TITLE>
</HEAD>
<BODY>
<H1>This is a simple form which invokes a CGI script,
cookie.cgi
</H1>
<P>
<HR>
<FORM method="POST" action="cookie.cgi">
What is your name: <input name="name"><P>
What is your age: <input name="age"><P>
What is your id: <input name="id"><P>
Press <input type="submit" value="here"> to submit your query.
</FORM>
</BODY>
</HTML>
```

Figure 9.26 *cookie.c.*

```
1   /* cookie.c - source code for cookie.cgi
2   Author: M. L. Liu.
3   This script, requested by cookie.html, creates a cookie
4   for each name-value pair in the query string
5   */
6
7   #include <stdio.h>
8   #ifndef NO_STDLIB_H
9   #include <stdlib.h>
10  #else
11  char *getenv();
12  #endif
13
14  #define MAX_ENTRIES 10000
15
16  typedef struct {
17    char *name;
18    char *val;
19  } entry;
20
21  char *makeword(char *line, char stop);
22  char *fmakeword(FILE *f, char stop, int *len);
23  char x2c(char *what);
24  void unescape_url(char *url);
25  void plustospace(char *str);
26
27  main(int argc, char *argv[]) {
28    entry entries[MAX_ENTRIES];
```

(continued on next page)

```
29    register int x,m=0;
30    int cl;
31
32    if(strcmp(getenv("REQUEST_METHOD"),"POST")) {
33      printf("This script should be referenced with a
34        METHOD of POST.\n");
35      exit(1);
36    }
37    cl = atoi(getenv("CONTENT_LENGTH"));
38
39    for(x=0;cl && (!feof(stdin));x++) {
40      m=x;
41      entries[x].val = fmakeword(stdin,'&',&cl);
42      plustospace(entries[x].val);
43      unescape_url(entries[x].val);
44      entries[x].name = makeword(entries[x].val,'=');
45    }
46
47 /* A Set-cookie header line is generated for each name-value
48 pair. Each line creates a cookie with default attributes.
49 */
50    for (x=0; x<=m; x++)
51    {
52      printf("Set-cookie: %s=%s%c\n",
53      entries[x].name, entries[x].val,'\0');
54    }
55 /*** IMPORTANT: NO BLANKS BEFORE OR AFTER THE EQUAL SIGN ***/
56 /*** Set-cookie request must precede response header ***/
57    printf("Content-type: text/html%c%c",10,10);
58    printf("<form method = POST action = cookie2.cgi>\n");
59    printf("<body bgcolor=\"#CCFFCC\">");
60    printf("Press <input type =submit value =here> to
61      create the cookie\n");
62    printf("</form>\n<hr></html>");
63 }
```

Figure 9.27 presents the source code for the next CGI script, *cookie2.cgi*, which is requested by the Web form dynamically generated by *cookie.cgi* (see line 58 of Figure 9.26). The CGI script *cookie2.cgi* retrieves the name-value pair string placed in the environment variable *HTTP_COOKIE* (lines 41, 51–57), then simply displays the strings. In an actual application, the state data thus retrieved will be used in the application logic.

Figure 9.27 *cookie2.c.*

```
1 /* cookie2.c - source code for cookie2.cgi
2 Author: M. L. Liu.
3 This CGI script, invoked by the Web page generated by
4 cookie.cgi, receives the state data placed in cookies
5 created by cookie.cgi.
6 */
7
```

(continued on next page)

```
 8  #include <stdio.h>
 9  #ifndef NO_STDLIB_H
10  #include <stdlib.h>
11  #else
12  char *getenv();
13  #endif
14
15  #define MAX_ENTRIES 10000
16
17  typedef struct {
18    char name[128];
19    char val[128];
20  } cookieEntry;
21
22  char *makeword(char *line, char stop);
23  char *fmakeword(FILE *f, char stop, int *len);
24  char x2c(char *what);
25  void unescape_url(char *url);
26  void plustospace(char *str);
27
28  void getword(char *word, char *line, char stop);
29
30  main(int argc, char *argv[]) {
31    cookieEntry cEntries[MAX_ENTRIES];
32  /* storage for the name-value pairs retrieved
33    from HTTP_COOKIE */
34    register int x,m=0;
35    int cl;
36    char* cookieString;
37
38  /* Code for query-string omitted for simplicity */
39
40  /* retrieve state data from cookies */
41    cookieString = getenv("HTTP_COOKIE");
42    if(cookieString == NULL) {
43      printf("No cookie information received.\n");
44      exit(1);
45    }
46    printf("Content-type: text/html%c%c",10,10);
47
48    printf("<body bgcolor=\"#CCFFCC\">");
49    printf("<H1>Cookie received</H1>");
50    printf("The cookie string is: %s\n", cookieString);
51    for(x=0;cookieString[0] != '\0';x++) {
52      m=x;
53      getword(cEntries[x].val,cookieString,';');
54      plustospace(cEntries[x].val);
55      unescape_url(cEntries[x].val);
56      getword(cEntries[x].name,cEntries[x].val,'=');
57    }
58
59    printf("<p>The following name/value pairs are received
60      from cookies:<p>%c",10);
61    printf("<ul>%c",10);
62    for(x=0; x <= m; x++)
```

(continued on next page)

```
63        printf("<li> <code>%s = %s</code>%c",
64            cEntries[x].name, cEntries[x].val,10);
65     printf("</form>\n<hr></html>");
66  }
```

Data Privacy and Security Concerns

Cookies have been employed extensively in commercial Web applications. Cookies are a more sophisticated mechanism for session data maintenance than hidden form fields. However, their use has generated controversy.

First, cookies can be written to files on a user's computer without the knowledge or explicit approval of the user. (It is possible for a user to instruct the browser not to accept cookies; unfortunately, doing so may cause problems when the Web site browsed expects to be able to use cookies.) Although cookie files are small in size, the buildup of a large number of such files does take up system resources.

Second, cookies can be exploited to gather personal information on Web users, without their knowledge or approval. Privacy advocates have voiced concern that cookies can be used to collect the "profile" (interest pattern) of a browser user. The "State Management" section in [research.att.com, 18] provides a detailed explanation of how cookies may be used to build a user profile.

Moreover, persistent cookies, stored in a file that is easily accessible, can also reveal personal information to users who share a computer, thus posing a serious security and privacy threat.

For these reasons, HTTP/1.1 made specific provisions to address these concerns. Unfortunately these provisions have not been widely adopted, so privacy concerns regarding the use of cookies remain.

This concludes our introduction to Internet applications. In Chapter 11 we will study more advanced protocols and facilities, including **servlets** and **Web services**.

Summary

This chapter introduced you to Internet applications and the key protocols that support them. A summary of the topics covered follows.

- The Hypertext Markup Language (HTML) is a markup language used to create documents that can be retrieved using the World Web Web. The language allows a document to be marked up for the presentation or display of the information contained in a document.
- The XML (Extensible Markup Language) allows a document to be marked up for structured information.

■ The HTTP (Hypertext Transfer Protocol) is the transport protocol on the Web.

  ● HTTP is a protocol that allows the transfer of Web contents of virtually unlimited types. HTTP is a connection-oriented, stateless, request-response protocol. An HTTP server, or Web server, runs on TCP port 80 by default. HTTP clients, colloquially called Web browsers, are processes that implement HTTP to interact with a Web server to retrieve documents phrased in HTML, whose contents are displayed according to the documents' markup.

  ● In HTTP/1.0, each connection allows only one round of request-response: A client obtains a connection, issues a request; the server then processes the request, issues a response, and closes the connection thereafter.

  ● HTTP is text-based: The requests and responses are character strings. Each request and response is composed of four parts: the request/response line; a header section; a blank line; the body.

    A request line takes the following form:

    <HTTP method><space><Request-URI><space><protocol specification> \r\n

    The key HTTP methods are *GET* and *POST*.
    A header is composed of one or more lines, each line taking the form

    <keyword>: <value> \r\n

    The request body contains data that needs to be transferred to the server in association with the request.

  ● An HTTP response is composed of the response or status line, a header section, a blank line, and the body.

    The status line takes the form

    <protocol><sp><status-code><sp><description> \r\n

    The response header is composed of one or more lines, each line in the form

    <keyword>: <value> \r\n

    The body of the response follows the header and a blank line and contains the contents of the Web object requested.

■ The Common Gateway Interface (CGI) protocol is a protocol to augment HTTP in supporting run-time–generated Web contents. Using the CGI protocol, a Web client may specify an external program, known as a CGI script, as the target Web object in an HTTP request. When requested, the Web server fetches the CGI script and activates it as a process, passing to the process input data transmitted by the Web client. The Web script executes and transmits its output to the Web server, which returns the Web-script–generated data as the HTTP response to the Web client.

■ A Web form is a special kind of Web page that (1) provides a graphical user interface that prompts the user for input data, and (2) when a Submit button on the page is pressed by the user, invokes the execution of an external program on the Web server host.

The input data is gathered in a URL-encoded query string, which is sent to a Web script specified in the *ACTION* tag of the Web form.

■ To allow session data to be shared among the Web scripts invoked during a Web session, a number of mechanisms have emerged, which can be classified as server-side facilities and client-side facilities. Client-side facilities include the use of hidden-form tags and so-called cookies.

■ The use of hidden-form tags and cookies raises privacy and security concerns.

Exercises

1. In the context of Web-based applications, what role does each of the following languages/protocols play? HTML, MIME, XML, HTTP, CGI.

2. When an HTTP server sends the contents of a document to a client in a response body, it uses the *Content-Length* header line to specify the byte length of the body. For static documents, the byte length is provided by the file system. But for dynamically generated Web pages, such as those generated by a CGI script, the length must be determined at run time, on the fly.

   a. For a dynamically generated Web page, how can the server come up with the content length specified in the *Content-Length* header? Remember that header lines appear before the body in a HTTP response.

   b. Look up how HTTP/1.1 address this problem and summarize what you found. (See section 4.4 of RFC 2068 [ietf.org, 10].)

3. Compile *HTTPClient.java*, the code sample shown in Figure 9.6. Run it to contact a Web server whose name you know to (a) fetch a file you know that exists, and (b) fetch a file you know that does not exist. Capture the output of each run on hard copy. Analyze the lines in the response from the server in each case and identify the different parts (status line, header line(s), and body) in each case.

4. Repeat the previous exercise using *URLBrowser.java*, as shown in Figure 9.7.

For the rest of the exercises, you will need to have access to the following:

■ A Web server host that supports CGI (and you will need to find out from the system administrator of that host on which directory you may file your Web pages and CGI scripts), and

■ A C compiler (such as *gcc*, the GNU C compiler—see *http://www.gnu.org/ software/gcc/gcc.html*) that generates machine code for the Web server host.

5. Experiment with the *Hello CGI* example presented in Figures 9.10 and 9.11.

   a. Obtain the source files for the *Hello CGI* example presented in Figures 9.10 and 9.11.

   b. Install *hello.html* on the Web server, making sure to open its access to world-readable.

   c. Compile *hello.c* (with *util.c* for the query-string processing routines) to generate an executable *Hello.cgi*. (The command is *gcc hello.c util.c -o hello.cgi*.) Install *hello.cgi* on the Web server, making sure to open its access to world-readable and world-executable.

   d. Open a browser and specify the URL for *hello.html*. When the page is displayed, press the button to submit the form and invoke *hello.cgi*.

   e. Summarize the experiment and report the result.

6. Write a client program that invokes *Hello.cgi*.

   a Write it using the stream socket API.

   b. Write it using the *URL* class.

   Hand in the program listings.

7. Experiment with the Web form example presented in Figures 9.14, 9.15, and 9.16.

   a. Obtain the source files for *getForm.html*, *getForm.c*, *postForm.html*, and *postForm.c*.

   b. Install *getForm.html* on the Web server.

   c. Compile *getForm.c* with *util.c* to generate an executable *form.cgi*. Install *form.cgi* on the Web server.

   d. Browse *getForm.html*. Enter some data that includes at least one blank character. Press the Submit button.

   e. What is displayed in the URL field of the browser (usually at the top of the screen)? Copy the display and identify the part that corresponds to the query string. Is the string URL-encoded? How can you tell?

   f. Are the data that you input in step d echoed correctly?

   g. Modify *form.html* to specify the *POST* method in the *FORM* tag (instead of *GET*). Reinstall *form.html* on the Web server.

   h. Compile *postForm.c* with *util.c* to generate an executable *form.cgi*. Install *form.cgi* on the Web server.

   i. Browse, enter data, and submit *form.html*.

   j. What is displayed in the URL field of the browser (usually at the top of the screen)?

   k. Are the data that you input in step i echoed correctly?

   l. Summarize this experiment and your observations. Include comments on the differences in the behaviors of the *GET* and *POST* methods.

   m. Why is it not a good idea to use the *GET* method to send data, such as your social security number or credit card number, with an HTTP request? (*Hint*: Observe the URL field in the browser's display when you run the *getForm* sample.)

8. Write a client program that directly invokes *Form.cgi* with the *GET* method specified, using either the stream socket API or the *URL* class.
   Hand in the program listings. (*Hint*: Use a simple query string in your code, such as "name=Donald%20Duck&quest=gold%20medal." It may also be helpful to review Example 3 of the HTTP request in section 9.3.)

9. Write a client program that directly invokes *Form.cgi* with the *POST* method specified, using either the stream socket API or the *URL* class.

10. Experiment with the hidden-form example presented in Figures 9.21, 9.22, and 9.23.

    a. Obtain the source files for *form.html*, *hidenForm.c*, *hiddenForm2.c*.

    b. Install *form.html* on the Web server.

c. Compile *hiddenForm.c* with *util.c* to generate an executable *hiddenForm.cgi*. Install *hiddenForm.cgi* on the Web server.

d. Compile *hiddenForm2.c* with *util.c* to generate an executable *hiddenForm2.cgi*. Install *hiddenForm2.cgi* on the Web server.

e. Browse *form.html*. Enter a name and press the Submit button. When the dynamically generated Web page is displayed, use the *View source* option of the browser to look at the source code of the Web page (as generated by *hiddenForm.cgi*). Do you see the hidden data embedded in the source code?

f. Does the session data (the name entered in the static form) get passed to the last Web script?

g. Summarize the experiment and your observations.

11. Experiment with the *cookie* example presented in Figures 9.25, 9.26, and 9.27.

   a. Obtain the source files for *form.html*, *cookie.c*, and *cookie2.c*.

   b. Install *form.html* on the Web server.

   c. Compile *cookie.c* with *util.c* to generate an executable *cookie.cgi*. Install *cookie.cgi* on the Web server.

   d. Compile *cookie2.c* with *util.c* to generate an executable *cookie2.cgi*. Install *cookie2.cgi* on the Web server.

   e. Browse *form.html*. Does the session data (the name entered in the static form) get passed to the last Web script?

   f. Summarize the experiment and your observations.

12. This exercise experiments with the *cookie* example presented in Figures 9.25, 9.26, and 9.27 to investigate the use of the *path* and *domain* attributes with cookies.

   On the server, duplicate the *form.html* file in two separate folders, *cookie1* and *cookie2*, respectively, so that the URL to these pages will differ by their paths, such as *www.alpha.org/cookie1/form.html* and *www.alpha.org/cookie2/form.html*.

   a. Open two browser sessions on your computer. Browse to *form.html* in the *cookie1* folder in both sessions, but enter different data (for example, name = "alpha" in one and name = "beta" in the other) in each. What are the respective settings of the *path* and *domain* attributes of the cookie generated in each session? In each session, which cookie(s) will the browser send to *cookie2.cgi* via the server?

   What do you expect the outcome to be? Describe your observations. Explain the outcome.

   b. Open two browser sessions on your computer. Browse to *form.html* in the *cookie1* folder in one session, then to *form.html* in the *cookie2* folder in the other session. Enter different data (for example, name = "alpha" in one and name = "beta" in the other) in each. What are the settings of the *path* and *domain* attributes of the cookie generated in each session? In each session, which cookie(s) will the browser send to *cookie2.cgi* via the server? What do you expect the outcome to be? Describe your observations. Explain the outcome.

c. Modify the source for the CGI script (in *cookie.c*) so that the cookies are generated with a path of "/".

Open two browser sessions on your computer. Browse to *form.html* in the *cookie1* folder in one session, then to *form.html* in the *cookie2* folder in the other session. Enter different data (for example, name = "alpha" in one and name = "beta" in the other) in each. What are the settings of the *path* and *domain* attributes of the cookie generated in each session? In each session, which cookie(s) will the browser send to *cookie2.cgi* via the server? What do you expect the outcome to be? Describe your observations. Explain the outcome.

d. Suppose you install *form.html*, *cookie.c*, and *cookie2.c* on another server, say *www.beta.org*, so that you have two sets of identical files, one on *www.alpha.org* and the other on *www.beta.org*. If you open two separate browser sessions on your computer, browse to *www.alpha.org/ form.html* in the first session and *www.beta.org/cookie2/form.html* in the second session. Enter "alpha" as the name in the first session, and "beta" in the second. What are the settings of the *path* and *domain* attributes of the cookie generated in each session? In each session, which cookie(s) will the browser send to *cookie2.cgi* via the server? What do you expect the outcome to be? Explain.

13. This exercise experiments with the *cookie* example presented in Figures 9.25, 9.26, and 9.27 to investigate the use of the *expires* attributes with cookies.

Modify the source for the CGI script (in *cookie.c*) to add an *expires* attribute to the *Set-Cookie* header line, such as:

```
expires Mon, 09-Dec-2002 13:46:00 GMT
```

so that the cookies will be written to a file (instead of existing temporarily during the lifetime of a browser session). Open two browser sessions on your computer. Browse to *form.html* in the *cookie* folder in both sessions but enter different data in each (for example, name = "alpha" in one and name = "beta" in the other).

What are the respective settings of the *path* and *domain* attributes of the cookie generated in each session? In each session, which cookie(s) will the browser send to *cookie2.cgi* via the server?

What do you expect the outcome to be? Describe your observation. Explain the outcome.

14. The cookie hunt:

Close your browser and restart it to begin a new session. Run the *cookie* suite that creates cookies written to a file (as described in the previous exercise). Enter an unusual string (e.g., "xyxyxyx") in the form field. When run, this should create a cookie containing the quirky string that you entered.

On your system, use a system utility to look for a file that contains your quirky string. (On a UNIX system, you may use the *grep* command. On a Windows system, the *search* or *file-find* utility can be used.) Did you find it? If so, copy the contents of the file and identify the elements in it.

15. Read the "State Management" section in [research.att.com, 18].

    a. Summarize the concerns that privacy advocates express about the use of cookies.

    b. Provide, with explanations, a sample HTTP session during which cookies can be used to build a profile consisting of (i) the user's credit card number, and (ii) a trace of the URLs of the Web sites that the user visits during the session.

    c. What are the specific provisions made in HTTP/1.1 to address these concerns? Summarize them. (You may want to consult [ietf.org, 10] in addition to [research.att.com, 18].)

The rest of the exercises are for students who are proficient with the C language or other languages that can be used to implement CGI scripts. Students who are not familiar with these languages may skip these exercises. You will have an opportunity to practice these exercises using the Java language in Chapter 11.

16. Modify the *cookie* sample files to implement a suite of Web pages and CGI scripts for the simple shopping cart illustrated in Figure 9.17. The state data that need to be maintained are (a) a customer ID, and (b) a merchandise name.

17. Either (a) write a CGI script or (b) find a freeware CGI script (try the Login program at http://tectonicdesigns.com/freecgi) that allows you to provide password protection to your home page. When the URL for your home page is entered to a browser, the display should look as shown below. If the password is correct when the form is submitted, your home page will be displayed. Install the script and test it. Describe your work and explain how it provides password protection.

    Note: The CGI script will need to output a line as follows:

    ```
    <html><head><META HTTP-EQUIV="REFRESH" CONTENT="0;URL=<url for your
    home page>"></head></html>\n
    ```

    to transfer to your home page after the password has been verified.

References

1. Hobbes' Internet Timeline, *http://www.zakon.org/robert/internet/timeline/*

2. A Little History of the World Wide Web, *http://www.w3.org/History.html*

3. ISO 8879:1986, Information processing—Text and office systems—Standard Generalized Markup Language (SGML), International Organization for Standardization, *http://www.iso.org/*

4. People of the W3C, *http://www.w3.org/People/*

5. RFC 2109 HTTP State Management Mechanism, *http://www.ics.uci.edu/pub/ietf/http/rfc2109.txt*

6. Welcome to CERN, *http://public.Web.cern.ch/Public/*

7. HTTP: A protocol for networked information, *http://www.w3.org/Protocols/HTTP/HTTP2.html*

8. RFC 1945, Hypertext Transfer Protocol—HTTP/1.0, *http://www.faqs.org/rfcs/rfc1945.html*

9. RFC 1521, MIME (Multipurpose Internet Mail Extensions) Part One, *http://www.faqs.org/rfcs/rfc1521.html*

10. RFC 2068, Hypertext Transfer Protocol—HTTP/1.1, *http://www.ietf.org/rfc/rfc2068.txt*

11. The World Wide Web Consortium, *http://www.w3.org/*

12. RFC 959, File Transfer Protocol (FTP), *http://www.ietf.org/rfc/rfc0959.txt?number=959*

13. RFC 1866, Hypertext Markup Language 2.0, *http://ftp.ics.uci.edu/pub/ietf/html/rfc1866.txt*

14. NCSA—A Beginner's Guide to HTML, *http://archive.ncsa.uiuc.edu/General/Internet/WWW/HTMLPrimerAll.html*

15. Extensible Markup Language (XML), *http://www.w3.org/XML/*

16. A Quick Introduction to XML, *http://java.sun.com/xml/jaxp-1.1/docs/tutorial/overview/1_xml.html*

17. The Original HTTP as defined in 1991, Tim Berners-Lee, *http://www.w3.org/Protocols/HTTP/AsImplemented.html*

18. Balachander Krishnamurthy, Jeffrey C. Mogul, and David M. Kristol. Key Differences between HTTP/1.0 and HTTP/1.1, *http://www.research.att.com/~bala/papers/h0vh1.html*

19. The Common Gateway Interface, *http://hoohoo.ncsa.uiuc.edu/cgi/overview.html*

20. The Common Gateway Interface Specification, *http://hoohoo.ncsa.uiuc.edu/cgi/interface.html*

21. CGI Tutorial, *http://www.comp.leeds.ac.uk/nik/Cgi/start.html*

22. RFC 1738, The Uniform Resource Locators, *http://www.w3.org/Addressing/rfc1738.txt*

23. URL Encoding, *http://www.blooberry.com/indexdot/html/topics/urlencoding.htm*

24. Hypertext Markup Language 2.0—Forms, *http://www.w3.org/MarkUp/html-spec/html-spec_8.html*

25. Client Side State—HTTP Cookies, Netscape Inc., *http://home.netscape.com/newsref/std/cookie_spec.html*

26. *What is Jabber?*, Jabber Software Foundation, *http://www.jabber.org/about/overview.htm*

## CHAPTER 10

The Common Object Request Broker Architecture

In Chapter 7 you were introduced to the distributed objects paradigm. Among the topics covered there was the architecture for an archetypal distributed objects system, illustrated by the Java RMI.

In this chapter, we present an alternate architecture—a standard architecture—for a distributed objects system. The architecture is known as the **Common Object Request Broker Architecture (CORBA)**. The reasons for our interest in CORBA are twofold: First, it provides a case study to illustrate two similar but contrasting architectures for a given concept, distributed objects. Second, CORBA provides an example of an architecture designed to maximize interoperability.

CORBA is a distributed object architecture designed to allow distributed objects to interoperate in a heterogeneous environment, where objects can be implemented in different programming languages and/or deployed on different platforms. CORBA differs from the architecture of Java RMI in one significant aspect: RMI is a proprietary facility developed by Sun Microsystems, Inc. and supports objects written in the Java programming language only. In contrast, CORBA was developed by the **Object Management Group (OMG)** [corba.org, 1], an industrial consortium, and was designed to maximize interoperability. It is important to understand that CORBA is *not* in itself a distributed objects facility; instead, it is a set of protocols. A distributed object facility that adheres to these protocols is said to be **CORBA compliant**, and the distributed objects that the facility supports can interoperate with objects supported by other CORBA-compliant facilities.

CORBA features a very rich set of protocols [Siegel, 4], the coverage of many of which is beyond the scope of this book. We will instead focus on the key concepts of CORBA as they relate to the distributed objects paradigm. We will also study a facility based on CORBA: the **Java Interface Definition Language (IDL)**.

10.1 The Basic Architecture

Figure 10.1 illustrates the basic architecture of CORBA [omg.org/gettingstarted, 2]. As a distributed objects architecture, it bears considerable resemblance to the RMI architecture. Logically, an **object client** makes method calls to a distributed object. An object client interfaces with a proxy—a **stub**—while the object implementation interfaces with the server-side proxy—a **skeleton**. Unlike with Java RMI, an additional layer of software, known as the **Object Request Broker (ORB)**, is required. On the client side, the ORB layer software serves as an intermediary between the stub and the client system's network and operating system software. On the server side, the ORB layer software serves as an intermediary between the skeleton and the server system's network and operating system software. Using a common protocol, the ORB layers on the two sides are able to resolve the differences in the programming languages of the objects, as well as the differences in the platforms (networks and operating systems) on the two hosts, to assist in data communication between the two sides. A **naming service** is used by the client to locate an object.

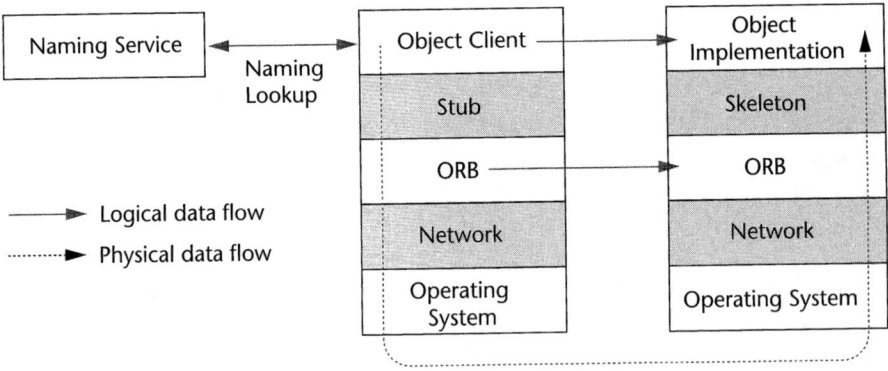

Figure 10.1 Basic CORBA architecture.

10.2 The CORBA Object Interface

A distributed object is defined using a software file similar to the remote interface file in Java RMI. Since CORBA is language independent, the interface is defined using a universal language with a distinct syntax, known as the **CORBA Interface Definition Language (IDL)**. You will find the syntax of CORBA IDL similar to that of Java and C++, but keep in mind that an object defined in a CORBA IDL file can be implemented in a large number of diverse programming languages, including C, C++, Java, COBOL, Smalltalk, Ada, Lisp, Python, and IDLScript [omg.org/gettingstarted, 2]. For each of these languages, OMG has a standardized mapping from CORBA IDL to the programming language, so that a compiler can be used to process a CORBA interface to generate the proxy files needed to interface with an object implementation or with an object client written in any of the CORBA-compatible languages.

Figure 10.2 illustrates an application where the object client is a program written in Java while the object implementation is written in C++. Notice that the stub is generated by mapping the CORBA object interface to a stub in Java, while the skeleton is generated by mapping the CORBA object interface to a C++ skeleton. Although implemented in different languages, the two ORBs can interoperate thanks to the common protocol observed by the two ORBs.

A large number of proprietary as well as experimental ORBs are available [corba.org, 1; puder.org, 19].

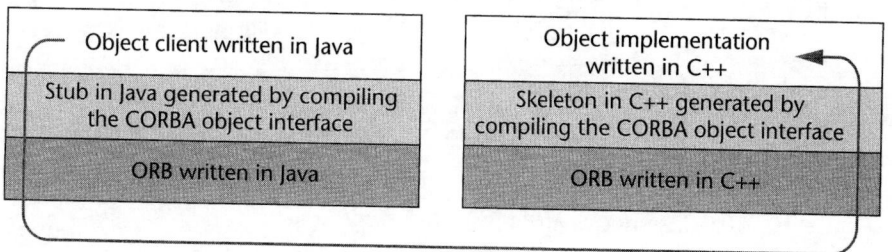

Figure 10.2 Language independence in CORBA.

10.3 Inter-ORB Protocols

To allow ORBs to be interoperable, the OMG specified a protocol known as the **General Inter-ORB Protocol (GIOP)**, a specification that provides a general framework for interoperable protocols to be built on top of specific transport layers. A special case of the protocol is the **Internet Inter-ORB Protocol (IIOP)**, which is the GIOP applied to the TCP/IP transport layer.

The IIOP specification includes the following elements:

1. **Transport management requirements.** These requirements specify what is needed for connection and disconnection, and the roles that the object client and object server play in making and unmaking connections.

2. **Definition of common data representation.** A coding scheme needs to be defined for marshaling and unmarshaling data of each IDL data type.

3. **Message formats.** Different types of message formats need to be defined. Messages allow clients to send requests to object servers and receive replies. A client uses a request message to invoke a method declared in a CORBA interface for an object and receives a reply message from the server.

In computer architecture, a bus is the equivalent of a highway on which data travels to and from each component within a computer. In networking, a bus is a central cable that interconnects devices.

An ORB that adheres to the specifications of the IIOP may interoperate with any other IIOP-compliant ORBs over the Internet. This gives rise to the term **object bus**: The Internet is seen as a bus that interconnects CORBA objects, as illustrated in Figure 10.3.

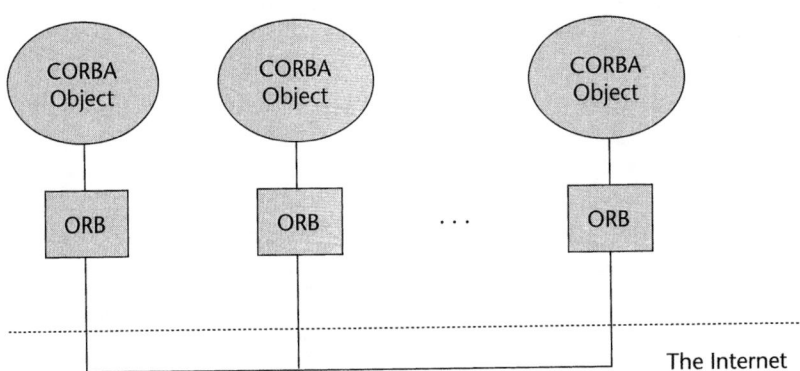

Figure 10.3 The Internet as an object bus.

10.4 **Object Servers and Object Clients**

As in Java RMI, a CORBA distributed object is exported by an **object server**, similar to the object server in RMI. An **object client** retrieves a reference to a distributed object from a naming or directory service (to be described) and invokes the methods of the distributed object.

10.5 **CORBA Object References**

Also as in Java RMI, a CORBA distributed object is located using an **object reference**. Since CORBA is language independent, a CORBA object reference is an abstract entity mapped to a language-specific object reference by an ORB, in a representation chosen by the developer of the ORB.

For interoperability, OMG specifies a protocol for the abstract CORBA object reference object, known as the **Interoperable Object Reference (IOR)** protocol. An ORB that is compatible with the IOR protocol will allow an object reference to be registered with and retrieved from any IOR-compliant directory service. CORBA object references represented in this protocol are called **Interoperable Object References (IORs)**.

An IOR is a string that contains encoding for information including the following [omg.org/technology, 5]:

- The type of object.
- The host where the object can be found.
- The port number of the server for that object.
- An object key, a string of bytes identifying the object. The object key is used by an object server to locate the object.

An IOR is a string that looks like this:

```
IOR:000000000000000d49444c3a677269643a312e3000000
0000000000100000000000000004c00010000000000015756c74
72612e6475626c696e2e696f6e612e6965500000963000000002
83a5c756c7472612e6475626c696e2e696f6e612e69653a67
7269643a303a3a49523a67726964003a
```

The representation consists of the character prefix "IOR:" followed by a series of hexadecimal numeric characters, each character representing 4 bits of binary data in the IOR. The details of the representation are not important to our discussion; interested readers may refer to the references for such details.

10.6 CORBA Naming Service and the Interoperable Naming Service

In Chapter 7, when we studied Java RMI, we introduced the RMI registry as a directory service for distributed RMI objects. CORBA specifies a directory service for the same purpose. The **Naming Service** [omg.org/technology, 5; java.sun.com/j2se, 16] serves as a directory for CORBA objects, playing a role that is analogous to the RMI registry, except that the CORBA Naming Service is platform independent and programming language independent.

The CORBA Naming Service

The Naming Service permits ORB-based clients to obtain references to objects they wish to use. It allows names to be associated with object references. Clients may query a Naming Service using a predetermined name to obtain the associated object reference.

To export a distributed object, a CORBA object server contacts a Naming Service to **bind** a symbolic name to the object. The Naming Service maintains a database of names and the objects associated with the names.

To obtain a reference to the object, an object client requests that the Naming Service look up the object associated with the name (this process is known as **resolving** the object name). The API for the Naming Service is specified in interfaces defined in IDL, and includes methods that allow servers to bind names to objects and clients to resolve those names. To be as general as possible, the CORBA object naming scheme is necessarily complex. Since the namespace is universal, a standard naming hierarchy is defined in a manner similar to the naming hierarchy in a file directory, as shown in Figure 10.4. In the naming scheme, **naming context** corresponds to a folder or directory in a file hierarchy, while object names correspond to a file. The full name of an object, including all the associated naming contexts, is known as a **compound name**. The first component of a compound name gives the name of a naming context, in which the second component is accessed. This process continues until the last component of the compound name has been reached.

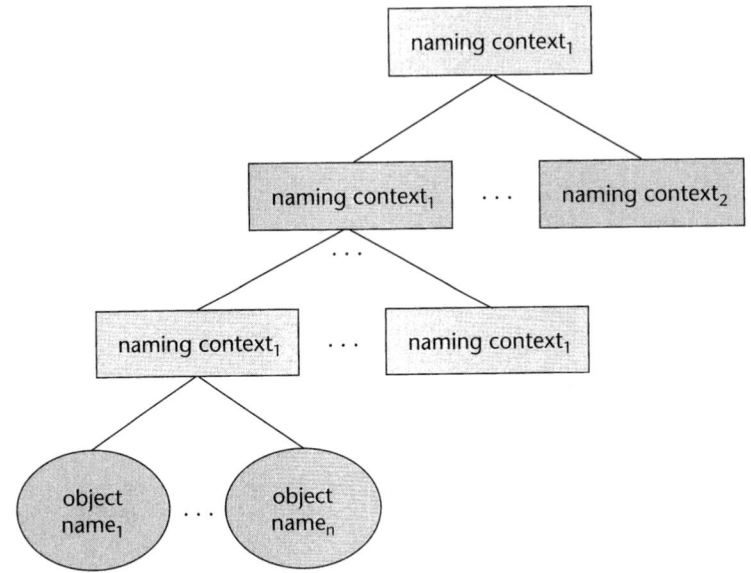

Figure 10.4 The CORBA naming hierarchy.

The syntax for an object name is as follows:

<naming context>.<naming context>. ... <naming context>.<object name>

where the sequence of naming contexts leads to the object name.

Figure 10.5 shows an example of a naming hierarchy. As shown, an object representing the men's clothing department is named *store.clothing.men*, where *store* and *clothing* are naming contexts, and *men* is an object name.

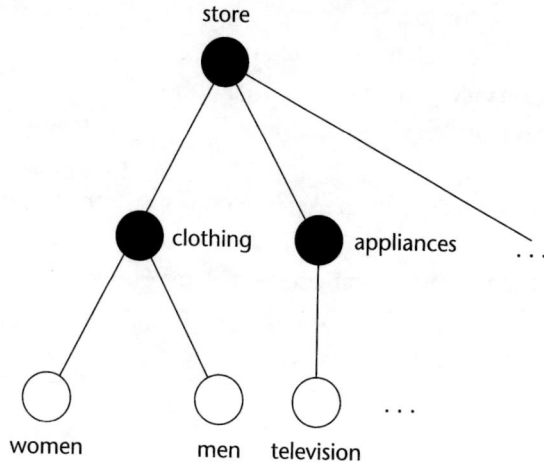

Figure 10.5 An example of a CORBA naming hierarchy.

Naming contexts and name bindings are created using methods provided in the Naming Service interface.

The Interoperable Naming Service

The **Interoperable Naming Service (INS)** [omg.org/technology, 5; java.sun.com/j2se, 16] is a URL-based naming system based on the CORBA Naming Service. It allows applications to share a common initial naming context and provide a URL to access a CORBA object. Using this system, a URL such as *corbaname::acme.com:2050#store/clothing/women* can be used to access the object named *store/clothing/women* from the naming service running at port 2050 of the host with the domain name *acme.com*.

10.7 CORBA Object Services

Within the specifications for CORBA are those for distributed objects that provide services commonly needed in distributed applications. Following are some of the services [corba.org, 1]:

- **Concurrency Service**—a service that provides concurrency control
- **Event Service**—for event synchronization
- **Logging Service**—for event logging
- **Naming Service**—an object directory service, as described in the previous section
- **Scheduling Service**—for event scheduling
- **Security Service**—for security management

- **Trading Service**—for locating a service by type (instead of by name)
- **Time Service**—a service for time-related events
- **Notification Service**—for event notification
- **Object Transaction Service**—for transactional processing

Each service is defined in a standard IDL that can be implemented by a developer of the service object, and the service object's methods can be invoked by a CORBA client.

As an example, the CORBA specification of Time Service describes the following functionalities:

- Enabling the user to obtain current time together with an error estimate associated with it
- Ascertaining the order in which "events" occurred
- Generating time-based events based on timers and alarms
- Computing the interval between two events.

The Time Service consists of two services, each defined in a service interface:

1. The **Time Service** manages Universal Time objects and Time Interval objects and is represented by the **TimeService** interface. The service provides a facility for keeping a record of time for CORBA applications.

2. The **Timer Event Service** manages Timer Event Handler objects and is represented by the **TimerEventService** interface, which provides methods for setting and canceling a timer set in absolute, relative, or periodic time.

Based on these specifications, numerous CORBA Time Service objects have been developed by vendors, researchers, and individuals.

10.8 Object Adapters

In the basic architecture of CORBA, the implementation of a distributed object interfaces with the skeleton to interact with the stub on the object client side. As the architecture evolved, a software component in addition to the skeleton was added to the server side: an **object adapter** (see Figure 10.6). An object adapter simplifies the responsibilities of an ORB by assisting an ORB in delivering a client request to an object implementation. When an ORB receives a client's request, it locates the object adapter associated with the object and forwards the request to the adapter. The adapter interacts with the object implementation's skeleton, which performs data marshaling and invokes the appropriate method in the object.

There are different types of CORBA object adapters. The **Portable Object Adapter (POA)** [citeseer.nj.nec.com, 8] is a particular type of object adapter that is defined by the CORBA specification. An object adapter that is a POA enables an object implementation to function with different ORBs, so that the object implementation becomes portable across different platforms.

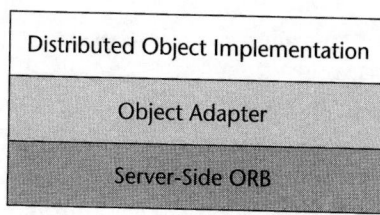

Figure 10.6 An object adapter.

10.9 Java IDL

Given the CORBA specifications, a software developer may implement any component specified in the CORBA framework. Indeed, a large number of CORBA facilities are available [corba.org, 1], many of which can be obtained at no cost. Some of these facilities are developed by commercial vendors, some by researchers, and still others by individuals.

As an example of such a facility, we will introduce **Java IDL**. Java IDL is part of the Java 2 Platform, Standard Edition (J2SE). The Java IDL facility includes a **CORBA Object Request Broker** (ORB), an **IDL-to-Java compiler**, and a subset of **CORBA standard services**. It should be noted that in addition to the Java IDL, Java provides a number of CORBA-compliant facilities [java.sun.com/j2ee, 7], including **RMI** over **IIOP** [java.sun.com/j2se/1.3, 9], which makes it possible for a CORBA application to be written using the RMI syntax and semantics. With your knowledge of RMI and CORBA, you should be able to learn the RMI over IIOP facility on your own. In the rest of this chapter, we will explore the Java IDL as a sample CORBA toolkit.

Key Java IDL Packages

Java IDL provides a number of packages containing interfaces and classes for CORBA support [java.sun.com/j2se/1.4, 17]:

- Package *org.omg.CORBA* contains interfaces and classes that provide the mapping of the OMG CORBA APIs to the Java programming language
- Package *org.omg.CosNaming* contains interfaces and classes that provide the Naming Service for Java IDL
- *org.omg.CORBA.ORB* contains interfaces and classes that provide APIs for the Object Request Broker.

Java IDL Tools

Java IDL provides a set of tools needed for developing a CORBA application [java.sun.com/products, 18]:

- *idlj*—the IDL-to-Java compiler (*Note*: Use of a former rendition of this compiler, *idl2java*, is discouraged.)
- *orbd*—a server process that provides a Naming Service and other services
- *servertool*—provides a command-line interface for application programmers to register/unregister an object, and start up/shut down a server
- *tnameserv*—an older transient Java IDL Naming Service whose use is now discouraged.

An Example CORBA Application

The following example application illustrates the use of the IDL facilities provided with Java 2 Standard Edition (J2SE) version 1.4 [java.sun.com/j2se/1.4, 20]. If you are using an earlier version of Java, such as J2SE 1.3, the syntax and mechanics described here will be different. The example illustrates a CORBA object that provides a method that returns the "Hello world" string. The example, while simplistic, serves to illustrate the basics.

In the example, the distributed object name is *Hello*. When developing your application, you may substitute an alternate object name wherever the word *Hello* appears in the description.

The CORBA Interface File

The starting point of a CORBA application is developing a CORBA interface file written in OMG's IDL, or simply called an IDL file. Recall that the IDL is a universal language, so the syntax of such an interface file is the same regardless of which CORBA facility you use. Figure 10.7 shows a sample IDL file that specifies an interface called *Hello*. The interface specifies two methods: Method *sayHello* requires no argument and returns a character string (note that *string* is spelled with a lower-case *s*; the *string* data type is a CORBA IDL data type); the *shutdown()* method deactivates the ORB and is recommended to be included in all CORBA service interfaces. The words *module, interface, string,* and *oneway* are reserved words in IDL. A *module*, as the word implies, specifies a software module. One or more interfaces may be declared within each module, and one or more method declarations may appear within each interface. The *oneway* modifier specifies that the *shutdown* method requires only communication from the client to the server (and no communication from the server to the client).

The IDL file should be placed in a directory dedicated to the application. The file is compiled using the compiler *idlj* using a command as follows:

```
idlj -fall Hello.idl
```

Figure 10.7 *Hello.idl.*

```
1  module HelloApp
2  {
3    interface Hello
4    {
5      string sayHello();
6      oneway void shutdown();
7    };
8  };
```

The *-fall* command option is necessary for the compiler to generate all the files needed for the rest of the example, which, in this case, are provided in a subdirectory named *HelloApp*. In general, these files can be found in a subdirectory named <some name>*App* when an interface file named <some name>.*idl* is compiled. In our example, if the compilation is successful, the following files can be found in a *HelloApp* subdirectory:

1. *HelloOperations.java*
2. *Hello.java*
3. *HelloHelper.java*
4. *HelloHolder.java*
5. *_HelloStub.java*
6. *HelloPOA.java*

These files are generated by the *idlj* compiler automatically as a result of a successful compilation; the files require no modifications by you. We will briefly explain each of these files in the following paragraphs. For this book, you need not be concerned about the specific coding in each file.

HelloOperations.java, the Operations Interface

The file *HelloOperations.java* (Figure 10.8), known as a **Java operations interface** in general, is a Java interface file mapped from the CORBA IDL interface file (*Hello.idl*).

The file contains the methods specified in the original IDL file: In this case the methods are *sayHello( )* and *shutdown()*.

Figure 10.8 *HelloApp/HelloOperations.java.*

```
1  package HelloApp;
2
3
4  /**
5  * HelloApp/HelloOperations.java
6  * Generated by the IDL-to-Java compiler
7  * version "3.1" from Hello.idl
8  */
9
10 public interface HelloOperations
11 {
12   String sayHello ();
13   void shutdown ();
14 } // interface HelloOperations
```

Hello.java, the Signature Interface File

The file *Hello.java* (Figure 10.9) is known as the **signature interface file**. It extends the standard CORBA classes *org.omg.portable.IDLEntity, org.omg.CORBA. Object,* and an application-specific interface, *HelloOperations,* as described in the previous section.

Figure 10.9 *HelloApp/Hello.java.*

```
1  package HelloApp;
2
3  /**
4  * HelloApp/Hello.java
5  * Generated by the IDL-to-Java compiler (portable),
6  * version "3.1" from Hello.idl
7  */
8
9  public interface Hello extends HelloOperations,
10     org.omg.CORBA.Object,
11     org.omg.CORBA.portable.IDLEntity
12 {
13 } // interface Hello
```

The signature interface file combines the characteristics of the Java *operations* interface (*HelloOperations.java*) with the characteristics of the CORBA classes that it extends.

HelloHelper.java, the Helper Class

The Java class *HelloHelper* (Figure 10.10) provides auxiliary functionalities needed to support a CORBA object in the context of the Java language. In particular, a method, *narrow* (see line 49) allows a CORBA object reference to be cast to its corresponding type in Java, so that a CORBA object may be operated on using syntax for Java object. A full discussion of the syntax and semantics in the file is beyond the scope of this book.

Figure 10.10 *HelloApp/HelloHelper.java.*

```
1  package HelloApp;
2
3
4  /**
5  * HelloApp/HelloHelper.java
6  * Generated by the IDL-to-Java compiler (portable),
7  * version "3.1" from Hello.idl
8  */
9
10  abstract public class HelloHelper
11  {
12    private static String _id = "IDL:HelloApp/Hello:1.0";
13
14    public static void insert
15        (org.omg.CORBA.Any a, HelloApp.Hello that)
16    {
17      org.omg.CORBA.portable.OutputStream out =
18        a.create_output_stream ();
19      a.type (type ());
20      write (out, that);
21      a.read_value (out.create_input_stream (), type ());
22    }// end insert
23
24    public static HelloApp.Hello extract (org.omg.CORBA.Any a)
25    {
26      return read (a.create_input_stream ());
27    } //end extract
28
29    private static org.omg.CORBA.TypeCode __typeCode = null;
30    synchronized public static org.omg.CORBA.TypeCode type ()
31    {
32      if (__typeCode == null)
33      {
34        __typeCode = org.omg.CORBA.ORB.init().
35          create_interface_tc
36          (HelloApp.HelloHelper.id (), "Hello");
37      }
38      return __typeCode;
39    } //end type
40
```

(continued on next page)

```
41   public static String id ()
42   {
43     return _id;
44   } // end id
45
46   public static HelloApp.Hello read
47       (org.omg.CORBA.portable.InputStream istream)
48   {
49     return narrow (istream.read_Object (_HelloStub.class));
50   } //end read
51
52   public static void write
53       (org.omg.CORBA.portable.OutputStream ostream,
54       HelloApp.Hello value)
55   {
56     ostream.write_Object ((org.omg.CORBA.Object) value);
57   } //end write
58
59   public static HelloApp.Hello narrow
60       (org.omg.CORBA.Object obj)
61   {
62     if (obj == null)
63       return null;
64     else if (obj instanceof HelloApp.Hello)
65       return (HelloApp.Hello)obj;
66     else if (!obj._is_a (id ()))
67       throw new org.omg.CORBA.BAD_PARAM ();
68     else
69     {
70       org.omg.CORBA.portable.Delegate delegate =
71         ((org.omg.CORBA.portable.ObjectImpl)obj).
72         _get_delegate ();
73       HelloApp._HelloStub stub = new HelloApp._HelloStub ();
74       stub._set_delegate(delegate);
75       return stub;
76     } // end else
77   }// end narrow
78
79 }// end class
```

HelloHolder.java, the Holder Class

In IDL, a parameter may be declared to be *out* if it is an output argument and *inout* if the parameter contains an input value as well as carries an output value.

The Java class called *HelloHolder* (Figure 10.11) contains a reference to an object that implements the *Hello* interface. The class maps an *out* or an *inout* parameter in IDL to Java syntax.

Figure 10.11 *HelloApp/HelloHolder.*

```
1  package HelloApp;
2
3  /**
4   * HelloApp/HelloHolder.java
5   * Generated by the IDL-to-Java compiler (portable), version "3.1"
6   * from hello.idl
7   * Sunday, December 29, 2002 3:41:50 PM PST
8   */
9
10 public final class HelloHolder implements org.omg.CORBA.portable.
       Streamable
11 {
12   public HelloApp.Hello value = null;
13
14   public HelloHolder ()
15   {
16   }
17
18   public HelloHolder (HelloApp.Hello initialValue)
19   {
20     value = initialValue;
21   }
22
23   public void _read (org.omg.CORBA.portable.InputStream i)
24   {
25     value = HelloApp.HelloHelper.read (i);
26   }
27
28   public void _write (org.omg.CORBA.portable.OutputStream o)
29   {
30     HelloApp.HelloHelper.write (o, value);
31   }
32
33   public org.omg.CORBA.TypeCode _type ()
34   {
35     return HelloApp.HelloHelper.type ();
36   }
37
38 }
```

_HelloStub.java, the Stub File

The Java class *HelloStub* (Figure 10.12) is the stub file, the client-side proxy, which interfaces with the client object. It extends *org.omg.CORBA.portable. ObjectImpl* and implements the *Hello.java* interface.

Figure 10.12 *HelloApp/_HelloStub.java.*

```
1  package HelloApp;
2
3
4  /**
5   * HelloApp/_HelloStub.java
6   * Generated by the IDL-to-Java compiler (portable),
7   * version "3.1" from Hello.idl
8   */
9
10 public class _HelloStub extends
11     org.omg.CORBA.portable.ObjectImpl
12     implements HelloApp.Hello
13 {
14
15   public String sayHello ()
16   {
17     org.omg.CORBA.portable.InputStream $in = null;
18     try {
19       org.omg.CORBA.portable.OutputStream $out =
20         _request ("sayHello", true);
21       $in = _invoke ($out);
22       String $result = $in.read_string ();
23       return $result;
24     } catch (org.omg.CORBA.portable.ApplicationException $ex)
25       $in = $ex.getInputStream ();
26       String _id = $ex.getId ();
27       throw new org.omg.CORBA.MARSHAL (_id);
28     } catch (org.omg.CORBA.portable.RemarshalException $rm) {
29       return sayHello ();
30     } finally {
31       _releaseReply ($in);
32     }
33   } // sayHello
34
35   public void shutdown ()
36   {
37     org.omg.CORBA.portable.InputStream $in = null;
38     try {
39       org.omg.CORBA.portable.OutputStream $out =
40         _request ("shutdown", false);
41       $in = _invoke ($out);
42     } catch (org.omg.CORBA.portable.ApplicationException $ex)
43       $in = $ex.getInputStream ();
44       String _id = $ex.getId ();
45       throw new org.omg.CORBA.MARSHAL (_id);
46     } catch (org.omg.CORBA.portable.RemarshalException $rm) {
47       shutdown ();
```

(continued on next page)

```
48        } finally {
49            _releaseReply ($in);
50        }
51   } // shutdown
52.
53   // Type-specific CORBA::Object operations
54   private static String[] __ids = {
55      "IDL:HelloApp/Hello:1.0"};
56
57   public String[] _ids ()
58   {
59      return (String[])__ids.clone ();
60   }
61
62   private void readObject (java.io.ObjectInputStream s)
63          throws java.io.IOException
64   {
65      String str = s.readUTF ();
66      String[] args = null;
67      java.util.Properties props = null;
68      org.omg.CORBA.Object obj =
69         org.omg.CORBA.ORB.init (args, props).
70         string_to_object (str);
71      org.omg.CORBA.portable.Delegate delegate =
72         ((org.omg.CORBA.portable.ObjectImpl) obj).
73         _get_delegate ();
74      _set_delegate (delegate);
75   }
76
77   private void writeObject (java.io.ObjectOutputStream s)
78          throws java.io.IOException
79   {
80      String[] args = null;
81      java.util.Properties props = null;
82      String str = org.omg.CORBA.ORB.init
83         (args, props).object_to_string (this);
84      s.writeUTF (str);
85   }
86 } // class _HelloStub
```

HelloPOA.java, the Server Skeleton and Portable Object Adapter

The Java class *HelloPOA* (Figure 10.13) is a combination of the skeleton (the server-side proxy) and the portable object adapter. It extends *org.omg. PortableServer.Servant*, and implements the *InvokeHandler* interface and the *HelloOperations* interface.

Figure 10.13 *HelloApp/HelloPOA.java.*

```
1  package HelloApp;
2
3
4  /**
5  * HelloApp/HelloPOA.java
6  * Generated by the IDL-to-Java compiler (portable),
7  * version "3.1" from Hello.idl
8  */
9
10 public abstract class HelloPOA extends
11   org.omg.PortableServer.Servant
12   implements HelloApp.HelloOperations,
13   org.omg.CORBA.portable.InvokeHandler
14 {
15
16   // Constructors
17
18   private static java.util.Hashtable _methods =
19     new java.util.Hashtable ();
20   static
21   {
22     _methods.put ("sayHello", new java.lang.Integer (0));
23     _methods.put ("shutdown", new java.lang.Integer (1));
24   }
25
26   public org.omg.CORBA.portable.OutputStream _invoke
27       (String $method, org.omg.CORBA.portable.InputStream in,
28       org.omg.CORBA.portable.ResponseHandler $rh)
29   {
30     org.omg.CORBA.portable.OutputStream out = null;
31     java.lang.Integer __method =
32       (java.lang.Integer)_methods.get ($method);
33     if (__method == null)
34       throw new org.omg.CORBA.BAD_OPERATION
35       (0, org.omg.CORBA.CompletionStatus.COMPLETED_MAYBE);
36
37     switch (__method.intValue ())
38     {
39       case 0: // HelloApp/Hello/sayHello
40       {
41         String $result = null;
42         $result = this.sayHello ();
43         out = $rh.createReply();
44         out.write_string ($result);
45         break;
46       }
47
48       case 1: // HelloApp/Hello/shutdown
49       {
50         this.shutdown ();
51         out = $rh.createReply();
```

(continued on next page)

```
52              break;
53          }
54
55          default:
56             throw new org.omg.CORBA.BAD_OPERATION
57               (0,org.omg.CORBA.CompletionStatus.COMPLETED_MAYBE);
58      }
59
60      return out;
61   } // _invoke
62
63   // Type-specific CORBA::Object operations
64   private static String[] __ids = {
65     "IDL:HelloApp/Hello:1.0"};
66
67   public String[] _all_interfaces
68        (org.omg.PortableServer.POA poa, byte[] objectId)
69   {
70     return (String[])__ids.clone ();
71   }
72
73   public Hello _this()
74   {
75     return HelloHelper.narrow(
76       super._this_object());
77   }
78
79   public Hello _this(org.omg.CORBA.ORB orb)
80   {
81     return HelloHelper.narrow(
82       super._this_object(orb));
83   }
84
85 } // class HelloPOA
```

The Application

Other than the IDL file (*Hello.idl*), the files you have seen so far are those generated automatically when the IDL file is compiled with the compiler *idlj* and require no modification by you. Next we will look at source files for the application that must be created by you, as the application developer.

Server-Side Classes

On the server side, two classes need to be provided: the servant and the server. The servant, *HelloImpl*, is the implementation of the *Hello* IDL interface; each *Hello* object is an instantiation of this class.

The Servant As presented in Figure 10.14, the servant is a subclass of
HelloPOA. The servant contains the definition for each method declared in the
IDL interface: in this example, the *sayHello* and *shutdown* methods. Note that
the syntax for writing these methods is the same as that for ordinary Java
methods: logic for interacting with the ORB, and for data marshaling is provided by the skeleton, whose code is included in *HelloPOA.java* (Figure 10.13).

Figure 10.14 *HelloApp/HelloImpl.java.*

```
 1  // The servant — object implementation — for the Hello
 2  // example Note that this is a subclass of HelloPOA, whose
 3  // source file is generated from the compilation of
 4  // Hello.idl using j2idl.
 5
 6  import HelloApp.*;
 7  import org.omg.CosNaming.*;
 8  import org.omg.CosNaming.NamingContextPackage.*;
 9  import org.omg.CORBA.*;
10  import org.omg.PortableServer.*;
11  import org.omg.PortableServer.POA;
12
13  import java.util.Properties;
14
15  class HelloImpl extends HelloPOA {
16     private ORB orb;
17
18     public void setORB(ORB orb_val) {
19        orb = orb_val;
20     }
21
22     // implement sayHello() method
23     public String sayHello() {
24        return "\nHello world !!\n";
25     }
26
27     // implement shutdown() method
28     public void shutdown() {
29        orb.shutdown(false);
30     }
31  } //end class
```

The Server Figure 10.15 presents the code for a sample object server. The server
process is responsible for creating and initializing the ORB (in this case, the Java
IDL ORB), activating the Portable Object Adapter Manager, creating an instance
of the object's implementation (a servant), and registering the object with the
ORB. Note that in Java's implementation, the Naming Service is provided by the
ORB. In the sample code, the Interoperable Naming Service is employed for registering the object, with the name *"Hello"* (lines 25–37). After announcing that
the object server is ready, the server waits to receive client requests forwarded by
the ORB (lines 39–43).

Figure 10.15 *HelloApp/HelloServer.java.*

```
1  // A server for the Hello object
2
3  public class HelloServer {
4
5    public static void main(String args[]) {
6      try{
7        // create and initialize the ORB
8        ORB orb = ORB.init(args, null);
9
10       // get reference to rootpoa & activate the POAManager
11       POA rootpoa =
12         (POA)orb.resolve_initial_references("RootPOA");
13       rootpoa.the_POAManager().activate();
14
15       // create servant and register it with the ORB
16       HelloImpl helloImpl = new HelloImpl();
17       helloImpl.setORB(orb);
18
19       // get object reference from the servant
20       org.omg.CORBA.Object ref =
21         rootpoa.servant_to_reference(helloImpl);
22       // and cast the reference to a CORBA reference
23       Hello href = HelloHelper.narrow(ref);
24
25       // get the root naming context
26       // NameService invokes the transient name service
27       org.omg.CORBA.Object objRef =
28         orb.resolve_initial_references("NameService");
29       // Use NamingContextExt, which is part of the
30       // Interoperable Naming Service (INS) specification.
31       NamingContextExt ncRef =
32         NamingContextExtHelper.narrow(objRef);
33
34       // bind the Object Reference in Naming
35       String name = "Hello";
36       NameComponent path[] = ncRef.to_name( name );
37       ncRef.rebind(path, href);
38
39       System.out.println
40         ("HelloServer ready and waiting ...");
41
42       // wait for invocations from clients
43       orb.run();
44     }
45
46     catch (Exception e) {
47       System.err.println("ERROR: " + e);
48       e.printStackTrace(System.out);
49     }
50
51     System.out.println("HelloServer Exiting ...");
52
53   } // end main
54 } // end class
```

The Object Client Application

Figure 10.16 presents a sample object client for the *Hello* object. The sample is written as a Java application, although a client program can also be written as an applet or a servlet.

The client code is responsible for creating and initializing the ORB (line 14), looking up the object using the Interoperable Naming Service (lines 16–22), invoking the *narrow* method of the *Helper* object to cast the object reference to a reference to a *Hello* object implementation (lines 24–27), and invoking remote methods using the reference (lines 29–33). The object's *sayHello* method is invoked to receive a string as return value, and the object's *shutdown* method is invoked to deactivate the service.

Figure 10.16 *HelloApp/HelloClient.java.*

```
1   // A sample object client application.
2   import HelloApp.*;
3   import org.omg.CosNaming.*;
4   import org.omg.CosNaming.NamingContextPackage.*;
5   import org.omg.CORBA.*;
6
7   public class HelloClient
8   {
9     static Hello helloImpl;
10
11    public static void main(String args[]){
12      try{
13        // create and initialize the ORB
14        ORB orb = ORB.init(args, null);
15
16        // get the root naming context
17        org.omg.CORBA.Object objRef =
18          orb.resolve_initial_references("NameService");
19        // Use NamingContextExt instead of NamingContext
20        // part of the Interoperable naming Service.
21        NamingContextExt ncRef =
22          NamingContextExtHelper.narrow(objRef);
23
24        // resolve the Object Reference in Naming
25        String name = "Hello";
26        helloImpl =
27          HelloHelper.narrow(ncRef.resolve_str(name));
28
29        System.out.println
30          ("Obtained a handle on server object: "
31          + helloImpl);
32        System.out.println(helloImpl.sayHello());
33        helloImpl.shutdown();
34
35      }
```

(continued on next page)

```
36        catch (Exception e) {
37          System.out.println("ERROR : " + e) ;
38          e.printStackTrace(System.out);
39        }
40     } //end main
41
42  } // end class
```

In the rest of the chapter we present the algorithms for developing a CORBA application using Java IDL.

Compiling and Running a Java IDL Application

For the end-of-chapter exercises, you will be compiling and running Java IDL applications. Following is a description of the procedure.

Server Side

1. Move into the directory that contains the IDL file *Hello.idl*.
2. Run the IDL-to-Java compiler, *idlj*, on the IDL file. This step assumes that you have included the path to the *java/bin* directory in your path.

   `idlj -fall Hello.idl`

   You must use the *-fall* option with the *idlj* compiler to generate all the client- and server-side support files. The generated files provide standard functionality and require no modification by you.

   With the *-fall* command line option, the files generated by the *idlj* compiler for *Hello.idl* are

   - *HelloPOA.java*
   - *_HelloStub.java*
   - *Hello.java*
   - *HelloHelper.java*
   - *HelloHolder.java*
   - *HelloOperations.java*

   These files are automatically placed in a subdirectory, which is named *HelloApp* in this example.
3. Compile the *.java* files in the directory *HelloApp*, including the stubs and skeletons.

   `javac *.java HelloApp/*.java`
4. Start the Java Object Request Broker Daemon, *orbd*, which includes a Naming Service server.

   To start *orbd* on a UNIX system, enter at the system prompt:

   `orbd -ORBInitialPort <port number>&`

On Unix systems, a "daemon" is a task that runs in the background in response to events.

On a Windows system, enter the following at a command prompt:

```
start orbd -ORBInitialPort <port number>&
```

Note that `<port number>` is the port on which you want the name server to run; it should be a port number above 1024, say, 1234.

5. Start the *Hello* server.

   To start the *Hello* server on a UNIX system, enter the following (all on one line) at the system prompt:

```
java HelloServer -ORBInitialPort 1234 -ORBInitialHost localhost
```

On a Windows system, enter the following (all on one line) at a command prompt:

```
start java HelloServer -ORBInitialPort 1234 -ORBInitialHost localhost
```

The *-ORBInitialHost* option specifies the host on which the IDL name name server is running. The *-ORBInitialPort* option specifies the name server (*orbd*) port as described in Step 4.

Client Side

1. Obtain and compile the *Hello.idl* file on the server machine:

```
idlj -fall Hello.idl
```

Copy the directory containing *Hello.idl* (including the subdirectory generated by *idlj*) to the client machine.

2. In the *HelloApp* directory on the client machine, create *HelloClient.java*. Compile the **.java* files, including the stubs and skeletons (which are in the directory *HelloApp*):

```
javac *.java HelloApp/*.java
```

3. On the client machine, run the *Hello* application client as follows (all on one line): `java HelloClient -ORBInitialHost <nameserverHost>`

```
-ORBInitialPort <name server port>
```

The `<nameserverHost>` is the host on which the IDL name server is running. In this case, it should be the domain name or IP address of the server machine.

Client Callback

Recall that RMI provides the capability for client callback, which enables a client to register with an object server so that the server may initiate a call to the client subsequently, upon the occurrence of some event. The same capability is available with Java IDL. Reference [java.sun.com/products, 18] provides a code sample for such an application.

10.10 Trade-offs

A key lesson of this book is that in distributed computing (and in computing in general) there are typically numerous ways to accomplish the same task. This chapter introduces you to such an example. As you can see, and as you will experience when you tackle some of the exercises at the end of this chapter, the same application (say, a distributed game) can be implemented using Java RMI or a CORBA toolkit such as Java IDL. It is hoped that at this point, having studied both facilities, you will be able to make an intelligent comparison of the two and articulate the trade-offs, as you will be asked to do for one of the exercises.

Summary

This chapter has introduced you to the Common Object Request Broker Architecture (CORBA) and a specific facility based on the architecture: Java IDL.

The key topics introduced with CORBA are:

- The basic CORBA architecture and its emphasis on object interoperability and platform independence
- The Object Request Broker (ORB) and its functionalities
- The Inter-ORB Protocol (IOP) and its significance
- CORBA object reference and the Interoperable Object Reference (IOR) protocol
- The CORBA Naming Service and the Interoperable Naming Service (INS)
- Standard CORBA object services and how they are provided
- Object adapters, portable object Adapters (POA), and their significance

The key points presented in conjunction with Java IDL are:

- Java packages are available that contain interfaces and classes for CORBA support.
- Tools provided for developing a CORBA application include *idlj* (the IDL compiler) and *orbd* (the ORB and name server).
- An example application named *Hello* was presented to illustrate the basic Java IDL syntax.
- Steps for compiling and running an application was presented.

CORBA toolkits and Java RMI are comparable and alternative technologies that provide distributed objects. An applicaton may be implemented using either technology, but there are trade-offs between the two.

Exercises

1. In the context of CORBA, what do the following acronyms stand for? For each acronym, provide the extended name and a brief description: CORBA, ORB, GIOP, IIOP, IOR, INS, POA.

2. Provide a block diagram to illustrate the CORBA architecture. The diagram should include these components: a distributed object, the object server, the object client, the skeleton, the stub, the ORB, and the object adapter.

   Provide a block diagram to illustrate the Java RMI architecture, including the equivalent components: the distributed object, the object server, the object client, the skeleton, the stub.

   Based on your diagrams, write a paragraph to describe the main differences in the two architectures. Try to explain the differences.

3. Compared to Java RMI, what are the main strengths of a CORBA facility, if any? What are its weaknesses, if any?

4. Follow the algorithm presented in the chapter to compile and run the *Hello* example on one machine. Write a report describing your experience, including any difficulty you encountered and how you resolved it.

5. Follow the algorithm presented in the chapter to compile and run the *Hello* example on two machines. Write a report to describe your experience, including any difficulty you encountered and how you resolved it. (You may find reference [java.sun.com/j2se/1.4, 13] helpful.)

6. Use Java IDL to build a server and client suite that implements the *Daytime* protocol.

7. Using Java IDL, write an application for a prototype opinion poll system. Assume that only one issue is being polled. Respondents may choose *yes, no,* or *don't care*. A server application accepts the votes, keeps the tally (in transient memory), and provides the current counts to those who are interested.

   a. Write the interface file first. It should provide remote methods for accepting a response to the poll, providing the current counts (e.g., "10 yes, 2 no, 5 don't care") upon request.

   b. Design and implement the server (i) to export the remote methods, and (ii) to maintain the state information (the counts).

   c. Design and implement the client application to provide a user interface for accepting a response and/or a request, and to interact with the server appropriately via remote method invocations.

   d. Test your application by running two or more clients on different machines (preferably on different platforms).

   e. Hand in listings of your files, which should include your source files (the interface file, the server file(s), and the client file(s)) and a *README* file that explains the contents and interrelationship of your source files and the procedure for running your work.

8. Create a Java IDL application for conducting an election. The server exports two methods:

   - *castVote*, which accepts as a parameter a string containing a candidate's name (Gore or Bush), and returns nothing, and

   - *getResult*, which returns, in an *int* array, the current count for each candidate.

   Test your application by running all processes on one machine, then test it by running the client and server on *separate* machines. Turn in source code for the remote interface, the server, and the client.

9. Build a distributed two-player tic-tac-toe game using (a) Java RMI with client callbacks, and (b) Java IDL with client callbacks.

   Design your applications so that the client is as "thin" as possible; that is, the client should carry as little state data and contain as little code as possible. The server maintains the game state and synchronizes the players' turns.

   Turn in (a) design documents, including UML class diagrams, (b) source listing, and (c) a report comparing the trade-offs between the two technologies, in terms of ease of implementation, language independence, platform independence, and execution overheads.

References

1. *Welcome To The OMG's CORBA Website, http://www.corba.org/*

2. CORBA FAQ, *http://www.omg.org/gettingstarted/corbafaq.htm*

3. CORBA for Beginners, *http://cgi.omg.org/corba/beginners.html*

4. Jon Siegel. CORBA 3 Fundamentals and Programming. New York, NY: John Wiley, 2000.

5. OMG Naming Service specification, *http://www.omg.org/technology/documents/formal/naming_service.htm*

6. CORBA Naming Service Evaluation, Sean Landis and William Shapiro, *http://www.cs.umd.edu/~billshap/papers/naming.doc,* 1999.

7. CORBA and Java™ technologies, *http://java.sun.com/j2ee/corba/*

8. Irfan Pyarali and D. C. Schmidt. "An Overview of the CORBA Portable Object Adapter." ACM StandardView 6, (March 1998). *http://citeseer.nj.nec.com/pyarali98overview.html*

9. JavaTM RMI-IIOP Documentation, *http://java.sun.com/j2se/1.3/docs/guide/rmi-iiop/index.html*

10. Cetus Links: 18,452 Links on Objects and Components/CORBA, *http://www.cetus-links.org/oo_corba.html*

11. The Java Tutorial Trail: IDL, *http://java.sun.com/docs/books/tutorial/idl/index.html*

12. Java™ IDL, *http://java.sun.com/products/jdk/idl/*

13. Java IDL: The "Hello World" Example on Two Machines, *http://java.sun.com/j2se/1.4/docs/guide/idl/tutorial/jidl2machines.html*

14. Java IDL Sample code, *http://java.sun.com/j2se/1.4/docs/guide/idl/jidlSampleCode.html*

15. Java IDL: Naming Service,
    http://java.sun.com/products/jdk/1.2/docs/guide/idl/jidlNaming.html

16. Naming Service, Sun MicroSystems,
    http://java.sun.com/j2se/1.4/docs/guide/idl/jidlNaming.html

17. Java IDL Technology Documentation,
    http://java.sun.com/j2se/1.4/docs/guide/idl/index.html

18. Java IDL: Example 3, Hello World with Callback Object, *http://java.sun.com/products/jdk/1.4/docs/guide/idl/jidlExample3.html*

19. CORBA Product Profiles, *http://www.puder.org/corba/matrix/*

20. Java 2 Platform, Standard Edition (J2SE), *http://java.sun.com/j2se/1.4/*

11

Internet Applications— Part 2

In Chapter 9 we studied HTTP, CGI, and session state information maintenance for Internet (or Web) applications. Because of the popularity of Web applications, a plethora of protocols and toolkits have emerged. In this chapter we will explore some of the more recent protocols and mechanisms, including applets, servlets, and Simple Object Access Protocol (SOAP).

11.1 Applets

Simply put, **applets** [java.sun.com/docs, 1; java.sun.com/applets, 2; javaboutique.internet.com, 3; java.sun.com/sfaq, 17] are Java classes that are fetched by a browser from a Web server using HTTP and subsequently executed via a Java Virtual Machine in the browser's environment (see Figure 11.1).

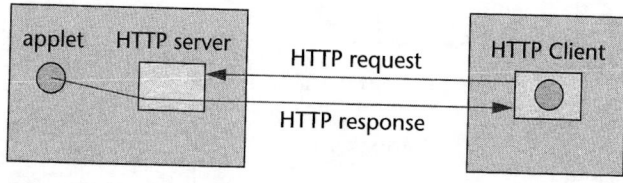

Figure 11.1 A Java applet is fetched using HTTP.

An applet is specified in an HTML page using an *APPLET* tag, as illustrated in Figure 11.2.

Figure 11.2 A Web page that specifies an applet.

```
<Html>
<Head>
<Title>Applet Example</Title>
</Head>

<Body>
This is what the applet displays when it is run:<br>
<Applet Code="HelloWorld.class" width=200 Height=100>
</Applet>
```

When the *APPLET* tag is parsed by the browser, it issues a request to the HTTP server specified in the applet tag or, if a server is not specified, to the current server (the server from which the Web page was downloaded) by default. The text of a sample of such an HTTP request follows:

```
GET /applets/HelloWorld.class HTTP/1.1
<blank line>
```

In the request, *HelloWorld.class* is the name of the class file for the applet. The HTTP server locates the class file and sends its contents to the client in the body of the HTTP response.

Upon receiving the class file for an applet, the browser runs it in its Java Virtual Machine (JVM) and displays its output.

Figure 11.3 illustrates a Web session during which a Web page containing an *APPLET* tag is fetched by a browser. The applet class is subsequently transferred from the server to the client (the browser), on whose host the applet class is executed and the result displayed.

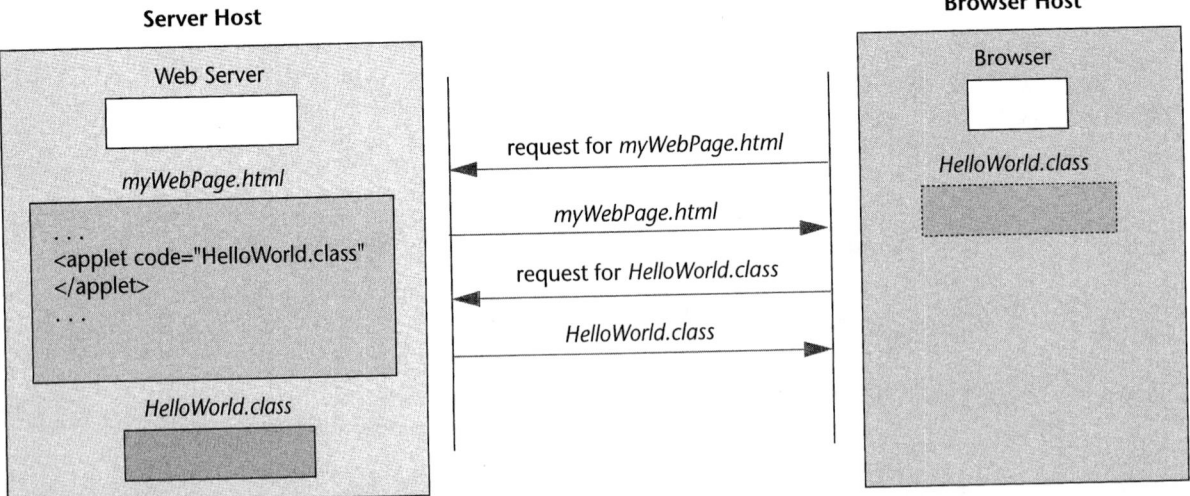

Figure 11.3 A Web session involving an applet.

An applet is a special type of Java program that is loaded by either a browser or an *appletviewer*. Each applet extends the Java *Applet* class, which is a subclass of Java's *awt.Container* class, a class that supports drawing graphics. Consequently, applets can be coded relatively easily to draw graphics. Figure 11.4 illustrates the source code for an applet that draws a string "Hello world" when run.

An *appletviewer* is a program provided in the Java SDK for running an applet without using a browser.

Figure 11.4 *HelloWorld.java*, the source code for an applet.

```
import java.applet.Applet;
import java.awt.Graphics;

public class HelloWorld extends Applet
{
    public void paint(Graphics g)
    {
        g.drawString("Hello world!", 50, 25);
    } //end paint

} //end class
```

In practice, the code for an applet can be far more complex, involving elaborate graphics and event handling.

An applet is best tested using an *appletviewer* before you try to run it using a browser. When you test an applet on a browser, it will be helpful for you to look at the messages displayed on the Java console screen. The Internet Explorer, for example, allows you to do so if you select the "Java console enabled" option in the Tools—Internet options menu.

Because applets are downloaded from a remote host and run on a local host, their execution is subject to restrictions for security reasons. (In Chapter 8 we looked at similar concerns for RMI stub downloading.) One such restriction is that an applet ordinarily is not allowed to read or write files stored on the computer on which it is executing. Another is that an applet is not allowed to make network connections except to the host from which it originated (see Figure 11.5). There are other restrictions [java.sun.com/sfaq, 17] imposed to limit the damage that can be done to the host system by a potentially malignant object downloaded from an untrusted source.

Applets are interesting programs. However, in the context of distributed computing, applets are of limited significance; they are introduced here primarily for completeness. Interested readers should consult these references [java.sun.com/docs, 1; java.sun.com/applets, 2; javaboutique.internet.com, 3; java.sun.com/sfaq, 17] for further details. Program code for sample applets can be obtained from numerous sources, such as [java.sun.com/sfaq, 17].

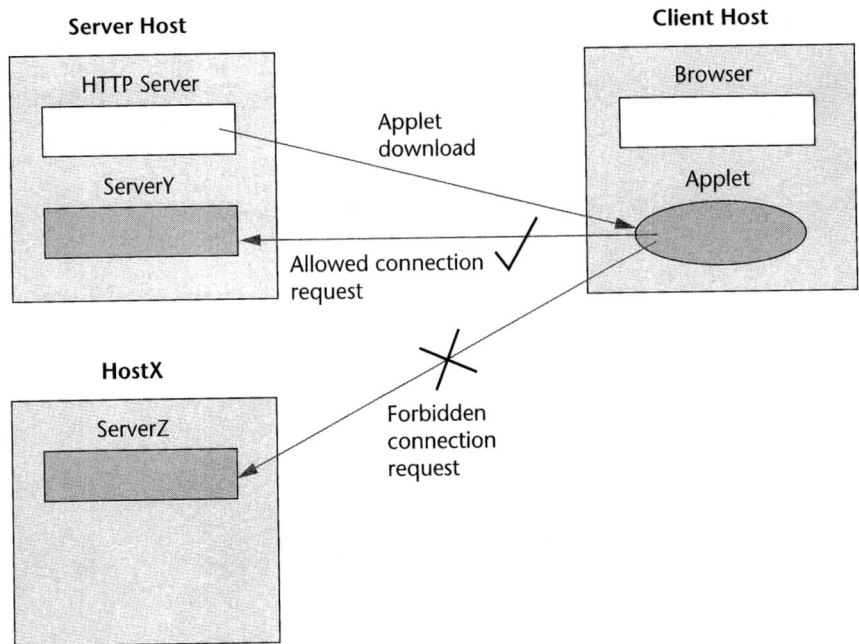

Figure 11.5 An applet is forbidden from making foreign network connections.

11.2 Servlets

Servlets are another type of Java program. Whereas applets are transferred from a server to an HTTP client, to be executed on the client host, servlets are extensions of a server and are executed on the server host. In Chapter 9 we studied one form of server extension programs: CGI scripts. As you recall, CGI scripts are external programs that extend the capabilities of an HTTP server to support customized action for the processing of a Web form. Playing a role similar to that of a CGI script, an **HTTP servlet**—a special form of servlet—executes on the server host as the action triggered by a client's request. Unlike a CGI script, however, a servlet can be used to extend *any* server that practices a request-response protocol. Servlets are most commonly used with HTTP servers, in which case they are referred to as **HTTP servlets**.

In the rest of this section we will focus on HTTP servlets, which we will simply refer to as servlets; readers should keep in mind that a special form of servlets is being discussed.

Architectural Support

Unlike CGI scripts—which run on an HTTP server host with no additional system architectural support—the execution of servlets requires the existence of a module known as a **servlet engine** or **servlet container** (see Figure 11.6).

Each servlet is executed in a context provided by the servlet engine running on the server host.

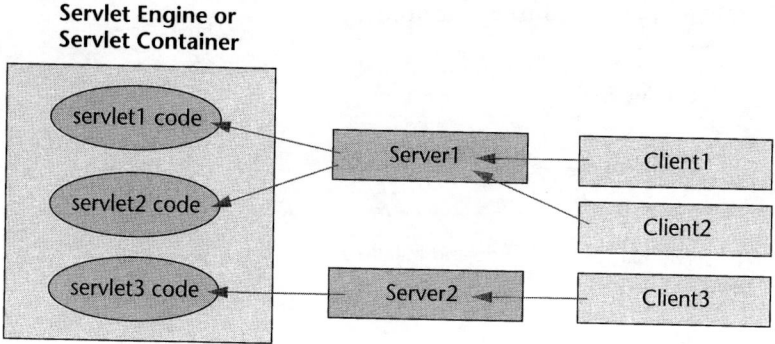

A servlet container or servlet engine is required. The servlet engine can be part of a server, or a module external to a server.

Figure 11.6 Servlet support architecture.

Figure 11.7 illustrates the life cycle of a servlet. The code of a servlet, which is a Java class, is loaded into the servlet engine. The execution of the servlet is then initiated by the server as a result of a client's request. Subsequently, the server acts as an intermediary between the client and the servlet: The client issues requests to the servlet through the server, and the servlet sends responses to the client via the server. Depending on the implementation of the server, a servlet may persist for as long as there are requests issued to it, or it may persist indefinitely until the server is shut down. **Persistence** is another difference between a servlet and a CGI script: A CGI script is reloaded each time a client issues a request for it, whereas a single instance of a servlet will run for at least as long as there are requests issued to it. Because of this persistence, a servlet can hold stateful data across clients sessions during its lifetime. For example, it is possible to use an instance variable to keep count of how many times a request has been issued to a servlet since its loading.

A servlet is an object of the *javax.Servlet* class, which is part of an extended Java class library called *javax*; the Javax library is not included as part of the basic Java Development Kit (JDK) but can be downloaded separately [java.sun.com/products/servlet/download.html, 5].

A number of implementations exist that provide the servlet architecture. The following two are readily available:

■ The *JSWDK* (**Java Server Web Development Kit**) [java.sun.com/products/servlet/archive.html, 4] is a free package provided by Sun Microsystems when the servlet technology was first introduced. *JSWDK* is meant to be a **reference implementation**, which means that it is provided by Sun Microsystems to illustrate the technology but is not intended to be used in production. Its simplicity makes this package an ideal starting point for students. Unfortunately, the package is now available only from Sun's archival site, and its availability in the future cannot be assumed.

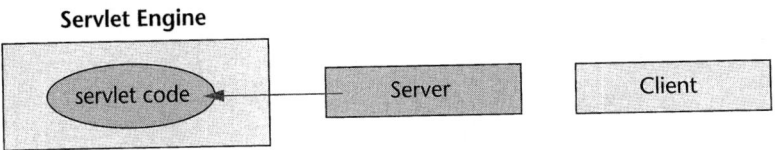

The server loads servlet code and initializes the servlet, possibly as a result of a client's request.

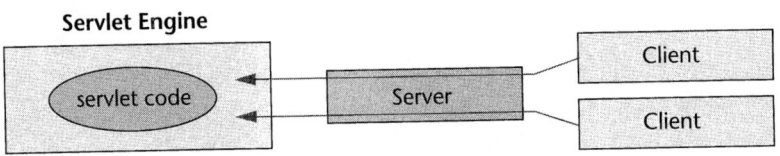

Via the server, the servlet handles zero or more client requests.

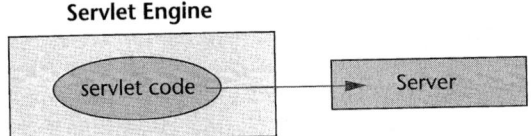

The server removes the servlet when there are no more client requests for it. (Some servers do this step only when they shut down.)

Figure 11.7 The lifetime of a servlet.

■ **Apache Tomcat** [jakarta.apache.org, 6] is a free, open-source implementation of Java Servlet and JavaServer Pages technologies developed under the Jakarta project at the Apache Software Foundation.

Servlet support is also available on commercial application servers such as WebLogic, iPlanet, WebSphere.

Among the methods specified with each servlet object are

■ *init( )*—invoked by the servlet engine when a servlet is initialized

■ *shutdown( )*—invoked by the servlet engine when a servlet is no longer needed

■ *service( )*—invoked by the servlet engine when a client request is forwarded to the servlet

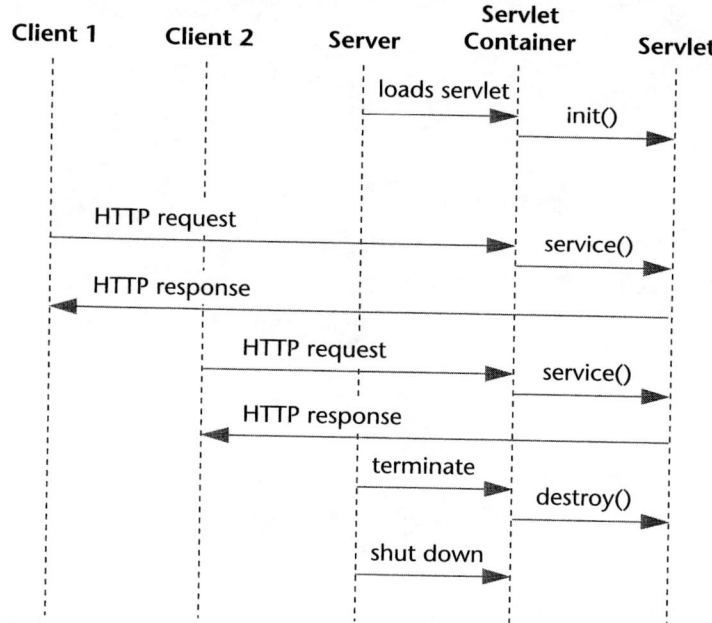

Figure 11.8 Interactions among clients, server, servlet container, and servlets.

The sequence diagram in Figure 11.8 illustrates the interactions among the HTTP server, the servlet container, a servlet, and concurrent clients that issue requests to the servlet via the server.

Servlet Programming

The programming of an HTTP servlet [Hunter and Crawford, 19] is simplified by the abstraction provided by the Servlet API, in a set of classes and interfaces. The central abstraction in the Servlet API is the *Servlet* interface, which contains the *init( )*, *destroy( )*, and *service( )* methods that have already been mentioned. Abstraction for HTTP servlets is further provided in a Java abstract class *HTTPServlet*, which is a subclass of the *Servlet* interface, as illustrated in Figure 11.9 [jakarta.apache.org, 6].

As a subclass of the generic servlet, an HTTP servlet inherits the methods *init( )*, *destroy( )*, and *service( )*. For the servlet's role as an extension of the HTTP server, additional methods are defined [java.sun.org/products/servlet/2.2, 7], two of which are shown in Table 11.1.

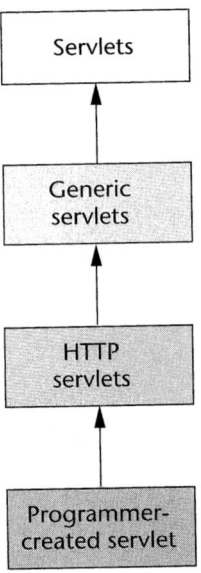

Figure 11.9 Java class hierarchy of a servlet object.

Table 11.1 Key HTTP Servlet Methods

Method	Description
protected void doGet(HttpServletRequest req, HttpServletResponse resp)	Called by the server (via the *service* method) to allow a servlet to handle a *GET* request.
protected void doPost(HttpServletRequest req, HttpServletResponse resp)	Called by the server (via the *service* method) to allow a servlet to handle a *POST* request.

As you recall from Chapter 9, an HTTP request may invoke an external program (such as a CGI script) and pass parameters to the program using either the *GET* method or the *POST* method. Similarly, a servlet can be invoked via an HTTP request, with parameters passed to the servlet in a query string, in the same manner as described in Chapter 9. To review: If an HTTP request specifies a *GET* method, a query string is affixed to the request's URI, and deposited by the HTTP server to the environment variable *QUERY_STRING*; if the request specifies a *POST* method, the query sting is placed in the body of the request, and the HTTP server writes the string to the standard input of the external program (a CGI script or a servlet).

With servlets, the details of parameter passing are encapsulated in the *HTTPServletRequest* class. When a servlet is requested with *GET*, the HTTP server calls the *doGet* method of the servlet; the server calls the *doPost* method of the servlet if the servlet is requested with *POST*. Helpful methods in the *HTTPServletRequest* class facilitates the extraction of parameters from the query string, regardless of whether the request was made specifying the *GET* or *POST* method.

Figure 11.10 shows the source code for an example Web form that invokes a servlet. In the example, the Web form specifies the *POST* form method. When the Web form is submitted, the HTTP server will load the code for the servlet (filed under the name *formServlet*) in the servlet container. The servlet container initializes the servlet by invoking its *init( )* method, then calls its *service( )* method. As illustrated in Figure 11.11, the *ser-vice( )* method in turn invokes the *doPost( )* method in the servlet, executing the code programmed therein. If the code outputs a response, the response is passed from the servlet via the HTTP server to the browser. Had the form specified the *GET* method instead, the *doGet( )* method in the servlet would be invoked instead.

Figure 11.10 Source code for a sample Web form that invokes a servlet.

```html
<html>
<head>
<title>A Web form which invokes a servlet</title>
</head>
<body>
<H1>This is a simple form which invokes a servlet</H1>
<P>
This is a sample form which demonstrates the use of
web form processing using a Java servlet.
<P>
<font color = red>
<HR>
<form method="post"
action="http://localhost:8080/examples/servlet/formServlet">
<H2> Pop Quiz: </H2>
What is thy name: <input name="name"><P>
What is thy quest: <input name="quest"><P>
What is thy favorite color:
<select name="color">
<option selected>chartreuse
</select>
<P>
What is the weight of a swallow: <input type="radio" name="swallow"
value="african" checked> African Swallow or
<input type="radio" name="swallow" value="continental"> Continental
Swallow
<P>
What do you have to say for yourself
<textarea name="text" rows=5 cols=60></textarea>
<P>
Press <input type="submit" value="here"> to submit your query.
</form>
<hr>
</body>
</html>
```

HTTP Client Host

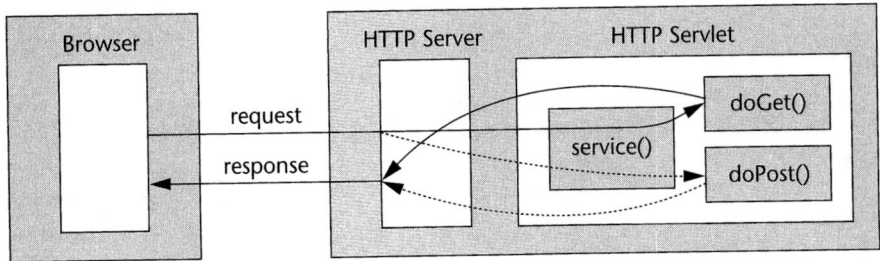

Figure 11.11 The *doPost* and *doGet* methods in an HTTP servlet.

As shown in Table 11.1, the *doPost* or *doGet* method receives, as parameters, references to two objects: first, an *HttpServletRequest* object and, second, an *HttpServletResponse* object. An object of the first type encapsulates an HTTP request, as discussed in Chapter 9. An object of the second type encapsulates an HTTP response, also discussed in Chapter 9. Inside the servlet, information in the request is extracted using appropriate methods in the *HttpServletRequest* object, some of which are shown in Table 11.2. The information is processed, and a response is formulated using appropriate methods in the *HttpServletResponse* object. Some of the key methods in the *HttpServletResponse* class are listed in Table 11.3.

Table 11.2 Selected Methods in an *HttpServletRequest* Object

Method	Description
public *String* getHeader(String name)	Returns the value of the specified request header as a *String*.
public *String* getMethod( )	Returns the name of the HTTP method with which this request was made, for example, *GET, POST,* or *PUT.*
public *String* getQueryString( )	Returns the query string sent with the request.
public *String* getParameter(String name)	Returns the value of a request parameter as a *String,* or *null* if the parameter does not exist.
public *Enumeration* getParameterNames()	Returns an *Enumeration* of *String* objects containing the names of the parameters contained in this request. If the request has no parameter, the method returns an empty *Enumeration*.
public *String*[ ] getParameterValues(String name)	Returns an array of *String* objects containing all of the values the given request parameter has, or *null* if the parameter does not exist.

Table 11.3 Selected Methods in an *HttpServletResponse* Object

Method	Description
public void *setContentType(String type)*	Sets the content *type* of the response being sent to the client. This method should be called first before a *PrintWriter* object is obtained for the response.
void *addHeader(String* name, and *String* value)	Adds a response header line with the given name and value.
void *sendError(int sc, String msg)*	Sends an error response to the client using the specified status code and descriptive message.
void *setHeader(String name, String value)*	Sets a response header with the given *name* and *value*.
void *setStatus(int sc)*	Sets the status code for this response.
public *ServletOutputStream getOutputStream()* throws *java.io.IOException*	Returns a *ServletOutputStream* object suitable for writing binary data in the response. The servlet container does not encode the binary data. Either this method or *getWriter( )* may be called to write the body, but not both.
public *PrintWriter getWriter()* throws *java.io.IOException*	Returns a *PrintWriter* object that can send character text to the client. Either this method or *getOutputStream()* may be called to write the body, not both.
public void *sendRedirect (String location)* throws *java.io.IOException*	Invokes the execution of the servlet at the URL specified in the location string. The redirection should be invoked before the response (if any) of the current servlet is written to the *HTTPServletResoponse* object. The execution of the current servlet will continue after the redirection.

Figure 11.12 shows the source code for a sample servlet. The code makes use of the methods introduced in Tables 11.2 and 11.3 to process the HTTP request generated when the Web page shown in Figure 11.10 is submitted. If you compare this code with the code for the CGI script *GetPost.c* (Figure 9.16) introduced in Chapter 9, you will see that the same application logic is expressed in each sample and that the abstraction provided by Java makes this code far more readable. Note that this sample overrides the *doPost* method, since the Web form that invokes this servlet specifies the *Post* form method.

Figure 11.12 Source code for a sample form-processing servlet.

```
1  // A sample web form processing servlet
2  // Author: M. Liu
3
4  import java.io.*;
5  import javax.servlet.*;
6  import javax.servlet.http.*;
7
8  public class FormServlet extends HttpServlet {
9
10   public void doPost (HttpServletRequest request,
11       HttpServletResponse res)
12       throws ServletException, IOException (
13
14     //The content type of the response body
15     // should be set first
16     res.setContentType("text/html");
17
18     //Get an output stream to write the response body
19     ServletOutputStream out = res.getOutputStream();
20
21     out.println("<html>");
22     out.println("<head><title>Servlet Response" +
23       "</title></head>");
24     out.println("<body>");
25     out.println("<body bgcolor=\"beige\">");
26     out.println("<P>Hello, </FONT><FONT FACE=" +
27       "\"Arial\" SIZE=5 COLOR=\"#ff0000\">");
28     //Retrieve the value of the parameter named "name"
29     out.println(request.getParameter("name") +
30       "</P></FONT>");
31     out.println("<br>");
32     out.println("<hr><br>");
33     //Retrieve the value of the parameter named "quest"
34     out.println("<UL><LI>Quest: " +
35       request.getParameter("quest") + "</LI>");
36     out.println("<LI>Color: " +
37       request.getParameter("color") + "</LI>");
38     out.println("<LI>Swallow Type: " +
39       request.getParameter("swallow") + "</LI>");
40     out.println("<LI>And you said: " +
41       request.getParameter("text"));
42     out.println("</UL><BR>");
43     out.println("<HR>");
44     out.println("<P><h3>Request processed from: " +
45       "<font color =\"#00AAFF\">");
46     out.println(request.getRemoteHost() +
47       "</FONT></h3></P>");
48     out.println("</body></html>");
49   }
50 } //end class
```

State Information Maintenance in Servlet Programming

Back in Chapter 9 when CGI script was introduced, we studied the means by which state information can be passed among scripts. Since CGI scripts are independent programs, special mechanisms are required to allow the sharing of information among them. You may recall that some of the mechanisms described in Chapter 9 are the use of **hidden form fields** and **cookies**.

A servlet has a wider selection of such mechanisms, some of which are presented below, including the use of (1) servlet variables, (2) hidden form fields, (3) cookies, and (4) session objects.

Servlet Variables

As has already been mentioned, servlets are **persistent**: A single instance of the servlet program, once loaded into the servlet engine, is run until the the servlet is destroyed. Hence it is possible to store state information in the variables of a servlet. However, it is not common for a programmer to maintain state information this way, for the following reasons:

1. A programmer has no control over the lifetime of a servlet. Depending on the implementation of the server that interacts with the servlet engine, a servlet may persist for a certain duration, or it may persist indefinitely until the servlet engine is shut down.

2. Since a single copy of the servlet is run at a given time, state information stored in the variables of a servlet will be global to all clients, making it difficult to separate the state data for concurrent sessions.

Figure 11.13 presents the source code for a servlet that uses an instance variable to maintain a counter throughout the lifetime of the servlet. The counter is incremented each time that the servlet is run. You can experiment with it by running it multiple times, successively or concurrently, as you will be asked to do in one of the exercises at the end of this chapter.

Figure 11.13 *Counter.java.*

```
1  // An example which illustrates the use of
2  // servlet variables for storing state information.
3  // M. Liu
4
5  import java.io.*;
6  import javax.servlet.*;
7  import javax.servlet.http.*;
8
9  public class Counter extends HttpServlet {
10
11     int counter = 0;
12
13     public void doGet(HttpServletRequest request,
14         HttpServletResponse response)
```

(continued on next page)

```
15          throws ServletException, IOException {
16        response.setContentType("text/plain");
17        PrintWriter output = response.getWriter();
18
19        counter++;
20
21        output.println("This servlet has been" +
22          " accessed " + counter + " times.");
23      } //end doGet
24    } //end class
```

Counter.java is not thread safe, since the increment operation of the variable counter (line 19) is interruptible, so that one concurrent increment may overwrite another. Figure 11.14 is a thread-safe version of the servlet that uses a synchronized method to ensure that only one invocation of the servlet may access and increment the counter at a time.

Figure 11.14 *Counter.java.*

```
1   // A servlet which maintains a counter for
2   // the number of times that it has been
3   // accessed since its loading.
4   // M. Liu
5
6   import java.io.*;
7   import javax.servlet.*;
8   import javax.servlet.http.*;
9
10  public class Counter2 extends HttpServlet {
11
12    public int counter = 0;
13
14    public void doGet(HttpServletRequest request,
15        HttpServletResponse response)
16        throws ServletException, IOException {
17      response.setContentType("text/plain");
18      PrintWriter output = response.getWriter();
19      increment(output);
20    } //end doGet
21
22    private synchronized void increment(PrintWriter output){
23      output.println("This servlet has been" +
24        " accessed " + counter + " times.");
25      counter++;
26    } //end increment
27
28  } //end class
```

Hidden Form Fields

The use of hidden form fields, as described in Chapter 9, can be applied in exactly the same way with servlets as with CGI scripts to pass state information. HTML statements containing the hidden form fields can be written to an output stream of a *PrintWriter* associated with the *HTTPServletResponse* to contain the state data to be delivered to a subsequent servlet in a query string. The following code fragment illustrates the output of a line in the HTTP response that contains a hidden form field whose name is *ID* and whose value is that retrieved from the variable *someValue*:

```
response.setContentType("text/plain");
PrintWriter output = response.getWriter( );
output.println("<INPUT TYPE=\"HIDDEN\" NAME=ID VALUE=" + someValue);
```

Cookies

Cookies, too, can be applied in the same manner as with CGI scripts. Java provides classes and methods to facilitate such use.

The class, *HttpCookie*, represents the cookies presented in Chapter 9. The key methods of the class are described in Table 11.4.

Table 11.4 Key Methods of the *Cookie* Class

Method	Description
public *Cookie(String name, String value)*	Constructs a cookie with a specified name and value.
public *String getDomain( )*	Returns the domain name set for this cookie.
public *int getMaxAge( )*	Returns the maximum age of the cookie, specified in seconds. By default, -1 indicates that the cookie will persist until the browser is shutdown.
public *String getName( )*	Returns the name of the cookie.
public *String getPath( )*	Returns the path on the server to which the browser returns this cookie.
public *String getValue( )*	Returns the value of the cookie.
public void *setDomain(String pattern)*	Sets the domain attribute of this cookie.
public *setMaxAge(int expiry)*	Sets the expires attribute of this cookie to a time period in the specified number of seconds.
public void *setPath(String uri)*	Sets the path attribute of this cookie.
public void *setValue(String newValue)*	Assigns a value to a cookie.

The *HttpRequest* class provides a method, *getCookies*, for retrieving the cookie(s) sent with an HTTP request, as shown in Table 11.5.

Table 11.5 The *getCookie* Method of the *HttpRequest* Class

Method	Description
public *Cookie*[ ] *getCookies*( )	Returns an array containing all of the *Cookie* objects that the client sent with this request.

Figures 11.15 through 11.18 present a set of source code that illustrates the basic implementation of a shopping cart using servlet programming.

Figure 11.15 The Web form *cart.html*.

```
<HTML>
<HEAD>
<TITLE>Fruits Online</TITLE>
</HEAD>
<BODY bgcolor=#CCffCC>
<CENTER><H1>We have these goodies</H1></CENTER>
<HR>
<FORM ACTION="http://localhost:8080/examples/servlet/Cart" METHOD="POST">
<TABLE CELLSPACING="5" CELLPADDING="5">
<TR>
  <TD ALIGN="center"><B>Add to Cart</B></TD>
  <TD ALIGN="center"></TD>
  <TD ALIGN="center"></TD>
</TR>
<TR>
  <TD ALIGN="center"><INPUT TYPE="Checkbox"
      NAME="item_a" VALUE="apple    $1"></TD>
  <TD ALIGN="left">apple</TD>
</TR>
<TR>
  <TD ALIGN="center"><INPUT TYPE="Checkbox"
      NAME="item_b" VALUE="orange   $2"></TD>
  <TD ALIGN="left">orange</TD>
</TR>
<TR>
  <TD ALIGN="center"><INPUT TYPE="Checkbox"
      NAME="item_c" VALUE="pear     $3"></TD>
  <TD ALIGN="left">pear</TD>
</TR>
</TABLE>
<HR><BR>
<CENTER>
Press
<INPUT TYPE="Submit" NAME="Cart1_submit" VALUE="Submit">
to submit your order.
</CENTER>
</FORM>
</BODY>
</HTML>
```

Figure 11.16 The *Cart* servlet.

```
1   import javax.servlet.*;
2   // Source code for Cart servlet, invoked when the
3   // web form cart.html is submitted
4   // M. Liu
5
6   import javax.servlet.http.*;
7   import java.io.*;
8   import java.util.*;
9
10  public class Cart extends HttpServlet
11  {
12    public void doPost(HttpServletRequest request,
13        HttpServletResponse response)
14        throws ServletException, IOException
15    {
16      response.setContentType("text/html");
17      ServletOutputStream out = response.getOutputStream();
18      out.println("<html>");
19      out.println("<head><title>Servlet Response" +
20        "</title></head>");
21      out.println("<body>");
22      Cookie c;
23
24      /* Retrieve form data */
25      Enumeration keys;
26      String name, value, prefix;
27      keys = request.getParameterNames();
28      while (keys.hasMoreElements())
29      {
30        name = (String)keys.nextElement();
31        prefix = name.substring(0,4);
32
33        if (prefix.equals("item"))
34        // This test is necessary to eliminate
35        // input fields that are not items.
36        {
37          /* Retrieve the parameter value */
38          value = request.getParameter(name);
39          /* Create a cookie */
40          out.println("<H4>Setting cookie: " + name +
41            " " + value + "</H4>");
42          c = new Cookie(name, value);
43
44          /* Set it to expire in 1 day */
45          /* c.setMaxAge(1*24*60*60); */
46          response.addCookie(c);
47        }//end if
48      } //end while
49      out.println("</body></html>");
50
```

(continued on next page)

```
51        /* Issue a redirect to send the cookies and
52           invoke another servlet to generate a display
53           of the items in the shopping cart */
54        response.sendRedirect("Cart2");
55
56
57    } //end doPost
58 } //end class
```

Figure 11.17 The *Cart2* servlet.

```
1  // Servlet to view what is in the shopping cart (as recorded by
2  // the use of cookies in the Cart servlet.
3  // M. Liu, based on various sources
4
5  import javax.servlet.*;
6  import javax.servlet.http.*;
7  import java.io.*;
8  import java.util.*;
9
10 public class Cart2 extends HttpServlet
11 {
12    /* View items in shopping cart */
13    public void doGet(HttpServletRequest request,
14        HttpServletResponse response)
15        throws ServletException, IOException {
16
17      response.setContentType("text/html");
18      ServletOutputStream out = response.getOutputStream();
19      out.println("<html>");
20      out.println("<head><title>Servlet Response" +
21        "</title></head>");
22      out.println("<body>");
23      out.println("<body bgcolor=\"beige\">");
24      out.println("Contents of your shopping cart<UL>");
25
26      /* Retrieve the cookies */
27      Cookie cookies[];
28
29      cookies = request.getCookies();
30      if (cookies != null)
31      {
32        for (int i = 0; i < cookies.length; i++)
33        {
34          /* Note: It is important to identify the cookies
35             by name, as there may be other cookies in use
36             for this site */
37          if (cookies[i].getName().startsWith("item"))
38          {
39            out.println("<LI>" + cookies[i].getName() +
40              "\t" + cookies[i].getValue());
41          }
```

(continued on next page)

```
42            } // end for
43         } // end if
44
45         out.println("</UL>");
46         out.println("<HR>");
47         out.println("</body></html>");
48
49      } // end doGet
50
51   } // end Cart
```

Figure 11.18 *Cart2.html.*

```
<html>
<center>
<FORM ACTION="Cart2" METHOD="GET">
<h1>View items currently in cart...</h1>
<p>
Press
<INPUT TYPE="Submit" NAME="Cart2_submit" VALUE="Submit"> to view
contents in your shopping cart.
</CENTER>
</FORM>
</BODY>
</HTML>
```

Figure 11.15 is the source code for a Web form *Cart.html*. When browsed, the form displays three items available for selection.

When the form is submitted, the servlet *Cart* (Figure 11.16) is initiated. In the example, the servlet is assumed to run on the local host. However, the domain name and port number may be replaced with those of an alternate server. The names of the request parameters passed from the Web form are obtained using the *getParameterNames* method (line 27), and then each parameter's value is obtained using the *getParameter* method (line 38). For each parameter whose name starts with the appropriate prefix ("item," in our example), the name and value are used to create a new cookie (line 42), which is added to the response using the *addCookie* method (lines 46). If orange is selected, for example, the cookie generated will have the name set to "item_b," and the value set to "orange $2." There are statements in the code (lines 44–45) to set the cookies to last for one day, although these statements are currently commented out.

The *sendRedirect* method of the *HttpServletResponse* object is called to invoke a subsequent servlet, *Cart2*. The *Cart2* servlet dynamically generates a Web page that displays the contents of the shopping cart.

In *Cart2.java* (Figure 11.17), the cookies are retrieved using the *getCookies* method of the *HttpServletRequest*, one by one (lines 29–43). Note that only cookies named with the appropriate prefix ("item") are processed. The value of each cookie is presumed to contain the name and price of a selected item. A description of this item is then included in the dynamically generated Web page.

Figure 11.18 shows a Web form *Cart2.html* that, when submitted, invokes the *Cart2* servlet directly to allow a browser user to view the contents of the shopping cart during a session.

Since a servlet is persistent, one may wonder if the use of cookies, as illustrated in the shopping cart example, will result in the commingling of session information, causing the contents of one customer's shopping cart to show up in another's? Consider customer A and customer B, who are browsing *cart.html* concurrently from different computers. Each customer's HTTP request will result in the invocation of the same instance of the *Cart* servlet, which generates the cookies for each customer's selections. Customer A's request results in cookies being generated based on the request parameters sent with A's request, while Customer B's request results in cookies being generated based on the request parameters sent with B's. A's cookies are stored by the browser on A's computer. Likewise, B's cookies are stored on B's computer. The cookies are sent by each browser with subsequent HTTP requests (to the host of the *Cart* servlet) issued by its user, hence there is no confusion in the data for the separate shopping carts.

However, the situation is different if the concurrent sessions are conducted on the same computer. There is an exercise at the end of the chapter in which you can investigate and experiment with this scenario.

Session Object

The Servlet API provides a special mechanism for maintaining state information specific to a particular HTTP client session. The mechanism is known as **session objects**. A session object implements the *HttpSession* interface. A servlet may create such an object and then use the object as a repository of state data throughout a client session. To differentiate concurrent sessions, each session object must be uniquely identified. The identifier is automatically assigned by the servlet container and is transparent to the users. Throughout a client session, the session identifier is passed between the server and the client using a cookie or some other mechanism. Once a session object has been created, a servlet may deposit into it one or more objects that contain session data. Each object added to the session object is specified with a name. The object may then be retrieved by another servlet—or even the same servlet—that is invoked subsequently in the same client session.

A session object will persist for an active interval that can be set by code, or the interval is set to a default value that is implementation dependent. When the interval expires, the servlet container will invalidate the session object so that its contents may no longer be accessed. The invalidation of a sesson object can also be initiated in a program; it is good practice to do so in the code at the end of a session.

Table 11.6 presents key methods that can be invoked with an *HTTPSession* object. The *setAttribute* method is used to add session data to a session object, while the *getAttribute* method or optionally the *getAttributeNames* method can be called to retrieve session data from an existing session object. The *setMaxInactiveInterval* method allows one to set an active time interval for a session object, while the *invalidate* method will invalidate the session object.

Table 11.6 Key Methods of the HTTPSession Interface

Method	Description
public *Object* getAttribute(*String* name) throws *java.lang.IllegalStateException*	Returns the object bound with the specified name in this session, or null if no object is bound under the name.
public *Enumeration* getAttributeNames( ) throws *java.lang.IllegalStateException*	Returns an *Enumeration* of *String* objects containing the names of all the objects bound to this session.
public void *setAttribute* (*String name*, Object value) thows *java.lang.IllegalStateException*	Binds an object to this session, using the name specified. If an object of the same name is already bound to the session, the object is replaced.
public void *invalidate*( ) throws *java.lang.IllegalStateException*	Invalidates this session and then unbinds any objects bound to it.
public void *setAttribute* (*String name,Object value*) throws *java.lang.IllegalStateException*	Binds an object to this session, using the name specified. If an object of the same name is already bound to the session, the object is replaced.
public *int* getMaxInactiveInterval( )	Returns the maximum time interval, an integer specifying the number of seconds that the servlet container will keep this session open between client accesses. After this interval, the servlet container will invalidate the session. The maximum time interval can be set with the setMaxInactiveInterval method. A negative time indicates the session should never timeout.
public void setMaxInactiveInterval (*int interval*)	Specifies the time, in seconds, between client requests before the servlet container will invalidate this session. A negative time indicates the session should never time out.
public *String getId*( )	Returns a string containing the unique identifier assigned to this session. The identifier is assigned by the servlet container and is implementation dependent.
public void *invalidate*( ) throws objects *java.lang.IllegalStateException*	Invalidates this session anb then unbinds any bound to it.

A session object can be created and subsequently retrieved using the *getSession* method of the *HttpRequest* class, as shown in Table 11.7.

Figures 11.19 and 11.20 revisits the source code for the *Cart* and *Cart2* servlets, previously presented in Figures 11.16 and 11.17. In this set of sample code, a session object (instead of cookies) is used to maintain the items in the shopping cart.

Table 11.7 The *getSession* Method of the *HttpRequest* Class

Method	Description
public *HttpSession* getSession(*boolean create*)	Returns the current *HttpSession* associated with this request or, if there is no current session and the *create* parameter is set true, returns a new session.
	If *create* is false and the request has no valid *HttpSession*, this method returns null.

Figure 11.19 The *Cart* servlet using a session object.

```
1   import javax.servlet.*;
2   // Source code for Cart servlet invoked when the
3   // Web form cart.html is submitted
4   // M. Liu
5
6   import javax.servlet.http.*;
7   import java.io.*;
8   import java.util.*;
9
10  public class Cart extends HttpServlet
11  {
12    public void doPost(HttpServletRequest request,
13        HttpServletResponse response)
14        throws ServletException, IOException {
15
16
17      /* Retrieve the session object or create
18         a new one */
19      HttpSession session = request.getSession(true);
20
21      Integer itemCount =
22        (Integer) session.getAttribute("itemCount");
23      Vector items =
24        (Vector) session.getValue("items");
25      /* If no item has been selected so far,
26         set the count to zero and create a vector. */
27      if (itemCount == null) {
28        itemCount = new Integer(0);
29        items = new Vector( );
30      }
31
32      // It is recommended that you obtain the session
33      // object prior to writing any output.
```

(continued on next page)

```
34          PrintWriter out = response.getWriter( );
35          response.setContentType("text/html");
36
37          /* Retrieve the request parameters */
38          Enumeration keys;
39          String name, value, prefix;
40          int count = itemCount.intValue( );
41          keys = request.getParameterNames();
42          while (keys.hasMoreElements())
43          {
44            name = (String)keys.nextElement();
45            prefix = name.substring(0,4);
46            out.println("name=" + name + " prefix=" +
47            prefix);
48            if (prefix.equals("item"))
49            {
50              // add item to list of items
51              value = request.getParameter(name);
52              out.println("adding to items:" +
53                value + " count=" + count);
54              items.add(value);
55              count++;
56            }//end if
57          } //end while
58          itemCount = new Integer(count);
59          session.putValue("itemCount", itemCount);
60          if (items != null)
61            session.setAttribute("items", items);
62
63          /* Issue a redirect to invoke another servlet
64             to generate a display of the items in the
65             shopping cart */
66
67          response.sendRedirect
68            ("http://localhost:8080/examples/servlet/Cart2");
69      } //end doPost
70
71  } //end class
```

Figure 11.20 The *Cart2* servlet using a session object.

```
1  // Servlet to view what is in the shopping cart (as recorded
2  // by the use a session object in the Cart servlet)
3  // M. Liu, based on various sources
4
5  import javax.servlet.*;
6  import javax.servlet.http.*;
7  import java.io.*;
8  import java.util.*;
9
10 public class Cart2 extends HttpServlet {
11
```

(continued on next page)

```
12   /* View items in shopping cart */
13     public void doGet(HttpServletRequest request,
14         HttpServletResponse response)
15         throws ServletException, IOException {
16
17
18         // Retreieve the session object, if any
19         HttpSession session = request.getSession(false);
20         Integer itemCount;
21         Vector items = null;
22         if (session == null)
23         {
24             //no session object has been created
25             itemCount = new Integer(0);
26         }
27         else
28         {
29             itemCount =
30                 (Integer) session.getValue("itemCount");
31             items =
32                 (Vector) session.getValue("items");
33         }
34         // It is recommended that you obtain the session
35         // object prior to writing any output.
36         PrintWriter out = response.getWriter( );
37         response.setContentType("text/html");
38
39         out.println("<html>");
40         out.println("<head><title>Servlet Response" +
41           "</title></head>");
42         out.println("<body>");
43         out.println("<body bgcolor=\"beige\">");
44         out.println
45           ("Contents of your shopping cart " +
46           " using session object<UL>");
47
48         int count = itemCount.intValue( );
49         /* Retrieve the items from the session object*/
50         for (int i = 0; i < count; i++)
51             out.println("<LI>" + items.get(i));
52
53         out.println("</UL>");
54         out.println("<HR>");
55         out.println("</body></html>");
56
57     } // end doGet
58
59   } // end Cart2
```

This concludes the introduction to servlets. The material that has been presented provides an overview of the technology. At the end of the chapter, you will find exercises that allow you to experiment with servlets.

A technology that is closely related to servlet is **Java Server Page** (JPS) [java.sun.com, 25], which allows you to create a Web page with embedded servlet code. The use of JSP can significantly simplify the coding for generating Web pages dynamically in a servlet. Interested readers should consult references [java.sun.com, 25] and [javaboutique.internet.com, 26].

11.3 Web Services

In Chapter 3 we introduced the *network service* paradigm for distributed computing. Using this paradigm, an application performs some of its tasks by making use of ready-made services available on the network. In such an application, network services can be integrated dynamically, on an as needed basis.

This paradigm has been extended to **Web services**, a technology that has emerged recently. Web services provide network services transported by HTTP, and they are promoted as a new way to build network applications from distributed components (services) that are language and platform independent. Protocols and APIs for the technology are still evolving. In this section, we will look into one of the protocols, the **Simple Object Access Protocol (SOAP)** [w3.org, 9], and we will look at one sample API, the **Apache SOAP API**.

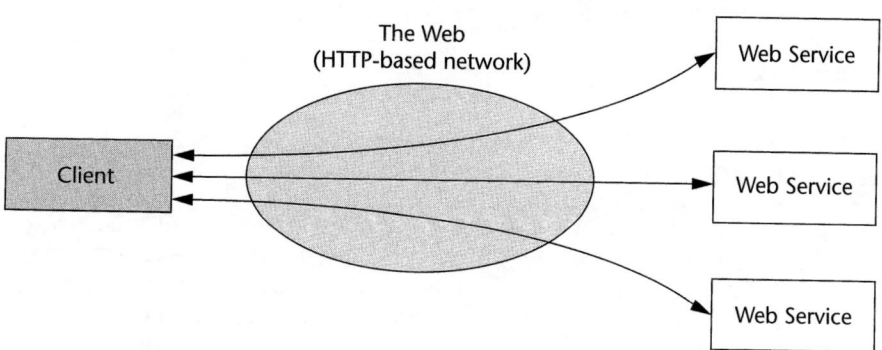

Figure 11.21 The conceptual model of Web services.

Figure 11.21 illustrates the conceptual model of Web services. A Web service is provided by a server object and is accessed by a client. The server and client exchange messages in accordance with standard protocols developed for Web services. Figure 11.22 depicts the protocol hierarchy. Logically, the server and client exchange messages at the **application layer**. Physically, a series of protocols are required to support the message exchange. A **service discovery protocol** allows the service to be registered and located. The functionalities provided at the **service description layer** allow a service to be described to the directory. The **messaging layer** supports the mechanisms for interprocess communication, including the functionalities for data marshaling. The **transport layer** delivers the messages. Finally, the **network layer** represents the network protocol hierarchy for the physical transmission and routing of data packets.

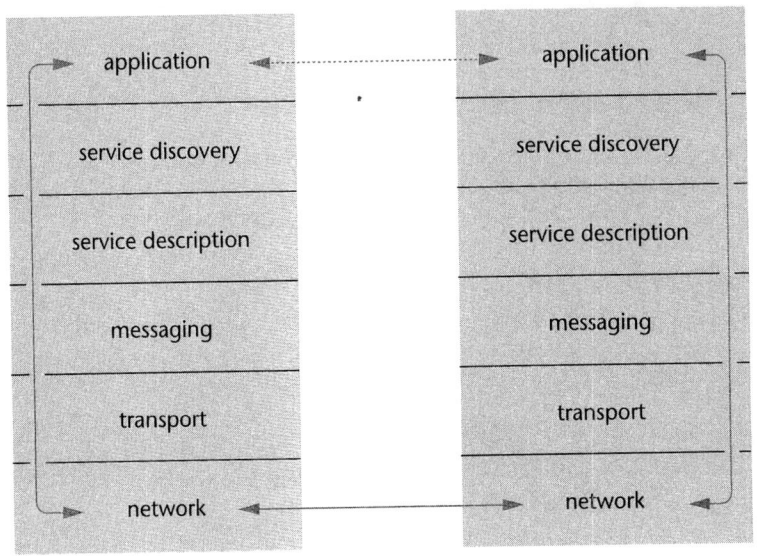

Figure 11.22 The Web service protocol hierarchy.

Jabber is an open, XML-based protocol for instant messaging and presence [jabber.org, 23].

Figure 11.23 illustrates the prevalent protocols used for Web services. For service discovery, the standard protocol is called **UDDI (Universal Description, Discovery, and Integration)** [uddi.org, 21]. The syntax and semantics for describing services are specified using the **WSDL (Web Service Description Language)** [w3.org, 22]. At the message layer, **XML**-encoded messages are exchanged according to **SOAP** [mole.informatik.uni-stuttgart.de, 9; sun.com, 10; Edwards, 11]. At the transport layer, **HTTP** serves to transmit the requests and responses, **SMTP** or **Jabber** is used to transmit messages, and **TCP** is used to transmit the data. Finally, **IP** is the network layer protocol.

Figure 11.24 illustrates the software architecture for a Web service. A service listener on the server host listens for service requests transmitted over the Web. When a request is received, it is forwarded to a proxy for the service. The proxy invokes the application logic in the service object and relays the return value to the caller.

Although each of the protocols mentioned in Figure 11.23 is of interest, SOAP is particularly relevant to our ongoing discussion. The rest of this chapter will concentrate on the SOAP protocol and its applications.

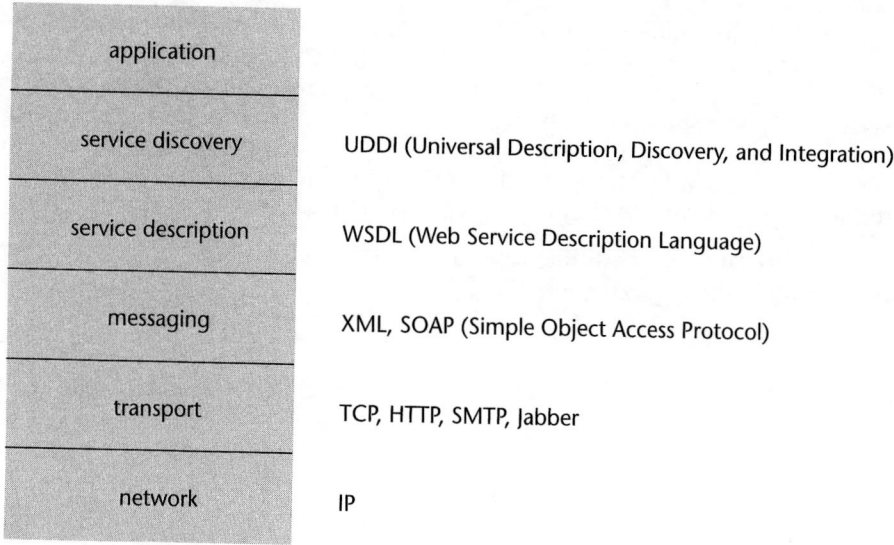

Figure 11.23 Web service protocols.

Figure 11.24 Web service software architecture.

11.4 **The Simple Object Access Protocol (SOAP)**

In past chapters we have studied the distributed objects paradigm, including two protocols/architectures that support the paradigm: Java RMI and CORBA. SOAP is a protocol that incorporates the distributed objects paradigm and Internet protocols. Specifically, it is a protocol that extends HTTP to allow access to distributed objects that represent Web services.

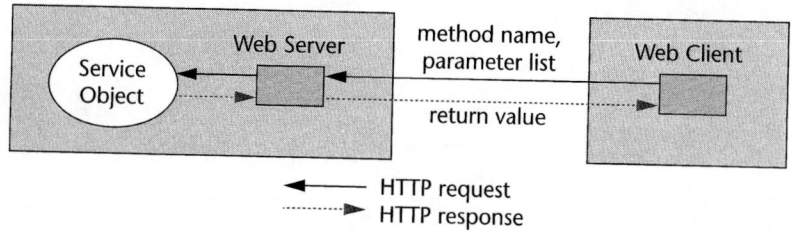

Figure 11.25 The SOAP model.

Figure 11.25 illustrates the model for the Simple Object Access Protocol. A Web client issues an HTTP request, whose body contains a SOAP formatted message that represents a method call to a service object. The request is transmitted to a Web server, which forwards the request, along with parameters for the method call to the named method. The method is then invoked. Upon its completion, the value returned by the method is sent to the Web server and then transmitted to the Web client in the body of the HTTP response.

For interoperability, SOAP messages are encoded in XML. Each SOAP message has a simple format, as depicted in Figure 11.26.

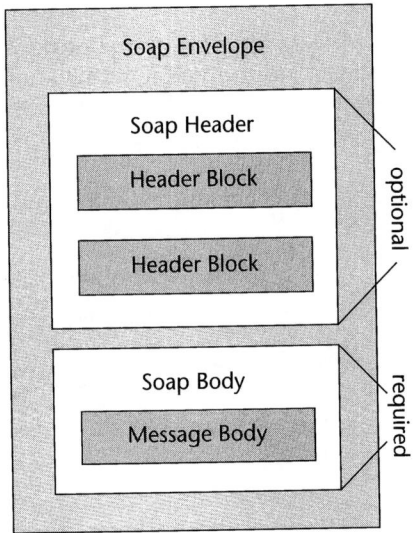

Figure 11.26 The layout of a SOAP request message.

Each SOAP message is carried in an HTTP request or response, as will be explained in the following sections.

A SOAP Request

Figure 11.27 illustrates the syntax of a HTTP request that carries a SOAP request. The elements of the HTTP request are described in the following paragraphs.

Figure 11.27 A HTTP request that carries a SOAP request (*Source:* [soapware.org, 11]).

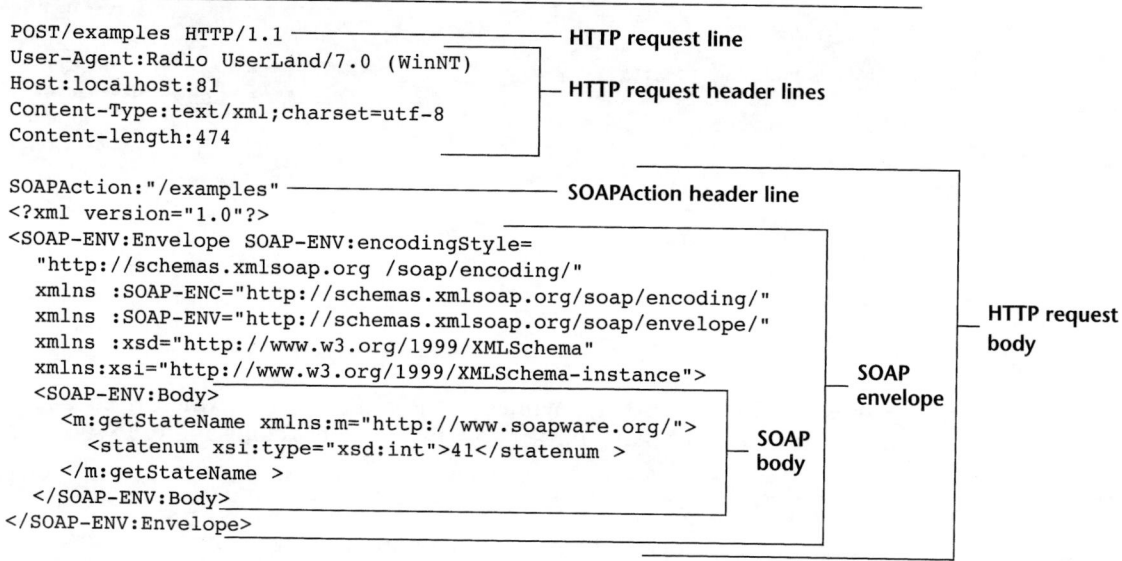

HTTP Request Header Lines

The URI in the first line of the HTTP request header should specify the object to which the remote method call is directed. In the example above, the remote object is /examples. The *User-Agent* and *Host* header lines must be specified.

The *Content Type* should be specified as *text/xml*. The *charset* is a specification of the character representation employed; the default is *US-ASCII*. Other acceptable *charset* specifications are *UTF-8* and *UTF-16*, which are Unicode encoding schemes.

The *Content Length*, if specified, should be the byte length of the request body.

The *SOAPAction* header line specifies the remote object to which the request is to be directed. The interpretation of this header element is up to the program. In most cases, the URI (specified in the first header line) and the *SOAPAction* header will have the same value.

Figure 11.28 A SOAP request (*Source:* [soapware.org, 11]).

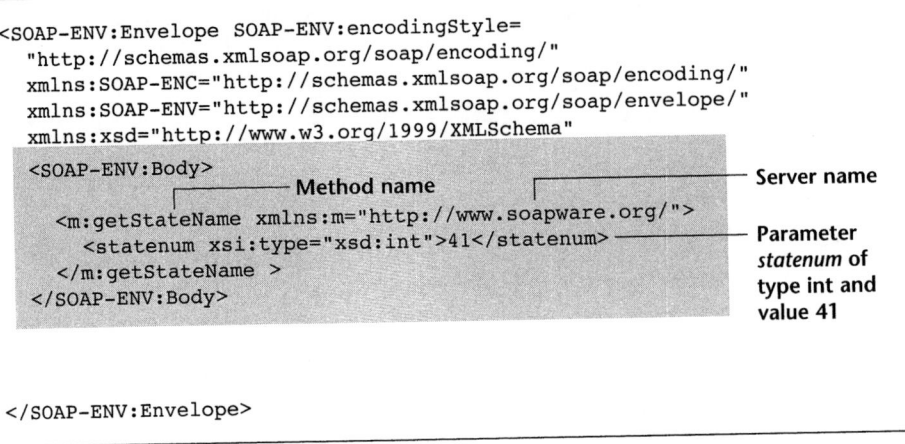

```
<SOAP-ENV:Envelope SOAP-ENV:encodingStyle=
   "http://schemas.xmlsoap.org/soap/encoding/"
   xmlns:SOAP-ENC="http://schemas.xmlsoap.org/soap/encoding/"
   xmlns:SOAP-ENV="http://schemas.xmlsoap.org/soap/envelope/"
   xmlns:xsd="http://www.w3.org/1999/XMLSchema"
```

```
  <SOAP-ENV:Body>
                              ─── Method name                            ─── Server name
    <m:getStateName xmlns:m="http://www.soapware.org/">
      <statenum xsi:type="xsd:int">41</statenum> ─── Parameter
    </m:getStateName >                                   statenum of
  </SOAP-ENV:Body>                                       type int and
                                                         value 41
```

```
</SOAP-ENV:Envelope>
```

The Request Body

Figure 11.28 highlights the syntax of the request body, which is encoded in XML. There are two parts in the body: the SOAP envelope and the SOAP body.

The SOAP Envelope   This SOAP envelope is defined with the *<SOAP-ENV:Envelope>* element. The element contains a set of required attributes specifying the encoding scheme and envelope style.

The SOAP Body   The SOAP body is defined with the *<SOAP-ENV:Body>* tag. The SOAP body contains a single element, which represents the method call. Specified within the element are the method name (*getStateName* in our example), the name of each parameter (*statenum* in our example), the value of each parameter (4 in our example), and the data type of each parameter.

Data Types

SOAP has a rich set of language-independent data types that are based on XML Schema data types. The full coverage of the data types is beyond the scope of this book; interested readers are referred to [w3.org, 24].

Table 11.8 summarizes a subset of the key scalar data types supported by a subset of SOAP 1.1.

Table 11.8 Sclar XML Schema Data Types (*Source:* [soapware.org, 11])

Attribute Value	Type	Example
xsd:int	32-bit signed integer	–12
xsd:boolean	A boolean value, 1 or 0	1
xsd:string	A string of characters	hello world
xsd:float or xsd:double	A signed floating point number	–12.214
xsd:timeInstant	Date/time	2001-03-27T00:00:01-08:00
SOAP-ENC:base64	base64-encoded binary	eW91IGNhbid0IHJlYWQ gdGhpcyE=

Non-scalar data types, including objects, structs, arrays, vectors, and enumeration are also supported in SOAP. Some of these types are discussed in the following sections.

Structs A value can be a **struct**, which is specified by an XML element that contains subelements. Structs can be nested and may contain any other data type, including an array.

Following is an example of a two-element struct:

```
<param>
  <lowerBound xsi:type="xsd:int">18</lowerBound>
  <upperBound xsi:type="xsd:int">139</upperBound>
</param>
```

The names of struct elements are significant; the order of the elements is not.

Arrays A value can be an array, which is specified by an XML element with a *SOAP-ENC:arrayType* attribute whose value begins with *ur-type*[<the number of array elements>].

The following is an example of a four-element array:

```
<param SOAP-ENC:arrayType="xsd:ur-type[4]"
xsi:type="SOAP-ENC:Array">
<item xsi:type="xsd:int">12</item>
<item xsi:type="xsd:string">Egypt</item>
<item xsi:type="xsd:boolean">0</item>
<item xsi:type="xsd:int">-31</item>
<param>
```

The order of array elements is significant; the names of the elements are not.

A **struct** is a type of data structure in the C language and its derivative C++. It is also called a *record*.

Objects An object can be transmitted in a SOAP request/response if the service provider defines and registers the object type as a subtype, and the two sides provide the appropriate object serializer and de-serializer, respectively. The name of the subtype is then declared as the *xsi:type* attribute of the parameter.

A SOAP Response

Figure 11.29 shows an HTTP response that contains a successful SOAP response. The HTTP header follows the usual format. Note that the content type is *text/xml*.

Figure 11.29 An HTTP response that contains a successful SOAP response (*Source:* [soapware.org, 11]).

```
HTTP/1.1 200 OK
Connection: close
Content-Length: 499
Content-Type: text/xml; charset=utf-8
Date: Wed, 28 Mar 2001 05:05:04 GMT
Server: UserLand Frontier/7.0-WinNT

<?xml version="1.0"?>
<SOAP-ENV:Envelope SOAP-
ENV:encodingStyle="http://schemas.xmlsoap.org/soap/encoding/" xmlns:SOAP-
ENC="http://schemas.xmlsoap.org/soap/encoding/"
xmlns:SOAP-ENV="http://schemas.xmlsoap.org/soap/envelope/"
xmlns:xsd="http://www.w3.org/1999/XMLSchema"
xmlns:xsi="http://www.w3.org/1999/XMLSchema-instance">
   <SOAP-ENV:Body>
     <m:getStateNameResponse xmlns:m="http://www.soapware.org/">
       <Result xsi:type="xsd:string">South Dakota</Result>
       </m:getStateNameResponse>
     </SOAP-ENV:Body>
   </SOAP-ENV:Envelope>
```

Figure 11.30 highlights the SOAP response contained in the HTTP response. As with the SOAP request, the response is composed of two parts: the **envelope** and the **body**.

The syntax for the envelope is the same as with the request. The syntax for the body is also analogous to that of the request. The single element contained in the *<SOAP-ENV:Body>* has a name that matches the name of the method that was called, with the word *Response* attached to the end of the method name (*getStateName* in our example). The data type (string) and value (South Dakota) of the returned value is contained in the *Result* subelement.

Figure 11.30 A SOAP response (*Source:* [soapware.org, 11]).

```
<?xml version="1.0"?>
<SOAP-ENV:Envelope SOAP-ENV:
  encodingStyle ="http://schemas.xmlsoap.org /soap/encoding/"
  xmlns:SOAP-ENC="http://schemas.xmlsoap.org /soap/encoding/"
  xmlns:SOAP-ENV="http://schemas.xmlsoap.org /soap/envelope/"
  xmlns:xsd="http://www.w3.org/1999/XMLSchema"
  xmlns:xsi="http://www.w3.org/1999/XMLSchema-instance">

  <SOAP-ENV:Body>            ── Method name                    ┌── Server name
    <m:getStateNam eResponse xmlns:m="http://www.soapware.org/">
       <Result xsi:type="xsd:string">South Dakota</Result> ──── Returned
    </m:getStateName Response >                                   value
  </SOAP-ENV:Body>

</SOAP-ENV:Envelope>
```

A SOAP method call may fail, perhaps due to errors in the specification of the method name or parameters. When a method call cannot be completed successfully, the HTTP response (see Figure 11.31) contains a SOAP body that defines a fault code and a fault string. The fault code (*SOAP-ENV:Client* in our example) identifies the fault, while the fault string provides a description of the fault.

Figure 11.31 An HTTP response that contains a failed SOAP method call (*Source:* [soapware.org, 11]).

```
HTTP/1.1 500 Server Error
Connection: close
Content-Length: 511
Content-Type: text/xml; charset=utf-8
Date: Wed, 28 Mar 2001 05:06:32 GMT
Server: UserLand Frontier/7.0-WinNT

<?xml version="1.0"?>
<SOAP-ENV:Envelope SOAP-
ENV:encodingStyle="http://schemas.xmlsoap.org/soap/encoding/" xmlns:SOAP-
ENV="http://schemas.xmlsoap.org/soap/envelope/"
xmlns:xsd="http://www.w3.org/1999/XMLSchema"
xmlns:xsi="http://www.w3.org/1999/XMLSchema-instance">
  <SOAP-ENV:Body>
    <SOAP-ENV:Fault>
      <faultcode>SOAP-ENV:Client</faultcode>
      <faultstring>Can't call getStateName because there are too many
       parameters.</faultstring>
    </SOAP-ENV:Fault>
  </SOAP-ENV:Body>
</SOAP-ENV:Envelope>
```

Apache SOAP

Apache Axis is "a follow on to Apache SOAP" [xml.apache.org, 20]. It is a reimplementation of Apache SOAP, with supposedly improved run-time performance.

As you can see from the preceding description, writing code to directly generate the XML syntax for SOAP requests and responses would be tedious and error-prone. Hence numerous APIs for SOAP have emerged that provide the necessary abstraction to facilitate programming involving SOAP requests/responses. Among the SOAP toolkits available are *Apache SOAP* and *Apache Axis* for Java programming; and *SOAP::Lite* for Perl programming. Microsoft's .net also supports SOAP.

The rest of this section will provide an overview of the Apache SOAP API [xmethods.com, 12; 106.ibm.com, 13; xml.apache.org, 14; xml.apache.org, 15] for building a service client and for building a service object. We will first look at some important classes from Apache SOAP, and then we will look at some sample programs.

The *RPCMessage* Class

The Apache SOAP API provides a class called *RPCMessage* to encapsulate a SOAP request. An object of this class contains the following instance fields: *targetObjectURI*, *methodName*, *params*, and *header*, representing the various fields in a SOAP request. The class has methods for setting and retrieving the value of each of these fields.

The *Call* Class

The *Call* Class is a subclass of the *RPCMessage* Class, and represents a remote method call. An object of this class can be created in a SOAP client program, which may then call the *invoke* method to make the remote method call. Table 11.9 presents the specification of the *invoke* method.

Table 11.9 The *invoke* method of the *Call* Class

Method	Description
public *Response invoke* (*URL* url, *String* SOAPActionURI) throws *SOAPException*	Invoke this call at the specified URL

The *Parameter* Class

An object of the *Parameter* class represents a parameter as well as the return value of a method call. In the client program, an object of this class is created for each remote method parameter by invoking the constructor of this class, whose specification is shown in table 11.10. In the server, an object of this class is constructed for the return value.

Table 11.10 The constructor of the *Parameter* class

Constructor	Description

public *Parameter*(*String* name,
    Class type,
    Object value,
    String encodingStyleURI)
	Create a Parameter object of the given name, data type, value, and encoding style.

The *Response* Class

An object of the *Response* class represents the response to a method call. Both the client and the server use *Response* objects to represent the result of a method invocation. The server formulates the response. The client extracts information from the response. The key methods of the *Response* class are presented in Table 11.11.

Table 11.11 Key method of the Response Class

Method	Description
public *Parameter* getReturnValue( )	This method is invoked by a client to receive the value returned by the method call.
public boolean *generatedFault*( )	This method is invoked by a client to seee if a method call has resulted in an error. The method returns true if an error has occurred.
public *Fault getFault*()	This method can be invoked by a client to analyze the error that caused the failure of a method call.

The *Fault* Class

An object of the *Fault* class represents the contents and semantics of a <SOAP-ENV:Fault> element, and is returned by the *getFault* method issued by a client. In our sample code, the method *getFaultString* (table 11.12) is invoked by a client to receive a description of the error that caused a method call to fail.

Table 11.12 The getFaultString method of the Fault Class

Method	Description
public *String getFaultString*( )	Returns a string that contains a brief description of the error that caused the failure of a method call.

Ready-Made Web Services

The idea of Web services is to allow software developers to make use of ready-made services. As envisioned, such services will range from for-profit services provided by commercial vendors (such as credit card validation) to free services provided by a user community (such as network games or language translation).

A number of free Web services are currently available for those who are interested in experimenting with the technology. Reference [xmethods.net, 16] provides a list of such services, many of which are accessible using the Apache SOAP API.

An example of such a service is described in [xmethods.net, 16] and shown in Figure 11.32.

Figure 11.32 Description of a sample ready-made Web service.

```
XMethods ID 8
Service Owner:xmethods.net
Contact Email:support@xmethods.net
Service Home Page:
Description:Current temperature in a given U.S.zipcode region.
SOAP Implementation:Apache SOAP
```

With each service listed in [xmethods.net, 16], a service profile is provided, as shown in Figure 11.33.

Figure 11.33 Description of a sample ready-made Web service.

Method Name	`getTemp`
Endpoint URL	`http://services.xmethods.net:80/soap/servlet/rpcrouter`
SOAPAction	
Method Namespace	`URI urn:xmethods-Temperature`
Input Parameters	`zipcode string`
Output Parameters	`return float`

The profile contains information for invoking the service, including the URL of the service object (http://services.xmethods.net:80/soap/servlet/rpcrouter, in the example), the name of the method (*getTemp*, in this case) or methods provided by the service, and the parameters (a string) and return value (a float) of the method.

Invoking a Web Service Using Apache SOAP

Figure 11.34 shows the source code for a sample program that invokes a SOAP service.

In lines 1–6, the client program imports the various packages required by Apache/SOAP. To prepare for an invocation of a method provided by the Web service, the program instantiates a *Call* object and assigns values to its fields using the object's methods (lines 26–34):

```
Call call = new Call(); // prepare the service invocation
call.setEncodingStyleURI( Constants.NS_URI_SOAP_ENC );
call.setTargetObjectURI("urn:xmethods-Temperature" );
call.setMethodName( "getTemp" );
```

The *setTargetObjectURI* method is specified with a URI that identifies the SOAP service object on the remote host. In our example, the URL is the one listed with "Method Namespace" in Figure 11.33.

To prepare the arguments for the invocation, an object of the *Parameter* class is instantiated for each parameter. Each *Parameter* object is initialized with the name of the argument, the data type of the argument, the value of the argument, and the encoding style for the argument (the default is null), as on lines 37–38:

```
Parameter aParam = new Parameter("zipcode", String.class, zipcode, null);
```

The parameter name(s) ("*zipcode*") and data type(s) (*String.class*) are listed in the Web service description shown in Figure 11.33. For simplicity, the input parameter value is hard-coded on line 14 in the sample code, but it can be obtained at run time.

The list of parameters is collected in a *Vector* (lines 39–40):

```
Vector params = new Vector ();
params.addElement (aParam);
```

And the vector is then bound to the *Call* object (line 41):

```
call.setParams( params );
```

To make the Web service method call, the *invoke( )* method of the *Call* object is specified with a URL (line 44):

```
Response response = call.invoke( url, "" );
```

where *URL* refers to an object of the Java URL class, instantiated with the Web service's URL (lines 12–13):

```
URL url = new URL( "http://localhost:8080/soap/servlet/rpcrouter" );
```

The URL can be found in the Web service description (listed as Endpoint URL in Figure 11.33). The method invocation should be checked for errors (lines 47–53), and, if none occurred, the returned value(s) can then be used in the processing of the rest of the program (lines 57–59).

Figure 11.34 A sample Web service client.

```
1  import java.io.*;
2  import java.net.*;
3  import java.util.*;
4  import org.apache.soap.util.xml.*;
5  import org.apache.soap.*;
6  import org.apache.soap.rpc.*;
7
```

(continued on next page)

```
 8  public class TempClient{
 9
10     public static void main(String[] args) {
11       try {
12         URL url= new URL(
13             "http://services.xmethods.com:80/soap/servlet/rpcrouter"
14         String zipcode= "93420";
15         float temp = getTemp(url, zipcode);
16         System.out.println("The temperature is " + temp);
17       }
18       catch (Exception e) {
19         e.printStackTrace();
20       }
21     } //end main
22
23     public static float getTemp (URL url, String zipcode)
24         throws Exception {
25
26       Call call = new Call ();
27
28       // SOAP encoding specification
29       String encodingStyleURI = Constants.NS_URI_SOAP_ENC;
30       call.setEncodingStyleURI(encodingStyleURI);
31
32       // Set service locator parameters
33       call.setTargetObjectURI ("urn:xmethods-Temperature");
34       call.setMethodName ("getTemp");
35
36       // Create parameter vector
37       Parameter aParam =
38         new Parameter("zipcode", String.class, zipcode, null);
39       Vector params = new Vector ();
40       params.addElement (aParam);
41       call.setParams (params);
42
43       // Invoke the service
44       Response resp = call.invoke (url,"");
45
46       // Process the response
47       if (resp.generatedFault ()) {
48         // The call was unsuccessful
49         Fault f = resp.getFault(); // an error occurred
50           System.err.println( "Fault= " + f.getFaultCode() +
51           ", " + f.getFaultString() );
52         throw new Exception( );
53       }
54       else {
55         // The call was successful.
56         // Extract return value and return the result
57         Parameter result = resp.getReturnValue ();
58         Float readOut=(Float) result.getValue();
59         return readOut.floatValue();
60       }
61     } //end getTemp
62
63  } //end class
```

Implementing a Web Service Using Apache SOAP

A Web service is defined using a Java interface, which contains declarations of the methods provided by the service. Figure 11.35 shows the interface *ITemp* for a sample Web service, *Temp*, which provides the *getTemp* method called by our sample client in Figure 11.34.

Figure 11.35 A Java interface for a simple Web service.

```
1   // A sample SOAP service object interface
2   // This method accepts a string containing a zip code,
3   // and returns the temperature of the area.
4
5   public interface ITemp
6   {
7     float getTemp( String zipCode);
8
9   } //end interface
```

The interface of a Web service is implemented as a Java class. Figure 11.36 shows a sample definition of the class *Temp*, which implements the *ITemp* interface. For simplicity, a fixed value is returned.

Figure 11.36 The implementation of a simple Web service.

```
1   // A sample SOAP service object inplementation
2
3   public class Temp implements ITemp
4   {
5     public float getTemp( String zipCode )
6     {
7       /**/ System.out.println
8       ( "Temperature for zip code " + zipCode + " requested.");
9       return 74.5F; // returns a constant for simplicity
10
11    } // end getTemp
12
13  } //end class
```

A SOAP service needs to be deployed on its host system. The procedure for deployment is implementation dependent. For Apache SOAP, the information can be found in references [xmethods.com, 12] and [xml.apache.org,14].

Summary

This chapter has presented three protocols and mechanisms for Internet applications.

Applets

- An applet is a Java class whose code is downloaded from a Web server and then run in a browser's environment on a client host.
- An applet is requested by a browser when it scans a Web page and encounters a class specified with the *APPLET* tag.
- For security reasons, the execution of an applet is subject to restrictions: By definition, an applet is prohibited from access files in the file system on the client host and from making network connections to a host other than the one from which it originated.

Servlets

- A servlet is an extension to a request-response server. An HTTP servlet is, like a CGI script, an extension to an HTTP server.
- An HTTP servlet is a Java class whose code is loaded into a servlet container on the server host, and is then initiated by the HTTP server in response to an HTTP request for a servlet.
- Unlike CGI script, an HTTP servlet is persistent: A CGI script is reloaded each time a client issues a request for it, whereas a single instance of a servlet will run for at least as long as there are requests issued to it.
- For servlet programming: The *HTTPServletRequest* class encapsulates an HTTP request, while the *HTTPServletResponse* class encapsulates the response.
- For state information maintenance, a servlet can use the mechanisms available to a CGI script, such as hidden form fields or cookies. In addition, state information can be maintained as follows:
  - The servlet's instance variables may hold global data.
  - A session object containing session data objects may be created and maintained on the host where the servlet is run.

Simple Object Access Protocol

- SOAP is a protocol that makes use of HTTP requests and responses to effect remote method calls to Web services.
- A SOAP method call is embedded in an HTTP request and is encoded in XML; the return value of a method call is embedded in an HTTP response and encoded in XML.
- A number of SOAP APIs are available for programming Web services and client method calls. The Apache API was introduced in this chapter.

Exercises

Note: Some of these exercises require a Web server that supports applets and servlets. For the servlet programming exercises, you may consider downloading and installing either the Apache Tomcat Server [apache.org, 18] or the Java *JSWDK* server on your PC.

Applet Exercises

1. Install *HelloWorld.html* and *HelloWorld.class* (compiled from *HelloWorld.java*) on a Web server to which you have access. If the server is a UNIX machine, be sure to set the permissions to these files to world readable and executable.
   Use a browser to browse *HelloWorld.html*. Describe the outcome and explain the events behind the scenes.

2. Modify *NetConnectApplet.java* to replace the host name www.alpha.edu with that of the Web server you are using for these exercises. Install *MyApplet.html* and *NetConnectApplet.class* (compiled from *NetConnectApplet.java*) on the Web server. Use your browser to browse *MyApplet.html*. Did the applet successfully make the socket connection?

3. Further modify *NetConnectApplet.java* to replace the host name www.beta.edu with that of another Web server, and uncomment the portion that is currently commented-out. Compile and file the new version on the Web server that you used for Exercise 2. Use your browser to browse *MyApplet.html*. Did the applet successfully make both socket connections? Describe and explain the outcome.

4. What are the two security-related restrictions on applets mentioned in this chapter? With each of the restrictions, explain why the restrictions are necessary.

General Servlet Exercises

1. Fill in the following tables to compare servlets with applets.

Implementation	Applet	Servlet
Programming language.		
What is the base class that the applet/server class should inherit from?		
Software support required to run the program (server side).		
Software support required to run the program (client side).		

(continued on next page)

Implementation	Applet	Servlet
Where is the program executed (server side/client side)?		
Show the text of a sample HTTP request to invoke the program.		
How is the program loaded for execution?		
Name a good use of this type of program in a Web application.		
Restrictions, if any, on this type of program (for security concerns).		
List other differences that you can think of.		

2. Fill in the table below to compare and contrast servlets with CGI scripts.

Implementation	Servlets	CGI Scripts
Programming language(s).		
Software support required to run the program.		
Show the text of a sample HTTP request to invoke the program.		
How is the program loaded for execution?		
Is the program persistent? (That is, is the same instance of the program run for multiple invocations?)		
Name the mechanisms that can be used for session data maintenance.		
List other differences that you can think of.		

Servlet Programming Exercises

The program files referred to in these exercises can be found in the *servlets\simple* folder in the program samples for this chapter.

1. Start the Apache Tomcat server [jakarta.apache.org, 6] if it has not already been started on your computer. Try out the servlet examples that come with the server by entering this URL in your browser:

```
http://<server host name>:8080
```

Choose the *Servlet Examples* link. You will see a set of servlet examples; for each you may view the source or choose to execute. Look at the source code of each, then execute it. Note the URL path displayed in the browser when the servlet is executed: This is the URL path that you should specify for your servlets. On the Apache Tomcat Server, the default path is http://localhost:8080/examples/servlet/. For example, browsing to http://localhost:8080/examples/servlet/HelloWorld will execute the *HelloWorldExample* servlet.

2. Open a directory on your PC to obtain the files in the *servlets\simple* folder. Compile *HelloWorld.java* and *Counter2.java*. Then file them into the designated servlets class directory. (On the Apache Tomcat Server, the default servlet class directory is TOMCAT_HOME\webapps\examples\WEB-INF\classes.)

   a. User the browser to run the *HelloWorld* servlet.

   b. To see that servlets can be run on a server host other than your *localhost*, use the browser on your system to run the *HelloWorld* servlet on your instructor's system or your neighbor's system.

   c. Compile the *Counter1.java* file, and install the resulting class file *Counter1.class* to the <servlet calss file directory>. Then browse to it using the <servlet URL path>. Refresh the browser repeatedly to run the *Counter1* servlet several times. Describe and explain the counter value displayed by the browser successively.

   d. Open another browser and browse to the *Counter1* servlet. Describe and explain the counter value displayed by the browser.

   e. Close the browser windows. Then open a new browser window and browse to the *Counter1* servlet. Describe and explain the counter value displayed by the browser.

   f. Stop the server and then restart it. Then refresh the browser window so that the *Counter1* servlet is reexecuted. Describe and explain the counter value displayed by the browser.

   g. Based on the experiments with *Counter1*, describe the lifetime of a servlet in the environment of the Jakarta Tomcat Server.

   h. Modify *Counter1.java* so that the counter value is incremented by 2 each time. Recompile and reinstall the class file. (*Note*: On some servers, such as JSWDK, you must shut down the server and restart it before the new servlet will take effect.) Show the code change.

   j. Compile *GetForm.java* and *PostForm.java*. Install the resulting class files to the server class file directory.

   k. Browse the page *GetForm.html* then *PostForm.html*. Did the servlets run properly? Compare the outputs—including the URL displayed in the browser—with those generated using CGI scripts.

3. Write an HTML Web form and the accompanying servlet for a simple login control for your home page.

The page displayed should be as follows:

> Please login:
>
> Name: [   ]
> Password: [   ]
> [Submit]

If the account data (for example: Name is "lucky" and Password is "12345") is correctly entered when the form is submitted, your home page will be displayed; otherwise, an "Invalid data" message should be displayed. Install the servlet and test it.

(*Note:* To transfer to your home page after the password has been verified, the servlet will need to output a line as follows:

```
<html><head><META HTTP-EQUIV="REFRESH" CONTENT="0;URL=<url for your
home page>"></head></html>
```

Don't forget that a double quote character within a string needs to be escaped via a preceding backslash.)

Show the source code of your servlet.

Using Cookies with Servlets

Note: Be sure to open a new browser session when you run or rerun each of these experiments, since the cookies generated in a session will persist throughout a session.

1. Copy the files in the *servlets\cookies* samples folder to a folder.

2. Comment out the statement at the end of *Cart.java* that redirects to the *Cart2* servlet.

3. Compile and install the *Cart* servlet. Browse *Cart.html* and select "orange." Check the output displayed when you submit the form.

4. Undo the changes made in step 2 so that the *Cart* servlet will redirect to *Cart2*. Compile and install the *Cart2* servlet.

Browse *Cart.html*. Select one item first. Check that it is in the shopping cart as displayed. Browse *Cart2.html* and check that the shopping cart is displayed correctly.

Use the back button in your browser to return to *Cart.html*. Select another item. Check your shopping cart again.

Use the back button in your browser again to return to *Cart.html*. Select the last item. Check your shopping cart again. Describe and explain your observations.

5. Uncomment the *setMaxAge* method call in *Cart.java* so that the cookies generated are nontransient. Compile and reinstall the *Cart* servlet. Open two separate browser sessions and browse to *Cart.html* in each page. Select an item in the first session, submit it, then select a different item in the second session. Submit the second page.

    Describe and explain your observations.

    To get rid of the nontransient cookies: Modify the *setMaxAge* method call so that the argument is zero. Compile and reinstall the *Cart* servlet. Open a fresh browser session and browse to *Cart.html*. Select all three items. When you submit the form, you should see an empty shopping cart.

6. Comment out the *setMaxAge* method call in *Cart.java* so that the cookies generated are transient. Modify the Web forms and servlets to (i) allow the user to choose the quantity of each item to buy (e.g., four oranges), and (ii) include in the display the total price of all items currently in the shopping cart.

    Suggested course of action:

    a. Modify *Cart.html* to add an input field for the quantity for each item, as follows:

```
<TR>
  <TD ALIGN="center"><INPUT TYPE="Checkbox"
    NAME="item_a" VALUE="apple $1"></TD>
  <TD ALIGN="left">apple</TD>
  <TD ALIGN="left">How many?
  <input name="quantity_item_a"></TD>
</TR>
```

    Browse the modified page to make sure that the display is correct.

    b. Second, modify *Cart.java* so that the quantity entered with each selected item is attached to the front of the cookie value, such as: 10 apple $1, for 10 apples selected.

       Temporarily comment out the last statement (the redirect call) in *Cart.java* so you can verify the string generated for each cookie value.

    c. Modify *Cart2.java*. For each cookie value string, parse the quantity and then the price. Maintain a cumulative sum of the total price. Output the total sum when all cookies have been processed.

       The recommended code for parsing each cookie value is as follows:

```
try {
  value = cookies[i].getValue();
  out.println("<LI>" + value);
  st = new StringTokenizer(value);
  quantity = Integer.parseInt(st.nextToken( ));
  st.nextToken("$\n");
  price = Integer.parseInt(st.nextToken());
  // add code to output the
  // cookie value and process
  // item quantity and item
  // value
}
```

(continued on next page)

```
catch (Exception ex)
//NumberFormat exception
{ } // simply skip that item
```

Using a Session Object with Servlets

(*Note:* Be sure to open a new browser session when you run or rerun each of these experiments, since the session object generated in a session will persist throughout a session.)

1. Copy the files in the *servlets\session* samples folder to a folder.

2. Comment out the statement at the end of *Cart.java* that redirects to the *Cart2* servlet.

3. Compile and install the servlet *Cart*. Browse *Cart.html* and select "orange." Check the output displayed when you submit the form. See if you can verify the output by looking at the code in *Cart.java*.

4. Undo the changes made in step 2 so that the *Cart* servlet will redirect you to *Cart2*. Compile and install the *Cart2* servlet.
   Browse *Cart.html*. Select one item first. Check that it is in the shopping cart. Browse *Cart2.html* and check that the shopping cart is displayed correctly.
   Use the back button in your browser to return to *Cart.html*. Select another item. Check your shopping cart again.
   Use the back button in your browser to return to *Cart.html* again. Select the last item. Check your shopping cart again.
   Describe and explain your observations. How do they differ from part 4 of the last set of problems, when cookies were used to store the contents of the shopping cart?

5. Open two separate browser sessions and browse to *Cart.html* in each. Make a selection in one browser, submit it, then make a different selection in the other browser, and submit it. Describe and explain your observations. How does the session behave differently from part 5 of the last set of problems, when cookies were used to store the contents of the shopping cart?

6. Modify the Web forms and servlets to (i) allow the user to choose the quantity of each item to buy (e.g., four oranges), and (ii) include in the display the total price of all items currently in the shopping cart.
   Suggested course of action:

   a. Modify *Cart.html* to add an input field for the quantity for each item, as follows:

   ```
   <TR>
   <TD ALIGN="center"><INPUT TYPE="Checkbox"
     NAME="item_a" VALUE="apple $1"></TD>
   <TD ALIGN="left">apple</TD>
   <TD ALIGN="left">How many? <input
     name="quantity_item_a"></TD>
   </TR>
   ```

   Browse the modified page to make sure that the display is correct.

b. Create a class called *Item*, which has the following instance data: item name, price, and quantity. *Item.java* is provided in the sample folder. Compile and move *Item.class* to the directory where the servlet class files reside.

c. Modify *Cart.java* so that each selection results in a reference to an *Item* object being added to the items vector. Temporarily comment out the last statement (the redirect call) in *Cart.java* so that you can see the value of the object being added to the session object.

Here's the suggested code:

```
while (keys.hasMoreElements())
{
  name = (String)keys.nextElement();
  prefix = name.substring(0,4);
  out.println("name=" + name + "prefix=" + prefix);
  if (prefix.equals("item"))
  {
    quantityName = "quantity_" + name;
    out.println("quantityName = " + quantityName);
    quantity = request.getParameter(quantityName);
    // add item to list of items
    value = request.getParameter(name);
    st = new StringTokenizer(value);
    name = st.nextToken("$\n");
    price = st.nextToken();
    out.println("adding name=" + name + " price=" + price +
      "quantity=" + quantity);
    items.add(new Item(name,Integer.parseInt(price),
      Integer.parseInt(quantity)));
    count++;
  }//end if
} //end while
```

Compile and install the *Cart* servlet.

When you are satisfied with the output, uncomment the redirect method call at the end of *Cart.java*.

d. Modify *Cart2.java*. For each *Item* object retrieved from the session object, extract the unit price and the quantity. Maintain a sum of the total price seen so far. Output the total sum when all *Item* objects have been processed.

Here's the suggested code:

```
for (int i = 0; i < count; i++) {
  nextItem = (Item)items.get(i);
  out.println("<LI>" + i + " " + nextItem.toString( ));
  total += nextItem.getPrice( ) * nextItem.getQuantity( );
}
```

Compile and install the *Cart2* servlet. Browse *Cart.html* and check the outcome.

7. Consider the use of session objects for session data storage. Why is it not necessary to use mututal exclusion to protect the retrieval and update of the session object?

SOAP Exercises

1. Browse the Web page http://www.xmethods.net/ [xmethods.net, 16]. Choose one of the "RPC style" services and write a Java client that uses the Apache SOAP API to call the service and display the returned value(s). Turn in the source code.

2. Consider the following HTTP request [soapware.org, 11]:

```
POST /examples HTTP/1.1
User-Agent: Radio UserLand/7.0 (WinNT)
Host: localhost:81
Content-Type: text/xml; charset=utf-8
Content-length: 474
SOAPAction: "/examples"
<?xml version="1.0"?>
<SOAP-ENV:Envelope SOAP-
ENV:encodingStyle="http://schemas.xmlsoap.org/soap/encoding/"
xmlns:SOAP-ENC="http://schemas.xmlsoap.org/soap/encoding/" xmlns:SOAP-
ENV="http://schemas.xmlsoap.org/soap/envelope/"
xmlns:xsd="http://www.w3.org/1999/XMLSchema"
xmlns:xsi="http://www.w3.org/1999/XMLSchema-instance">
    <SOAP-ENV:Body>
      <m:getStateName xmlns:m="http://www.soapware.org/">
      <statenum xsi:type="xsd:int">41</statenum>
      </m:getStateName>
    </SOAP-ENV:Body>
</SOAP-ENV:Envelope>
```

Mark up the text to identify the SOAP components in the request.

3. Consider the following HTTP response:

```
HTTP/1.1 200 OK
Connection: close
Content-Length: 499
Content-Type: text/xml; charset=utf-8
Date: Wed, 28 Mar 2001 05:05:04 GMT
Server: UserLand Frontier/7.0-WinNT
<?xml version="1.0"?>
<SOAP-ENV:Envelope SOAP-
ENV:encodingStyle="http://schemas.xmlsoap.org/soap/encoding/"
xmlns:SOAP-ENC="http://schemas.xmlsoap.org/soap/encoding/" xmlns:SOAP-
ENV="http://schemas.xmlsoap.org/soap/envelope/"
xmlns:xsd="http://www.w3.org/1999/XMLSchema"
xmlns:xsi="http://www.w3.org/1999/XMLSchema-instance">
    <SOAP-ENV:Body>
      <m:getStateNameResponse xmlns:m="http://www.soapware.org/">
      <Result xsi:type="xsd:string">South Dakota</Result>
      </m:getStateNameResponse>
    </SOAP-ENV:Body>
</SOAP-ENV:Envelope>
```

Mark up the text to identify the SOAP components in the response.

4. Write a SOAP service (interface and class) that provides two methods: (i) *add*, which accepts two integers and return the sum, and (ii) *subtract*, which accepts two integers and returns the difference.

Write a client program that invokes the two methods and processes the outcomes.

If possible, deploy the service that you created, then run your client program to test the service. Hand in the source listings and run output.

References

1. Overview of Applets, *http://java.sun.com/docs/books/tutorial/applet/overview/index.html*

2. Applets, *http://java.sun.com/applets/?frontpage-spotlight*

3. Java(TM) Boutique, Free Java Applets, Games, Programming Tutorials, and Downloads—Applet Categories, *http://javaboutique.internet.com/*

4. Java Servlet Technology Implementations & Specifications Archive, *http://java.sun.com/products/servlet/archive.html*

5. Java(TM) Servlet Technology—Implementations & Specifications, *http://java.sun.com/products/servlet/download.html*

6. The Apache Tomcat Server, *http://jakarta.apache.org/tomcat/index.html*

7. *javax.servlet.http.HttpServlet* class specification, *http://java.sun.com/products/servlet/2.2/javadoc/javax/servlet/http/HttpServlet.html*

8. Neil Gunton. "SOAP: Simplifying Distributed Development." *Dr. Dobb's Journal*, September 2001.

9. Simple Object Access Protocol (SOAP) 1.1, *http://www.w3.org/TR/SOAP/*

10. SOAP Tutorial, *http://www.w3schools.com/soap/default.asp*

11. Dave Winer and Jake Savin. SoapWare.Org: A Busy Developer's Guide to SOAP 1.1, *http://www.soapware.org/bdg*. UserLand Software, April 2, 2001.

12. A Quick-Start Guide for Installing Apache SOAP, *http://www.xmethods.com/gettingstarted/apache.html*

13. developerWorks: Web services: The Web services (r)evolution: Part 2, Hello world, Web service-style, *http://www-106.ibm.com/developerworks/library/ws-peer2/*

14. Apache SOAP Documentation: User's Guide, *http://xml.apache.org/soap/docs/index.html*

15. Apache SOAP V2.2 Documentation, *http://xml.apache.org/soap/docs/index.html*

16. XMethods—Web Service Listings, *http://www.xmethods.net/*

17. *java.sun.com*. Frequently Asked Questions—Applet Security, *http://java.sun.com/sfaq/*

18. Welcome!–The Apache Software Foundation, *http://apache.org/*

19. Jason Hunter and William Crawford. *Java Servlet Programming*. Sebastopol, CA: O'Reilly, 1998.

20. Apache Axis, *http://xml.apache.org/axis/*

21. *uddi.org, http://www.uddi.org/*

22. World Wide Web Consortium. Web Service Definition Language (WSDL), *http://www.w3.org/TR/wsdl*

23. Jabber Software Foundation, *http://www.jabber.org/*

24. World Wide Web Consortium. XML Schema Part 2: Datatypes, *http://www.w3.org/TR/xmlschema-2/*

25. Java Server Page Tutorial, *http://java.sun.com/products/jsp/pdf/jsptut.pdf*

26. Tutorial: Servlets and JSP, *http://javaboutique.internet.com/tutorials/jsp.html*

CHAPTER **12**

Advanced Distributed Computing Paradigms

In the previous chapters we have explored a number of the paradigms first introduced in Chapter 3, where a hierarchy of the paradigms was presented in a diagram repeated here as Figure 12.1.

Level of Abstraction

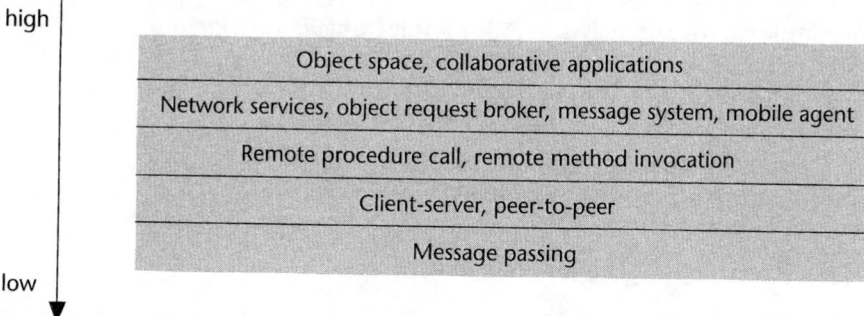

Figure 12.1 Distributed computing paradigms and their levels of abstraction.

This chapter presents some of the paradigms that are more advanced. Some of these paradigms are still being researched, while others are widely used in practice. Specifically, this chapter will provide an overview of the following distributed computing paradigms: **message queue system, mobile agents, network services, object spaces,** and **collaborative computing.**

12.1 Message Queue System Paradigm

The **message queue system paradigm**, also called **message-oriented middle-ware (MOM)**, is an elaboration of the basic message-passing paradigm. In this paradigm, a message system serves as an intermediary among separate, independent processes.

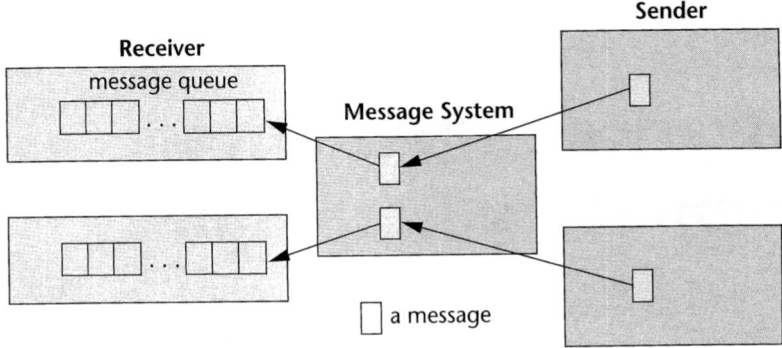

Figure 12.2 The message queue system paradigm.

Figure 12.2 illustrates the paradigm. Messages are sent to the message system, which acts as a switch for the messages, routing them to the appropriate receivers.

Through the message system, processes exchange messages asynchronously, in a decoupled manner. A sender deposits a message with the message system, which forwards the message to a message queue associated with each receiver. Once a message is sent, the sender is free to proceed with other tasks. The message is forwarded by the message system to the clients. Each client may extract a message from its queue on an as-needed basis.

Message queue system models can be classified into two subtypes, **point-to-point** and **publish-subscribe**, which are described below.

The Point-to-Point Message Model

The model illustrated in Figure 12.2 is the point-to-point message model. In this model, a message system forwards a message from the sender to the receiver's message queue. Unlike the basic message-passing model, the point-to-point message model provides a message depository that allows the sending and the receiving to be decoupled.

Compared to the basic message-passing model, this paradigm provides additional abstraction for **asynchronous operations**: There is no blocking on either the sender or the receiver.

The Publish/Subscribe Message Model

In this model, shown in Figure 12.3, each message is associated with a specific topic or event. Applications interested in the occurrence of a specific event may subscribe to messages for that event. When the awaited event occurs, the process publishes a message announcing the event or topic. The message queue system distributes the message to all its subscribers.

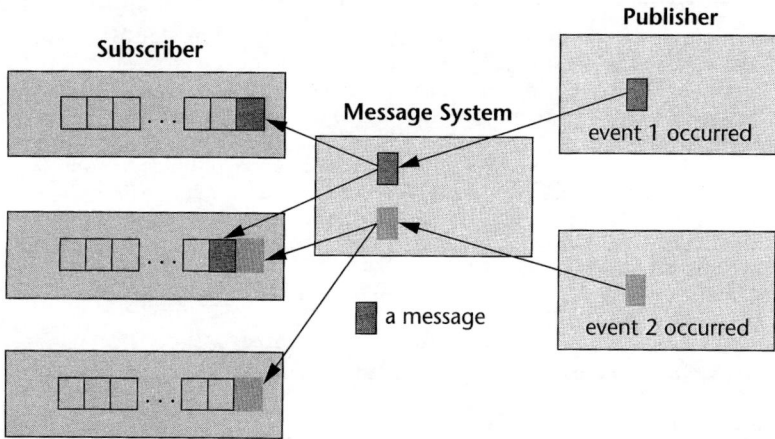

Figure 12.3 The publish/subscribe message system model.

Note that the publish/subscribe message model provides an abstraction for asynchronous **multicasting** or **group communication**. The **publish** operation allows a process to multicast to a group of processes, and the **subscribe** operation allows a process to listen for such a multicast.

The message-system paradigm is widely employed in commercial distributed applications. A large number of toolkits that support the paradigm are available. Some of them are:

- The IBM MQ*Series (renamed WebSphere MQ) [4.ibm.com, 3]
- Microsoft's Message Queue (MSQ) [microsoft.com, 2],
- Java Message Service (JMS) [java.sun.com, 1], available with J2EE SDK [java.sun.com, 4] version 1.3 and higher.

For students who are interested in a sample API that supports the message queue system model, the JMS is a good starting point.

Figure 12.4 and Figure 12.5 present a JMS programming sample. A *MessageSender* sends a message to a JMS message queue, while a *MessageReceiver* receives a message from the queue. To appreciate the asynchronicity that the message queue system provides, you should experiment with starting one or more copies of the

MessageReceiver, then start the *MessageSender*. Each of the clients should receive the message ("Hello World!") once it is sent. (*Note*: The example programs will only compile and run on a system installed with JMS; see [java.sun.com, 1] for information on downloading and installing JMS.)

Figure 12.4 A sample point-to-point message sender.

```
1  /**
2   * The MessageSender class sends a single "Hello World!"
3   * message to a Java Message System (JMS) queue  This
4   * program is to be run in conjunction with the
5   * MessageReceiver class, which receives the message
6   * via the JMS.
7   * To run the program: The JMS provider should be started,
8   * and a queue should have been created  The name of the
9   * queue should be specified as command-line argument
10  * when this program is run.
11  * M. Liu, based on examples in the
12  * tutorial http://java.sun.com/products/jms/tutorial/
13  */
14  import javax.jms.*; // for JMS classes
15  import javax.naming.*; // for JNDI classes
16
17  public class MessageSender {
18
19    public static void main(String[] args) {
20      String queueName = null;
21      Context jndiContext = null;
22      QueueConnectionFactory queueConnectionFactory
23        = null;
24      QueueConnection queueConnection = null;
25      QueueSession queueSession = null;
26      Queue queue = null;
27      QueueSender queueSender = null;
28      TextMessage message = null;
29      final int NUM_MSGS;
30
31
32      if ( (args.length != 1) ) {
33        System.out.println("Usage: MessageSender ");
34        System.exit(1);
35      }
36      queueName = new String(args[0]);
37      System.out.println("Queue name is " + queueName);
38
39      /* Create a JNDI InitialContext object if none
40         already exists */
41
42      try {
43        jndiContext = new InitialContext();
44      } catch (NamingException e) {
```

(continued on next page)

```
45        System.out.println("Could not create JNDI " +
46          "context: " + e.toString());
47        System.exit(1);
48      }
49
50      /* Look up connection factory and queue. If either
51         does not exist, exit. */
52
53      try {
54        queueConnectionFactory =
55          (QueueConnectionFactory)
56          jndiContext.lookup("QueueConnectionFactory")
57          queue = (Queue) jndiContext.lookup(queueName);
58      } catch (NamingException e) {
59        System.out.println("JNDI lookup failed: " +
60          e.toString());
61        System.exit(1);
62      }
63
64      try {
65        /* create connection */
66        queueConnection =
67          queueConnectionFactory.createQueueConnection
68
69        /* create session */
70        queueSession =
71          queueConnection.createQueueSession(false,
72          Session.AUTO_ACKNOWLEDGE);
73
74        /* create sender and a message object */
75        queueSender = queueSession.createSender(queue)
76          message = queueSession.createTextMessage();
77
78        /* set the message */
79        message.setText("Hello World!");
80        System.out.println("Sending message: " +
81          message.getText());
82
83        /* send it to the JMS */
84        queueSender.send(message);
85
86      } catch (JMSException e) {
87        System.out.println("Exception occurred: " +
88          e.toString());
89      } finally {
90      /* close the queue connection */
91        if (queueConnection != null) {
92          try {
93            queueConnection.close();
94          } catch (JMSException e) {}
95        }
96      } //end finally
97    } //end main
98  } //end class
```

Figure 12.5 A sample point-to-point message receiver.

```
1  /**
2   * The MessageReceiver class is to be used with
3   * the MessageSender class, which sends a message
4   * via the JMS.
5   * The same queue name as specified with MessageSender
6   * should be entered as command line argument.
7   * M. Liu, based on examples in the Java Message Service
8   * Tutorial,http://java.sun.com/products/jms/tutorial/
9   */
10
11 import javax.jms.*;
12 import javax.naming.*;
13
14 public class MessageReceiver {
15
16   public static void main(String[] args) {
17     String queueName = null;
18     Context jndiContext = null;
19     QueueConnectionFactory queueConnectionFactory
20       = null;
21     QueueConnection queueConnection = null;
22     QueueSession queueSession = null;
23     Queue queue = null;
24     QueueReceiver queueReceiver = null;
25     TextMessage message = null;
26
27     if (args.length != 1) {
28       System.out.println("Usage: java " +
29         "SimpleQueueReceiver <queue-name>");
30       System.exit(1);
31     }
32     queueName = new String(args[0]);
33     System.out.println("Queue name is " + queueName);
34
35     /* Create a JNDI InitialContext object if none
36        exists */
37
38     try {
39       jndiContext = new InitialContext();
40     } catch (NamingException e) {
41       System.out.println("Could not create JNDI " +
42         "context: " + e.toString());
43       System.exit(1);
44     }
45
46     /* Look up connection factory and queue. If either
47        does not exist, exit. */
48     try {
49       queueConnectionFactory =
50         (QueueConnectionFactory)
51           jndiContext.lookup("QueueConnectionFactory");
```

(continued on next page)

```
52        queue = (Queue) jndiContext.lookup(queueName);
53      } catch (NamingException e) {
54        System.out.println("JNDI lookup failed: " +
55          e.toString());
56        System.exit(1);
57      }
58
59      try {
60        /* create connection */
61        queueConnection =
62          queueConnectionFactory.createQueueConnection(
63        /* create session from connection */
64        queueSession =
65          queueConnection.createQueueSession(false,
66          Session.AUTO_ACKNOWLEDGE);
67        /* create a receiver */
68        queueReceiver = queueSession.createReceiver(queue);
69        queueConnection.start();
70        /* receive the message */
71        Message m = queueReceiver.receive(1);
72        message = (TextMessage) m;
73        System.out.println("Reading message: " +
74          message.getText());
75      } catch (JMSException e) {
76        System.out.println("Exception occurred: " +
77        e.toString());
78      } finally {
79        if (queueConnection != null) {
80          try {
81            queueConnection.close();
82          } catch (JMSException e) {}
83        }
84      }//end finally
85    }//end main
86 }//end class
```

Readers are referred to reference [java.sun.com, 1] for details of the JMS API and for additional examples, including those that illustrate the publish/subscribe model.

12.2 Mobile Agents

The **mobile agent** is a distributed computing paradigm that has interested researchers since the 1980s. Mobile agents have become commercially viable with recent technologies and have the potential for revolutionizing network applications.

In the context of computer science, an **agent** is an independent software program that runs on behalf of a network user.

A mobile agent is a program that, once it is launched by a user, can travel from host to host **autonomously** and can continue to function even if the user is disconnected from the network. Figure 12.6 illustrates the concept of a mobile agent.

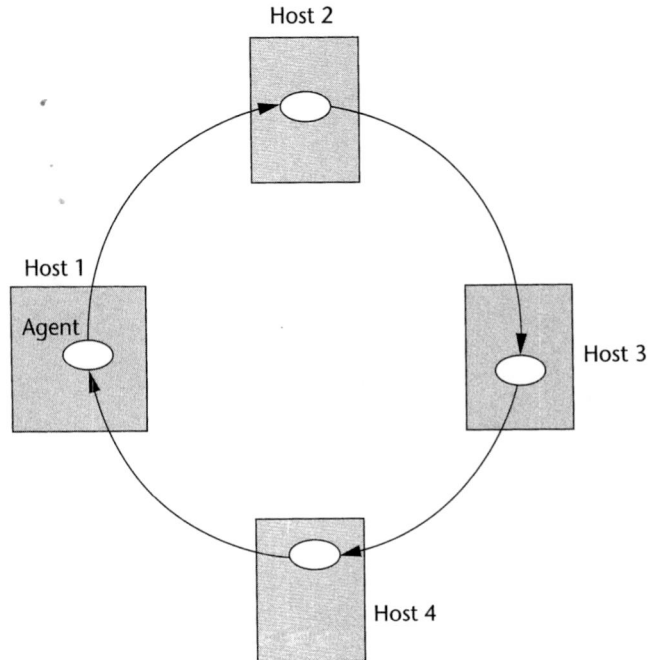

Figure 12.6 A mobile agent travels from computer to computer.

Basic Architecture

A mobile agent is a **serializable object**—an object whose data as well as state can be marshaled for transportation over the network. You may recall the term **data marshaling**, first introduced in Chapter 1, for the flattening and encoding of data structures so that they can be sent from one computer to another. An object can be similarly serialized and transmitted between hosts. Upon arrival, the object can be reconstituted and deserialized, with its execution state restored to when it was serialized, and then the object can resume execution on the newly-arrived host system.

The basic architecture for supporting mobile agents is illustrated in Figure 12.7. A serialized object, representing the mobile agent, is launched from a computer. The agent carries with it the following data items:

■ **Identifying information**—information that allows the agent to be identified.

■ **Itinerary**—a list of the addresses of the hosts that the agent is to visit.

■ **Task data**—data required by the agent to perform its tasks, or data collected by the agent.

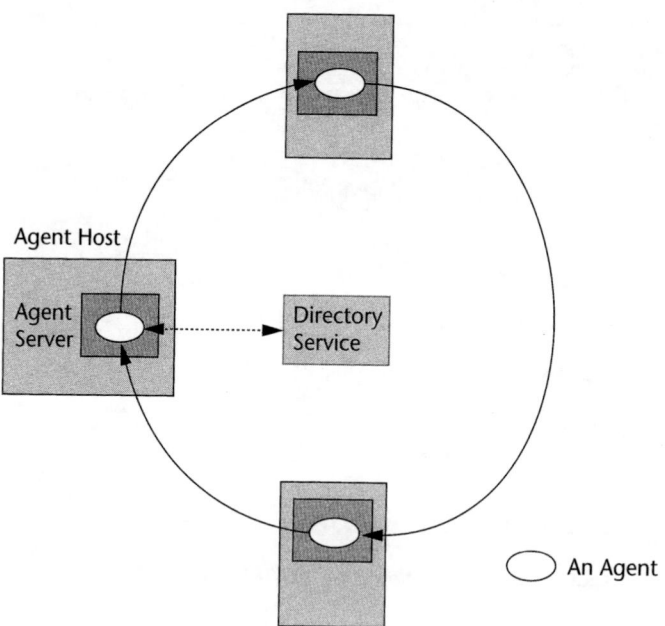

Agent Host

Agent Server

Directory Service

An Agent

Figure 12.7 A mobile agent travels from computer to computer.

The agent also carries the logic (code) to perform its tasks.

At each stop, the agent is received by a server. Through the agent server, the mobile agent makes use of the local resources to perform its tasks.

As part of the architecture, a directory service is required to allow the agent to look up the server at its next stop. When an agent has completed its task at one site, the agent object is serialized, and, with the assistance of the agent server, the object is transported to the next host on its itinerary.

There are a number of frameworks that have been built to provide the architecture for supporting mobile agents, including Aglet [Lange and Oshima, 5; aglets.sourceforge.net, 6], Concordia [merl.com, 7], and Grasshopper [grasshopper.de, 8]. For simplicity, however, we will demonstrate the concept of mobile agents using a serializable object and Java Remote Method Invocation. (*Note*: The implementation presented is for demonstrating the concept of mobile agents. For actual deployment, there are issues—to be discussed—that the demonstration does not address.)

Figure 12.8 presents a Java interface for the agent; the implementation of the interface is presented in Figure 12.9.

Figure 12.8 *AgentInterface.java.*

```
// An interface for a transportable object
// representing a mobile agent.
// M. Liu
import java.io.Serializable;
public interface AgentInterface extends Serializable {
  void execute();
}
```

Figure 12.9 *Agent.java.*

```
 1  // An implementation of a mobile agent
 2
 3  import java.io.*;
 4  import java.util.*;
 5  import java.rmi.*;
 6  import java.rmi.registry.Registry;
 7  import java.rmi.registry.LocateRegistry;
 8
 9  public class Agent implements AgentInterface {
10
11  int hostIndex; // which host to visit next
12  String name;
13  Vector hostList; // the itinerary
14  int RMIPort = 12345;
15
16    public Agent(String myName, Vector theHostList,
17        int theRMIPort ) {
18      name = myName;
19      hostList = theHostList;
20      hostIndex = 0;
21      RMIPort = theRMIPort;
22    }
23
24    // This method defines the tasks that the mobile agent
25    // is to perform once it has arrived at a server.
26    public void execute() {
27      String thisHost, nextHost;
28      sleep (2); // delay for visibility
29      System.out.println("007 here!");
30      thisHost = (String) hostList.elementAt(hostIndex);
31      hostIndex++;
32      if (hostIndex < hostList.size()) {
33        // if there is another host to visit
34        nextHost = (String) hostList.elementAt(hostIndex);
35        sleep (5); // delay for visibility
36        try {
37        // Locate the RMI registry on the next host
38          Registry registry = LocateRegistry.getRegistry
39            ("localhost", RMIPort);
```

(continued on next page)

```
40        ServerInterface h = (ServerInterface)
41           registry.lookup(nextHost);
42        System.out.println("Lookup for " + nextHost +
43           " at " + thisHost + " completed ";
44        sleep (5); // delay for visibility
45        // Ask the server at the next host to receive
46        // this agent
47        h.receive(this);
48     } // end try
49     catch (Exception e) {
50       System.out.println
51          ("Exception in Agent execute: " + e);
52     }
53   } // end if
54   else { //if all the stops have been made
55     sleep (5); // delay for visibility
56     System.out.println("Agent 007 has come home");
57     sleep (5); // delay for 5 visibility
58   }
59 }
60
61 // Method sleep suspends this object's execution for
62 // the specified number of seconds.
63 static void sleep (double time ){
64    try {
65       Thread.sleep( (long) (time * 1000.0));
66    }
67    catch (InterruptedException e) {
68       System.out.println ("sleep exception");
69    }
70 } // end sleep
71
72 } // end class Agent
```

The core of the agent implementation (Figure 12.9) is in its constructor (lines 16–22) and its *execute* method (lines 26–59). The constructor initializes the agent's state data, including the itinerary and an index to the next host to visit on its itinerary. The method *execute* contains the logic of the tasks that the agent is expected to perform at each host. In this demo, the tasks for the agent are simply to output a message to the standard output (line 56) and to look up the agent server at the next stop (lines 32–53).

The implementation of the agent server is shown in Figures 12.10 and 12.11.

Figure 12.10 *ServerInterface.java.*

```
// Agent Server interface file - M. Liu
import java.rmi.*;
public interface ServerInterface extends Remote {
  public void receive(Agent h)
     throws java.rmi.RemoteException;
}
```

The server exports itself to the RMI registry and provides a method, *receive*, which is invoked by the mobile agent when it is ready to be transported to the server. The method outputs a message to announce the arrival of the agent, then invokes the agent's *execute( )* method. Note that the *receive* method accepts as argument the serialized agent object.

Figure 12.11 *Server.java.*

```
1   // An implementation of an agent server
2   import java.rmi.*;
3   import java.rmi.server.*;
4   import java.rmi.registry.Registry;
5   import java.rmi.registry.LocateRegistry;
6   import java.net.*;
7   import java.io.*;
8
9   public class Server extends UnicastRemoteObject
10      implements ServerInterface{
11    static int RMIPort = 12345;
12    public Server() throws RemoteException {
13      super();
14    }
15
16    public void receive(Agent h) throws RemoteException {
17      sleep (3); // delay for visibility
18      System.out.println
19        ("*****Agent" + h.name + " arrived." );
20      h.execute();
21    }
22
23    public static void main(String args[]) {
24      InputStreamReader is = new InputStreamReader(System.in);
25      BufferedReader br = new BufferedReader(is);
26      String s;
27      String myName = "server" + args[0];
28      try{
29        System.setSecurityManager(new RMISecurityManager());
30        Server h = new Server();
31        Registry registry =
32          LocateRegistry.getRegistry(RMIPort);
33
34        registry.rebind( myName, h);
35
36        System.out.println("*****************************");
37        System.out.println(" Agent " + myName + " ready.");
38        System.out.println("*****************************");
39      }// end try
40      catch (RemoteException re) {
41        System.out.println("Exception in AgentServer.main: "
42          + re);
43      } // end catch
44    } // end main
```

(continued on next page)

```
45
46     // Method sleep suspends this object's execution for the
47     // specified number of seconds.
48     static void sleep (double time ){
49       try {
50         Thread.sleep( (long) (time * 1000.0));
51       }
52       catch (InterruptedException e){
53         System.out.println ("sleep exception");
54       }
55     } // end sleep
56  } // end class
```

Finally, a client program is needed to instantiate and launch the agent to its first stop on the itinerary. The implementation is shown in Figure 12.12.

Figure 12.12 *Client.java.*

```
1  //Client.java - client program for launching the mobile agent
2  // M. Liu
3
4  import java.io.*;
5  import java.util.*;
6  import java.rmi.*;
7  import java.rmi.registry.Registry;
8  import java.rmi.registry.LocateRegistry;
9
10 public class Client {
11    static int RMIPort = 12345;
12    public static void main(String args[]) {
13
14      System.setSecurityManager(new RMISecurityManager());
15
16      try {
17        Registry registry = LocateRegistry.getRegistry
18          ("localhost", RMIPort);
19        ServerInterface h = (ServerInterface)
20        registry.lookup("server1");
21        System.out.println
22          ("Lookup for server1 completed " );
23        System.out.println("***Have a good trip, " +
24          " agent 007.");
25
26        Vector hostList = new Vector();
27        hostList.addElement("server1");
28        hostList.addElement("server2");
29        hostList.addElement("server3");
30        Agent a = new Agent("007", hostList, RMIPort);
31        h.receive(a);
32        System.out.println("***Nice job, agent 007");
33      }
```

(continued on next page)

```
34       catch (Exception e) {
35          System.out.println("Exception in main: " + e);
36       }
37    } //end main
38 } //end class
```

As a distributed computing paradigm, the mobile agent is radically different from the other paradigms that we have studied. In other paradigms, independent processes collaborate by exchanging data over their network links. With mobile agents, a process is transported, carrying with it the shared data as it visits individual processes on its itinerary. Figure 12.13 illustrates this distinguishing characteristic.

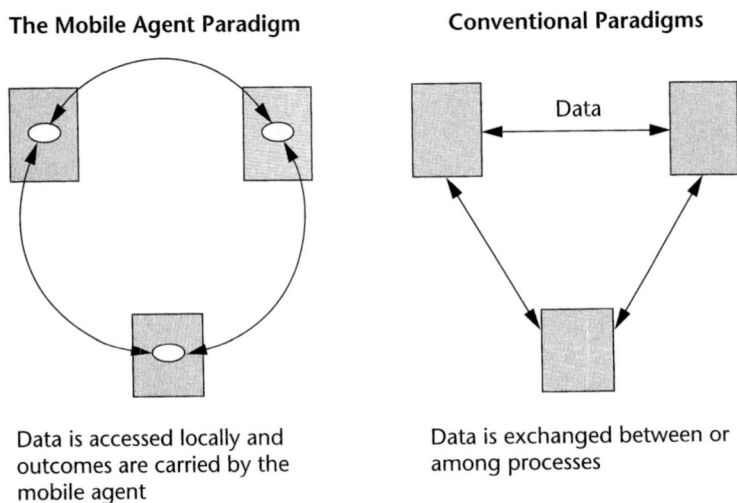

The Mobile Agent Paradigm

Data is accessed locally and outcomes are carried by the mobile agent

Conventional Paradigms

Data

Data is exchanged between or among processes

Figure 12.13 Contrasting the mobile agents paradigm with conventional paradigms.

Advantages of Mobile Agents

The mobile agents paradigm provides the following key advantages:

▪ Mobile agents allow efficient and economical use of communication channels, which may have low bandwidth, high latency, and may be error-prone. In contrast, conventional paradigms require repeated exchange of data over network links. If a large amount of data is involved, the consumption of network bandwidth can be considerable, with a resultant delay in response time or latency. With mobile agents, a single serialized object is transmitted over the network, potentially reducing the consumption of network bandwidth. Moreover, since the mobile agent needs only to be transported once between two sites, the probability of failure owing to network faults is reduced. For these reasons, mobile agents are especially appropriate for wireless network links.

■ Mobile agents enable the use of portable, low-cost, personal communications devices to perform complex tasks even when the device is disconnected from the network. An agent can be launched from any device that supports the necessary architecture. Once launched, the agent is decoupled from its orginator and is capable of performing its tasks independent from the originating device. With proper implementation, a mobile agent may have the intelligence to bypass faulty hosts or seek temporary shelter on a reliable host.

■ Mobile agents allow asynchronous operations and true decentralization. The execution of a mobile agent is decoupled from its originating host and other participating hosts. Tasks are performed at individual sites in an asynchronous manner, and it is not necessary for any participant to play the role of a coordinator.

In spite of the advantages that mobile agents offer, the paradigm has not been widely deployed in commercial or industrial applications. One of the main drawbacks of the paradigm is that it can pose a security threat for the participants.

There are concerns for both the agent hosts and the mobile agents. From the point of view of the hosts that receive an agent, malicious or unauthorized agents can misuse and destroy system resources. Unrestrained, a malicious agent can wreak havoc on a host in the same way that computer viruses do. From the point of view of an agent, malicious hosts can destroy or alter an agent's data or logic. For example, the itinerary of a mobile agent can be destroyed or altered by a malicious host, so that the agent cannot continue with its journey. Or, the data carried by an agent may be altered so that the agent carries with it erroneous information.

Security in mobile agent systems is an active area of research [mole.informatik.uni-stuttgart.de, 9]. Some of the countermeasures that have been proposed are:

■ **Authentication.** An agent must authenticate itself to a host, and an agent server must authenticate itself to the agent.

■ **Encryption.** An agent encrypts its sensitive data.

■ **Resource access.** A host enforces strict access control to its resources.

Mobile-Agent Framework Systems

A number of mobile-agent framework systems are now available. In addition to providing the architecture for transporting mobile agents, these systems address issues such as security concerns, transactional support, and management of agents. Readers who are interested in this topic should look into references such as [trl.ibm.com, 6], [concordiaagents.com, 7], and [grasshopper.de, 8].

12.3 Network Services

In the **network services** paradigm [Edwards, 11], the network is viewed as an infrastructure for **services**, which "may include applications, files, databases, servers, information systems, and devices such as mobile appliances, storage, printers." Figure 12.14 illustrates this paradigm. A client application may make use of one or more of such services. Services can be added to and removed from the network autonomously, and clients can locate available services through a directory service.

The Simple Object Access Protocol (SOAP), which we studied in Chapter 10, is based on this paradigm. Jini, which predates SOAP, is a toolkit also based on this paradigm.

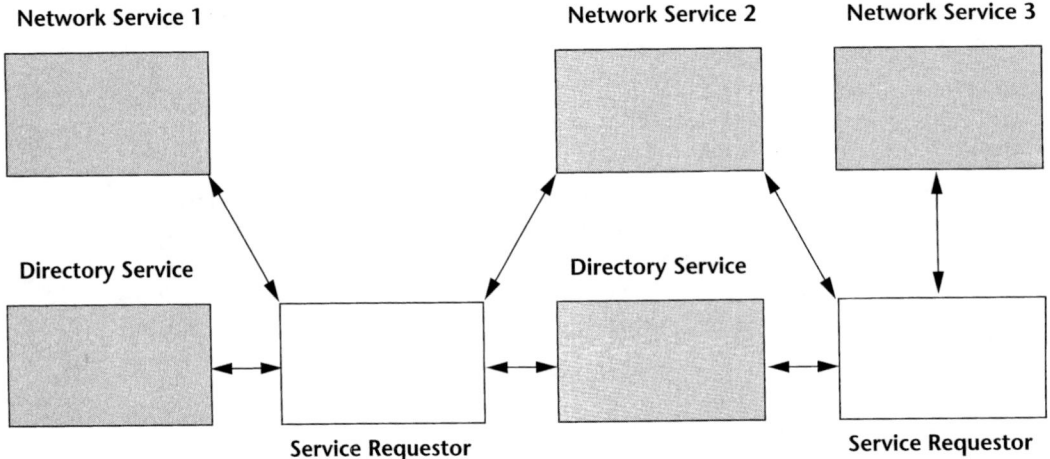

Figure 12.14 The network service paradigm.

Figures 12.15 and 12.16 illustrate the syntax for the implementation of a Jini service provider, which simply provides a *sayHello( )* method. Figure 12.17 shows the implementation for a client of the service. Note that Jini makes use of Remote Method Invocation, which we studied in Chapters 7 and 8.

Figure 12.15 *HelloServerInterface.java.*

```
1  // Interface for the HelloServer
2
3  import java.rmi.*;
4
5    public interface HelloServerInterface extends Remote {
6      public String sayHello() throws RemoteException;
7    }
8  }
```

Figure 12.16 *HelloServer.java.*

```
1   // A simple Jini server
2   // M. Liu, based on code sample from "Noel's Nuggets"
    // [cc.gatech.edu, 14]
3   import net.jini.core.entry.*;
4   import net.jini.core.lookup.*;
5   import net.jini.core.discovery.*;
6   import net.jini.lookup.entry.*;
7   import com.sun.jini.lookup.*;
8   import com.sun.jini.lease.*;
9   import java.io.*;
10  import java.rmi.*;
11  import java.rmi.server.*;
12
13  public class HelloServer extends UnicastRemoteObject
14      implements HelloServerInterface, ServiceIDListener {
15
16    public HelloServer () throws RemoteException {
17      super();
18    }
19
20    public String sayHello () throws RemoteException {
21      return ("Hello World!");
22    }
23
24    // This method listens for the ServiceID returned
25    // by the service directory when the ID is available.
26    public void serviceIDNotify (ServiceID id) {
27      System.out.println (" ServiceID received: " + id);
28    }
29
30    public static void main (String[] args){
31      HelloServer server;
32      Entry[] aeAttributes;
33      JoinManager manager;
34
35      try {
36        System.setSecurityManager
37          (new RMISecurityManager ());
38        // Creates the attributes as an array of entry
39        // objects that describe this service, and
40        // register with the lookup service via The
41        // JoinManager. The service ID, when ready,
42        // will be reported by the serviceID listener.
43
44        attributes = new Entry[1];
45        attributes[0] = new Name("HelloServer");
46        server = new HelloServer();
47        manager = new JoinManager (
48          server, attributes, server,
49          new LeaseRenewalManager()
50          );
51      }
52
```

(continued on next page)

```
53          catch (Exception ex) {
54             ex.printStackTrace( );
55          }
56       } //end main
57    } //end class
```

Figure 12.17 A *Jini* client.

```
1   // A simple Jini client
2   // M. Liu, based on a code sample from "Noel's Nuggets"
    // [cc.gatech.edu, 14]
3
4   import net.jini.core.entry.*;
5   import net.jini.core.lookup.*;
6   import net.jini.core.discovery.*;
7   import net.jini.lookup.entry.*;
8   import com.sun.jini.lookup.*;
9   import java.rmi.*;
10
11  class HelloClient{
12    public static void main (String[] args){
13
14       Entry[] attributes;
15       LookupLocator lookup;
16       ServiceID id;
17       ServiceRegistrar registrar;
18       ServiceTemplate template;
19       HelloServerInterface helloServer;
20
21       try {
22         System.setSecurityManager
23           (new RMISecurityManager ());
24
25         // Locate the Jini lookup service */
26         lookup = new LookupLocator("jini://localhost");
27         // Find the ServiceRegistrar
28         registrar = lookup.getRegistrar();
29         // Look up the service
30         attributes = new Entry[1];
31         attributes[0] = new Name ("HelloServer");
32         template = new ServiceTemplate
33           (null, null, attributes);
34         helloServer = (HelloServerInterface)
35           registrar.lookup(template);
36         //Invoke a method of the service
37         System.out.println(helloServer.sayHello());
38       }
39
40       catch (Exception ex) {
41          ex.printStaceTrace( );
42       }
43     }
44  }
```

The discussion we have presented barely touches on the fundamentals of Jini and does not begin to do justice to the sophisticated capabilities that this toolkit provides. An interesting concept in Jini is the use of "leases" (see line 49 in Figure 12.16). In a Jini system, each service is associated with a **lease renewal manager**. When a client locates a Jini service through a lookup service, the lookup service acts as a granter of leases to that service. The client can expect to be able to make request for the service as long as the lease has not expired. The use of leases allows the system to manage fault tolerance more effectively. (Faults in distributed systems and fault tolerance were introduced in Chapter 1.)

Readers who are interested in investigating Jini further are encouraged to consult references [Edwards, 11], [jan.netcomp.monash.edu.au, 12], [kedwards. com, 13], [cc.gatech.edu, 14], [corkill, 15], and [onjava.com, 20], which provide sample programs as well as instructions on downloading and installing the Jini toolkit.

12.4 Object Spaces

This section looks at a paradigm that arguably provides the highest level of abstraction: **object spaces**. The object spaces paradigm has its origin in David Gelernter's Linda Tuplespace [Ahuja, Carriero, and Gelernter, 17] and is the basis of Blackboard systems in the field of artificial intelligence [Corkill, 15]. In the object spaces paradigm, a **space** is a shared, network-accessible repository for objects. Instead of communicating with each other, processes coordinate by **exchanging objects** through one or more spaces. Figure 12.18 illustrates this concept. Processes interact by sharing state data in one or more objects and by updating the state of the objects as needed.

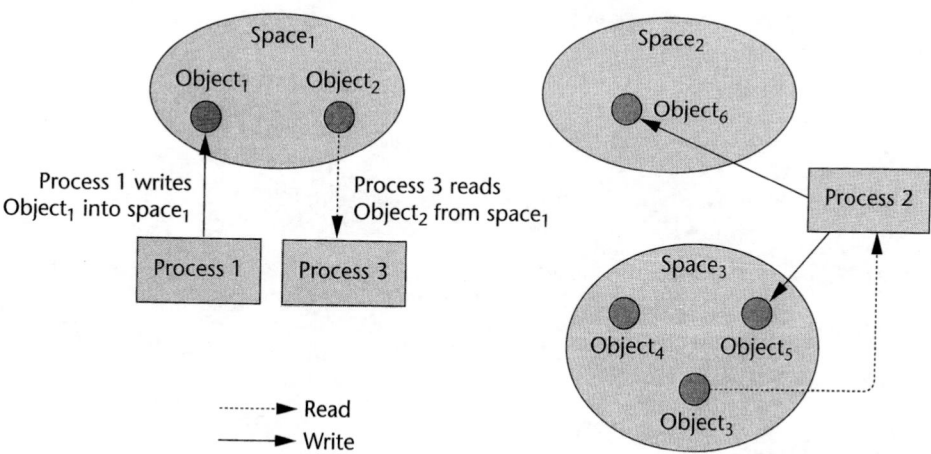

Figure 12.18 The object spaces paradigm.

A process may deposit an object into a space. Unlike in other message models, processes do not modify objects in the space or invoke an object's methods directly. A process wishing to access an object will make use of a directory service to locate the object in a space. To modify an object, a process must explicitly *remove* it, update it, and *reinsert* it into the space.

The object spaces paradigm is an active area of research. A Java-based toolkit, JavaSpaces, which provides a framework based on this paradigm, is available for experimentation.

In the JavaSpaces API, an interface called *Entry* is provided. An *Entry* object can be written to or read from a space. Figures 12.19 through 12.21 illustrate a simple sample program that makes use of an *Entry* object that contains a message ("Hello World!") and a counter. The server creates the *Entry* object, then writes it to a default object space. The client reads (takes) the object from the space and increments the counter, before writing it back to the space. Note that JavaSpaces makes use of the JINI API introduced in section 12.3.

Figure 12.19 A sample *JavaSpaces entry* class.

```
1   // A JavaSpaces Entry class for a space object
2   // M. Liu, based on code samples provided in:
3   // JAVASPACES PRINCIPLES, PATTERNS, AND PRACTICE [18]
4
5
6
7   import net.jini.core.entry.Entry;
8
9   public class SpaceObject implements Entry {
10    public String message;
11    public Integer counter; //An object is required.
12
13    public SpaceObject( ) {
14    }
15
16    public SpaceObject(String message) {
17      this.message = message;
18      counter = 0;
19    }
20
21    public String toString( ) {
22      return content + " read " + counter + " times.";
23    }
24
25    public void increment( ) {
26      counter = new Integer(counter.intValue() + 1);
27    }
28  } //end class
```

Figure 12.20 A sample program that initiates a *JavaSpaces* object.

```
1  // A program which initiates a JavaSpaces entry.
2  // M. Liu, based on code samples provided in:
3  // JAVASPACES PRINCIPLES, PATTERNS, AND PRACTICE [18]
4
5
6
7  import net.jini.core.lease.Lease;
8  import net.jini.space.JavaSpace;
9
10 public class HelloWorld {
11   public static void main(String[] args) {
12     try {
13       SpaceObject msg = new SpaceObject("Hello World!");
14
15       JavaSpace space;
16       space = (JavaSpace)space();
17       space.write(msg, null, Lease.FOREVER);
18
19       SpaceObject template = new SpaceObject();
20       while (true) {
21         SpaceObject result = (SpaceObject)
22           space.read(template, null, Long.MAX_VALUE);
23         System.out.println(result);
24         Thread.sleep(1000);
25       } //end while
26     }
27     catch (Exception ex) {
28       ex.printStackTrace();
29     }
30   }
31 } //end class
```

Figure 12.21 A sample *JavaSpaces* client.

```
1  // A client program which accesses a JavaSpaces entry.
2  // M. Liu, based on code samples provided in:
3  // JAVASPACES PRINCIPLES, PATTERNS, AND PRACTICE [18]
4
5
6
7  import net.jini.core.lease.Lease;
8  import net.jini.space.JavaSpace;
9
10 public class HelloWorldClient {
11   public static void main(String[] args) {
12     try {
13       JavaSpace space = (JavaSpace)space();
```

(continued on next page)

```
14          SpaceObject template = new SpaceObject();
15          // Repeatedly retrieve the object from the space,
16          // update it, then deposit the object in the space
17          while (true) {
18            // Read the object from the space.
19            SpaceObject result = (SpaceObject)
20              space.take(template, null, Long.MAX_VALUE);
21            result.increment();
22            // Write the object to the space
23            space.write(result, null, Lease.FOREVER);
24            Thread.sleep(1000);
25          }//end while
26        }
27        catch (Exception ex) {
28          ex.printStackTrace();
29        }
30      }
31 } //end class
```

Of particular interest is that mutual exclusion is a built-in characteristic of the object spaces paradigm, since a shared object can be accessed by only one party at a time. Reference [Ahuja, Carriero, and Gelernter, 17] provides excellent examples illustrating applications that can be built using this paradigm.

Readers interested in JavaSpaces are urged to consult references [java.sun.com, 18], [jiniworld.net, 19], [onjava.com, 20], and [Halter, 23].

Ongoing Developments

This chapter presented a number of advanced distributed computing paradigms, most of which are still in the realm of research. It is a certainty that more paradigms and toolkits will emerge. For example, **peer-to-peer** is a paradigm that has recently received wide attention; a number of systems/APIs has been developed to support the paradigm, including the JXTA project [jxta.org, 16]. Another paradigm, **collaborative computing**, uses the concept of channels to enable independent processes to collaborate in real-time; the Java Shared Data Tookit (JSDT) [java.sun.com, 21] can be used "to create network-centric applications, such as shared whiteboards or chat environments. It can also be used for remote presentations, shared simulations, and to easily distribute data for enhanced group workflow."

It is hoped that you, as a reader of this book, will have acquired the basic concepts and understanding that will enable you to explore new or unfamiliar paradigms and APIs in distributed computing.

Summary

This chapter provided an overview of the following advanced distributed computing paradigms:

- The Message Queue System paradigm, which supports asynchronous sending and receiving of messages through the use of message queues. A framework that supports the paradigm is the Java Message System (JMS).

- The mobile agents paradigm, which supports the use of transportable programs. Although mobile agents can be implemented directly using Remote Method Invocation, the use of frameworks such as Aglet, Concordia, and Grasshopper is recommended.

- The network services paradigm, which views the network as a federation of service providers and service consumers. An application may consume one or more services, on an as needed basis. The Simple Object Access Protocol (SOAP) is a protocol based on this paradigm. Java's Jini is a sophisticated toolkit that supports this paradigm and makes use of the interesting concept of leasing a service.

- The object spaces paradigm, which provides logical spaces to which objects can be deposited and retrieved by collaborators. JavaSpaces is a toolkit that supports the paradigm.

There are other paradigms and technologies that were not covered, including peer-to-peer, and collaborative computing.

Exercises

1. Follow the instructions in [java.sun.com, 1] to install Java Message System (JMS) on your computer.

   a. Experiment with the *HelloWorld* sample presented in Figures 12.4 and 12.5.

      — Compile the source files.

      — Start a receiver, then a sender. Describe and explain the outcome.

      — Start two receivers, then a sender. Describe and explain the outcome.

   b. Repeat part a to experiment with the point-to-point sample provided in [java.sun.com, 1].

   c. Repeat part a to experiment with the publish/subscribe sample provided in [java.sun.com, 1].

2. Describe an application that can make use of one or more point-to-point message queues. Explain how the application benefits from the use of the message queue(s) in terms of ease of implementation.

3. Describe an application that can make use of one or more publish/subscribe message queues. Explain how the application benefits from the use of the message queue(s) in terms of ease of implementation.

4. Follow the instructions in the README file in the mobile agents sample folder to run the mobile agents demo presented in Figures 12.8 through 12.12. Describe and explain the outcome.

5. Investigate the Aglet framework [trl.ibm.com, 6], a mobile-agent framework.

   a. How does the Aglet framework provide for code transportation?

   b. What other services does the Aglet framework provide besides code transportation?

   c. Download and install the package, then experiment with the samples provided.

6. Consider the following applications listed below. Describe how each of these paradigms (message queue system, mobile agents, and object spaces) can be applied to support the application. Note that you are not asked to provide an implementation. Your description should be framed in terms of the generic paradigm, not a specific API.

   The applications to be considered are:

   a. Monitoring a shipment of goods being carried by a vehicle en route to warehouses and stores.

   b. A chat room.

   c. An online auction.

   d. A service to enable your university to provide course information to students. The information is updated frequently.

7. Perform research on JXTA [jxta.org, 16] and write a report on the peer-to-peer paradigm that it supports. Include in your report a description of the architecture, the API, and sample programs. Where would you place this paradigm in the hierarchy of distributed computing paradigms?

8. Perform research on the Java Shared Data Toolkit [pandonia.canberra.edu.au, 22] and write a report on the distributed computing paradigm that it supports. Include in your report a description of the architecture, the API, and sample programs. Where would you place this paradigm in the hierarchy of distributed computing paradigms?

References

1. Java Message Service Tutorial, *http://java.sun.com/products/jms/tutorial/*

2. Microsoft MSMQ Home Page, *http://www.microsoft.com/msmq/default.htm*

3. IBM's MQ-Series, *http://www-4.ibm.com/software/ts/mqseries/*

4. Java™ 2 Platform, Enterprise Edition, *http://java.sun.com/j2ee/*

5. D. Lange and M. Oshima. "Seven Good Reasons for Mobile Agents." *Communications of the ACM*, March 1999.

6. IBM Aglet. *http://www.trl.ibm.com/aglets/*

7. Concordia. *http://www.concordiaagents.com/*

8. Grasshopper 2, *http://www.grasshopper.de/index.html*

9. Security in mobile agent systems, *http://mole.informatik.uni-stuttgart.de/security.html*

10. Jini™ Network Technology, *http://www.sun.com/jini/*

11. Keith Edwards. *Core Jini*. Upper Saddle River, NJ: Prentice Hall PTR, 2000.

12. Jan Newmarch's Guide to JINI Technologies, *http://jan.netcomp.monash.edu.au/java/jini/tutorial/Jini.xml*

13. Jini Planet, *http://www.kedwards.com/jini/*

14. Noel's Nuggets, *http://www.cc.gatech.edu/~kris/cs7470/nuggets/*: Jini tutorial, with examples and instructions.

15. Daniel D. Corkill. "Blackboard Systems." *AI Expert 6*, no. 9 (September 1991): 40–47.

16. Project JXTA, *http://www.jxta.org/*

17. Sudhir Ahuja, Nicholas Carriero, and David Gelernter. "Linda and Friends." *Computer*, August 1986: 26–34.

18. Eric Freeman, Susanne Jupfer, and Ken Arnold. *JavaSpaces: Principles, Patterns, and Practice*. Reading, MA: Addison-Wesley, 1999. *http://java.sun.com/docs/books/jini/javaspaces/*

19. The Nuts and Bolts of Compiling and Running JavaSpaces Programs, *http://www.jiniworld.net/document/javaspace/The Nuts and Bolts of Compiling and Running JavaSpaces(TM).htm*

20. O'Reilly Network, First Contact: Is There Life in JavaSpace?, *http://www.onjava.com/pub/a/onjava/2001/04/05/javaspace.html?page=1*

21. Java Shared Data Toolkit Home Page, *http://java.sun.com/products/java-media/jsdt/*

22. Jan Newmarch. *Jan Newmarch's Guide to JINI Technologies.* *http://pandonia.canberra.edu.au/java/jini/tutorial/Jini.xml*

23. Steven L. Halter. *JavaSpaces Example by Example.* Upper Saddle River, NJ: Prentice Hall. 2002.

Epilogue

I hope you have found the materials presented in this book as interesting as I did when, as a student, I was first introduced to the field of distributed computing. By no means, however, has this book done justice to the vast range of topics that fall under the broad umbrella of distributed computing.

Distributed computing is a vibrant field, with new ideas and technologies constantly being introduced, and old ideas and technologies constantly being rediscovered. It is a certainty that anyone involved in it will be continually challenged with new models, theories, and tools. It is my sincere hope that this book has contributed to your understanding of the fundamental concepts and principles of distributed computing so that you will be prepared for lifelong learning in the field.

There are many areas that merit further attention. **Fault tolerance** is a topic that is of great importance to any researcher or practitioner in distributed computing. Likewise, the significance of the area of **security** cannot be overstated. **Distributed algorithms** is a topic that I teach to more advanced students, many of whom have found it particularly stimulating. I urge you to explore these topics further as you broaden your knowledge of the field of distributed computing.

M. L. Liu

Index